Hermeneutics & Deconstruction

D1557983

Selected Studies in Phenomenology
and Existential Philosophy 10

Board of Editors

Hermeneutics & Deconstruction

Edited by
Hugh J. Silverman
and Don Ihde

State University of New York Press

Published by
State University of New York Press, Albany

1985 State University of New York

For information, address State University of New York
Press, State University Plaza, Albany, N.Y., 12246

Library of Congress Cataloging in Publication Data
Main entry under title:

Hermeneutics and deconstruction.

(Selected studies in phenomenology and existential
philosophy ; 10)
    Includes index.
    1. Hermeneutics—Addresses, essays, lectures.
2. Deconstruction—Addresses, essays, lectures.
I. Silverman, Hugh J., 1945– II. Ihde, Don, 1934–
III. Series.
BD241.H36 1985   149   84-8801
ISBN 0-87395-979-5
ISBN 0-87395-980-9 (pbk.)

10 9 8 7 6 5 4 3 2 1

CONTENTS

WAS HEISST LESEN?

Martin Heidegger, 1954

Was heisst Lesen? Das Tragende und Leitende im Lesen ist die Sammlung. Worauf sammelt sie? Auf das Geschrieben, auf das in der Schrift Gesagte. Das eigentliche Lesen ist die Sammlung auf das, was ohne unser Wissen einst schon unser Wesen in den Anspruch genommen hat, mögen wir dabei ihm entsprechen oder versagen.

Ohne das eigentliche Lesen vermögen wir auch nicht das uns Anblickende zu sehen und das Erscheinende und Scheinende zu schauen.

WHAT IS CALLED READING?

What is [calls forth] reading? That which is sustaining and directive in reading is gatheredness. To what is it gathered? To what is written, to what is said in writing. Authentic reading is a gatheredness to that which, unbeknown to us, has already claimed our essence, regardless of whether we comply with it or withhold from it.

Without authentic reading we are also not able to see what has us in sight nor to gaze upon any appearance or semblance.

(Translated by J. Sallis)

INTRODUCTORY REMARKS

Hermeneutics and deconstruction have come to occupy a dominant place in contemporary continental philosophy, particularly as it is practiced in North America. Although these two different ways of philosophizing are, to a large extent, mutually exclusive, nevertheless they are often juxtaposed. They both constitute responses to and readings of the phenomenological traditions inaugurated by Husserl and Heidegger. While hermeneutics is concerned primarily with *interpretation* and the meaning of what is interpreted, deconstruction is concerned with *reading* and the marked limits of texts. Hermeneutics places itself in the relation between the interpreter and the interpreted. Deconstruction traces the places of indecidability, marginality, and supplementarity in texts. To the extent that hermeneutics establishes a signifying middle ground in the act of interpretation and in the understanding that it seeks to produce, deconstruction operates in the differential intermediate zone of textuality so as to elucidate the fabric of the text and its limit conditions.

While both deconstruction and hermeneutics can be traced to Heidegger, the latter seeks to carry on the Heideggerian tradition whereas the former provides a re-reading of it. Hermeneutics draws upon the nineteenth century tradition of Biblical interpretation (as in Schleiermacher), extends it to the understanding of life and history (in Dilthey), and then offers access to the meaning of Being (Heidegger), the world (Dilthey and Heidegger), artworks (Gadamer), and narratives or historical texts (Ricoeur). Deconstruction investigates the goals and ends of phenomenology as articulated by Husserl on the one hand and by Heidegger on the other, but it also picks up features of (and re-reads) semiology and structuralism, psychoanalysis and theories of the subject, literature and literary theory. Deconstruction offers strategies for reading all sorts of texts in all sorts of contexts. Hermeneutics offers the hope of producing the meaning of various objects and artifacts — natural and cultural.

The juxtaposition of hermeneutics and deconstruction typically takes the form of a confrontation between Heidegger and Derrida. Yet it is an odd confrontation. It is not just that Heidegger was nearly a quarter of a century older than Derrida. It is also that there is no real conflict between them — the opposition is neither internal nor external. If there is any substantial critique, it is from Heidegger — of Derrida — from the grave. For Derrida, Heidegger is a text, not a master, a place in the history of textuality not a competitor. For Heideggerians, such as Caputo and Sheehan, the debate is very much alive. It was Heidegger who announced the "end of philosophy" (along with Hegel) — Derrida reads such an "end" as an indecidable: as telos, as termination, as accomplishment, as eschatology. Whereas this volume begins by asking about "the end of philosophy" it ends with a post-Derridean reading — the "only hope" for continental philosophy when it comes to what comes after "the end of philosophy."

The essays incorporated into this volume are selected from among those read at the twentieth (1981 at Northwestern University), twenty-first (1982 at Pennsylvania State University), and twenty-second (1983 in St. Louis) annual conferences of the Society for Phenomenology and Existential Philosophy. The pre-occupation with issues in hermeneutics, in deconstruction, and in their inconnections was a dominant problematic for these three conferences. A second volume (number 11 in the series) will focus on "descriptions" representing a very different current of discussion at these same annual meetings. Since the Society moved to concurrent sessions in 1981, a wide range of rich and energetic interchange has been occurring at SPEP. Indeed even many excellent papers and presentations cannot be included in these two volumes.

As to the debates within the present collection of essays, an attempt has been made to give fair representation to both the hermeneutic and the deconstructive modes of philosophical practice. The issue is raised in connection with the question of the "end of philosophy" as debated by philosophers associated with rather different continental traditions: Magnus with Nietzschean perspectivism, Seebohm with Kantian and Husserlian foundationalism, and Schrag with Heideggerian interpretive ontology. Out of this debate, we have offered some consideration of the implications of hermeneutics as a practice and the differences between the interpretation of texts and the interpretation of things (Nicholson and Heelan). In the essay by Descombes, a quasi-deconstructive reading of the very paradoxes of interpretation makes it evident that the difference between seeing and reading is not as simple as it may seem.

The third part demonstrates some of the dimensions of hermeneutic study — with respect to Being, Life, and World — by three of its most well-known proponents (Marx, Rodi, and Murray). Although Marx asks about the history of Being, a separate section is devoted to narratives and historical discourse by a Husserlian (Carr) and a deconstructionist (Blanchard). On the one hand, the position of the narrator is interrogated as the voice from the outside; on the other hand, the narrative is examined in terms of the voice in the text.

The last three parts focus more specifically on the controversy in and around deconstruction. An analytic philosopher asks about the "mystery of the text" and highlights the play in deconstruction (Margolis). Lingis looks at Derrida's more recent writings on Freud and the pleasure principle. He offers a Merleau-Pontean reading of the libido and Derrida's inscription of a segment of his own life. Gasché, more closely associated with deconstruction, examines the connection between Heidegger and Derrida with respect to the problem of metaphoricity. This opens the door for the debate between Caputo, Sheehan, and Holland on the relative merits of the Heideggerian and Derridean approaches. Although Holland's paper was presented a year later, she picks up a number of questions raised by various readings of Derrida – in addition to those of Caputo and Sheehan. The last part offers examples of the possibility of a post-Derridean reading. In one case, texts from Kant to Heidegger are re-examined in Derridean fashion for their 'abysmal' dimensions (Watson). In another, Derrida's own texts are put into play – Ormiston's encounter with Derrida is neither sympathy nor criticism, but something in-between. The final essay by Olkowski returns to Derrida's Heidegger – as mediated by the art theorist Meyer Schapiro. She asks about the orientation of thought after Derrida – in the reading of texts – at/in/after the "end of philosophy" and the beginning of the writing of a new orientation, a new inscription in another place.

Hugh J. Silverman
SUNY – Stony Brook

Part I.
The End of Philosophy

1. The End of 'The End of Philosophy'

Bernd Magnus

"The report of my death was an exaggeration." (Cable from Europe to the Associated Press, 1899. Samuel Langhorne Clemens, a.k.a. Mark Twain.)

The end of philosophy has become a respectable, even a fashionable topic of philosophical conversation at professional meetings. The unintended irony of this situation can scarcely have escaped notice. As a result, my contribution may be more usefully construed as a paper about the end of the end of philosophy. To accomplish this I shall need, first, to locate the symposium topic in philosophic space, to distinguish various senses of "the end of philosophy" in order to identify the sense which is causing much of the fuss. I shall then turn briefly to Nietzsche to illustrate what is gained and what is lost at the end of philosophy's own end.

There are many senses in which philosophy may be said to be brought to an end, and may even be said not to exist at all any longer; and it would help to get clear on some of these senses.

(1) There is the sense of end as *Vollendung*, the sense of philosophy completing itself, surpassing all previous achievements and setting them aside.[1] It is the unstated but powerful motivating conviction that a final vocabulary has been achieved, that a given text, discourse, or framework has a privileged attachment to reality, that this particular theory is not still another commentary but is instead the vocabulary in which mute reality would have chosen to describe itself, if only it could have. I take this to be the most common sense of "end of philosophy." Following Sellars,[2] Rorty[3] and Putnam,[4] I shall call this sense "the God's eye view."

The God's eye view may plausibly be said to inspire Aristotle's correction of Plato, Descartes' search for indubitable foundations, Kant's attempt to circumscribe the boundaries of intelligible discourse, Hegel's *Aufhebung* of the whole of the tradition, Comte's issuing in of the Positive Age, the early positivists' search for an ideal language and their verifiability criterion of cognitive meaningfulness,[5] and Husserl's early *Wesensanschauungen*,[6] for example. This most typical sense of "end" as *Vollendung* — completion or consummation — is no mere historical relic, however. The God's eye view often inspires those who yearn for eidetic reductions without hyletic trace or residue, as well as those in analytic philosophy of language who would wed essentialism to the so-called new theory of direct reference, Saul Kripke for example. *Vollendung* is not an end of philosophy devoutly to be wished; for if a final solution to philosophical questions were achieved, philosophy would become distinguishable from theology primarily with reference to what each took as its sacred text.[7] *That* there would have to be such a privileged text or texts — whose meaning and application it would become our job to review — should be obvious.

The God's eye view sense of the end of philosophy is peculiar precisely because in the sense of *Vollendung* it may be said to be coextensive with the history of philosophy itself. For it just *is* one common feature of our philosophic heritage that, at critical moments, each succeeding philosopher implies that he[8] has gotten it all right for the first time, and perhaps forever.[9]

(2) A second sense of "the end of philosophy" is what I shall call "the Politburo solution." Imagine, if you would, a world in which a philosophy in our first sense — the God's eye view — were to become dogma. Imagine further that it is part of this triumphant particular God's eye view to regard unfettered, open inquiry as subversive activity. Having gained hegemony, this God's eye view brands departments of unfettered inquiry subversive; and with it all philosophy departments are closed. While one should not confuse the end of philosophy with the end of philosophy departments, in time the result in my chilling New World scenario would be much the same. Philosophy books are suddenly burned or banned, new "revolutionary" thoughts are treason, collective forgetfulness reigns supreme. Philosophy as we know it shall have come to an end.

The Politburo solution sense of "the end of philosophy" is a permanent political possibility.[10] It has sometimes even been achieved.

(3) Less obvious than either the God's eye view or the Politburo solution as senses of the end of philosophy is skepticism. Skepticism, when construed as the claim that knowledge is not possible, is often

taken to be a philosophical position itself. And in its traditional academic form it certainly has been parasitic upon philosophy proper.[11] Its parasitology requires philosophy for its own existence, it has sometimes been said. And yet one can imagine a world in which the standard for knowledge claims is set so high that all we are left with is reasonable belief. In such a world knowledge *qua* apodictic certainty is not possible. Such a world would certainly be incompatible with the God's eye view. Indeed, if philosophy is understood as a search for a permanent neutral matrix, or ultimate foundation, or apodicticity, or a final framework and vocabulary, then skepticism just *is* the end of philosophy.

There are two more perhaps trivial senses of "the end of philosophy" worth mentioning. One sense is (4) the *de facto* cultural loss of philosophical activity, texts and memory, for reasons which have nothing whatsoever to do with philosophy itself – for example, the loss of "philosophy" during certain periods of the Middle Ages. Another is (5) the potential end of philosophy with the end of the human species in a possible nuclear war of global annihilation.[12].

(6) Finally, there is a sixth sense of "the end of philosophy." This may be characterized as the view that (a) there is no subject-matter called "philosophy," (b) there is no proper philosophic method, (c) there are no solutions to problems called "philosophical" and (d) the history of philosophy just *is* the failed attempt to define philosophic problems, the failed search for infallible methods and a series of failed proposed solutions.[13]

I take it that the sense of urgency and irritation which attaches to our symposium topic is the current vogue of this sixth sense in some quarters, particularly in France and in the United States. And I should like briefly to suggest two theses in this connection: the first thesis is that this sixth sense of "the end of philosophy" – let us call it the therapeutic, hermeneutic or pragmatist's sense – is best understood as an attempt to set aside the first sense, the foundationalist's God's eye view of philosophy. My second, perhaps more controversial thesis is that our common tendency to view sense six as philosophical nihilism is due to our own foundationalist hopes and expectations.

If the therapeutic/hermeneutic/pragmatic sense of the end of philosophy – the sense that there are no philosophical problems, properly speaking, no single philosophical method or set of solutions, and that the history of philosophy shows this to be the case – if this is understood superficially and uncharitably it results in paradox or silence. For if the therapist *argues* that there are no philosophical problems, method, or solutions he may be said to be doing philosophy itself,[14] because he must take the whole of the history of philosophy as evidence to argue his deconstructive thesis and he must show by philosophical analysis that proposed solutions have been mere pseudo-solutions. Or he must, like Heidegger, destroy and recapitulate the history of ontology, or deconstruct the metaphysics of presence à la Derrida — both decidedly philosophical undertakings, it seems to me. One other alternative open to the therapeutic philosopher is to cease to argue or to discuss philosophy at all. But in that case the therapist is no longer doing philosophy at all; he may be writing novels or playing bridge instead. And it is hard to see how not doing philosophy at all can count either as a thesis about or as a demonstration of the end of philosophy, unless we philosophize as we sleep. Finally, if in not doing philosophy the therapist points out that what he is now doing illustrates the end of philosophy, he runs the risk of being hailed as doing philosophy properly for the first time; he thus enlarges the subject while wishing instead to change it.

A more plausible account of the therapist's intention therefore is to regard him as attempting to displace traditional philosophical convictions, urging us to acknowledge and set aside our God's eye view hopes and preconceptions. To accomplish this we must give up at least the following, he might argue:

1. We are urged to give up the view that "philosophical problems" arise naturally upon reflection. Instead, philosophy names no natural kind, no activity intrinsic to our species, but is an historic, principally Western achievement.

2. Giving up #1 entails giving up the view that there is a fixed, permanent philosophical agenda, a set of problems which defines philosophy, a common paradigm which transcends natural languages, dictions, frameworks, idioms, distinctions and interests. We are asked to give up the textbook picture of philosophy as a United Nations translation service in which the living converse with the honored dead.

3. We are aksed to give up the notion of an inherent division of labor among disciplines, a division which marks philosophy neatly off from the arts and sciences, and the sciences from the arts. We are asked instead to view philosophy as a cultural genre — a voice in the conversation of mankind, in Oakeshott's phrase borrowed by Rorty — and to give up altogether the generic distinction between *Natur und Geisteswissenschaften*, between the natural and human sciences.[15].

4. If there is no metahistorical philosophical agenda, we are also asked to recognize that there are no final solutions to putative philosophical questions. Rather, in philosophy as elsewhere in culture, interests ebb and flow, and topics of conversation change. For example, philosophers trained in analytic circles three decades ago were worried

about the problem of the counterfactual conditional, the nature of analyticity, and the emotive meaning of ethical terms. Some of their European counterparts were at the same time concerned about the death of phenomenology in its existential incarnations, the proper definition of existentialism, and whether a pure domain of apodictic noemata could be grasped. The debates have shifted; scarcely anyone is concerned with such issues today. Philosophical issues are not solved it would appear; we simply – perhaps not "simply" – change the subject.

5. If there are no final solutions to philosophical questions then we must also come to see that there is no final vocabulary – no ultimate principles, distinctions, insights and frameworks – which defines rationality in virtue of its privileged attachment to reality, no vocabulary which is reality's own (potential) ultimate self-description.

6. Finally, we must be cautious about the generality and use of mirroring metaphors which have shaped our common representational vocabulary – instituted by Plato and codified by Descartes – which leads us to think of philosophy chiefly in representational terms. Talk of correctness or representation may be replaced, for example, with talk about what we are warranted or justified in asserting.[16]

Some of us may be inclined to think that giving up the six items I have just enumerated is equivalent to giving up philosophy itself. For it is surely to admit that there is no distinct permanent *Fach* which is philosophy's own, that there is no univocal philosophic method – what we today call argument analysis, for example, resembles "rhetoric" in the classical quadrivium – and that no answers to putative philosophical problems have withstood the test of time. But it is certainly fair to ask what is left after God's eye view assumptions have been displaced. An adequate answer, I regret to say, would take far too long, so I must content myself again with simple slogans.

The end of the God's eye view involves, paradoxically, the end of the end of philosophy; this may require, in Rorty's terms, a post-Philosophical culture, one in which philosophy understands itself as the interpretation, integration and self-reflection of the arts and sciences. Or, put in Hegel's terms, post-Philosophical philosophy is its own time reflected in thought, not in the sense that its own age is the object of reflection but that we see its age through its work – just as most of us have come to understand the Greeks essentially through Plato's and Aristotle's eyes. Philosophy in a post-Philosophical culture will be characterized – in Sellars' unhelpful phrase – as seeing how things, in the widest possible sense of the term, hang together, in the widest possible sense of the term. In such a culture the notion of corresponding to some brute *Ding an sich* will have lost its force. There will be no constraints upon philosophical inquiry save conversational ones, shaped by our shared need to cope.

I can illustrate my second thesis — that philosophical therapists are viewed as nihilists because they threaten our God's eye view yearnings — by turning briefly to two ways to characterize Nietzsche's perspectivism and then drawing a moral from these very characterizations.

Here is one way in which Nietzsche's perspectivist remarks have been construed: Nietzsche's perspectivism is, roughly, his theory of knowledge. On this account, there are four distinguishable claims: (1) no accurate representation of the world as it is in itself is possible; (2) there is nothing to which our theories stand in the required correspondence relation to enable us to say whether they are true or false; (3) no method of understanding our world — the sciences, logic, or moral theory — enjoys a privileged epistemic status; (4) human needs always help to "constitute" the world for us. Nietzsche tends to conflate some or all of these claims. But the most serious difficulty for Nietzsche's perspectivism lies elsewhere: the notorious self-reference problem. Are we to understand his many naturalistic theses as accurate representations of the world as it is in itself, as corresponding to any facts of the matter, as privileged perspectives, ones which are conditioned by no need whatsoever? If we are, then Nietzsche's perspectivism is self-contradictory in all four versions mentioned. But that is just to say that the theories Nietzsche offered either are not to be taken perspectivally — in which case his perspectivism must be abandoned — or they are only perspectives — in which case they may not be true and may be superseded. But to say that that they may not be "true" is just to say that what he maintains may be "false"; but then how can he maintain that there is nothing to which our theories stand in the required correspondence relation to enable us to determine whether they are true or false? Nietzsche's remarks about truth, interpretation and perspective seem to suffer from the liar's paradox disease. And similarly, if every great philosophy is really only "the personal confession of its author and a kind of involuntary and unconscious memoir," as Nietzsche asserts in *Beyond Good and Evil*, then what is Nietzsche confessing? What is his involuntary and unconscious memoir *really* about? Perhaps the best way to understand Nietzsche's perspectivism, then, is to construe it in a neo-Kantian way, as providing a transcendental standpoint in which putative "facts" about human needs and human neurophysiology play a role not unlike that of Kant's categories and forms of intuition. Think of it as the empirical turn gone transcendental. In admittedly different ways, this seems to be the framework common to the work of Danto, Wilcox and Schacht; or perhaps it is the framework toward which their work points.

Here is another, second and different way to construe Nietzsche's perspectivist remarks: Nietzsche's "perspectivism" is not a *theory* of anything, and it is certainly not a theory of knowledge. To say that there are only interpretations (or perspectives) is just to rename all the old facts "interpretations" (or "perspectives"). Similarly, to say that "truth" is "error" is not to offer a theory of truth so much as it is to rename it. The point of the renaming is to help us set aside the vocabulary of accurate representation which still holds us in its Platonic thrall. So Nietzsche's tropes concerning "truth" and "error," "fact" and "interpretation" are best understood as rhetorical devices to help us confront our preconception that there must be something like a final truth about reality as such which it is the goal of philosophy to disclose. A theory of knowledge is not something Nietzsche has; the yearning for its possession is what he parodies. Knowledge is the sort of thing about which one ought to have a theory primarily when the Platonic picture — the God's eye view — has seduced us, primarily when we construe "knowledge" in terms of visual metaphors — of the mind's eye seeing the way things really are — primarily if we see philosophy as culture's referee, as allowing or barring moves made elsewhere in culture which claim to be items of knowledge. Yet precisely this picture of philosophy is what Nietzsche urges ought to be set aside. "Knowledge" and "truth" are simply compliments paid to successful discourse. To give an account of such success is always to say why this *specific* item — e.g., the superiority of the heliocentric over the geocentric account of planetary motion — is "true" or "known." There can be explanations and illustrations of successful discourse on a case by case basis, explanations and illustrations of the relative attraction of various concrete proposals; but there can only be a misconceived "theory of" successful discourse. Again in admittedly different ways, this seems to me to be a useful way of capturing an orientation common to Derrida, Alderman, Allison, Deleuze and Rorty, for example.

God's eye view philosophers and commentators are likely to be attracted to different versions of my first characterization of perspectivism because they regard offering theories of knowledge, as well as theories about the nature of the universe, and theories of the ideal life as philosophical tasks proper, tasks it is our duty to undertake. From their perspective one has difficulty grasping how anyone would or should *care* about Nietzsche's remarks concerning perspectivism, or eternal recurrence and the Übermensch, for that matter, unless these remarks are recast either as proposing a theory – in some sense – or as contributions to a theory of knowledge, the universe, and the ideal life.

Therapeutic philosophers and commentators are likely to be attracted to different versions of my second characterization of perspectivism. Such readers will regard as quaint, or worse, attempts to interpret Nietzsche as a philosopher who proposes new answers to textbook philosophic questions. They will already have concluded that what are called the "perennial problems of philosophy" are just each generation's revisionist reading of the great monuments of the past, ritual gesture to our honored dead, to make them conform to the current generation's interests by reading their works as addressed to the very same matters which engage our current attention; but that is always a revisionist metahistory on their view. Such post-Philosophical philosophers will conclude that those who read Nietzsche as a philosopher who addresses textbook questions are really only trying to make his concerns and insights conform to their own foundationalist conception of philosophy as a Platonic-Cartesian-Kantian undertaking; they will see that as an attempt to situate Nietzsche within the metaphysics of presence, rather than initiating its self-cancellation. And they will regard this as pointless and naive, since Nietzsche attempted to liberate us precisely from the notion that the Platonic-Cartesian-Kantian enterprise is still worth undertaking, that the metaphysics of presence still has any point, that there *are* problems of knowledge, or morals or ontology which are left over after the present state of "knowledge" – social practices – have been subtracted from our common vocabulary. They will read Nietzsche as having performed the therapeutic function of showing us that only on a certain optional conception of "philosophy" are there any metahistorical "perennial problems" at all; and they will regard him as among the first in a long line of liberating voices – along with James' and Dewey's, Heidegger's and Wittgenstein's, Derrida's, Gadamer's, Kuhn's, Rorty's and Foucault's – which tried to tell us that we can abandon without loss the need to satisfy our God's eye view yearning, our felt need to see philosophy as reality's potential canonical self-description.

Which commentators are right, those with God's eye view expectations or therapeutic ones? Can one decide such a question?

There is no fact of the matter that I know of which will tell us who is right here. If God's eye view foundationalists continue to prevail over therapists, particularly within analytic trend-setting departments in the United States, then it will be business as usual. If the therapeutic lineage prevails, on the other hand, that will mean primarily that Nietzsche and James will be read more earnestly than (the *begeisterte* side of) Hegel and (the dialectical materialist side of) Marx, that Dewey and Heidegger will be read more earnestly than Russell and Husserl, that the later Wittgenstein will be read as having defeated his own *Tractatus* decisively, that Derrida, Rorty, Gadamer, Kuhn and Foucault will be read with as much seriousness by students of philosophy as is now expended on Quine, Kripke, Husserl and Rawls at leading American universities. In such a culture we shall then come to see the God's eye view as something which held us captive for more than two thousand years but by which we are no longer seduced; we shall have seen through our need to ground our practices in some infallible abiding presence; in brief, we shall have given up philosophy as an epistemology-centered discipline along with the spectator theory of knowledge; and "if that day comes, it will seem as quaint to treat a man's knowledge as a special relation between his mind and its object as it now "does to treat his goodness as a special relation between his soul and God."[17]

2. The End of Philosophy: Three Historical Aphorisms

Thomas M. Seebohm

Marx's *Introduction to the Critique of Hegel's Philosophy of the Right* is one of the earliest texts in which the "end of philosophy" is a central topic.[1] He refers here, however, to a debate which had already begun when he wrote the *Introduction*. Thus this symposium could be understood as the celebration of an anniversary: 150 years of the "end of philosophy movement." This invites historical reflections. Considering the 150 years, one discovers that almost every significant thinker of this period – Marx, Comte, Nietzsche, Dilthey, Husserl, Wittgenstein, Carnap, Heidegger, Adorno, Gadamer, Derrida – deals with the end of philosophy or the end of metaphysics in one sense or another. To find a common denominator is very difficult. *Prima facie* the common denominator is that each position accuses the foregoing positions to be still "metaphysical." Furthermore, a main weapon in the polemic is to be found in different types of ideology critique unearthing forgotten metaphysical presuppositions. But since each type of ideology critique presupposes for its validity the position from which it is used, the "victories" are only victories for those who share the position. Thus the situation resembles the situation which Kant described as the "battlefield of metaphysics" shortly before the beginning of the "end of philosophy movement." This implies that for each position in that movement the understanding of what is at an end, and how it is at an end, is different.

Another common denominator of the movement is that the judgment "philosophy is at an end" is always also understood as an historical judgment. Though none of the aforementioned thinkers will admit that this is essential for his thesis, I want to try to analyze the judgment as an historical judgment hoping that this can lead to something more.

An analysis of a judgment has to cover three aspects: (1) the meaning of the predicate term, (2) the meaning of the subject term, and (3) the situation in which the judgment can be uttered with a claim for validity. From the historical point of view (1) is the question: what does "to come to an end" mean for literary traditions in general? A literary tradition is a set of texts which, either explicitly or implicitly, refer to each other according to their chronological order with respect to a certain topic. To see it that way has the advantage of including after the end of that tradition also the texts which proclaim the end of that tradition just because they refer to it. Accordingly (2) has to be answered by saying something about the topics, but also about the different approaches to the topics developed in the tradition. To answer question (3), one has also to take into account the viewpoints under which the tradition has been declared to be incompetent, i.e. literature which had rejected that tradition already at the time in which it was still alive. Furthermore it has to be asked whether such attempts were sometimes successful and why they failed in the long run. Only on the background of such information can it be asked what the factor in the situation is which justifies the judgment that the tradition is from now on forever at an end. Factors or reasons which had been given before are not sufficient because they actually did not succeed in putting an end to the tradition. (3) will have, therefore, two parts. There is no possibility of giving a corroborated account for my answers to the three questions. Hence I call what I will have to say "aphorisms."

First Aphorism, Concerning "to be at an end"

"To be at an end" has different meanings with respect to literary traditions and especially with respect to the literary tradition of philosophy.

(I) One can distinguish between phases in which a literary tradition was productive and those in which what was produced is reproduced in positive applications. History teaches that the productive phases of philosophy are rare and extremely short — two or three generations — and that the phases of reproduction are very long. "Philosophy is at an end" is, seen from here, a judgment which implies that philosophy has exhausted all of its possibilities and that philosophical activity in the future is restricted to reproduction and corroborating interpretation. Such a judgment can only be justified if there is a philosophical system in which it can be shown that all possibilities are indeed exhausted, i.e. in which a full account of the tradition can be given. Hegel's system claims to be such a system. It is such a system which is, therefore, what has to be reproduced again and again in the future. Since an account for all possible approaches in philosophy cannot be given with the aid of the methods used in these approaches themselves it will always include the meaning of "philosophy is at its end" mentioned below in (II.A.b.).

(II) "Is at its end" implies a negative application of the tradition, i.e. the pregiven tradition is in part or as a whole rejected as incompetent and outdated. Such a rejection can either be a rejection only of the approaches used in the tradition (A) or include the rejection of the topics in addition (B).

(A) The Cartesian revolution in philosophy was of type (A). As all later revolutions of this type, it distinguishes its own approach from all previous approaches as the scientific versus the prescientific approach. There are as many variants of such "revolutions" as there are ideas about what "scientific" can mean with respect to philosophy.

(a) What "scientific" means is determined with the aid of an investigation of what it means with respect to pregiven disciplines which are already on the secure path of science. It is, in addition, assumed that all problems connected with the topics of philosophy can be solved by the new scientific method.

(b) What "scientific" means with respect to philosophy is *toto genere* different from what it means with respect to other sciences. Philosophy as a science in this sense requires a completely new, hitherto unknown attitude. Examples are speculative thinking in the sense of German Idealism and Husserl's epoche. If the claim is added that the new attitude can give an account not only for all topics of the tradition but also for all approaches and methods used there determining their rights and their limits, then the meaning of "is at its end" in (II.A.b.) will merge with the meaning (I).

(c) The method of philosophy has to be scientific in the sense of (a), but the specific understanding of "scientific" which emerges has the consequence that most of the topics of traditional philosophy become meaningless because they cannot be formulated in the language of science. Philosophy is reduced to epistemology. Its method is reduced to mathematico-logical analysis.

(B) The negative application of a tradition is most radical when it is claimed that its topics are meaningless and worthless because there exists no approach in which they can be treated meaningfully. Furthermore the claim can be made that to be fascinated by such topics has evil consequences. To be fascinated by them means to develop a faulty and destructive attitude to life and its real values. There can be no doubt that the judgement "philosophy is at its end" in the last 150 years is of type (II.B.). History teaches us, however, that the history of philosophy was always accompanied by other literary traditions which passed a similar verdict on philosophy. The third aphorism will come back to this point.

Second Aphorism Concerning "what" is at its End

A complication has to be taken into account before answering this question. Kant proclaimed the end of metaphysics as a theoretical science already at the end of the eighteenth century. Immediately after that his critical philosophy was itself criticized by a radical scepticism influenced by Hume but also by motives belonging to the antiphilo-sophical traditions in which the incompetency of philosophy had been asserted before Hume.[2] German Idealism is on the one hand the attempt to deal with that situation and presents itself on the other hand as an "end of philosophy" position of the type (II.A.b.). Some closer considerations will be necessary in the third aphorism. For the second aphorism it is essential to keep in mind that the "end of philosophy movement" was in its beginning a reaction to a phase in the history of philosophy in which the end of philosophy in the sense (I) and (II.A.b.) was already reflected in philosophy itself. Thus an answer to the question "what is at an end" should restrict itself at least in the beginning to the phase of the tradition which ends with Kant's precritical philosophy.

A general historical answer to the question "what is philosophy" can restrict itself to a list of the basic topics which philosophical literature has dealt with in general. But it is not necessary to give defini-tions of the topics; for their concepts changed in the course of the history of philosophy, together with the approaches under which they were considered. It is sufficient to mention their names and the relations they had to each other. The answer must be sufficient only for the purpose of determining whether a certain text belongs to the literary tradition which represents philosophy. All historical research beyond that point is concerned already with the characteristics of philosophy in a certain period of its development, and not with the general concept of philosophy to the extent in which it can be determined for history.

A broader and a narrower sense of "philosophy" has to be distinguished. Philosophy in the broader sense included the sciences, mathematics and physics. It is often said that they split from philosophy after they matured, but already Aristotle had taught that the type of knowledge given in these disciplines is different from the type of knowing belonging to philosophy in the narrower sense. That physics belongs to philosophy in the broader sense was still recognized in Kant's time. Physics was called *philosophia naturalis*.

Philosophy in the narrower sense was divided into theoretical and practical philosophy, metaphysics or first philosophy, and ethics. In Kant's time this division was undercut by another one within metaphysics itself. There was on the one hand general metaphysics or general ontology dealing with the transcendentals and the categories as determinations of being. General ontology was supposed to lay the ground for epistemology and the sciences which belong to philosophy in the broader sense. On the other hand there was special metaphysics dealing with being as totality, being as transcending all beings. Special metaphysics delivered viewpoints for practical philosophy which had in addition its own principles. Finally there was general consent that the goal of philosophy was practical, the good life, and that theoretical life being itself an activity has its value only to the extent in which it serves that purpose.[3]

As metaphysics is, hence, the cornerstone of traditional philosophy, a rejection of metaphysics, such as in (II.A.c.), is a rejection of philosophy itself. The approach to metaphysical problems is what determined the positions of the different philosophical schools in the history of philosophy. Two common denominators can thus be identified. There was agreement that metaphysics was about foundations, principles. Foundationalism is characteristic for metaphysics, regardless of the fact that there was disagreement with respect to the question how and to what extent principles can be known. Foundationalism, in the sense used here, is by no means restricted to the type of foundationalism which asks for a clear and distinct knowledge of some first principles from which all other metaphysical knowledge has to be deduced. It includes also cases in which e.g. knowledge of first principles is supposed to be gained by some kind of induction and/or dialectical investigations in the scholastic sense. The second general assumption is that the principles are eternal and determine a fixed framework in which the question "what is man" and man's relation to being, which is of practical significance, can be answered. Even Kant's approach, which reduces metaphysics to a metaphysics of experience and recognizes the logical possibility of other types of experience with different ontological categories, works with the tacit assumption that the system of categories which determines human experience will never change.[4] Such an assumption implies, however, that there is a fixed structure of the universe and humanity which remains the unchanged foundation of all change.

Third Aphorism: The Situation

Part I

As mentioned above, the history of philosophy is accompanied throughout by literary traditions which declare its incompetency. Kant observed that dogmatic metaphysics has had scepticism as its contender from the very beginning.[5] The relation of philosophy and scepticism can be characterized as follows. The application of sceptical methods, namely to develop diaphonies and antinomies in metaphysical questions and to argue for both sides with equal rigour, is a necessary tool of a thorough philosophical investigation. The philosopher is in this case interested either in finally making a decision for one side of the controversy, or in discovering ambiguities in basic concepts which are responsible for the development of an antinomy in a critical approach. The sceptic is not interested in such solutions. Diaphonies are for him the indicator of the incompetence of philosophy. He will try to reestablish them for every philosophical solution offered.

Already Sextus Empiricus had shown that the attempt to give a formal refutation of scepticism is futile. The sceptical thesis is not that knowledge is impossible, the thesis is rather that even this thesis is undecidable.[6] The real weakness of scepticism as a theoretical enterprize is that it is parasitic on philosophy. It can succeed only with respect to pregiven forms of philosophy, but it cannot bring philosophy to a definite end. Fichte pointed out that the claim that the true principles never will be found in the future because they have not been found in the past "is a presumption whose refutation is below the dignity of serious considerations."[7] The justification of such a claim can only be given on the basis of a confirmed theory of human knowing which exhausts all of its possibilities and establishes a firm conclusion about its impossibility, i.e. which has to utter the thesis which the refined sceptic has to avoid in order to safeguard his enterprize against the formal refutation of scepticism. Furthermore, philosophy has a practical goal, the good life. The sceptical activity as theoretical activity does not offer an alternative in this respect. It was, however, the additional thesis of all serious sceptics that philosophy cannot reach this goal but is, on the contrary, an obstacle to finding *ataraxia*, the tranquillity of the soul.[8] That means that the theoretical activity of scepticism against philosophy can be connected with other attitudes which claim as well that philosophy does not reach its practical goal and is even an hindrance of grasping that goal, a task which can only be fulfilled in attitudes foreign to philosophy.

Pneumatism or mysticism was the most powerful tradition which made such a claim. It succeeded in Byzantium — and in medieval Russia — in virtually blotting out philosophy for centuries. It succeeded in blotting out philosophy in the islamic culture forever. The sceptical work of deconstructing philosophy and to declare its incompetency was done in the latter case by Al Ghasali.[9] These two cases are for the historical point of view of highest interest for the evaluation of the judgment "philosophy is at its end." The history of the western European culture can lead to the false conclusion that philosophy, if it is established, will come to an end as a cultural activity only in a general collapse of the culture, and that the early, really dark, middle ages are an instance of such a collapse. It is, however, very much a question of whether the real factor for the vanishing of philosophy in this period is the collapse of the state or, on the other hand, pneumatism. The parallel vanishing of philosophy in Byzantium is not accompanied by a general collapse of the culture. That means that philosophy can come to an end if at some period the thrust in its theoretical competency breaks down and a powerful contender is capable to establish an ideal of the good life in other than philosophical terms. History teaches that this actually was the case for long periods and even that a revival of philosophy may never take place after it has been uprooted in a culture.

Pneumatism or mysticism can express its claims in many ways. For a brief sketch, the concepts can be considered which were used in the cases mentioned above in which pneumatism was most successful. They were developed in the monastic-gnostic tradition of minor Asia. According to this view philosophy cannot reach its theoretical goal, the source of being, because philosophy, science, and externally practiced religion are activities of the psychic man. The psychic man tries to overcome the flesh, the hyletic man. He will, however, always fail and fall back to the hyletic level because in his thinking he reaches only for external grounds and means. The source of being, God, can be reached, on the contrary, only in a higher "thinking" which reveals the source of being in silent meditation which is the fruit of the highest form of human praxis, the ascetic life. Thus philosophy as such must be considered as the most subtle source of evil, a seduction which is an obstacle in the way on which man can reach his final destination.[10]

Philosophy has, however, after an attack by pneumatism, a chance of a renaissance. The pneumatic is communicable only on the psychic level. Mystical literature using religious paradigms sketches out a fixed structure of the universe and the place of man in it. A further conceptual corroboration leads to dogmatic theology and dogmatic theology can give shelter for metaphysics. The rise of the prophetical religions was as such not a threat of the survival of philosophy as long as there was an interest in dogmatic theology and this interest was dominating; for a radical rejection of philosophy requires that the interest in dogmatic theology be replaced − and even itself be rejected − by pneumatism. This was the case in the monastic schools even in western Europe in the early middle ages.[11] The reason why philosophy did not survive in Islam might be that the interest in dogmatic theology has been weak also in periods in which pneumatism was not governing.

The second contender against philosophy in the tradition is humanism. Its claims against philosophy were first explicitly formulated in the hellenistic period. The wisdom of the humanist is grounded in two factors. The first is universal philological knowledge of the tradition. It includes everything: poetry, religious knowledge, the sciences, philosophy and also viewpoints against philosophy − sceptical viewpoints as well as pneumatical viewpoints − and the art of rhetoric. The applied art of rhetoric is the second factor. It is the art of applying all philologically obtained knowledge in the proper situation, and thus also of broadening such knowledge in its application. The wisdom of the humanist is in this way grounded in the unity of interpretation and application which is at work in all human activities. Rhetoric functions in the sciences as the *ars inveniendi*.[12]

The humanist uses sceptical viewpoints in order to invalidate the claim of philosophy to have an access to knowledge which is special.[13] Truth is, in the case of philosophy as well as in jurisprudence, the sciences, and poetry, that which surfaces in the process of the rhetorical application in concrete situations. Thus the wisdom of the humanist is higher than the philosopher's wisdom. It is universally practical, i.e. it knows where philosophical viewpoints can and cannot be applied and is hence capable of doing what philosophy cannot do, namely to develop concrete guidelines for the good life in concrete situations.

The chances for a renaissance of philosophy after periods in which humanism has dominated are similar to those it has vis-a-vis pneumatism. Traditional humanism works with the tacit assumption that the tradition provides us with an ideal of humanity and its place in the universe which does not change and which has a fixed structure. It is that fixed structure which in the final instance provides the basis for the validity claims of humanism. The conceptual explication of this structure − and hence the validity claim − would lead back to philosophy, and the philosophical literature in which such attempts are made belong to the tradition recognized by the humanist. The attempt of the humanist to safeguard himself with sceptical viewpoints against such a temptation shares the general weakness of scepticism mentioned above.

Part II

It is easy to rediscover certain *topoi* of the older anti-philosophical literature in the contemporary "end of philosophy movement." The following list is by no means complete: "Philosophy fails in dealing with concrete human reality." "We need a more thoughtful thinking beyond philosophy which has access to being." "Metaphysics is a source of evil, especially of dehumanizing technology." "Objective validity of knowledge is an untenable ideal." "Truth emerges in the unity of interpretation and application." "'True' is a compliment paid to successful speech." "With 'philosophy' one should not refer to a specific discipline but rather to an activity connecting all disciplines."

A *prima facie* response for such findings could be the following. Though these *topoi* are used by scholars who are called philosophers and belong to institutions which are called "departments of philosophy," it should be recognized that they characterize their position with *topoi* which are largely parallel to those of the humanists of the philological-rhetorical syndrome which turns against philosophy. Others have strong family resemblances with *topoi* of the pneumatists position. As mentioned, this position is not excluded from humanism, it is included here as well as scepticism.[14] If that is the case then, in order to avoid misnomers, one could recommend certain reorganizations — some of which already exist in liberal arts colleges. Instead of a department of philosophy one should have a program in the humanities. Such a program shoud be interdisciplinary. There should be chairs for the history of philosophical literature. In addition, one would want to establish a chair for a professional deconstructor of all attempts to restore traditional metaphysics and a chair for hermeneutics and rhetorics. The task of the latter would be to teach how philosophical literature, alongside with other literatures, has to be read and interpreted according to the aforementioned principles.

Such a *prima facie* response does not take into account that *topoi* can be transferred from one context to another and that, in the process, they receive a different meaning and a different significance. Such a transfer must have taken place if the judgment that "philosophy is at its end" is to have validity with respect to the present situation and, hence, a situation which is different from the one in which a judgment concerning the incompetency of philosophy was uttered in the tradition. As shown above, the situation in the tradition never justified a judgment about a definitive end of philosophy. Thus there must be a new factor in the present situation which grounds the judgment "philosophy is at its end."

A search for this factor has to take into account that philosophy had reestablished itself, immediately before the beginning of the contemporary "end of philosophy movement," by claiming the end of all traditional philosophy in the sense (I) and (II.A.b.). Some aspects of this idea of philosophy are of significance. (a) Philosophy has to reestablish itself beyond completed scepticism. (b) Philosophy has to give a coherent account of the whole sphere of erudition, *Bildung*, i.e. all contents of traditional humanism. (c) Philosophy as speculative thinking can establish itself beyond pneumatism, *Geistreligion*. The implication is (d) that philosophy has to give an account not only for the history of philosophy, but also of human culture in general, including the contenders of philosophy in the past.[15]

Looking into the beginning of the "end of philosophy movement" in the nineteenth century as a turn away from this reestablishment of philosophy, one can identify the factor asked for. The turn is not the simple turn towards concrete human reality in which a fixed ideal of humanity is tacitly presupposed as in traditional humanism. In Marx as well as in Comte the turn is a turn towards concrete *historical* human reality. The point of departure is, hence, (d). The turn is not grounded in any argument. It is based in an *experience*, the *experience of history*.

This analysis can be supported by pointing to two other turns of a similar kind. Husserl also tried in the beginning of the twentieth century to reestablish philosophy on the level (I) and (II.A.b.). In the beginning, i.e. in 1913, he still thought that he could deal with history and historicism in the same way he dealt with psychology and psychologism. At the end of his life he realized that the threat coming from history was much more serious than he expected and that his original program was dropped by most of his alleged disciples who were in one way or the other fascinated by *historicity*.[16] The truncated type of philosophy which is the result of bringing philosophy to an end according to (II.A.c.) still flourished as scientific logico-mathematical epistemology at the beginning of the second half of the twentieth century. It came to an abrupt end in the last decades with the "discovery" that the concrete reality of the sciences can only be reached by studying the *history* of the sciences, a move very much appreciated by already existing "end of philosophy" positions.[17]

On this basis the thesis of the third aphorism can now tentatively be formulated. "Philosophy is at its end" is not only an historical judgment, it is also the judgment, the *verdict*, passed by history on philosophy. It is, so to speak, the revenge of history for the treatment it received by philosophy in the beginning. In order to have that revenge, history had only to sit back and watch itself growing. In the end it could raise a mirror for mankind in which mankind received an image of itself which ridiculed all attempts of the philosophers – and not only of the philosophers – to say something definitive about the human condition.

The experience of history has layers. Already on the first layer the image reveals the folowing – sometimes surpressed in the later development – objective characteristics. (1) One's own cultural tradition is not a unity but represents a development with levels which are incompatible. (2) Outside one's own tradition others are discovered which are as well incompatible with our culture. (3) In the far distance – historically as well as geographically – the cultures of the savage mind are discovered marking the beginning point of human history, and revealing that human history is itself only a small segment of the history of life and nature. The immediate and devastating consequences are: (a) Mankind is not temporally coexistent with the universe. Science moved mankind out of the center of the universe. History combined with science taught mankind that it was and is an episode in the history of nature. (b) In its own history mankind is of tremendous plasticity and can, hence, be developed in the future into something completely beyond its present stage. (c) Every self-understanding of mankind rests on a dark ground hidden in an impenetrable past.

Such an image destroys the presupposition of traditional philosophy, the assumption that there is an unchangable system of principles, *archai*, but it destroys also the tacit presuppositions of its traditional contenders concerning a fixed human condition. As said above, these tacit presuppositions grounded the possibility of a renaissance of philosophy in all periods in which it could survive only in the subculture. Since that grounding is no longer given, the judgment "philosophy is at its end" can claim to be a definitive judgment in the new situation. But it holds as well that the new "program in the humanities" can have nothing in common with the comfortable humanism of the tradition. Its victory over philosophy depends on the acceptance of the image of humanity provided by history.

As said, there are layers in the experience of history. On the first layer history is understood objectively and it is assumed that a proper "scientific" analysis of history will provide us with what is necessary for the understanding of the present phase of our cultural development and its near future. Such attempts had to use, however, some general ontology of history and change in general and hence a metaphysics of matter-in-change. Such assumptions are, however, not acceptable for the experience of history on the second level. History establishes itself on this level as universal human science, *universale Geisteswissenschaft.* This layer can be criticized from the first layer for being in danger of forgetting what history teaches us in combination with science about man's place in the universe and producing the illusion that we can restore some modified type of good old humanism. It can be criticized as well from the third layer for the assumption that there is something like objective validity in the human sciences. The essence of history − historicity − allows us claims for truth, even with respect to understanding the image of mankind given by history, only as claims valid in the unity of interpretation and application in the present situation; i.e. the image of mankind given by history as being inexhaustively plastic is itself in what it shows from case to case conditioned by historicity and, hence, of the same plasticity. What is reached here is a new type of "scepticism" which is no longer parasitic on philosophy. It is the outcome of a reflection on the experience of history and historicity. This is finally the situation grounding the validity of the judgment "philosophy is at its end."

Postscript

The task was to say something about "the end of philosophy." What remains is to make some remarks concerning my views regarding a possible revival which surfaced in the discussion. I cannot explain them in detail. They have to be offered as theses which cannot be justified here.

First, I do think that any attempt to secure the future of philosophy by going back to some past phases of its development, especially to the ancients, will not be successful. They will all evade the real problem philosophy has to face and represent, therefore, different types of escapism.

Secondly, it is not difficult to see that my account concerning the situation in which we find ourselves is throughout compatible with what has been said by Professor Magnus and Professor Schrag. I differ from them (1) with respect to the chosen terminology. I think that the affinities of modern thought to the philological-rhetorical syndrome on the one hand and to the experience of history on the other constitutes such a sharp opposition to philosophy in the sense of the tradition that to call this type of thinking "philosophy" is close to the creation of an equivocation. This might be, however, only a question of the introduction of proper *caveats* with which both have provided us sufficiently.

(2) I am by no means as comfortable with the situation as they seem to be. What they characterize as the new form in which philosophy will survive is for me a situation of radical instability. A program of education and learning grounded in the situation as I described it and really facing it as it has to be faced in its harsh reality might pretty soon create an "unhappy consciousness" in Hegel's sense but on a level which is much more radical. It may cause a turn to positive religion and pneumatism and dissolve itself in such a turn in the same way in which hellenistic scepticism turned into a weapon of apologetics and rhetorics into an instrument of preaching.

Finally, I think that philosophers must, as Hegel said, stick to their principle, foundationalism, *à corps perdue*[18] and that they have to do that not by escaping but by facing the experience of history. The brief sketch of the development of the layers of this experience in the end of the third aphorism indicates that this experience is by no means free from antinomies. But that means that *critique* is possible and necessary, a critique which asks back towards the structure of this experience, its foundations. It should not be forgotten that there is still the possibility of following the path outlined in (II.A.b.). What Kant, the German Idealists, and Husserl developed in this respect is insufficient given the present situation; but it can be developed further. Fichte's objection against the denial of the meaningfulness of the task of philosophy mentioned above may be still valid. Thus my conclusion is: philosophy can have a revival only if it can give a satisfactory critique of the experience of history in all of its aspects. Such a critique is still the task of the future. It is, in the meantime, no hindrance for the possibility of a future critical reflection, if the type of thinking created in the "end of philosophy movement" is pushed to its limits in ultimate radicality. A critique of an experience requires the full development of that experience. "The owl of Minerva spreads its wings only with the falling of the dusk." Is the dusk falling after 150 years of the "end of philosophy movement"?

3. Subjectivity and Praxis at the End of Philosophy

Calvin O. Schrag

S ince the announcement of the "end of philosophy" we have been besieged, almost daily, with reports about the "death of the subject". Our intention in this paper is to show that this report, in the words of Mark Twain's response to the news release of his death, is a "gross exaggeration." The subject is alive and well.

The report on the death of subject has come to us from many quarters. Michel Foucault in his announcement of the "death of man" has informed us that man, "an invention of recent date", will soon be erased − "like a face drawn in sand at the edge of the sea."[1] Roland Barthes in his funeral oration, "Death of the Author," has detailed the demise of the subject in literary theory.[2] Levi-Strauss has reported the expiration of the subject in yet another domain − in the republic of the human sciences. The principle task in the current human sciences, according to Levi-Strauss, is not to constitute the human subject but rather to dissolve it.[3] In Derrida's grammatology the subject is pretty much deconstructed to the bone, and if one can indeed still talk about a marrow which remains, it is in the shape of *écriture* − the event and form of writing.

Many of these strategies of dissolution and deconstruction exhibit, either consciously or unconsciously, a debt to Martin Heidegger, who was after all the first of the postmoderns to recommend a wholesale "destruction" (*Destruktion*) of the history of ontology proceeding by way of a "deconstruction" (*Abbau*) of traditional metaphysical and epistemological concepts.[4] In the wake of all this, the philosophical uses of "subject" and "subjectivity" are clearly brought under suspicion, and we are forced to ask, "Is there life after death of the subject?"

There are clearly many lessons to be learned from the masters of deconstruction and from the story which they tell. This story cannot be rehearsed here for it is a very involved one. Derrida's deconstructive strategy is not of a piece with that of Heidegger. Foucault and Barthes share many similar interests, but they follow different paths in pursuing these interests. Levi-Strauss is most unlike all the rest, assessing the dissolution of the subject as a fallout of a methodological decision on what counts as the doing of science. Our present task is not that of exploring the similarities and differences in the various deconstructionist postures, however important such a task might be, but rather that of isolating some of the central features germaine to the project of a recovery of the subject at the end of philosophy.

We enter the conversation about reflections on the end of philosophy with a general observation, laying down a general thesis. Reminiscent of Merleau-Ponty's assessment of the lesson to be learned from the phenomenological reduction – namely, that no complete reduction is possible – we propose that the main lesson to be learned from the contemporary flurry of deconstructionist strategy is that no complete deconstruction is possible. The disassemblage of the classical substance-attribute categorial scheme and the modern empirico-transcendental doublet does not entail a displacement of the subject in every sense you please. We wish to show, quite to the contrary, that the proper charge of such a disassemblage is to provide a clearing for a restoration of the subject. It opens the path to a transvalued subjectivity within a new space, making it possible to speak of a new humanism at the end of philosophy.

Our defense of this thesis proceeds along the lines of two stages of development. The first stage is what one might call a radicalization of the Cartesian way. The strategy in this first stage of exploration still moves within the space of traditional metaphysical and epistemological ruminations, but in such a way that it already gathers the resources for thinking beyond it. The second stage involves a break, a shift away from, a setting aside of the space of traditional philosophical inquiry in an effort to reclaim the subject as decentered subjectivity, restored within the contours and texture of another space – the hermeneutical space of communicative praxis. The first stage can be named the strategy of critical hermeneutics as deconstructionist critique; the second stage is that of a restorative hermeneutics, reclaiming the subject within the *ethos* of a new humanism.

The first stage takes shape as a reformulation and radicalization of the Cartesian argument for the ego-cogito. In addressing the topic of subjectivity it is our historical destiny to begin with Descartes for it was he who invented the modern concept of the subject as the source and center for his philosophy of mind. This invention of the subject, orchestrated as an argument for th ego-cogito, proceeds within the framework of a strategy of systematic doubt and the epistemic require-ments of intuition and deductive inference. All contents of experiential and rational truths can be subject to doubt, save the inescapable "fact" of a doubter. One can doubt and think away the reality of everything save the reality that one is doubting, that one is thinking. Thus the strategy of systematic doubt allegedly delivers an indubitable cogito, intuitively grasped in every performance of thought reflectively directed to itself. Thought presupposes a "who" that is thinking; doubt pre-supposes a "who" that is doubting.

There is, we suggest, a similar play operative in the strategy of deconstruction, yielding not the truth of Cartesian subjectivity, the "I think, therefore I am", but rather a deconstructionalist modification — "I deconstruct, therefore I am". In dismantling subjectivity as a posi-tional center and a zero-point consciousness, peeling away the sedimented layers of philosophical construction, some species of claim upon the subject remain in force. The very strategy of deconstruction serendipitously reinvents the subject and instructs us that no complete deconstruction is possible. Although this is a truth that has been forgot-ten by some of the latter-day deconstructionists, it was grasped clearly enough by Derrida. In his response to a question from Serge Doubrov-sky following the presentation of his essay on "Structure, Sign, and Play" at the 1966 international symposium at Johns Hopkins University, Derrida offered an unequivocal reply: "The subject is absolutely indis-pensable. I don't destroy the subject; I situate it. That is to say, I believe that at a certain level both of experience and of philosophical and scien-tific discourse one cannot get along without the notion of subject. It is a question of knowing where it comes from and how it functions".[5] If indeed the subject is "absolutely indispensable," as Derrida proclaims, then the question about its proper placement needs to be pursued with some diligence. This question takes on a particular urgency when it becomes a question about the "who" of experience and the "who" of philosophical and scientific discourse. And it is this question about the "who" that is the genuine bugbear.

It is precisely at this juncture, where one is compelled to ask and re-ask the question about the "who", that the Cartesian way founders. And it founders principally because the inquiry standpoint is still geared to a search for a *res*, a residuum, a center of consciousness, a stable presence that somehow supports the processual stream of thoughts. To fill the bill, delivering all these good things, Descartes invented the modern concept of mind in the guise of an unimpeachable ego-cogito. This concept of mind, however, still called upon the classical doctrine of substance to provide consciousness with a stable support, an abiding and ever-present ego, an Archimedian point of certainty.

This quest for a durable concept of mind within such a metaphysico-epistemological space, however, comes up short. It is precisely here that the Cartesian argument fractures, and fails in its effort to deliver a warrantability for the inference from the fact of thought to a substantial support for it. Hence, the truth of the ego-cogito as a thinking substance remains perpetually deferred. The search for the "who" as *knower, mind*, or *cognitive subject*, within the parameters of epistemological space, ends in failure.

Now the proper response to this unsettling state of affairs, we would urge, is not a further probing of epistemological space and its protocols of pure theory (categories, propositions, and beliefs), but rather a shift to another space and another strategy of questioning. In this shift the question of the "who" is addressed against the backcloth of the conversation, habits, skills and institutional involvements that limn the hermeneutical space of communicative praxis. What informs the quest for a restoration of subjectivity is no longer a system of beliefs, about which one can always remain skeptical, but a history of social practices. One can always suspend beliefs and their putative criteria for justification, but one cannot escape one's praxis – one's linguistic and institutional engagements. One can always defer theoretical judgments about oneself, but in the meantime one continues to speak, act, work, play, and assume social roles. This is the domain of communicative praxis, and it is here, we suggest, that we look for a possible restoration of subjectivity.

The general thesis that we will attempt to support is that the subject, deconstructed as a cognitive center in an epistemological space, undergoes a hermeneutical self-implicature in the space of communicative praxis. What we call the hermeneutical implicature of self takes the place of the Cartesian argument for the ego-cogito and its epistemic requirements of intuition and inference. This comprises a methodological shift, which may be more of a shift away from methodology than a shift to another methodology. The strategy of argumentation, proof, intuition, deduction, and inference (which has informed philosophical method since the time of Descartes) is set aside to make room for the play of interpretive discernment and description. This does not mean that argumentation, proof, and procedures of inference are intrinsic evils to be shunned; they are relativized and seen as efficacious only within the contours of the wider, global space of praxis. It is within this praxial space that the question about the "who" is properly asked, and it is asked in the more specific forms of "Who is speaking?", "Who is writing?", and "Who is acting?" Communicative praxis, as an amalgam of spoken and written discourse and action, implicates the subject as speaker, author, and actor. This hermeneutical self-implicature, it needs be underscored, functions not as a *foundation* for communicative praxis but rather makes manifest the odyssey of the subject as an emergent from it. The subject is restored as an implicate of communicative praxis – not as a *foundation* for it. The philosophical prejudice of foundationalism falls away with the dismantling of epistemological space.

In tracking the route of the self-implicature of the subject we begin with the subject as implicated in discourse. Discourse is the saying of something about something through the language of speaking and writing. Discourse displays, makes manifest, discloses a world of concerns in which objects and processes of nature and history are taken as meaning such and such. This is the referential moment of discourse. However, insofar as reference is here understood as the taking of something as something within a holistic context of patterns of human actions and involvements, it assumes a hermeneutical posture. It thereby needs to be distinguished from objectifying, propositional reference (either of a categorial or empirical sort) within epistemological space. Propositional reference atomizes and identifies. Hermeneutical reference displays and makes manifest. And that which it makes manifest are configurative wholes, occasioning an understanding of human behavior by placing it within a network of goals, intentions, and purposes. This making manifest proceeds against the backdrop of a play of metaphors, illustrating what Paul Ricoeur has suggestively named "Metaphorical reference".[6] Hermeneutical reference solicits the play of metaphor, and one must not forget that metaphor comports its own intentionality. It displays a world of the text and a horizon of meanings inscribed in the fabric of social practices. But discourse is not only *about* something; it is also *by* someone, who tracks the meanings of that which discourse is about, articulating the varied configurations of thought and action. This is the moment of hermeneutical self-implicature that accompanies the display and disclosure of hermeneutical reference. Finally, discourse is *for* someone – the interlocutor in a conversation, the audience in a public assembly, the potential reader of a text. This comprises the rhetorical moment of discourse – its directedness to the other.

This triadic intentionality of discourse (*about* something, *by* some-one, *for* the other), falling out as an interdependent complex of hermeneutical reference, self-implicature, and rhetorical address, furnishes the proper context for a comprehension of the traces of the subject within the praxial space of discursive transactions. It is within this context that the subject emerges and establishes its presence, not as an epistemological point, a positional interiority seeking commerce with an external world and an alien other, but as a developing event whose constitution bears the inscriptions of the prose of the world. The "who" of discourse is an achievement of praxis rather than a theoretically delivered given, a happening, an event of participatory life within a world of nature and history.

The "who" of discourse is set forth, both in speech acts and in the word of the text, through a saying of the pesonal pronoun "I". This pronoun figures in discourse not as a formal place-holder for a parade of particulars. "I" is not a class concept, like for example "tree", "gazelle", and "professor", waiting for particulars to instantiate them. The "I" of discourse is an index or indicator, making manifest the "who" of the saying. The "who" of speaking and writing is implicated in the performance of saying, not as a modal inference operative within a logic of classification but through a hermeneutical self-disclosure. The subject is implicated in his discourse in the way that an unfaithful husband implicates himself in his unmonitored conversation.

Now this hermeneutical implicature of the subject proceeds in tandem with the rhetorical moment of discourse – its directedness toward and disclosure of the other. Indeed, in the concrete participatory discourse of dialogue and public interaction the self and the other undergo a consummate co-constitution. Only after the dialogue is finished and the public exchange has run its course can one do a post-mortem and discern – and only with relative success – the episodical contributions of the "I" as the speaker and the "you" as the hearer. Subjectivity is thus achieved only with the other, through an acknowledgement of his actual or potential presence in the space of discursive praxis. No speaking subject is an island entire of itself. Every subject is a piece of the continent of other subjects, a part of the main of inter-subjectivity.

The discourse of the spoken word in its rhetorical posture thus provides its own traces of the subject in the life of dialogue and in the varied discursive transactions within the *polis*. But there is also a self-implicature operative in the written word. As Derrida reminds us, there is the inescapable requirement for a resituation of the subject within the tissues of *écriture*. It is thus that the question concerning the place and role of the author comes to the fore, which may be the most urgent and pressing question of our time. The proverbial "every schoolboy" of our day knows that the author as the monarchical legislator of textual meaning has been effectively effaced, by philosophers and theorists of literature alike. We have all cut our teeth on the intentional fallacy and have been duly apprized of the futility of chasing down the meaning of a text within the confines of authorial intentions. But heeding the sirens of the intentional fallacy does not as such displace the question about the status and function of the authorial subject. Michel Foucault, in his provocative essay, "What is an author?", urges some reflection on this matter:

> Is it not possible to reexxamine, as a legitimate extension of this kind of analysis, the privileges of the subject? Clearly, in undertaking an internal and architectionic analysis of a work (whether it be a literary text, a philosophical system, or a scientific work) and in delimiting psychological and biographical references, suspicions arise concerning the absolute nature and creative role of the subject. But the subject should not be entirely abandoned. It should be reconsidered, not to restore the theme of an originating subject, but to seize its functions, its intervention in discourse, and its system of dependencies.[7]

The authorial subject dethroned as absolute monarch of the text takes his place among the citizenry at large, along with the readers, interpreters, critics and above all the other authors whom he engages either tacitly or explicitly. The author still retains his "authority," but this is now manifest as an authority which is decentralized and shared with others, as the author himself undergoes a decentering within a network of interdependencies.

Communicative praxis, however, involves not only the discourse of the spoken and the written word, it also includes the nondiscursive display of dimensions of human action and social practices. Communicative praxis is textured by the amalgam of discourse and action. Hence, one needs also to look for the traces of the subject in the performance of individual and institutional acts. Hermeneutical self-implicature is operative both in discourse and action. On this point Paul Ricoeur has offered some suggestive leads in his detailed study on the phenomenology of the will. In describing the structure and dynamics of volition Ricoeur points us to what he calls the "prereflexive imputation of myself" in the act of decision. Decision implicates me in the motivation and in the act. *"Je me décide à . . ."*[8] The English rendering of this French syntax falls out roughly as "making up my mind in the act of decision." The German is syntactically closer to the French: *"Ich entsheide mich . . ."* The point at issue is that decision summons the self as agent in the action to be undertaken, as actor in the project to be realized. This "self-imputation" is prereflexive in that it is not a matter of theoretical observation by a present self explaining its presence to itself through a reflexive duplication. It is, as articulated by Ricoeur, a self-imputation via action rather than an observation of a state of affairs.[9] The trace of subjectivity is manifested in the decision-action configuration of praxis, rather than in the tortuous self-reflexivity of an epistemological subject attempting to deliver knowledge of itself. The actional route to subjectivity follows a detour around the deconstructed site of idealist, epistemologically oriented self-constitution.

This route to subjectivity, however, like that cleared by discourse, is at once a route to intersubjectivity, opening up a public space of shared projects and joint endeavors. The subject as agent is implicated not as a *voluntas solus ipse*, centered in a time-space point, in an abstracted here and now; it comes forth as a decentered and decen-tralized co-subject, cohabiting a world with other agents. The projects and social practices of the agentive subject are textured by its responses to the attitudes and actions of other subjects, both in the world of con-temporaries and the world of predecessors. The agent achieves its sub-jectivity only by acknowledging the space of the other and responding to the other's actions. This responsive action of the decentered subject, no less than its discourse, comports its own intentionality. The actions of the subject are meaningful because they are expressive of meanings ensconced in the social practices of a community of subjects. Hence, there is a rhetoric of action as there is a rhetoric of the spoken and the written word. Action like discourse comports a directedness to the other. The intentionality of action is an event of meaning occasioned by the interplay of co-subjects within a context of social practices.

We have been proposing that we look and listen for the subject within the interstial space of discourse and action, after the structures of epistemological space have been disassembled. The subject impli-cated by his discourse and action in the hermeneutical space of com-municative praxis is a subject decentered and decentralized, bearing the inscriptions of a language community and a community of social practices as it undergoes the odyssey of self and social formation. No longer a monarchical self that somehow has its seat of authority, its "authorship," within itself — in its private sense perceptions and its private thoughts — the decentralized subject is more like what James Ogilvy has characterized as a "heterarchical self" — a self authorized and constituted by the multiplicity of its responses and profiles within a public and historical world.[10] This demands new descriptions and new interpretations of the subject. The metaphysical and epistemological characterizations of the subject as a mental substance, a monad, a self-identical entity, a zero-point monological consciousness, or a transcendental ego, are no longer compelling. Multiplicity, temporality, historicity, embodiment, and dialogical consciousness may need to become the new marks of subjectivity. The traditional metaphysical and epistemological "marks of the mental," as Richard Rorty has rather persuasively argued, invite a spate of philosophical contradictions and aporias, and hence had best be set aside.[11] This comprises the deconstructionist turn that leads to the end of philosophy and the death of the subject. But there is life after death of the subject, the life of a new subjectivity, opening new horizons for a possible reclamation of humanism. The new descriptions of this restored subject, approaching the subject from the side of praxis, will need to be particularly attentive to the play of metaphor in the cultural life of man. We shall then see what Bruce Wilshire has shown in his recent book, *Role Playing and Identity*, namely, that the metaphors of the theatre can be more efficacious in disclosing the life of the subject than are the categories of metaphysics. The metaphors of the theatre are able to display the restored subject within the intertexture of the drama of everyday life, elucidated within the context of its enactment of roles, mimetic responsiveness, and the intentionality of embodiment.[12]

The project of the recovery of the subject that we have sketched in the wake of the subject's deconstruction as a nexus of philosophical concepts raises anew the question of a possible ontology of subjectivity. If such an ontology is to appear on the scene it will of necessity have to be an *interpretive/descriptive* rather than a *constructive* ontology. It will take shape as a *hermeneutical* and *praxeological* ontology rather than one informed by metaphysical and epistemological protocols. It will remain an *oblique* ontology, slanting off the solicitations of praxis. There is no direct route to be followed in pursuing the question of being be it the being of man or the being of nature, for the question of being remains indissoluably linked to the question of praxis. Yet there is more to a praxeology of the subject than a deconstruction of the metaphysical and epistemological concepts of "presence." Such a deconstruction indeed remains in effect, performed through the resources of the *critical* posture of hermeneutics. Hermeneutics as critical assumes the task of deconstructionist critique. Hermeneutics is indeed critical; but it is also restorative. It reclaims the subject in a transvalued way after the philosophical invention of it has ceased to hold our attention.[13]

Part II.
Hermeneutics and the
Question of Interpretation

4. Seeing and Reading: Aspects of their Connection

Graeme Nicholson

The basic point of my book, *Seeing and Reading* (*SR*), is that our experience of reading is bound deeply to our experience of seeing because both are interpretative. In Part One I study interpretation itself, trying to show what constitutes it and why human perception is interpretative. Part Two is a study of textual interpretation; it establishes the analogy between reading and seeing and shows how some central problems of hermeneutics can be solved by way of the analogy.

1. Projection

Why is our seeing interpretative? Because it is not really a passivity and receptivity, because in all our seeing we are making projections.

Suppose you are travelling on an express subway train and you go rattling through a local subway station. Your perception of the station, over a few seconds, is composed of a fleeting set of visual fragments accompanied by a rattle and a roar – but these fragments are quite sufficient for you. Consider the experience from the vantage of a slightly later moment, the experience of just-having-seen the local station, when it has been seen but not forgotten. Where you have just glimpsed the station, you connect its bright colour fragments with the blackness of the tunnel you have just entered. Both in the brief interval of rattling through the station, and in the instant of just-having-seen, you have been linking the station visually with the destination up ahead that you anticipate. Your perception is shaped by the project of travel, your actually being bodily underway, and your anticipation of a destination.

The project induces a negative achievement in your vision which I call a denuding of the seen object. The local station stop is visually denuded by your projection to the status of distance-indicator, which is the way the visual fragments are bonded to the black tunnel and the anticipated stop. From this perception innumerable possible perceptions of that station have been excluded. It is in just this way that we also visually denude the buildings we walk by on our way to work: we reduce them to facades, indicators of our lateness.

The point is not only relevant to travel. Figure-perception of a cup, a book or a little stone, is no less rooted in goals and interests that we project. With the seeing of such things, the potential grip of our hand is guiding the focus of our eye. Our own manual habits, and our more complex interests, shape the perception through and through.

The linguistic conditions for perception are to be treated in a parallel way. When a man is lurching toward me on a sidewalk, I see him as drunk because my language has facilitated a judgment of perception. Its terms permit *selection* of one entity from the field of vision; they afford *classification* (the entity is defined as a man); they permit a bond to the *predicate* "drunk," resulting in the actual perception that I have. Indeed, my practical interest to elude the fellow is also fused to the perceptual employment of my language; it leads me to see him not only as drunk but as *a* drunk. I project a social status and an essence on him. Language is our collective creation; it is brought by ourselves to the perceptual encounter; and is not inherent in matter or nature.

SR attempts an a priori argument to prove that perception is shaped by projections, both practical and linguistic. Even if an angelic host were witnessing the coronation of the Virgin — as Fra Angelico has painted it — they would be making practical and linguistic projections. Here I've only given some examples, but they should give some idea of the point.

2. Background Interpretation

Projection is the root of our visual interpretation. My study of perception was inspired by *Being and Time*, sec. 31 and 32, where Heidegger showed how interpretation (*Auslegung*) developed out of *Verstehen*. (Heidegger's term *Verstehen* should be translated "projection".) My point is that perception exemplifies his theory perfectly: we cannot see a thing without interpreting and that is because we gain no kind of access to anything without introducing projections.

We must realize however that the interpretations of perception are background interpretations. A philologist interpreting an ancient Greek love poem is employing some unusual skills in this work and relying on prior research, perhaps on the historical circumstances of the text's production. The unskilled and the unlearned would make no headway with Greek philology, but they could see the printed book lying there on the desk just as our scholar does. Our words "book" and "document" are names for things that we can handle, on which we can then exercise our philogical skills. I call the philologist's work foreground interpretation because it implements specialized skills that must be learned, and because it is the art of linking a commentary to a text which invites others to look again to discover whether they would accept the interpretation. The link is consciously and methodically made. That which is being made subject to the interpretation is initially given us in the simple mode of perception. When we just see something we do not employ a rare skill or special knowledge, but habits and language that are common to all; we hardly ever need to puzzle over a thing and construe it. Seeing is precisely the elementary encounter with entities which are made subject to further specialized foreground interpretation. The factors of visual interpretation are at work only in the background: we remain largely unaware of the practical interests and language that shape our seeing. They do not only shape our visual perception, but other sensory modes and indeed they shape our self-image and our thought process. Our self-awareness is likewise constituted by a projection and the employment of language. Background interpreting goes on behind my ego and self. It thus becomes impossible to suppose that it is I, myself, who make the interpretation of perception; rather an anonymous power of practical and linguistic projection has done it.

In my study of *Being and Time* I tried to combine the themes of projection and interpretation with the theme of disclosure. If our projections shaped our interpreting, could the latter still claim to be revelatory? In the case of perception, this poses the very question that matters the most: are we entitled to understand perception as *cognitive*? The means whereby a perception would claim truth-value, while being projective and interpretative, have been explored by Heidegger: it is by projection that we reveal, and by intervention that we let things be. *Seeing and Reading* tries to confirm this in the case of our visual interpretations, by reliance on a concept of illumination. Today I shall not enter into that issue, but step back to a point still more elementary.

3. Appearance

Wherever there is interpretation, there is a subject, something made subject to interpretation. We can specify the subject of philological interpretation as a text, document or book. But if perception is an interpretation of the background sort, and if perception gives us our most elementary access to the things that may then become subject to foreground interpretation, how shall we find the subject of the background interpretation? To call it a book or a cup is to make the interpretation already and to assume it; we have not identified the subject in a pre-interpreted state. One hypothesis here is that what we are interpreting when we see our own sense data — colour sensations are interpreted by our practical interests and our language as a subway station. The hypothesis is not exactly false; but *SR* argues that there has to be another subject for interpretation. An analogy may make the point briefly: the translator *can* be said to be interpreting the black marks of the Greek script in his text, but those inscribed marks do not sufficiently define what he is translating. It is a poem he is translating. The perceiver can likewise be said to interpret or process the data, but the actual subject of perceptual interpretation is no more identical with them than the poem is with the marks on my page.

The term "seeing," as I use it, refers to an act or an event. It is not a mere capacity or competence, but the exercise of the capacity. It is not a potentiality but an actuality of the highest grade. An attentive study of this event, a phenomenological study, will wish to resolve it first of all into its constituent events, rather than to reduce it to objects or things. Our projecting is one of the events that constitute seeing, but there is another co-constituent that I call "appearing." The appearing of something is a part of the seeing event just as surely as our projecting is. *SR* defends the theory that an appearance is the subject of perceptual interpretation. Appearance is not usually an event that takes place within our own organism — on the contrary, since seeing includes the appearing of a thing as well as a human projection, it follows that seeing is not an event immanent to our organism either.

SR seeks to analyze appearance at length; it introduces as just one topic a theory of objective affinity in the thing seen. There is an affinity within the subway station itself that qualifies it as an appearance, quite in advance of any projection or interpretation we make. Imagine please, first of all, the painting of a child in a red coat, and imagine a gallery-goer viewing it. He has the freedom to see it as dabs of paint applied some time ago to the canvas, at other times to see it as a child in a red coat. These are two interpretations of the phenomenon; but the gallery-goer cannot integrate them, see red paint dabbed there in bits *and* see a red coat, because coats are not made of paint. But when he sees the red coat the interpretation is motivated by the way the red on the canvas coheres: this bit of the red has an affinity with that bit of the red. Affinity of this bit of the red for that bit of the red is an element in the *appearance* that is at work in *advance* of the viewer's projection which generates the interpretation, Coat. To switch to everday thing-perception, when you look at a table or desk, you are led to project, often, a fourth leg that is hidden from your view, and you are led to suppose that the back of it will be of such-and-such colour and material. The expectation of a fourth leg is based on your prior experience of such objects. But your anticipation of colour and material on the unseen side is of different motivation. It is not induced from prior experience of such objects; indeed it has no logical character at all. It is a perceptual disposition, a maxim that the back of a thing will be something like its front. This is motivated by an affinity that lies within the thing that is seen: affinity of one portion of the overt and manifest surface for another portion of that surface, and another and another; the affinity leads us past the visible section altogether, first leading our anticipation to the fringe or halo at the visible "edge," then around that edge to the completely covert and hidden profile. There is a continuous affinity of sections that includes even the totally hidden portion of the thing. The hidden and covert portion is therefore a part of the appearance itself. Appearance *includes* the recessive and the hidden, because of affinity and continuity between the overt and the covert. A withdrawal and a mystery is proper to appearance itself and is therefore a part of every human perception (whether noticed or not). The hidden, recessive or covert that is a *part* of appearance has nothing to do, you will see, with the thing-in-itself that Kant so sharply distinguished from appearance. The hidden and covert aspects of the subway station you rattled through were present in your perception even though your projection sought to denude it of them. What is the medium in which the overt and the covert can be continuous? Borrowing from Heidegger, I call it the Open, and I seek to differentiate the spatial and temporal articulation of the Open from the space and time our projections introduce. I delineate a certain conflict and contest between the Open and human projections. The very fact that the hidden and the covert can *appear* (continuously with the manifest) testifies to a withdrawal that comes across to us. In our perception we gain access to a withdrawal and mystery that is occurring uninterruptedly and universally. All this constitutes appearance, the subject of interpretation.

4. Foreground Interpretation

To turn to the second topic, reading, let me draw attention first to an asymmetry. In the discussion of seeing, I meant something we are all doing all the time – seeing the people around us, the clouds, trees and so on. There is likewise a sort of reading that people of our culture practice all the time and this everyday and simple reading is a kind of interpretation too. However, I shall zero in on the most elaborate refinements of reading that exist: the philological disciplines that interpret materials extremely ancient, or from civilizations remote from our own or inscribed in languages least akin to ours. Let us envisage the situation where a text T is at hand; while the non-specialist can make nothing of it, the specialists themselves diverge, one saying that T means p and one saying that T means q. Where this question "What does T mean?" is posed seriously, and answers are judged critically, where one is seeking the truth, I speak of foreground interpretation, and this interests a philosopher most of all: the epistemology of reading, especially in its most challenging cases. If there are alternative readings or interpretations of T, are there grounds to suppose one of them is the true one? Of all hermeneutical issues, this one is basic.

My hypothesis is that this and other questions fundamental to hermeneutics can be answered by applying the study of seeing. Let me stress two aspects of this point: (a) The bond I am speaking of links one case of background interpretation, seeing, to one case of foreground interpretation, philology (though there are of course other cases of both groups). In exploring this particular bond we are exploring one common structure, interpretation itself, present both in a background and a foreground form. This is element in human existence that overreaches the gulf between what is conscious and what is unconscious. (b) This bond is such as to solve certain key problems in hermeneutics. There is not a mere *analogy* between seeing and reading – the latter is *founded* upon the former. The study assumes the form of a "foundational" thesis, even a "transcendental" one. The term "analogy of interpretation" means not just features shared by the two in common, but also the foundation. Here in this paper I shall bring out only two aspects of the connection: on the role of projection, and the role of appearance.

5. Ventriloguism and Other Projections

A young reader today who digs into Homer for the first time will notice him talking of "kings": it may be he projects mediaeval and

Arthurian attributes on Agamemnon; this is an erroneous reading. He could however project his experience of jealousy and passion back upon Agamemnon too − less obviously wrong. Right or wrong − every reading of everything will have a projective aspect: this is true of foreground interpretation too. The classicist corrects the student's false mediaeval impression of Greek kingship by engaging in a series of projections himself: we have to reconstitute the archaic institution of kingship. More − and the book argues *a priori* here − when we are making a translation or a commentary we are projecting upon the original the medium of our own language and our habituated mode of understanding. Even where our interpretation is just library research, neither published nor given in lectures, our thinking process brings a vast component from our own times into the encounter. Where I correct the amateur interpreter and say "No; T isn't saying p; it's saying q," my role is that of the ventriloquist, projecting my voice upon the text that was hitherto unable to speak. Foreground interpretation is just as projective as simple reading but this is not tragic necessity or ground for skepticism; our projection is a material contribution to the truth of an interpretation. We have to recognize the different lines of interpretation which it is necessary to introduce from time to time, to shed light on the texts before us. The scrutiny of their mode of discourse and genre must often complement mere decipherment and translation. Linguistic and poetic interpretation is drawing on our own sciences of linguistics and poetics. We often need to set a text in the circumstances of its time of composition − economic, social, political − and we often need to bring to bear upon it our researches into the history and psyche of the author, if there is one known to us. This is all projected on the text by the scholar. The vast enterprise of academic scholarship is a collective projection that makes material contributions to truth.

The projection in our reading replicates the role of projection in our seeing, even to the point that it introduces the possibility of truth in both domains. Where I see a coat, my language has made that perception possible and made its truth possible. Where I interpret a lyric as a cultic hymn, my projections are at work constituting truth. The relevance of the study of seeing here is to show how the interest we take in a subject places us in contact with it, able to reach the truth.

6. Material Interpretation

Today we are acquainted with scholarly interpretations of so many different methods and theories − psychological, anti-psychological, structuralist, post-structuralist — that it is a valuable inquiry (though daunting) to establish priorities among methods of scholarly interpretation. My argument leads to the conclusion that material interpretation is preeminent and that it can accommodate linguistic, historical and psychological interpretation in a secondary position, excluding certain other methods of interpreting as irrational. What I mean by "material" is the scrutiny of a text employing my own understanding of the subject matter of the text. For example, I am defending a philosopher's interpretation of the *Republic*, guided by the philosophical theory of justice, asserting the primacy of such an interpretation over an interpretation based on the psycho-analysis of Plato, or the political-economic study of fourth-century Athens, or the study of Plato's rhetoric by comparison to the rhetoric of Homer or Aristophanes. By "primacy" I do not mean exclusiveness, but the opposite: since many perspectives of interpretation are legitimate, we must seek how to unify them, and this can only be done where the leading role of material interpretation is conceded. In *SR*, I defend the view that every interpretation needs to identify a *nucleus* of meaning to which a broad periphery can be attached: material interpretation's primacy arises from that imperative. A material interpretation allows the text to show us this or that aspect of its subject matter; by our own further independent reflection about that subject matter, however, we may be led to notice what is specific about this text's treatment, what is characteristically, one-sidedly, Platonic about the view of justice in *Republic* IV; to do that is to *interpret* Plato.

Being led to our own encounter with the subject matter of a text brings our projection into the interpretation — we reach out to constitute the subject. But material interpretation also involves appearances and in this respect too creates the replica of perception. For where the reader attends to the text, a subject matter rises up to meet his interest; it appears. And where the material interpretation invokes that very subject matter in making a comment on the text, it beckons to an appearance too. It summons the apparition of Platonic justice or Homeric war.

But there is no reason to pursue material interpretation in abstraction from the historical, psychological and linguistic. Full and concrete interpretations will fuse material insights with those gained from linguistics, and other researches thereby re-enacting the fusion of this subject matter with these words which the author's original composition brought about.

I shall conclude with a few remarks about drama and lyric poetry with the aim of forestalling an unduly prosaic or philistine understanding of the term "subject matter".

Think of the *Agamemnon* of Aeschylus, and the great series of deeds that it imitates, and the repetitions of the drama that are made on the stage again and again. That great myth or story is a sequence of deeds, things done, and that the story is the primary focus of a material interpretation. The material interpreter will treat these deeds as worthy of interest *per se*, and make it clear how such doings bear on us all. Speeches, ideas, and character can be treated in relation to the deeds. The primary focus will not be a moral one, as in various allegorical interpretations; "subject matter" does not mean the *moral* of a tale.

With respect to lyric poems there is no need to take "subject matter" in a primitive way to be some moral or narrative subject. But it is necessary even with the most advanced poetry, to differentiate "subject matter" from the process of composition, from the life, thought and development of the author, from causally operative factual circumstances, and from whatever is original and whatever is unoriginal about language use. Not that we need even be able to put a single name on this subject matter. I know a poem that mentions the sun four times. The sun signifies something on each of these occasions, but no exhaustive interpretation can be made of these lines. The sun is an infinite signifier in that poem, one without closure. It is a mystery that is invoked by a signifier such as that, one with infinited reverberations. The reader feels an attraction to this mystery, and the material interpreter seeks to facilitate that attraction. I think there are texts, not just of drama and lyric and religion, but of philosophy too, that constitute pinnacles of our literature through such invoking of mysteries. In the present context I refer to them not only to point away from a narrowly pragmatic sense of "subject matter" but also to complete the analogy to the earlier discussion of appearance. We have seen that there is a withdrawal and covertness even in the appearances we encounter in perception. The textual replica of appearance includes also mysteries evoked by signs such as the sun, in which a subject is at once approaching us and withdrawing from us.

5. Perception as a Hermeneutical Act

Patrick A. Heelan

In a recent work[1] I have attempted to show that visual space tends to have a Euclidean geometrical structure only when the environment is filled with a repetitive pattern of regularly faceted objects carpentered to exhibit simple standard Euclidean shapes, and tends to have a hyperbolic structure when vision is deprived of these clues. I conclude that visual perception – and by analogy, all perception – is hermeneutic as well as causal: it responds to structures in the flow of optical energy, but the character of its response is also hermeneutical, that is, it has the capacity to 'read' the appropriate structures in the World, and to form perceptual judgments of the World about which these 'speak.' (Note: single quotes indicate that a term is to be taken in a special sense that will be clarified in the course of this paper.) The clues that are 'read' perceptually as giving a Euclidean visual space are engineered objects, such as streets and buildings with repetitive architectural elements, these scientific artifacts of human culture belong to a family of readable technologies central to the phenomenological and existential-hermeneutical analysis of natural science.[2]

I

The term "hermeneutics" has a variety of meanings. Its original meaning comes from theology, where hermeneutics was the method used to infer the mind of the ancient writer, usually of some part of the Sacred Scriptures, but also the meaning of liturgical and religious symbols, etc. The modern interest in hermeneutics stems from the work of W. Dilthey and the beginnings of the scientific study of history. For Dilthey, hermeneutics was the method of determining the mind of the historical author or agent. It is now generally agreed, however, that meaning is something possessed by interpreters independently of the historical author's intentions. Closer to the sense in which I shall use the term is that of H. G. Gadamer[3]; hermeneutics comprise the conditions and processes of the hermeneutical circle used by interpreters to obtain meaning from literary texts and cultural/historical phenomena, these involve confronting the text or cultural object with an antecedent domain of meaning suggested by clues (in the text or cultural object, or in its context) and then refining this sense in a dialectical fashion through the interplay of part and whole, text and context. Such constitutes a mode of inquiry often taken to be characteristic of the *Geisteswissenschaften.*

My interests, however, go beyond the methodological aspects of hermeneutics to the existential-hermeneutical structure of the interpreter, that is, of Dasein's Being in the World. I shall try to exhibit perception as the historical way in which Dasein's understanding of Being is articulated by the interpretation of 'texts' in the World according to the conditions and processes of the hermeneutical circle.[4] Although Heidegger did not elaborate a theory of perception applicable to the kinds of questions addressed by philosophers of perception, there is no doubt that he regarded perception in which the World is disclosed and articulated, and indeed all knowledge, as fundamentally hermeneutical. My goal is to arrive at the conditions and processes of perception as a hermeneutical activity, in such a way as to be able to address in specific detail philosophical questions of the sort addressed, say, by M. Merleau-Ponty, and to be able to perform a critical analysis of contemporary work in experimental psychology, such as, for example, the work of the late D. Marr and his associates.[5]

II

Although the capacity to perceive in a certain way is acquired by learning, acts of perception – the exercise of these capacities – have distinguishing phenomenological characteristics. Perception is a form of cognitive activity in which the object known is a state of the World given directly and, in some sense, causally, to embodied knowers.[5] States of the World are, by definition, real and public. The object known, therefore, is public, it is not the private possession of a percept, or other internal representation, or surrogate model of the object known. This public reality known in perception is expressed as the content of a perceptual judgment formulated in the common descriptive language of a linguistic community. It is, as I said above, *directly* known, since it is not mediated by deductive or inductive inferences from more elementary or primitive prior knowns presented in experience itself; it is not, however, unmediated in other respects. The existence of a causal factor has often been used to distinguish acts of perception from related experiential acts, such as acts of memory, fantasy or imagination, illusion, and hallucination.

Perceivers "pick up" information from the World, and the information they pick up is in some sense "present" in the World antecedent to the acts of perception in which it is appropriated by perceivers. Such information is then in some sense 'embodied' in the World; I refer to those embodiments of perceptual information as 'texts' (single quotes indicating a special meaning). Perceptual information is embodied in the World analogously to the way a meaning is embodied in a book or corpus of written works; a 'text,' like a text, is a structure of related differences within a larger and complex structure of diffentiable states that function like a language. The process of "picking up" perceptual information from the World then is similar to reading a text, because it delivers its meaning directly to the reader. Perception then is a way of 'reading' the 'texts' that nature (and, through science, people) provide; such perceptual 'texts' respond to correlative hermeneutical intentions in experienced 'readers,' or perceivers not merely, like linguistic texts, by directly delivering meaning, but by simultaneously exhibiting the meanings as states of the World.[7] Exhibitable (or fulfilled) meanings engendered by such 'texts' are perceptual; and the act of perception is the exhibition of a state of the World to perceiving embodied intentional human subjects capable of 'reading' from the 'texts,' some natural and some man-made, that it provides. Since reading a text is a paradigmatically hermeneutical activity, perception is itself hermeneutical. This argument will be developed below.

All hermeneutical processes, whether reading or (as I also claim) perception, possess the dual structure associated with the acquisition or expression of information. The term "information" is notoriously abused in much philosophical and psychological literature. It refers both to the signs that are read, and to the shared public meaning given to these signs by a properly skilled community of readers. I shall distinguish between them by calling the text or 'text,' "information$_1$," and its meaning or content, "information$_2$." Observe that in scientific and much philosophical literature, information is taken to denote a 'text' or sign (information$_1$), while usually but not always connoting some meaning (information$_2$); in everyday life and ordinary usage, however, information denotes a meaning (information$_2$), while sometimes but not always connoting some text or sign (information$_1$). In the literary analogue, syllables, phonemes, and other linguistic signs and marks on paper (information$_1$), cease *for the reader* to be objects in the World, like houses or trees, and once read for their meaning (information$_2$), they become more like *windows into a house* that by their (more or less) transparent quality give direct access to the contents of the house. One does **not perceive** the syllables of a text, as Polanyi points out,[8] one reads them. In a reading, the physical text (as information$_1$) disappears from direct view leaving no objective trace whatsoever, it becomes non-objective, and I take that to mean belonging to the conditions of the knowing subject, it becomes in fact a physical part of the embodied cognitive subject; the text (as information$_1$) becomes a part of a specific somatic information channel of the embodied reader; this is part of an information-theoretic system whose "resonant" states (information$_1$ states) code for informaion$_2$, in this case, for the meaning-as-read. The text and the associated somatic information channel of which it is a part belong to the conditions and processes of the paradigmatically hermeneutic activity of reading.

I shall state three important theses about the relationships between systems of information$_1$ and systems of information$_2$ which apply both to texts and to 'texts':

1). All information$_1$ systems are to some extent indeterminate; firstly, because there are always redundancies in the system that could be used to extend the system of related differentiable signs, and secondly, because any information$_1$ system can be embedded as a subsystem in a variety of larger information$_1$ systems; these latter contribute to the process of contextualization of the original system (cf. the indeterminacies of language as system of signifiers).

2). Consequently, any information$_2$ system carried by an information$_1$ system has a potentiality for surplus meaning that lies both in the underutilization or indeterminacy of the resources of the information$_1$ system, and in the variety of hermeneutical contexts which can be brought to its interpretation; to each context will correspond a particular embedding of the signifiers in some larger system.

3). There is no necessary unique one-to-one mapping between states of information$_1$ and states of information$_2$, only *affinities* between them[9]; the manner in which the information$_1$ system is utilized depends on the context chosen for its interpretation, and that depends on the human interests of those who use it, whether readers or perceivers.

Phenomenological analysis of perception can take two forms: (1) eidetic analysis of the objects of perceptual acts, and (2) existential-hermeneutical analysis of the act of perception as Dasein's way of Being; this seeks to uncover the hermeneutical role of Dasein in perception.[10]

III

An *eidetic analysis* of a perceptual object as understood by E. Husserl is the determination of the invariants (the perceptual essence) that serve as the law that generates the manifold of an objects's perceptual profiles. Eidetic analysis is then a study of the kinds of perceptual objects that could be found in our World. Such an analysis, according to Husserl, is to be performed under an *epoché* that brackets the existence of the object. This also brackets any condition, if there is such, that is not part of the objective content of the *eidos* but which may happen to govern the actual performance of acts of perception; in Husserl's view, eidetic analysis presupposes that the content of a perceptual act specifies all that is necessary for the performance of the act, including all the conditions for the correct identification of individual exemplifications of the essence.[11]

I shall address two questions. First: can an eidetic analysis be unique and definitive? Second: does an eidetic analysis of perceptual essence contain all that is necessary for the performance of any act of recognition and naming of individuals of that essence? To both of these questions, Husserl responded affirmatively; to the contrary, Heidegger and others, among them myself, say no.

Can an eidetic analysis be unique and definitive? An eidetic analysis of a perceptual object can never be unique, complete, and definitive, because it involves a reflective determination of a potential infinity of perceptual profiles. Such a determination is possible for a rule-governed mathematical object, but not for any structure of perceptual profiles, since perceptual profiles are never exact; to the extent that an exact ordering is sought, for example (in physical space) of the shape of a wheel or (in visual space) of the visual convergence of railway tracks, a mathematical model may be used, but to the extent that a mathematical model serves as part of the specification of a perceptual eidos, it is applies to perceptual experience only in an inexact or, better, a metaphorical way. An eidetic analysis then is always to some extent incomplete and underdetermined; this does not mean that it does not serve a useful purpose, but only that Husserl may have been mistaken about the purpose it serves.[12] The determination of an *eidos* is relative to the interests of the historical community of perceivers,

and is indeterminate to the extent that a decision has to be made as
to how far one should go in any eidetic analysis in order to define in
a way satisfactory to its inhabitants the furniture of a particular
historical World. Such a dependence on the historical and cultural community reveals one small corner of the hermeneutical web of
perception.

E. Ballard's study,[13] for instance, of the eidetic meaning of *distance*
and *closeness*, illustrates both the power and limitations of purely eidetic
analysis. His descriptions of the St. Louis Arch as a visual phenomenon
are striking for what they affirm, and equally for what they overlook.
The latter stem from inherent limitations in the method itself, such as
restricting the resources to those of language presently descriptive of
the life-world to the exclusion of scientific viewpoints. (These being
theoretical are thought to be incapable of serving a descriptive function).

IV

Does an eidetic analysis of a perceptual essence contain all that is
necessary for the performance of any act of recognition or naming of
individuals of that essence? An *existential-hermeneutical analysis* of the
act of perception requires that the performance of an act of perception
depends on the presence of a suitable 'text' in the environment. Consider, for example, as 'text', one of those structures in the optical field
that have the power to specify distance in visual space. Such a 'text'
is, like a linguistic text, an information-carrying code, but it is also like
a tool, a ready-to-hand, that "shapes" the perceptual object by conditioning our physical access to it; the perceptual object as manifest –
its essence – should then be a function of the physical information
channel – the 'text' – through which its outlines are contacted and
probed. This 'text', accessible perhaps to scientific observations, is not
accessible to the perceiver's own reflective powers while performing
eidetic analysis. An existential-hermeneutical theory of perception
should then assert that reflective intuition alone is not final in specifying the content of a perceptual essence; that recourse must also be had
to a 'text'. As long as the 'text' remains hidden, it will influence eidetic
analysis unconsciously, the way the structure of a carving tool unconsciously influences the forms an artist sculpts with its aid; it may also
exercise an influence in a way that frustrates the attempted eidetic
analysis.

What kind of thing is a 'text' ordered to perception? If what is revealed to perception is revealed by interpretation, then the 'text' is in some sense a sign. In methodological hermeneutics, a sign is first known and then interpreted.[14] In existential hermeneutics, the sign need not be first known; because if it were, its 'text' in turn would have to be known, and so on to absurdity; Truth is never totally unconcealed, Dasein has at all times a mystery at its core. The function of a 'text' in preunderstanding is to unite the subject to the object in anticipation of interpretation, it is that through which the object is "had" or "held" by the subject in advance of being recognized or named as an object for the subject, it operates within that moment of interpretative understanding called *Vorhabe*, in anticipation of *Vorsicht* and *Vorgriff*.[15] The kind of sign I am referring to is not generally a sensible appearance, though a sensible appearance may sometimes be taken as a sign; a sensible appearance is a profile of a perceptual object, part of what is meant by an object of that kind, part of its inner horizon; it presupposes the structure and possibility of the perceptual object. A sign, however, is not generally part of the inner horizon of an object; nor for that matter is it generally a present-at-hand. A sign is more like a window into a house, one looks through it to see the contents of the house, but the window itself is transparent, and therefore usually invisible. The window itself, moreover, is not part of the contents of the house. The window metaphor does not connote the affinities that must exist between sign and signified, therefore, it can be misleading. A better example is a text: a text as signifier is transparent within the act of understanding the text, it is part of a system of signs which is not itself part of the object understood by the act of interpretation. Understanding a text, however, is not a form of perceiving. A better example from the latter point of view is a drawing: the lines as signifiers are transparent to the object represented, while the object represented is exhibited to the viewer in a direct perceptual act. Although the 'text' is not something of which we are aware (though it may be accessible to somebody else or to us at other times), in the case of perception, it "shapes" the object like a tool by conditioning how we gain access to it; these are its affinities.[16]

In the case of visual spaces, for example, it is by no means obvious what these 'texts' are, that we 'read' visually. The study that I have done is one of the few that associates the variety of visual geometries we use with the kinds of cues or 'texts' from which these spaces are 'read.' An eidetic analysis then of visual shapes may by unsuccessful, because there are in fact different 'texts' associated with different geometrical spaces, and we may not know this, or appreciate or recognize that our perception is being solicited by an overlay of opposing cues.

The necessity at times to establish the 'text' for a specific kind of perception raises the question as to whether the 'text' itself can in principle be established as an item in the World on equal footing with other perceptual objects. The 'text' may be, at least in part, a scientific object, structured with the help of a mathematical model, and empirically accessible only through a process of measurement[17]; such for example are the psychophysical angular variables (η, x, β) present in the optical field associated with hyperbolic vision. It is then necessary for the coherence of a phenomenological/hermeneutical theory of perception, to hold that, even when 'texts' are theoretical scientific entities, they are in priciple perceptual objects, and that they can be exhibited through a 'reading' of scientific instruments. I have argued for such a position in my book, *Space-Perception and the Philosophy of Science*. The general thesis proposed there is: a scientific explanation is a description of conditions of possibility of a scientific *explanandum*, and comprises a 'reading' of 'texts' generated by the physical interaction of the scientific objects and a suitable readable technology; a suitable readable technology in this case is a scientific instrument capable of being 'read' in a way analogous to the reading of a text.[18] Such is the goal aimed at by science, and realized by every scientific theory that has become sedimented in our culture. It follows then that scientific entities, such as temperature or Euclidean space, *are* (or, *should become*) perceptual entities in the final accomplishment of a scientific inquiry, that is, when the scientific explanation becomes a sedimented possession of our culture. The belong to the World together with those entities given directly in unaided perception. The two theses about perception and scientific observation are themselves related in a hermeneutical circle, so that the denial of one involves the denial of the other.

In the case of visual spaces, the thesis implies that, just as Euclidean visual space depends for its cues on the presence of those repetitive architectural elements which are a feature of our carpentered environment, and which serve as measuring instruments or uniform space markers, so one 'reads' the presence and character of a scientific variable from the response of standard instruments or (what I call) readable technologies. Just as the square marble flagstones in a painting by Raphael or Perugino, are 'read' as exhibiting a space of infinite depth, so the level of mercury in a thermometer is 'read' as exhibiting the scientific (thermodynamic) temperature of the environment.[19] I shall not elaborate or defend this thesis here, but the elements of the proof can probably be inferred from what I have to say about perception in general.

V

The principal argument in favor of the hermeneutical character of perception is a comparison between perceiving and reading. Reading a text is a paradigm case of a hermeneutical activity. Reading and perceiving, when analysed phenomenologically for their existential-hermeneutical structures, show a common hermeneutical structure. (It will become clear that the same conditions and processes that apply to perception, apply also to scientific observation in the natural sciences.)

The argument goes this way: Reading is, or aims at, the *direct, self-evident, reception* of the meaning of a *text*. Perceiving, likewise, is, or aims at, the *direct, self-evident, reception* of the meaning of a 'text' which is in fact either a natural or artificial state of the World. Both reading and perceiving share the same set of hermeneutical *pre-conditions, subjective* and *objective*; they differ, however, with respect to the prior knowability of the signs, here, the text or 'text', and with respect to the relationship of the meaning presented to the World.

Reading as a *direct* reception of the meaning of a text implies that the words of the text, as marks on paper, are transparent to meaning. The words as physical signifiers are not in any sense objects of the reading — these are what is signified by the signifiers, nor is meaning inferred from a prior knowledge of what constitutes their being by deductive or inductive methods.

The meaning received from the text is *self-evident*; that is, the satisfactoriness of the reading is evident to the reader, the reading provokes no reflection to the extent that it satisfies the reader's interest in the text.

Reading is the *reception* of a meaning from the text; that is, the meaning is not experienced as invented or constructed, but as found.

What is read is a *text*; this is a set of words in some language, expressed correctly according to the rules of that language, and offered within the context of linguistic communication. The text serves an information-theoretic function; it is the embodiment of meaning, it is information$_1$.

The *subjective pre-conditions* for any interpretation are specified by Heidegger as threefold, *Vorhabe, Vorsicht*, and *Vorgriff*. *Vorhabe* takes hold of what it is to be interpreted — in this case, a text as an instrument of a historical World-speaking language, this is a moment prior to interpretation; *Vorsicht* and *Vorgriff* anticipate in conceptual categories the possibilities of articulated meaning, and connect these conceptual categories with clues in the text and context.

Hidden in *Vorhabe* will be the linguistic, behavioral, social, neurophysiological, and other skills which are used by the reader (A), but which are not part of the meaning that is read from the text. Such structures, generally studied by scientific methods, can themselves – according to the general thesis about the goal of scientific inquiry stated above – become revealed as perceptual objects in the World of readers. As such they could function as secondary 'texts' for one skilled in 'reading' them as signs. However, they remain inaccessible to the individual (A) who is reading while he/she is actually pursuing the task of reading, but they may be accessible to some different individual (X), or even to the reader (A) during intervals when he/she is not actually engaged in reading. Such factors then become a secondary 'text' associated with the first, and assist readers, such as A and X, to test and correct possible readings of the original text. The third party X plays a regulative role relative to the public intersubjective character of perceptual knowledge.[20] X is analogous to the Perfect Knower in Cartesian philosophy, with the difference, however, that A and X belong to a hermeneutical community of readers in which complementary cultural and historical traditions prevail, specifically, the humanistic tradition of A, and the scientific tradition of X.[21] Such is the structure of Dasein.

The *objective pre-conditions* for a reading of the text include those that pertain to the reader A, and those that pertain to a third party X. They include establishing the correctness and authenticity of the wording of the original text, the elements of the context that need to be taken into account by A for its interpretation, as well as the possible secondary 'texts' that may be relevant to X's testing and correcting of possible readings of the original text, and the 'contexts' of those 'texts.'

Turning now to perception, perception is a 'reading' (in a special sense) of a 'text' (in a special sense) that parallels in structure the reading of a literary text, and consequently, is hermeneutical. Unlike a literary text, its 'text' is usually not in evidence, it is usually not identifiable by the perceiver with a given Worldly structure simply by a redirection of attention in the perceptual field. Its 'text,' however, can be uncovered and its structure analysed by psychophysical studies.

Perceiving, like reading, is a *direct* form of knowing; it does not draw a conclusion by deductive or inductive inferences from more elementary and basic knowns presented in the experience, nor is it merely the possession of an internal representation or model of the object known.

Perception carries with it, its own *self-evidence*; it is unproblematic to the perceiver to the extent that it evidently satisfies his/her interests in the World.

The perceived object is experienced as *given directly* by the World; the vehicle of this giving is its 'text,' which imposes itself causally on the perceiver.

Acts of perception are then mediated by structures in the World — *'texts'* — which embody perceptual (or fulfilled) meaning in a way similar to the way a written text embodies a meaning. In that respect, to perceive is to 'read,' because perceiving makes use of 'texts.'

Reading and perceiving employ similar sets of subjective and objective pre-conditions.

Reading and perceiving, however, differ in the following respects: (1) 'texts' for perceiving need not be known prior to interpretation; (2) the 'texts' which are 'read' perceptually "shape" the perceptual object, they have affinities with their objects, they are "tools" of knowing; (3) some 'texts' are of natural origin, others are man-made, these latter include the responses of readable technologies, for example, the carpentered structures of our environment; (4) the meanings perceived (fulfilled meanings) are beings, exhibited as states of the World, while to the contrary a meaning obtained by reading a linguistic text is something only intended but not exhibited as a state of the World.

It is now clear how, even within a phenomenological approach, it is possible to speak of acts of perception as being causal as well as hermeneutical. Since perception is information-theoretic, perceptual meanings are embodied in physical structures, information$_1$ or 'texts,' that act causally on or through some energy field, such as the optical energy field, and through this on somatic and neurophysiological processes, to produce "resonant" states in some appropriate somatic information system on which the Worldly structure to be perceived is coded. The 'texts' being a part or function of the "resonant" states, are on the side of the perceiver's functional body (Merleau-Ponty's *la chair*).

Because these 'texts' function hermeneutically, that is, within interpretation, they are then transparent to the perceiver's gaze, they no more enter into the objective content of what is perceived than, say, features of a hammer enter into the description of the bookshelf one is making; they belong instead to the set of conditions on the part of the subject, and in the case of ordinary perception they happen to be inaccessible to the reflective gaze of the perceiving subject.

Within the existential-hermeneutical context, then, a common primordial hermeneutical structure underlies linguistic and perceptual knowing. In linguistic knowing, the text (or word) is identifiable as a Worldly structure of human construction; in perceptual knowing, the 'text' (or 'word') may not be identifiable with the same ease, but it exists nevertheless, to be disclosed to an appropriate, usually scientific, form of inquiry. It need not be of human construction; in ordinary perception it is not, in other cases it may be the product of a readable technology. Perception, then, has a certain primacy as a form of knowing, for it interprets the meaning of structures usually as yet hidden from the knower; this interpretation, however, needs for its expression the resources of language already possessed by the speaker or reader. In this respect, language is prior to perception. However, at any stage of cultural evolution the limits of perception constitute the frontier between the unconcealment of perceptual horizons, and the as yet concealed 'texts' in which these horizons are "held" for understanding (as *Vorhaben*) and interpreted without themselves yet becoming known. In this respect, language waits on the progress of perception.

VI

It is a characteristic of all hermeneutical activity, that it is never unique, final, definitive, and absolute. Since perception is hermeneutical, its contents, and *a fortiori* the contents of scientific observation, will never be unique, final, definitive, absolute, and apart from history and particular social and cultural milieux. From this it follows that there is a history of perception, of perceptual Worlds, of pictorial spaces in art, of those anomalous perceptions we call visual illusions and, perhaps not surprisingly since the recent trend in the history and sociology of science suggest this, a history even of scientific observation.[22]

6. The Fabric of Subjectivity

Vincent Descombes

M y concern in this paper will be to argue that the controversy between two schools of philosophy, the one which calls itself positivist and the other hermeneutic, can only lead to an impass. During the course of this dispute, which involves not only professional philosophers, but also people in social theory, history, anthropology and literary criticism, these two schools have been using two concepts, those of fact and interpretation. We may formulate this controversy in a pseudo-Kantian manner:

Thesis: one cannot begin an interpretation without previously having ascertained the facts.

Antithesis: There are no facts without an interpretation. This is just of course another way of restating Nietzsche's paradox: "In opposition to Positivism, which halts at phenomena and says: 'There are only *facts* and nothing more', I would say: No, facts is precisely what is lacking, all that exists consists of interpretation" (W.z.M., par. 481). This is paradoxical because one cannot abolish the category of fact without abolishing also the category of interpretation; the words "fact" and "interpretation" get their meaning from the contrast between a fact and an interpretation of this fact. I think that Nietzsche's dictum is para- doxical only if it is understood as an ontological statement (as maybe it was intended to be). It is no longer paradoxical if it means that a positivist who begins by stating that there are only facts will neces- sarily come to the conclusion that "facts are lacking and all that exists consists of interpretation." (There is of course no paradox in saying that the positivist thesis involves a paradox.)

I shall argue that the Positivist-Hermeneutic dispute is a deadlock as both schools appeal to the same principle, which I shall call a principle of subjectivity. I shall try to demonstrate this point through an example. And since I distrust *ad hoc* examples philosophers often seem to be fond of – such as "it is a fact that there is an armchair in my study" or "the cat is on the mat" – I prefer to turn to an example of a real historical dispute about facts, where the possibility of distinguishing fact from interpretation, or raw data from opinion, was a vital issue.

We have classical example of a question of fact in Pascal's *First Provinciale*. Let us first recall the setting briefly. As is known, Pope Innocent the 10th had condemned five propositions given as expressing the views of the Bishop Jansenius concerning divine Grace in his book *Augustinus*. In 1655, Arnauld (the author of the *Logique de Port-Royal* and the *Grammaire de Port-Royal*) published two *Letters* in defense of Jansenists, to contest the charge of heresy which was brought against them. His defense rested upon the distinction between what is called "le point de fait" (the point of fact) and "le point de foi" (the point of faith). The point of faith consisted in whether the 5 Propositions (as they were called in the course of the controversy) were heretical or not. The point of fact is whether the 5 Propositions are in Jansenius or not. The Jansenists, as good Catholics, said that they condemned the 5 Propositions as heretical. But they added that the ecclesiastical authorities were mistaken in attributing these 5 Propositions to Jansenius. It was therefore possible for them to remain faithful to the Church, while upholding the views of Jansenius on divine Grace and Salvation.

Now, it is clear that Arnauld's distinction between the point of fact and the point of faith, or again the juridical distinction between the *de facto* question and the *de jure* question, is equivalent to the 19th-century philological distinction between a fact and an interpretation. For an interpretation is opposed to a fact insofar as it is said to involve an evaluation of a fact, and evaluation implies the application of a rule to the fact, which brings us back to the concept of right. Arnauld's *Second Letter* was examined and eventually condemned by the doctors of the Sorbonne. Five excerpts from the *Letter* were used as evidence against Arnauld. The first four excerpts attested to Arnauld's refusal to grant the point of fact. The last excerpt dealt with a theological point and will not concern us here. So there were two charges against Arnauld: that he was "presumptuous" (*téméraire*) in refusing to grant the point of fact, and that he was wrong on the theological point. The first charge was the *question de fait*, and the second charge the *question de droit*. The problem I shall discuss in the first part of my paper is the following: in what respect is the so-called "question of fact" in the *First Provinciale* a factual question, that is to say, a question of qualifying an opinion, or interpreting it, as right or wrong?

Arnauld's distinction of the two types of question seems at first sight unproblematic. Jansenius is heretical if his views are reflected by the 5 Propositions, because these Propositions are wrong and because the Pope and the Bishops are entitled to condemn them. But it is first necessary to ascertain this fact before passing judgement on Jansenius. Condemning the 5 Propositions is a question of right, condemning Jansenius is a question of fact.

Now it is important to remember that Arnauld's trial at the Sorbonne was not Jansenius' trial. It is important because the question of fact in the *1st Provinciale* does not amount to "Is it true that the 5 Propositions are contained in Jansenius?" Instead, it deals with Arnauld's temerity in stating that "he had carefully perused the book of Jansenius and that he had not discovered the propositions condemned by the late pope; but that, nevertheless, as he condemned these propositions whereever they might occur, he condemned them in Jansenius, if they were really contained in that work." As Pascal put it: "The question here was, if he could, without presumption, entertain a doubt that these propositions were in Jansenius, after the bishops had declared that they were." In effect, Pascal tells us that the doctors had not wanted to discuss whether Arnauld's statements were true or false: ". . . they have declared that they had nothing to do with the veracity of his proposition, but simply with its temerity." What strikes us here is the formal difference between Arnauld's *point de fait* (namely, "Is it true that the 5 Propositions are in Jansenius?") and the *question de fait* as stated by Pascal (namely, "Is it presumptuous to write that the propositions are not in Jansenius, after the bishops had declared that they are?"). Let us call "factual" a proposition which has the same form as "the 5 Propositions are in Jansenius." If this is so, we shall avoid saying that Pascal's question of fact is a question about a fact. Indeed, Arnauld's temerity lies in his claim to possess the right to doubt that a given factual proposition is true, after the bishops have declared that the proposition is true. Thus, Pascal's question of fact is really a *quaestio quid juris*, a question of right. It is the question of Arnauld's right. Therefore, the examination by the Sorbonne of Arnauld's so-called "question of fact" is not an examination of a fact or an examination of a factual proposition, it is rather an examination of Arnauld's right to pronounce on the authorities' right to pronounce on a point of fact.

Up to this point we had two clear cases of a factual proposition:

(1) The 5 Propositions are in Jansenius.

(2) Arnauld has not discovered the 5 Propositions in Jansenius. Proposition (1) is factual proposition since it is according to both Arnauld and Pascal the exemplum of a *de facto* proposition. Proposition (2) is

a factual proposition if it is understood as reporting some biographical episode related to Arnauld's reading of the *Augustinus*. But if it is so understood, it has to be a proposition about Arnauld, not about the presence of the 5 Propositions in Jansenius. If proposition (2) is true, then it is a fact that Arnauld could not say of any proposition contained in the book that it were one or the other of the 5 Propositions. But the truth-conditions of proposition (1) and proposition (2) are not the same. Arnauld could have failed to discover the 5 Propositions because he missed them; and this is why he has a proviso saying that "he condemned these propositions wherever they might occur, he condemned them in Jansenius, if they were really contained in that work."

Now, the *proposition de fait* under examination at the Sorbonne was not: Has Arnauld failed to discover the 5 Propositions in the book? It was rather: Does Arnauld believe that what the bishops have declared is false? Arnauld doubts that the propositions are in the book, which means that he does not believe that they are (without going so far as to say that he believes they are not). Since he says he doubts it after the bishops have declared that they are, Arnauld does not believe the bishops. That is to say, Arnauld recognizes that the bishops have the right to condemn the 5 propositions, not the right to condemn Jansenius. The *question de fait* is thus not a factual question. I do not mean to say here that Pascal is mistaken in calling a question of fact what is really a *de jure* question. I mean to say that Pascal is trying to discuss a certain point as a question of fact, whereas the doctors understand it as a question of right. Pascal wants the doctors to examine, not Arnauld's temerity, but facts about Jansenius. On the other hand, the doctors do not want to be concerned with Jansenius, they want to pronounce only on Arnauld's opinions upon the point of fact.

Pascal wants to stay on the level of factual proposition, but he is brought by the dispute itself to the level of *de jure* proposition. This is because a fact is necessarily beyond dispute. It follows from the definition of a fact that a fact is expressed by a true proposition. As soon as someone calls into question what was considered a fact, this "fact" ceases to be a fact and becomes what certain people believe to be a fact. In other words, if there is any controversy about a fact, the question arises: who is to settle the matter and how? It is obvious that this last question is a question of right.

So the moral of my first point would be the following: it is useless to call upon facts in a controversy, since facts cannot become arguments without losing the privilege of remaining indisputable. A fact used as argument will share the fate of opinion or interpretation. What is claimed to be beyond all controversy is unable to resolve a controversy, and what has the capacity of resolving some controversy is not beyond all controversy.

After having recounted the examination of the *question de fait* and before coming to the discussion of the *question de droit*, Pascal introduces what pretends to be simply a digression, where he tells the public what would have been his opinion on the *question de fait* if he has intended to have one. "Should I be tempted, from curiosity, to ascertain whether these propositions are contained in Jansenius, his book is neither so very rare nor so very large as to hinder me from reading it over from beginning to end, for my own satisfaction, without consulting the Sorbonne on the matter." There are two points in Pascal's methodology which deserve notice. *First:* what we have here is a device for acquiring factual knowledge (N.B.: "should I be tempted to ascertain" translates "si la curiosité me prenait de SAVOIR"). We may put it in the following maxim: where the advice of authorities is contradictory, the layman has to rely on his private judgement. Whoever wants to *know* (*savoir*) whether a factual proposition is true has to observe for and by himself how things are. In other words: we do not need the doctors on the matter of a point of fact. We may call this a principle of verification (= VP). The emphasis is to be placed on the phrase "for himself," as opposed to "relying on someone else's report." So, it is a principle of personal verification. What I really know, I have come to know for myself, not for having been told by witnesses, teachers, and all other sources of authority. Such a VP may be formulated in an empiricist fashion, which gives us an epistemology of sense-data, or in a rationalist fashion, which gives us the Kantian idea of pure reason.

Second remark: While providing the VP as the true device for acquiring factual knowledge, Pascal tells us that he will not apply it to the present dispute. Had he applied the VP to the *question de fait*, he would have known whether the 5 Propositions are in the book or not. Since he has no intention to read the *Augustinus*, his present epistemic attitude towards the *question de fait* is a bare lack of knowledge. He simply does not know if the 5 Propositions are in Jansenius.

As an advocate of the Jansenists, Pascal wants to be in a position to say something more, because he wants us to suspect that the 5 condemned Propositions are not in Jansenius. He does not want us to say that we don't know whether the 5 Propositions are in the book, rather he wants us to say that we believe that they are not in the book. This he cannot obtain by applying the personal verification principle. The VP would allow Pascal to know whether the 5 Propositions are in the book by reading the book for himself. But the VP would not allow us to believe Pascal if he told us, after having read the book, that he knows for sure that the 5 Propositions are not in the book. This is to say that the VP has solipsistic implications. Not only does such a device not allow me, for example, to know if the copy of Jansenius' *Augustinus* that I am now reading in search of the 5 Propositions is really from Jansenius. I can't say I know it for myself, since I would have learned it from someone's report, namely from what was said on the front page of the book. But it would also be a useless move for Pascal to read the book, since Arnauld has already read it and told us the results of his reading without resolving the controversy. It is a fact that Arnauld has not found the 5 Propositions, but it is just Arnauld's opinion that the 5 Propositions are not in the book, since the matter is still in dispute. And because of this dispute, Arnauld did not say and could not say: "I know that the 5 Propositions are not in the book." He said instead "that he had not been able to find them, but that if they were in the book, he condemned them in the book."

Now, the personal verification principle, which is also a solipsistic verification principle, is a principle of subjectivity. By "subjectivity," I mean a modality of proposition which is expressed by phrases such as "in my opinion," "according to me," "in my view," "upon evidences which were presented to me," "to my knowledge," etc. The VP is a principle of subjectivity as it requires the possibility of inserting, in any factual proposition presented as a true proposition, a subjective clause answering the question: How do you know that it is true?

So what Pascal needs here is a principle of subjectivity, since he wants us not to believe what we are told (namely, that the 5 Propositions are in Jansenius). But this principle of subjectivity has to be a non-solipsistic principle of verification, because Pascal wants us to believe that if we had read the book, we would not have discovered the 5 Propositions. In other words, Pascal wants us to think that we do not need to read the *Augustinus*, because Arnauld has already read it in such a way that he did, so to speak, the reading for us.

We may find a formulation of a non-solipsistic principle of verification in what Pascal says at the end of his digression: "The world has become sceptical of late and will not believe things till it sees them." (*"En vérité, le monde devient méfiant, et ne croit les choses que quand il les voit."*) The grammatical subject of the sentence is *"le monde"* (the world), which, in colloquial English, translates into "people." So this sentence expresses a principle of subjectivity, since it requires the possibility of inserting a phrase like "insofar as one can see" in a factual proposition; but it is no longer a solipsistic principle of subjectivity, since the subject of the sentence is not just "I," but "the world." What we have here is the universal subjectivity of modern philosophy, namely what later Kant will call a transcendental consciousness, and Hegel the Spirit, the "Ich" which is a "Wir."

Let us have a look at the difference between the personal verification principle (If I want to know that p, I must see for myself) and what I would like to call the Distrust principle (the world has become sceptical of late and will believe that p when it sees that p). Both principles actually express a disappointment with authorities, which culminates in a decision to trust them no longer. But the VP is stated as if we had to dismiss believing in order to make room for knowing (which is the contrary of the Kantian *dictum* 'I had to remove *knowledge* in order to make room for *belief*'), whereas the Distrust principle (= DP) allows us to believe in something, namely in what we see, or to believe someone, namely ourselves. The VP opposes knowledge and belief, or reading the book and consulting the Sorbonne. The DP provides a criterion of justified belief in an age of confusion and disappointment. So the DP is the reversal of a Trust principle, which we find in the *First Provinciale* when Pascal tells us that most of his acquaintances have previously believed what they were told, namely that the 5 Propositions were in Jansenius. *"JE CROIS que je suivrais l'avis de la plupart des gens QUE JE VOIS, qui, AYANT CRU JUSQU'ICI, SUR LA FOI PUBLIQUE, que ces propositions son dans Jansenius, commencent à SE DEFIER DU CONTRAIRE, par le refus bizarre qu'on fait de les montrer, qui est tel, que JE N'AI ENCORE VU personne qui M'AIT DIT LES Y AVOIR VUES."*

The *Trust principle* allows us to believe what we have not seen on the grounds that we have been told by somebody else.

The *VP* allows us to say that we know something only when we have seen it.

The *DP* as it is stated by Pascal says that we (the world) are to believe what we see and only what we see. But the DP as it is applied allows us to believe things that we have not seen. Indeed Pascal writes that most of his acquaintances begin "to suspect the contrary," that is, not only *not to believe* that the 5 Propositions are in the book, but *to believe* that they are not there. And we want to know how it is possible to say that people believe what they see, while stating that they begin to believe that not-p without having seen for themselves that not-p.

How could I be justified in saying "I believe what I see" if what I believe (that the 5 Propositions are not in the book) is not what I have seen. Two questions now arise:

1.) What is here the difference between believing and seeing?

2.) What is the reference of the pronoun "I" in the sentence "I believe what I see"?

First question. It follows from what I have said that there has to be a difference between knowledge and belief. Now, *seeing* is a kind of *knowing*. So, we understand that people know what they see and believe what they do not see. But then, what is the difference between "people *know* what they see" and "people *believe* what they see"? It is important here to recall the traditional opposition established by theologians between faith (viz. belief) and vision. Aquinas raises the question: *Utrum obiectum fidei possit esse aliquid visum* ("whether the object of faith can be something seen") and answers in the negative. He quotes here the Apostle: *Fides est argumentum non apparentium* ("Faith is the evidence of things that appear not"). If Pascal maintains such a traditional opposition, he must concede that what we believe is necessarily something that we do not see. The DP as Pascal applies it uses the verb "to believe" in such a way that the object of belief is not something seen. But the DP as posited by Pascal seems to state something to the contrary. So we are back to the question: how does it make sense to say that one believes what one sees?

Well, does it make sense to say that I believe myself? We have already noticed that the VP says: Do not believe what other people tell you they know, go and see how things are for yourself. On the other hand, the DP says: Do not believe what other people tell you they know, believe what you have seen for yourself. But how am I supposed to apply the DP and consequently believe what I see? Is trust in oneself possible at all? It would be ridiculous to say: I could not find any trustworthy witness, so I eventually decided that the only witness to be trusted by myself would be myself. To take a few more examples, it does not make sense to say: since I could not find a servant, I decided to be my own servant (that would not mean that I have found a loyal servant, namely myself, but that I do not have a servant). Or: since I have no friends, I shall be my own friend (that would not help me). Again: since I have not received an invitation from anyone, I have decided to receive an invitation from myself. Or again: since I cannot find anyone to lend me money, I shall borrow the money from myself.

So it seems that our first question (How can I say that I believe what I see, instead of saying that I know what I see?) beings us to the *second question*: what is the reference of the pronoun "I" in the sentence "I believe what I see"? We have now two reasons to suspect that the first "I," in the sentence "I believe what I see," does not have the same reference as the second "I." The first reason is that Pascal and the world were prepared to believe something that they did not see. The second reason is that belief in one's self is somehow paradoxical.

Let us suppose that the two occurrences of the pronoun "I" do not refer to one and the same person. If this is so, the sentence "The world believes things when the world sees them" does not amount to "everybody believes things when everybody sees them." And the sentence "Pascal believes things when everybody sees them," will not be an instantiation of "the world believes things when the world sees them."

But Pascal does not suggest here that "the world" stands, in the sentence, for everybody. He is speaking of "most of his acquaintances" (*"les gens que je vois"*). Thus "the world" stands for *almost everybody*, not for everybody. A correct paraphrase of the DP would be then: almost everybody believes that p if almost everybody sees that p. And it has now become obvious that the two grammatical subjects in the sentence expressing the DP do not necessarily have the same reference, since the phrase "almost everybody" in "almost everybody believes that p" does not necessarily refer to the same persons as "almost everybody" in "almost everybody sees that p." Now, if the reference is not necessarily the same, who believes and who sees?

Let us follow Pascal's reasoning, which he presents as a paradigm of the world's reasoning. The answer to the question: who believes? is: *Pascal* believes. Next, Pascal tells who and what he believes. He tells us that he believes that the 5 Propositions are not in the book. But he does not tell us that he sees that they are not in the book. He tells us that he sees *people*: *"je crois que je suivrais l'avis de la plupart des gens que je vois," "je n'ai encore vu personne qui m'ait dit les avoir vues."* So Pascal sees people and believes them. He believes what he sees. But he does not believe what he sees in the sense that he believes that there are people; he believes the people he is seeing, which means that he believes what they say when they say that they have not seen what he, Pascal, has not seen either.

The correct application, therefore, of the DP to Pascal's case would be: Pascal, as a man of the world, believes that not-p because he sees that nobody has seen that p. Now, this seems to be going too far. Why don't we just have: Pascal does not believe that p because nobody has seen that p? If we could answer this question, we would know who it is that Pascal believes. In other words, we would know who is believed when one believes one's self. But we have seen that this "self" — as the philosophers say — is the modern subjectivity. So we would also know what it means to be a subject in the modern sense of the word.

But we can answer the question, since Pascal tells us that he and the Jansenists are looking for someone who says that he has himself seen the 5 Propositions in Jansenius. Of course, Pascal would not be satisfied with just any kind of testimony. The sort of witness he is looking for would have to be prepared to point out the 5 Propositions in the book. We would believe the doctors if they were prepared to point them out. But if we believed them, we would not ask them to show us the five propositions, because we would trust them. So why don't we trust them in the present case? It is because, by refusing to show the 5 Propositions when asked, they forbid us to see precisely what they ask us to believe. Thus, they claim to possess a knowledge from which we are forever excluded. Therefore, the difference between Arnauld, when he tells us that he had not been able to find the Propositions in the book, and the doctors at the Sorbonne, who refuse to point out the Propositions, is the following: Arnauld will allow us to occupy his place, since we are free to read the book if we want to verify whether he was right or wrong; but the doctors want us to stay in a position of believers who can only rely on testimony.

We are now able to say who is, or what is, this "subject" that modern philosophers appeal to as to an authority which will not deceive us. "I believe what I see." This sentence shows the fabric of subjectivity insofar as it makes sense only if we understand how the first and the second occurrences of the pronoun "I" do not refer to one and the same entity.

Let us take the first "I" as referring to the person I am. Then, the authority I believe is not *me* (since I have become sceptical of late). But it is *anyone* who can be considered as my witness to the facts. The sentence "I believe what I see" will mean: I believe what the person who stands for me says and sees. When my representative sees something, he sees it for me and it is as if I had seen it myself.

And if we understand that it is the second "I" in the sentence which refers to my person, then "I believe what I see" will mean that I may consider myself as the representative of anyone, as if I were a reporter, not for this or that newspaper, but for any newspaper, for the world itself. Now, "I believe what I see" will mean: what I see is to be believed by anyone, if my position as witness to the facts is that of a representative of anyone.

We have obtained two readings of the sentence "I believe what I see":

1.) "I believe anyone who says that he sees something, provided that I can consider him as my representative."

2.) "Anyone believes what I see, provided that I can be considered as a representative of anyone."

Now, anyone is not the same as *anyone else*. And we need "anyone" to mean here "anyone, including me." So we must bring together the two readings, and this will give us: "Anyone, including me, is justified in believing what anyone, including me, can see."

This is the fabric of subjectivity. The modern subject is neither I nor someone else, but a fictitious entity: it is someone else insofar as I could have been the person referred to by the phrase "someone else," and it is me so far as anybody else could have been in my place. One may wonder if it is reasonable to trust a fictitious entity. But that would be another story.

Part III.
Dimensions of
Hermeneutic Understanding

7. Hermeneutics and the History of Being

Werner Marx

In his lecture course *"Der Satz vom Grund,"* Heidegger states that "The history of Western thought rests in (*ruht in*) the mittance of Being" — *dem Seinsgeschick*. Further on he remarks: "The history of Western thought is characterized by what we call the mittance of Being (*Seinsgeschick*)." And finally, "The knowledge of history must be understood from the mittance of Being."

It follows from these quotations that whenever we refer to "history" in connection with Heidegger (as I do in the title of this essay), we can only mean history — *Geschichte* — as understood from "the mittance of Being."

But what does Heidegger's term "the mittance of Being" (*Seinsgeschick*) mean? We must first recall the significance of the word *"Geschick."* It implies what in German is called *"schicken."* This can be rendered in English as "to send." *"Schicken"* as *"auf den Weg schicken"* corresponds in English to "sending something on its way." This "sending something on its way" can take place for a specific reason or on specific grounds; it can, however, also take place without any reason or ground. Heidegger has the latter sense in mind when he employs the word *"schicken"* as "sending something on its way." This sending is a gratuitous sending on the way without reason or ground.

We must further note the German prefix *"ge-"* which denotes a "collection" of such free sendings. The neologism "mittance" does not convey this meaning. Lacking a better term, however, some translators have adopted it and so must we. German-English dictionaries render the German word *"Geschick"* as "fate," inducing many translators of Heidegger to interpret *Seinsgeschick* falsely. Here at the outset I cannot emphasize strongly enough that "fate" is not the meaning to which Heidegger refers. Thus I shall exclusively employ the term "mittance."

There is, furthermore, an additional sense involved in the way Heidegger employs the term *"Geschick."* The receiver of such a collection of mittances is man's thought and only his thought. *"Geschick"* means, for Heidegger, precisely and exclusively a *"Geschick an und in das Denken,"* i.e. a "sending towards and into thinking" whereby "thinking" comes to be *"geschickliches Denken,"* "thinking in accordance with a mittance."

I

While speaking until now of *"Geschick,"* I have of course had in mind a *"Geschick des Seins,"* a "mittance of Being." Furthermore, though not explicitly part of this expression, I have meant *"Geschick des Seins in seiner Wahrheit,"* the collection of sendings into thought which are those of Being in its "truth." At a later point I shall refer back to and explain the significance of truth — and more importantly, the significance of Being — within this specific context. For now, however, I shall inquire into the significance of the term *Seinsgeschichte* as *Seinsgeschick*, of the history of Being as the mittance of Being. How at this point can *Seinsgeschichte* as *Seinsgeschick* be ascertained in a formal manner without regard for the specific subject-matter involved? It means the collective sending of Being in its truth towards and into thought which thereby is *seinsgeschickliches* or *seinsgeschichtliches Denken*. This I shall call the historical thinking of Being with the understanding that this so-called "history" is comprised of the collection of the "mittances of Being in its truth to thought."

The later Heidegger's mode of thinking as a whole is often characterized correctly in an "historical thinking of Being." But such a blanket characterization does not distinguish between four directions or paths (*Wege*) in the later thought:

1. The historical thinking of Being which directs itself toward the fragments of the Presocratics. Here the aim is to determine the meaning of an experience *with* Being at the beginning of Western history, i.e. with the "creative" sense of Being in what Heidegger calls the "first beginning." I shall subsequently discuss the meaning of the term "creative." Examples of such interpretations by Heidegger are "The Anaximander Fragment" and the essays *"Logos"* and *"Aletheia."*

2. The historical thinking of Being that directs itself towards the texts of metaphysics. On this path Heidegger is concerned with thinking Being insofar as it has withdrawn its creative sense. Examples are the interpretations of Plato, Aristotle, Descartes, Leibniz, Kant, Fichte, Hegel, Schelling, and Nietzsche.

3. The thinking that does not direct itself interpretatively towards texts, but is rather concerned with the sense of metaphysics in its final form, i.e. with the meaning of the essence of technology and of the "turn in Being" as it prepares itself in technology. Examples are "The Question Concerning Technology" and "The Turning."

4. The "preparatory" thinking which assumes as its sole task the projection of the fundamental determinations of "another beginning" for experience and thought. This thinking concerns itself with the poetic works of Hölderlin, Trakl, and Georg, attempting to develop the determinants of the essence of the world, the thing, and their interrelationship, as well as that of the essence of language. Examples are the essays on Hölderlin, "The Thing," "Building Dwelling Thinking," and "The Way to Language."

In this paper, I will deal particularly with the structure of the second path of thought, i.e. with the thinking that directs itself interpretatively towards the texts of metaphysics. My question is this: Can we call this interpretative thinking "hermeneutics"? It is definitely not a theory of the traditional art of hermeneutics. Nor is it, as it was in *Being and Time*, the philosophical articulation of the self-interpretation of circumspectively understanding Dasein in the mode of everydayness – a prepredicative projective understanding of Being which is pre-structured by facticity and thrownness. Its concern is not the way-to-be which exclusively distinguishes Dasein, i.e. *Seinverstandnis* or "understanding-of-Being" whereby the subject-matter of such understanding is Dasein's own Being as Being-in-the-world and the Being of entities encountered in the world. Nor is it concerned with the circular structure of understanding (*Verstehen*) as the basis for the kind of hermeneutics which is an interpretative understanding that distinguishes between fore-having, fore-sight, and fore-conception (*Vorhabe, Vorsicht,* and *Vorbegriff*). In contrast to the conception of hermeneutics and interpretation in *Being and Time*, as well as those rooted in the definitions of "understanding" developed in *Being and Time* (such as those of Gadamer, Habermas, and Apel), it is my thesis that the historical thinking of Being which directs itself towards the texts of metaphysics has *only one goal*: to find and to exhibit "words of the withdrawal of the creative sense of Being."

That this should be the only goal of this direction of Heidegger's historical thinking of Being might seem rather strange at first. Perhaps even stranger, however, is Heidegger's insistance that the thought of one engaged in this kind of thinking must have undergone a radical transformation. Heidegger writes in *"Der Satz vom Grund:"* "It must have transformed itself out of the truth of Being into another saying." So I shall inquire, first of all, into how metaphysical thinking transforms itself and into what structure. Secondly, since according to Heidegger this transformation must result "out of the truth of Being," I shall then ask what the "truth of Being" means in this context. Finally I shall attempt to further clarify the purpose and goal of the "historical thinking of Being."

II

Let us then address ourselves to the first question: how would our current philosophical thinking have to transform itself into the historical thinking of Being? Heidegger has characterized this transformation as a "leaping." I shall therefore attempt to unfold the structure of this "leaping," and in so doing I shall go beyond what Heidegger himself has said.

1. "Leaping" means "leaping away" from all deductive or dialectical thought as well as from all forms of rationalistic thought. "Leaping" and the "leap" signify thought that intends to reach another realm by breaking away from thought that develops itself by way of a necessary continuity of steady progress. The historical thinking of Being does not follow from a philosophical propaedeutic (as, for example, Hegel's *Logic* followed from the *Phenomenology of Spirit* or as Schelling's Positive Philosophy followed from his Negative Philosophy).

2. Though "leaping" does signify the leaving behind of traditional thought, it still remains in a relation to it. After all, the historical thinking of Being is directed toward traditional texts and positions, standing thereby in relation to the tradition.

3. Whoever wishes to leap away must prepare for this leap. Thus, whoever wishes to leap away from rationalistic thought should *first of all* open his eyes to the fact that all pre-philosophical ways-to-be are directed toward rationalistic grounds and that the beings which they encounter are assumed by such thought to be rationalistically groundable. He must *then* attend to the fact that from its inception, philosophical thought as metaphysics has thought about states of affairs in the same way: all particular beings were considered by it as rationally grounded. After this preparation, the one who tries to carry out the historical thinking of Being finds himself "in the leap." From the posture of "Being-in-the-leap," he would be able to look back at the "region from which it leaped." It is important to realize that only from that vantage point can this thinking catch sight of what would otherwise never be seen. This is, for one thing, metaphysics as a whole and the determinations that govern it. Furthermore, the state of "Being-in-the-leap" allows

the historical thinking of Being to see that the whole of metaphysics manifests itself in different ways for metaphysical philosophers, i.e. in the form of various mittances to their thinking. Moreover, it can also be seen that all of these mittances of Being are modes of withdrawal of the creative meaning of Being in a sense which must be clarified presently. And this is now my central thesis: *To think of the whole of metaphysics and its different mittances as forms of withdrawal of the creative meaning of Being, this and this alone is the theme of the historical thinking of Being which directs itself towards the traditional texts of metaphysics.*

4. "Being-in-the-leap" also signifies something further, something which Heidegger himself does not make clear. He who has leaped away and is in-the-leap is attuned neither in an everyday nor in a scientific manner. In order to understand the significance of the "historical thinking of Being," one must recognize that this "leaping away" abandons both everyday and scientific attunements. The leap leaves behind the secure and familiar region, the supposedly unshakable foundation of *ratio*. Obviously, only a non-everyday, non-scientific attitude is moved by that with which everyday and scientific attunements are never concerned. The attunement of a scientist − for example that of an historian who works on his material from the standpoint of historical objectivism − is precisely not the attunement of an "historical thinking of Being" in the comportment of "Being-in-the-leap." Only for the attunement of the historical thinking of Being is that which "has been" "present." And the presence of that which "has been" is what the historical thinking of Being must "appropriate anew." The historical thinking of Being is therefore always a renewed appropriation of what has been and is as such present. There is a great deal said about this renewed appropriation in the literature on Heidegger without it being seen that a non-everyday attunement is required for it.

5. Leaping as "appropriating anew" signifies that the historical thinking of Being" as a leaping away is at the same time a "leaping forward." But into which realm does the historical thinking of Being leap forward? Heidegger's answer is that it leaps forward into the realm of "that which approaches it as worthy of thought" (*das Denkwürdige*) and of "that which is to be thought" (*das Zu-Denkende*). But what is "that which is both worthy of thought and to be thought?" The answer is "that which gives the measure or the standard for thought" (*der Maßstab*) − what for Heidegger is the "truth of Being." I might further remark in regard to the structure of the historical thinking of Being that it is particularly distinguished in that "it is able to behold what is 'audible.'" This paradoxical characterization is intended to preclude any ideas of physiological or bodily hearing or sight. Beholding-hearing (*zuhörendes*

Sehen) is for Heidegger in turn grounded in a "belonging-to" (*Zugehören*). To what, however, does the historical thinking of Being in its beholding-hearing belong? The answer is that it belongs to the "truth of Being."

Heidegger has nowhere said so, but this further qualifies the thesis of this lecture. The "historical thinking of Being" in a text of metaphysics — which has transformed itself into the attunement of "Being-in-the-leap," i.e. into a "beholding-hearing" because it experienced itself as belonging to the "truth of Being" — this thinking is different from all other methods of interpretation because, in its interpreting, it keeps in mind the "truth of Being," envisages it so to speak. But what do we mean, within the present context, by the "truth of Being?"

III

The expression "the truth of Being" designates various aspects of the same thing. This can be confusing. Here I shall deal with only two of these aspects. Let us first turn our attention to the word "truth." As is well known, truth designates for Heidegger the occurrence of an unconcealing, a making-manifest, which thereby establishes a clearing that is at the same time permeated by concealment. This concealment either never discloses itself or discloses itself in such a manner that concealment in the forms of mystery and errancy hold sway over and continue to permeate the particular beings which are unconcealed. It is important to emphasize, within the context of our inquiry, that concealment is the source of the oblivion characterizing all of metaphysics; and, moreover, that this illustrates how the truth of Being as a mittance to metaphysics is a sending which takes place in the form of a withdrawal.

Now that we have turned our attention to truth, we can return to the expression "the truth of Being" to ask what Being means here. In my opinion, Heidegger scholars have often failed to recognize that the so-called "contents" of a truth so conceived consist of a creative occurrence, one experienced and sedimented first in certain key words from Presocratic texts. The phrase "truth of Being" makes reference to these "words." The first of the aforementioned forms of the historical thinking of Being, that which directs itself towards the "sense" of these words as expressions of the occurrence called "Being," tries to grasp this. Such "words of Being" are, for example, *physis, eon, logos,* and *moira.* Unfortunately, there is no time here to demonstrate how these words of Being partake in what my early book, *Heidegger and the Tradition,* refers to as the "creative sense."

The early Heidegger, in *Being and Time,* attempts to overcome the

Cartesian "ontology of Being present-at-hand" by employing such determinants as "Being-ready-to-hand" and "Being-authentic." The later Heidegger achieves something similar by means of the creative sense in the "words of Being." Unless one is cognizant that it is precisely the creative character of Being which has withdrawn itself under the dominion of metaphysical thought, there can be no proper understanding of what Heidegger means by oblivion in the form of a "withdrawal" (*Entzug*) brought about by metaphysics. Heidegger himself has not made this clear. Nor has he made clear another point of great importance for my thesis. I argued earlier that historical thinking in its interpretation of metaphysical texts has in mind the truth of Being. Such can now be understood as precisely the creative sense of Being — that which underlies the "words of Being" at the beginning of Western thought. This is why the second of the four aforementioned forms of the "historical thinking of Being," viz. that which directs itself to the texts of metaphysics, is founded upon the assumption that all metaphysical texts are "mittances" of Being insofar as its creative power has withdrawn. For this reason, it is obvious that the interpretation of metaphysical texts must yield words expressing "the withdrawal of the creative sense of Being." For example, the result of Heidegger's interpretation of Hegel's *Phenomenology of Spirit* is the neologism "Subjectivity." The result of his Nietzsche interpretation is the expression "will to will," and that of his interpretation of Leibniz is *ratio* in its modern sense. As I will soon show, these words of withdrawal bring Heidegger's thought onto the fourth of the pathways mentioned above, viz. that of "preparatory thinking," having as its sole end the projection of "another beginning" for thought and experience for mankind.

At this point it is worth noting that Heidegger himself calls the interpretation of a traditional text a "dialogue," a "discourse within the tradition and with it." As he says in the lecture course "What Is Called Thinking?", an interpreter is obliged "to have first entered into what has been said, into the way the matter stands which comes to language in the text." In the lecture "The Anaximander Fragment" he demands that the interpreter, "listening, lets himself into that which comes to language in the saying." This listening, however, is not the same as the "Beholding-hearing" (of the truth of Being) of which we spoke earlier. The former simply concerns the appeal — *der Zuspruch* — of language, which "beckons at first to us and then again at last to the essence of any matter at issue." The interpreter must follow this beckoning and bring to light what hitherto has been covered over and left unsaid. He must say the unapparent and thus bring it to appearance.

In a dialogue the issue of a text presents itself to the interpreter in the form of language. Thus the interpreter, addressed by the tradition, finds himself in an ambiguous situation. That is, he understands the issue from his horizon and from language. More precisely, he understands from an understanding of the present world already sedimented in language, already presupposing much which is not transparent to him.

With this idea of dialogue, Heidegger accordingly demands that the interpreter deal not only with those issues presented in the text, but that he also contribute on his own to the subject matter of interpretation. There is a difference between the commonly accepted view of hermeneutics and this view of interpreting metaphysical texts. In "The Anaximander Fragment," for instance, Heidegger emphasizes that the primary task of an interpreter or translator is to determine whether the mittance, the collection of sendings of Being to thought, remains the same as it was for the thought of a given past philosopher.

Here we see it confirmed that Heidegger's "historical interpretation of Being" is concerned only with mittances. As we have emphasized, these mittances are manifest in metaphysical thought only as Being withdraws the creative sense it showed in the first beginning. This is the real reason why Heidegger, in interpreting the texts of metaphysics, proceeds immediately from a conviction that the text is evidence of the self-withdrawing truth of Being. (To be sure, we do not find this conviction amongst the metaphysicians themselves.) The sole task in interpretation is to show how a particular mittance is a matter of the withdrawal of creative Being.

But now let me make this more clear with reference to Leibniz's metaphysical thought as Heidegger presents it. In *"Der Satz vom Grund,"* Heidegger proceeds without question from the assumption that Leibniz's thought is a manifestation of withdrawal. The task then is to show *how* it is subject to the claim of the mittance of self-withdrawing Being. I should again note that as a consequence of the withdrawal of the truth of Being, the creative occurrence of Being is not manifest. Instead, only particular beings are visible, and these become visible for metaphysics only in the light of projections which guide its views. The guiding projection for Leibniz's metaphysics is *ratio* in the modern sense of a rational ground. In this light, particular beings manifest themselves as rationally fathomable. Seeing them in this manner, Leibniz states of the particulars that "No being is without a rational ground" — *nihil est sine ratione*. Indeed Leibniz's thought is so determined by this mittance that he even considers it equivalent to the principle that the rational ground be conveyed to the representing Ego in the form of a judgment "which is sufficient." Under this *principium reddenda rationis sufficientis*, thought is taken to be that which "gives account," is "rational." The task of the historical thinking of Being is therefore to interpret this assertion as evidence of the withdrawal of the creative sense of Being, and thereby to illustrate the effect which the principle of "giving account," this form of rationality, has had upon modern philosophy and science.

The historical thinking of Being also shows how Kant is dominated by the same mittance as Leibniz. The direction and realm of the Kantian inquiry are likewise determined by the guiding projection of *ratio* in its double sense of reason and ground. But at the same time, the historical thinking of Being also demonstrates how the subjectivity of the subject emerges as the authentic realm of the projection of *ratio*; how transcendental consciousness allows the objectivity of objects to be "delivered" in such a way that it thereby co-represents itself as self-consciousness.

I cannot pursue the question of how, for the historical thinking of Being, objectivity develops into subjectivity — a subjectivity whose *ratio* is defined by the *principium rationis* as a withdrawal due to the mittance of Being. But in this process, our age finally develops into the "atomic age." For as Being withdraws itself in its creative sense, reason's claim to authority, as developed in modern science, becomes the universal and complete reckoning of everything as calculable.

The intention of these examples, however, has been simply to illustrate how Heidegger's historical thinking, in its interpretation of the texts of metaphysics, is concerned only with developing words to express the withdrawal of the creative sense of Being.

But how does this historical thinking of Being come to reach the point where it transforms itself anew? At the beginning of this lecture I mentioned that our current thinking would have to be transformed in order to become an "historical thinking of Being." I spoke of a "leap" such that thinking, in the attunement of "Being-in-the-Leap," could appropriate anew what "has been." I also quoted a passage which demands "that thinking transform itself out of the truth of Being into another Saying." However, as this passage goes on to say, "*It requires the leap* before thinking has transformed itself out of the truth of Being into another Saying." Hence, as I have stated, this leaping must leap forth into "that which is worthy of thought and must be thought" and this leaping forth is the truth of Being.

Now it can be shown how radically Heidegger conceives of this transformation of thought. Indeed with Heidegger, the historical thinking of Being in its interpretation of the texts of metaphysics is required to "jump" into the realm of the truth of Being. Thinking can free itself from the withdrawal of creative Being by jumping directly into *that* realm which, while interpreting texts of metaphysics, remains in the mode of a beholding-hearing. This jump only succeeds when thinking fully transforms itself, "out of the truth of Being," into its creative meaning. As the historical thinking of Being, thinking is now able to prepare for another beginning. Thought is able to think and to say Being *as* Being.

What does this mean? I can best explain it with reference to the interpretation of Leibniz as a form of the withdrawal of the creative sense of Being. The further transformation of thinking which "hears and beholds" the creative sense itself not only has the creative sense of Being in mind, i.e. beheld. It also hears and beholds "in another key." In contrast to the usual key in which it hears "*Nothing* is *without* ground," it now hears "Nothing *is* without *ground*." The emphasis shifts from "nothing" to "is" and from "without" to "ground." Transformed in this manner, thinking hears an accord of "is" and "ground," i.e. an accord of "Being" and "ground." In the new key, Leibniz's principle of sufficient reason signifies that "Such a thing as ground belongs to Being," and that this belonging-to means that Being itself is grounding in the manner of a groundless occurrence.

Here we have a particularly radical instance of the historical thinking of Being which directs itself toward the traditional texts of metaphysics. I have intentionally cited this instance in order to illustrate how Heidegger's interpretation of these texts springboards the historical thinking of Being toward a new beginning. This "preparatory thinking" is meant to give the truth of Being a new creative content. We know well that Heidegger gives to it the content of the *Geviert* or four-fold through whose mirror play he tries to save the things from *Verwahrlosung*, the devastation of their true way to be. By thinking the four-fold into the things, Heidegger tries to make it possible for some future form of mankind to live poetically with them on this planet. Heidegger conceives his thought as belonging to the "truth of Being" and takes seriously, for his historical thinking of Being, the task of guardianship and attendance which lies in this belongingness. If we are to understand Heidegger, we must keep in mind why he feels justified in hearing the text in a key different from, and even opposed to, the usual one. Only in this way can one understand the violence of his interpretations, so unlike that of his early hermeneutics.

It is obviously futile for a critique of the later Heidegger to ask whether this or that interpretation is "correct." Heidegger would have admitted the "incorrectness" of his interpretations in this sense. But his real concern is something very different with regard to the tradition. As we have seen, the tradition concerns him only as a point of departure, in his words a "realm-for-leaping-away-from." This leaping-away is justified by the need for "guardianship of and attendance to the truth of Being." A critique is consequently meaningful only if it points to immanent inconsistencies, to something unthought within Heidegger's complete project, or else if it can externally call the whole project into question, showing, for instance, a sense in which the project itself can be condemned as "utopian."

Heidegger's conviction is that mankind stands under the claim of the total withdrawal of the creative meaning of the truth of Being. Moreover, as long as this is so, man must respond to this claim. Thought today must respond to the claim of the mittance of the essencing of technology. As a result, we cannot help but think in a rationalistic, even in a calculating way. Of course, we can then ask what this "must," this necessity entails, and do so in an immanent and critical manner. For after all, it has been possible for Heidegger's own thought to transform itself into the historical thinking of Being, somehow freeing itself from the claim of the mittance of technology. His own thinking is able to leap away from rationally grounding thought. Heidegger himself does not discuss this possibility, the "freedom" of the historical thinking of Being to withdraw itself from the prevailing claim of the mittance, perhaps because the traditional meaning of freedom has been submerged slowly under what for Heidegger is the truth of Being. However, the real reason, I believe, is that Heidegger was never really struck by the wonder of freedom.

IV

By way of a conclusion, I still have to answer the questions of whether and in what sense the historical thinking of Being, which directs itself towards the texts of metaphysics, might be characterized as a "hermeneutics."

Heidegger himself declares explicitly that his late thought is not a hermeneutics. However, along with his efforts to think the essence of language in a different way from the tradition, he remarks that, — in its address, which he takes to be a non-human occurrence, in its silent Saying (der Sage), — there lies the relation of a "message" to a "messenger." Hermes is the messenger who receives a message and passes it on. In this sense, Heidegger speaks of a "hermeneutic relation" which lies in Saying. Indeed my very thesis here is that the historical thinking of Being beholdingly listens to the silent address of the truth of Being, to its creative sense. In this manner thinking keeps Being in mind, has it before its eyes whenever it interprets a text of metaphysics as a mittance of self-withdrawing Being.

My suggestion is that the "historical thinking of Being" as *messenger* keeps this message "in mind." Therefore, not only can it think the text as a "withdrawal of the creative sense of Being," but it is also able to transform itself into a different saying of Being. For that reason it does not seem to me inappropriate to call Heidegger's historical thinking of Being a "hermeneutics." But such a hermeneutics, however attentive to a text, receives and conveys a message never heard before.

Postscript

The conception of understanding (*Verstehen*) which Heidegger introduced in *Being and Time* is developed in various ways by the hermeneutics of his followers. This proves to be of considerable value not only in philosophy, but also for the humanities, the social sciences, and other fields as well. Despite this applicability of Heidegger's early thought, who would be in a position to "carry out" the hermeneutics offered by the later Heidegger and depicted here? Who could claim that his thinking fits in with Heidegger's own determination of "thought after the turning" (*die Kehre*)? Thinking, Heidegger claims, owes its power to the "lightening-like" *Ereignis*, the disclosure of "appropriation" (as Albert Hofstadter translates it). But can anyone carry out the leap of which we have spoken? Can one place oneself in the posture of being-in-the-leap and also make the "jump" that would then take him into the "saying of Being?"

This problem goes to the very heart of the situation in which many philosophers find themselves today. My own diagnosis has often been that we are condemned to philosophize "between tradition and another beginning." The reference here to "another beginning" indicates an "otherness" or "new way of experiencing and thinking" towards which our age strives. I refer, for example, to the thought of Rosenzweig, Buber, Jaspers, Cartre, Marcel, Maritain, and above all Heidegger. (I do not include Husserl who, in the *Crisis*, maintains that his transcendental phenomenology completes and fulfills a tradition of rational thought which was initiated in the Greek view of reality and developed further in Kant's transcendental idealism.)

At this point, I cannot even begin to delineate the tradition which includes (in Hegel and Hegelianism as well as in their antipodes Marx, Nietzsche, and Freud) the final witnessing of the onto-theological metaphysics of reason. Today, however, we are left to philosophize in the realm of an "in-between." Whether one practices linguistic or analytic, social or practical philosophy – to name but a few of the major directions in contemporary thought – philosophy itself remains for the most part committed to the power of reason – albeit somewhat diminished by the thought of Marx, Nietzsche, and Freud.

Nonetheless, some of us who philosophize within this "in-between" endeavor to understand, approach, and even carry out another kind of thinking. We are convinced that the steps which lead the later Heidegger to a so-called "turning" make a great deal of sense. However, as I observed earlier, we find ourselves incapable of taking the same steps on our own. What then are we to do? Shall we continue interpreting and dissecting Heidegger's terms, comparing his positions with those of his protagonists in the tradition? Or are we simply to try imitating him?

The book on Heidegger which I wrote some twenty years ago concludes by listing numerous tasks for a *Weiterdenken*, a thought which carries on and takes further. However, recently, in my foreword to the second German edition, I was forced to admit that in Germany, where interest has been diverted from Heidegger, further thought of this kind has become quite rare. (While Heidegger scholarship has grown considerably in the United States, I am not sufficiently familiar with it to pass judgment on its overall impact.) This prompts me to ask how such thought would go about its task? And if philosophy "in between the tradition and another beginning" is indeed unable to truly assimilate Heidegger's way of thinking, then what method would be available to it?

In view of this problem, I now suggest the following two steps toward a *Weiterdenken*. First, we must clarify the *Sachverhalt*, the subject matter underlying Heidegger's fundamental determinants. And second, we must examine those determinants – admittedly from a vantage point still under the sway of traditional thought – to see whether they can be found lacking either in conception or in their channels of expression. One might discover, for example, that the subject-matter underlying Heidegger's determinant "responding" (*Entsprechen*) is akin to what underlies the traditional concept of freedom. Furthermore, by "thinking further," the Heideggerian *Entsprechen* might even be given a wider scope. The result, in this particular instance, would, at least partially, resolve the problem of freedom that troubled us earlier. Or, to take another example, it could be shown that the problem of death in the later Heidegger has a decisive significance in relation to Being and Nothingness, one that Heidegger himself does not see. (In a recent article concerning "mortals" (*Sterblichen*), I tried to show this by investigating the subject matter underlying death as a fundamental determinant.)

These are examples of what I have called "further thought." In closing this essay, however, I leave the following questions unanswered: Can the hermeneutics of the later Heidegger–*Seinsgeschick* and *seinsgeschichtliches Denken*, the mittance of Being and the historical thinking of Being – be thought further? Or must we be satisfied with a realization that Heidegger, and only Heidegger, can carry out this task?

(Translation reviewed by K. Itzkowitz.)

8. Hermeneutics and the Meaning of Life: A Critique of Gadamer's Interpretation of Dilthey

Frithjof Rodi

In the history of hermeneutics Heidegger's emphasis on understanding as the basic trait of Dasein seems to be a decisive turning-point. Hermeneutical theory, heretofore primarily methodological, is extended – or radicalized – into a fundamental-ontological problematic. Through Gadamer's efforts to ground philosophical hermeneutics in *Wahrheit und Methode*, emphasis on this turning-oint has become a permanent part of the way the relation between philosophy and the human sciences through the last hundred years is regarded in the history of philosophy. Under Gadamer's influence, we have become used to making a distinction between "traditional" and "philosophical" hermeneutics: "The concept of understanding is no longer a methodological one as with Droysen. Nor, as in Dilthey's attempt to provide a hermeneutical ground for the human sciences, is understanding an inverse operation that simply follows behind life's tendency toward ideality. Understanding is the original character of the being of human life itself."[1] This new approach – Gadamer points out – was possible through Heidegger's ontological reflection, which "revealed the projective character of all understanding and conceived the act of understanding itself as the movement of transcendence, of moving beyond being."[2]

Wahrheit und Methode characterizes the historical consciousness developed throughout the 19th century as an attitude which could not grasp the full philosophical dimension of understanding because it was obsessed by the ideal of method and scientific objectivity. In elaborating on this point Gadamer draws a sharp line which divides the history of hermeneutics. Schleiermacher, Droysen, Dilthey and others belong to what he calls "traditional hermeneutics." It is only with the rise of the phenomenological movement that the philosophical dimension of understanding is discovered. Gadamer says repeatedly that the radical new point of departure does indeed "ask quite a lot" from the stand-point of traditional hermeneutics,[3] and he points to the "almost angry polemic" with which Emilio Betti reacted to this new point of depar-ture in his foundational works on hermeneutics.[4]

"Traditional hermeneutics," according to Gadamer, "has incorrectly limited the horizon within which understanding belongs."[5] More specifically, what this means is that in traditional hermeneutics, throughout its development from Schleiermacher to Dilthey and then on to Emilio Betti, the theory of understanding, as an objectivistic and psychologistic theory, is restricted to the possibility of apprehending objective intentions of meaning. In contrast, Gadamer is concerned to work out the structure of hermeneutical experience as it bears on the general relation of man to the world. Following the early Heidegger, the term 'hermeneutics' is thus no longer applied to denote a methodology, "but as a theory of real experience which thinking is."[6]

Under the influence of the criticisms which have been aimed at this theory by the proponents of "traditional" hermeneutics, such as Emilio Betti, E. D. Hirsch[7] and, more recently, Thomas Seebohm,[8] Gadamer has attempted to take the edge off this opposition through a series of further elucidations and emendations. He emphasized that his own point of departure was so far removed from being a methodology for the human sciences that a critique of it at the methodological level would be utterly irrelevant to it. His inquiry into "what happens to us above and beyond our own volition and praxis"[9] thus claims a different dimension from the outset. He also firmly repudiates the objections raised by Habermas and Apel on the one hand, but also by Albert on the other, that his hermeneutic reflection means "undermining scientific objectivity."[10]

But there remains an obvious ambiguity. Although Gadamer empha-sizes that he is not concerned with a methodology for the human sciences, and that accordingly any comparison whatever of the respec-tive points of departure is excluded *eo ipso*, he does remain constantly critical – indeed, often almost polemical – over against that position to which he contrasts his own hermeneutical reflection as *philosophical* hermeneutics (as opposed to a merely epistemological or methodological one). The relevant difference can be understood in either of two ways: if two utterly different *levels* of reflection are being distinguished – namely the epistemological-methodological one of "traditional" hermeneutics and the fundamental-ontological one of philosophical hermeneutics – then by mutual recognition of the entirely different approaches a relationship of indifference and neutral coexistence is possible. *Or*, alternately, a distinction is made between two *stages* within the development of hermeneutical theory. Then it is taken as a matter of course that the later stage represents a higher level of reflection, on which the earlier stage is "overcome."

The first way of regarding the distinction seems to be indicated by all those passages where Gadamer acknowledges the legitimacy of scientific method and the dignity of objectivity, and where he designates as a "crude misunderstanding" the charge that "the slogan 'truth and method' denigrates the methodological rigor of modern science."[11] The second alternative is supported, not only by Gadamer's clearly pejorative use of the terms "methodologism", "objectivism", etc., but especially by the way in which *Wahrheit und Methode* treats the history of hermeneutics. It argues the thesis that "an overcoming of the epistemological approach through phenomenological research"[12] was necessary in order to attain the proper philosophical dimension of the problem of understanding. This decisive change of outlook appears as a preparatory step towards Gadamer's own project "of transcending the restricted horizon of methodological interests in the theory of science" and rendering thematic, in the context of a philosophical problematic, "also the conditions and limits of science within the totality of human life."[13]

As regards the term 'traditional hermeneutics,' the question arises to what extent it implies the claim that the epistemological theory of understanding has become *obsolete* through the fundamental-ontological approach. It is precisely this point in the discussion between Gadamer and his critics where precious little clarity has been achieved. On the one hand, Gadamer neither can nor wants to contest the legitimacy of epistemological and methodological reflections accompanying research in the human sciences. On the other hand, he leaves no doubt that he is not prepared to take seriously any hermeneutical theory which has not endeavoured to make the step from historical to "*wirkungsgeschichtliches*" consciousness. This postulate has far-reaching consequences; I should like to indicate some of them by considering as an example the question of the pertinence of Wilhelm Dilthey's philosophy.

II

If we want to get a picture of the effects arising from Gadamer's Dilthey-interpretation, it is worthwhile to glance at the various writings which appeared around 1970 from young philosophers, in part students of Gadamer, who were at that time getting into the general controversy about hermeneutics. Thus we find, for example, R. Bubner, in an early paper entitled *"Über die wissenschaftstheoretische Rolle der Hermeneutik"* ["On the Role of Hermeneutics in Scientific Theory"],[14] repeating Gadamer's thesis that Dilthey, like Hegel, is characterized by the certainty of a philosophical absoluteness in the form of a universality opened up to us in understanding.

Bubner continues:

> This a precisely the point where Gadamer turns away from Dilthey's view of hermeneutics. The old self-certainty of comprehensive philosophical insight returns in the guise of a methodology with which the human sciences become established as legitimate and original modes of knowledge. In this methodology, however, what becomes virulent is that naive prejudice of methodological consciousness according to which securing the procedure also guarantees access to truth. In short, contemporary hermeneutics suspects Dilthey's methodology of bearing of false claim to absoluteness and — in spite of his assertions to the contrary — inadequate recognition of the finitude of knowledge in the context of historical human life.[15]

In a similar vein, Jürgen Habermas said in 1967 that Gadamer had demonstrated Dilthey to have

> indulged in the illusion that there is an all-comprehensive faculty for understanding, through reproduction, any and every objectivated meaning.[16]

In a "Discussion on Method" of young Tübingen philologists in 1971, it was claimed that Gadamer describes "the wrong path which historical-hermeneutical thought from Schleiermacher through Dilthey has taken, which ended in the blind alley of positivistic historicism."[12] This series of examples could be extended almost indefinitely. As regards the *topos* of "overcoming," Karl-Otto Apel speaks of the "overcoming of the psychologistic theory of Schleiermacher and Dilthey by Gadamer"[18] and of the "detour through Schleiermacher's and Dilthey's doctrine of identical re-experiencing,"[19] to which Gadamer had put an end. Apel regards the strength of philosophical hermeneutics – in spite of his many reservations of principle *vis à vis* Gadamer – as lying "in its critique of the objectivistic methodological ideal of historicism."[20]

In recent years, Gadamer has himself been working towards a more subtle and differentiated account of these matters, which also involves the concept of "overcoming." In the Epilogue to his 1979 Hegel Address in Stuttgart, he suggests, referring to Heidegger's relationship with classical metaphysics, that a philosophical "overcoming" can also mean an inseparable bond between the new and the old. The old is then not simply that which is left behind, but rather a partner over against which we can delineate our own position. Gadamer closes this Epilogue with the following remark, which is important to the question we are considering:

> I hardly need to add that in my own work in *Wahrheit und Methode* I proceeded similarly and delineated my own position in such a contrastive (and one-sided) manner-over against Schleiermacher whose hermeneutics I separated from his dialectics, and over against Dilthey whom I judged by the consequences of Heidegger and Nietzsche . . .[21]

Also in his major article on "Hermeneutik" in *Historisches Wörterbuch der Philosophie*[22] his discussion as regards Dilthey is more subtle and differentiating. It hardly allows of any wholesale dismissal of traditional hermeneutics as a "wrong path" or even merely a "detour." Also in the "Nachwort" to the later editions of *Wahrheit und Methode*, he had already admitted the (perhaps unavoidable) one-sidedness, being aware of new trends in Dilthey research which had led to a new interest in the program of a "critique of historical reason."[23]

Thus as regards the "overcoming" of traditional hermeneutics through philosophical hermeneutics, we can say that Gadamer's contrastive delineation of his own position over against the hermeneutical reflections of Schleiermacher and Dilthey has by no means settled the matter conclusively, but rather has led to new horizons in the problematic of hermeneutics. Any attempt to deal seriously with Dilthey cannot avoid the question raised by Gadamer; and yet, conversely, Gadamer's book has by no means rendered such an attempt superfluous.

There are two closely-related problems which deserve especial attention within a reconsideration of Dilthey's views if one has in mind the points raised by Gadamer: the question of the ambiguity of Dilthey's concept of *Wissenschaft* and the charge of objectivism. They are both closely connected with the broader problem of "methodologism" in the human sciences, which touches the whole of "traditional hermeneutics."

The following remarks are intended merely to indicate the direction which a meta-critique of the Gadamerian critique might take.

1. *As regards the ambiguity of Dilthey's concept of Wissenschaft.* In his account of Dilthey's "entanglement in the impasses of historicism,"[24] Gadamer is primarily concerned to show how a genuine commitment to life-philosophy in Dilthey conflicts with his ideal of Wissenschaft – which derives from very different sources. The reflectivity of life, i.e., the tendency – inherent in the *praxis* of life itself – to view itself reflexively and to make itself transparent is an implicit precondition for Dilthey's hermeneutical grounding of the human sciences. "Hence for Dilthey the connection between life and knowledge is an original datum."[25] And yet – Gadamer continues – in his grounding Dilthey could not maintain this principle of reflection immanent in life. Rather, he relativized it by focusing on the opposition between the *Unergründlichkeit,* i.e., the *unfathomability,* of life and the security of valid knowledge obtained through *Wissenschaftlichkeit.* In this opposition, in which the productive tension between life and knowledge is given up on favor of an ideal of *Wissenschaftlichkeit* oriented to the natural sciences, the influence of romantic hermeneutics asserted itself in him. It was in this context that he attempted to "harmonize the mode of knowledge of the human sciences with the methodological criteria of the natural sciences."[26] This is, Gadamer maintains, a primarily defensive tendency. The *Unergründlichkeit,* the unfathomability of life, this "frightful countenance," is set against "the human mind seeking protection and clarity . . . the scientifically-developed capacity of understanding."[27] This rationalistic ideal, stemming from an "unresolved Cartesianism," would in the final analysis lead Dilthey to "conceive the investigation of the historical past as deciphering and not as living historical experience."[28]

The primary objection to this interpretation – which is in fact one-sided – is that in presupposing a purely negative concept of *Unergründlichkeit* it generates the alternatives: security vs *Unergründlichkeit;* and it maintains that Dilthey surrenders the productive tension between life and knowledge in favor of a security through science.

A more subtle and differentiating interpretation would have to procede on the basis of some comments Georg Misch has given as far back as 1923 on Dilthey's concept of *"Unergründlichkeit".*[29] Today we are able to say a great deal more about this by considering the additional material now available in the editions of Dilthey's posthumous papers. Of especial interest here is what has been labelled the *"Berliner Entwurf"* for a second volume of the *Einleitung in die Geisteswissenschaften (Introduction to the Human Sciences).*[30] In various passages here, Dilthey's treatment of the problem of the *Unergründlichkeit* of life shows Gadamer's thesis to be untenable. This "Berlin Draft" which begins with a sketch for the continuation of the historical part of the *Einleitung*, contains an outline for a description of the task of philosophy in the present age. Because of the impotence of idealism *vis à vis* modern tendencies, philosophy has become the *"Selbstbesinnung* of society",[31] the positive content of which is to develop a "philosophy of reality and of life."[32] For only philosophy is capable of providing "coherence, communication and grounding of the particular areas of intellectual activity; but it can by no means do so through finding answers to transcendental questions, but rather solely through a fuller, more mature consciousness of reality."[33] This reality – and this is the central point for our line of argument – is not simply intelligible *(gedankenmäßig)*. Dilthey continues: "This reality is meaningful in its vitality, and yet it is at the same time unfathomable. It is because of this *Unergründlichkeit* of life that it can be expressed only in imagery."[34] The *Unergründlichkeit* which Dilthey intends here is not that it is fearful and senseless *Unergründlichkeit* of a chaotic world-will *à la Schopenhauer*, whose horror can only be alleviated by the rationality of science. This concept of the *"unfathonable"* is not a metaphysical concept whereby a world is constructed which is bottomless and thus abysmal and fearful. Rather, it is a gnoseological concept which expresses the idea that reality can be rendered amenable and transparent to thought only to the extent that the preconditions of thought are given in life itself. This is the meaning of Dilthey's much-quoted statement that "Beyond life thought cannot go." In the "Berlin-Draft" he writes:

> Thinking cannot go back behind life whose function it is. Life always remains a precondition of knowledge, of the consciousness or awareness contained in that life. As a precondition of knowing, it is itself not open to analysis through knowledge. Thus the foundation of all knowing in which its preconditions are inextricably contained, is life itself – in its totality and fullness and power. The character of life is visible in the structure of everything alive. Its meaning arises from this. It is *unergründlich*."[35]

I have quoted this passage so extensively because here the relationship between the principle of *Unergründlichkeit* and Dilthey's famous claim that thought cannot go beyond life emerges more clearly than in his earlier published writings. In the context of a more subtle Dilthey-interpretation, it is inconceivable to play off the principle of *Unergründlichkeit* against Dilthey's ideal of *Wissenschaft* and to maintain that this central area of Dilthey's theory of science hence contains an ambiguity.[36] Instead, it remains correct to say, with Georg Misch, "that recognizing the *Unergründlichkeit* of life" must become "a central element in the theory of knowing".[37] And, further, that it is precisely through this intention that Dilthey's philosophy — in spite of his exclusion of transcendental theses — does not slide into positivism.

2. *Objectivism.* The "Berlin Draft" also provides more light on another aspect of our problem. When Dilthey emphasizes that life is unfathomable and yet still at the same time intelligible, he always adds that there are forms of imagery and symbols [*Bilder- und Symbolsprachen*] which are capable of expressing the meaning of life, notwithstanding its *Unergründlichkeit*.

> To realize this, to make this clear by uncovering its basis, to develop its consequences: that is the beginning of a philosophy which is adequate to the great phenomena of literature, religion and metaphysics, in that it recognizes their basic oneness in their innermost nature. They all express the same life, the first in images, the second in dogmas, and the third in concepts; for even the dogmas are, properly conceived, not concerned with something outside this world."[38]

This is not yet being said in the context of a typology of *Weltanschauugen*, of world-views, although we can already see how that will later be developed along these lines. Here, however, Dilthey is concerned with a more general account of the function of a philosophy whose task it is — in the face of modern relativism and scepticism — to draw the proper conclusion from the nexus of intelligibility and *Unergründlichkeit*.

> What is required in this epoch is that we live only through what is accessible to reflection, what is experienceable, and that we be guided by it. But we also 'strive' to make this visible in its *unfathomable* depths and its unfathomable context."[39]

In its polar structure, this undertaking is far removed from a "naive prejudice of methodological consciousness" to the effect that by establishing the security of a procedure it has also guaranteed access to truth."[40] It is clear that Dilthey does not regard the principle of *Unergründlichkeit* as absolving him of his obligation to scientific methodological rigor and openness to corroboration in his own work. And yet it is characteristic of his hermeneutical theory that he also regards the concrete tasks of understanding as being related back to the limits set by the *unfathomable* meaning of life. This is, to be sure, not an innovation original to Dilthey, but rather derives from Schleiermacher's insight that the task of understanding is an infinite one, and is never open to more than approximative solutions. In his study of Schleiermacher's philosophy, Manfred Frank has aptly pressed this point over against Gadamer's critique.[41] Gadamer's thesis that Schleiermacher "assumes something like complete understanding" is,[42] in light of this, no more tenable than is his account of the position taken by romantic hermeneutics and its consequence, which he represents as being incumbent on Dilthey as well:

> "The perfect understanding of texts is as possible as the perfect understanding of another person. The author's meaning can be divined directly from his text. The interpreter is absolutely contemporaneous with his author."[43]

Neither Schleiermacher, nor Boeckh or Dilthey ever made this claim. Especially Dilthey was always aware of the limits of historical understanding. So he considered it the main task of his first book *Leben Schleiermachers* to bridge the gap between his own generation and the cultural heritage of Schleiermacher, Humboldt and Goethe, whose thinking and feeling in its core had become "utterly alien to our present age." What he aimed at was not absolute understanding of the past but restoring some of the historical continuity "between their achievements and the tasks of today." – "I do not want just to narrate: I want to convince. It is my wish that before the reader's eye the image of this great personality will appear; but at the same time, a nexus of well founded, lasting ideas should arise, applicable (*eingreifend*) to the theoretical as well as the practical life of the present age."[44] His aim was "*Wiederverständnis*[45] of the past, – a kind of re-understanding which could not be based on a relationship of absolute contemporaneousness with his authors. Rather it was determined by that tension between "*Zugehörigkeit*" and "*Zeitenabstand*" which Gadamer has so convincingly shown to be the basic constituent of hermeneutical experience.

"Not just to narrate, to convince." This is not Ranke's ideal of absolute objectiveness. It is not – to use Gadamer's words – the purely reconstructionist's approach. If we accept Gadamer's opposition of "reconstruction" vs "integration" as two fundamentally different ways of dealing with the past,[46] and if we allot the reconstructionist's approach to what he calls "traditional hermeneutics," then we are inclined to see a decisive watershed – not so much between Dilthey and his successors, but rather between philological "reconstruction" in general and philosophical "integration" within that tradition of Nineteenth Century thought which has made the term "historicity" a key word of hermeneutics.

(Translated by K. H. Heiges.)

9. Hermeneutics of the World

Michael Murray

When the concept of world first came to prominence in the context of Heidegger's existential phenomenology, it signaled an important break with the dominant modern tradition and was hailed as a positive new direction.[1] What is the present status of the notion of world in philosophical discourse? Has it been eclipsed and why does it seem little discussed or no longer productively developed? Is this because it has been assimilated, or because the notion has been rejected, refuted or supplanted and replaced by some other? Can we discover its analogue in different philosophical contexts, such as later analytic thought, or has it suffered the special tribulation of deconstruction? I want to raise this broad set of questions — broader than I can fully treat here — as a way of glancing over some of the major versions of this idea and in whose compass I shall try to formulate a new version that enjoys certain advantages over its comparables and over its wholesale disregard. Eventually I want to show the promise that the new hermeneutics has for contemporary literary theory, based on such a conception of world.

The concept plays a strategically important role in *Being and Time* where human Dasein is defined as constituted by its being-in-the-world, and where the worldhood of its world gets phrased in a preliminary way as the totality of significance and involvement of Dasein, such that neither world nor Dasein would mean anything without this inherence.[2] This fundamental state is missed by "traditional ontology," which Heidegger claims "operates in a blind alley if, indeed, it sees this problem at all" (SZ, p. 65). He projects an investigation of why it was not only at the beginning, but recurrently ever since, that Western ontology has overlooked the world phenomenon (SZ, p. 100). In the *Basic Problems of Phenomenology*, Heidegger reiterates that "elucidation of the world concept is one of the most central tasks of philosophy," adding that philosophy till now has failed to recognize the concept or phenomenon.

In *The Essence of Reasons* Heidegger ventures a sketch of the conceptual history of world, from the Presocratic *cosmos* to the Pauline and Johannine versions to its translation and alteration into the *mundus* of Augustine and Aquinas, and then through Baumgarten, Leibniz, and Kant.[3] From this sketch it becomes clear that Heidegger's own usage, which has its own variants and adaptation in his writings later and earlier, coincides with none at the explicit conceptual level. On the other hand one can see within this context how the special mission of his own project could strike him and just how Heidegger situates it with respect to the tradition.

1. The first of these senses is that of the early Greek *cosmos*, which signifies the How of beings as a whole, with special emphasis on its process character. We could call this an ontological sense of world.

2. The second is the New Testament sense of *cosmos* which specifically demarcates the human condition as the state of man without god, giving rise to the pejorative religious sense of "worldliness" and "man of the world." This is an anthropological-religious sense of world.

3. The second sense persists in Augustine's sense of *mundus*. But the latter also signifies the totality of created being (*ens creatum*), which is the domain of being created by God, and this sense survives as a major sense of the term all the way through Aquinas, Baumgarten and Leibniz. However broad, this represents a regional, or regional-ontological sense of world.

4. Kant's explicit use of *Welt* appears in a double usage that descends from the Greek and Christian senses. The first lies in the context of rational cosmology, where cosmology in turn is defined as one of the three disciplinary studies of special metaphysics (along with other devoted to the soul and god). Thus it too remains a *regional* delimitation of world. The second use occurs within the context of pragmatic anthropology, where it refers to man but emancipated from the older pejorative sense of the worldly man and the *amator mundi*. Rather Kant accents the positive sense of 'man of the world' as "a co-player in the great play of life."[4] This latter is thus an anthropological-secular sense of world. Of course for Heidegger these contributions do not yet display Kant's real importance. The real aim of the Kantian *Critique* does not consist in its cosmological or in its anthropological results (in either of the two senses), for Kant's work seeks the foundations of all metaphysics. His approach, which we should call transcendental-ontological, conceives not the domain of created being but the aggregate of "appearances" and their giveness to finite intuition, i.e., the possibility of the cognitive relation between man and things. Analogously, the orientation of Heidegger's analysis in *Being and Time* is neither

cosmological nor anthropological; *in-der-Welt-sein* identifies the fundamental structure of relation between things as a whole (however understood and determined) and man such that he always finds himself within that which is (*das Seiende*) as a whole. The existential-phenomenological sense of world functions to link man and being antecedent to their transformation into subject and object.[5]

This allows us to see just how Heidegger situates his own notion of world in the context of the philosophical tradition. He goes on to distinguish between a pre-philosophical and a philosophical conception of world. The first includes all those ancient, medieval, or contemporary notions of a totality of things *within* the world (be they nature, things, universes or sets). But the philosophical sense accordingly defines the sense of world within which intra-worldly things are intra-worldly and does so in terms of their structure of occurrence and appearance. Positively speaking, Heidegger defines world in *Basic Problems of Phenomenology* as "that which is already previously unveiled and from which we return to the beings with which we have to do and among which we dwell."[6] Heidegger's most intensive consideration of the world concept in *Basic Problems* leads him to an appeal to poetry, which is, he says, "nothing but the elementary emergence into words, the becoming-uncovered of existence as being-in-the-world." He cites a passage from Rilke's *Malte Laurids Brigge* portraying the hues and stains on an old wall, exposed by destruction, the layers of fading paint, the musty damp, and the bodily odors of its inhabitants, the signs of activity, weather, and time.[7] Hinted at in this allusion is an essential connection between the transcendental philosophical project and the subsequent turn toward poetry in Heidegger's thinking about world.

One can distinguish several fairly distinct stages in Heidegger's thinking about world:

1. world as totality of significance and involvement that makes up Dasein's being-in-the-world, and provides the formal existential conception defined in *Being and Time*.

2. world not as a unitary, but as a conflicted co-concept along with that of earth, which links together something like a formal determination with a material determination ("Origin of the Work of Art," 1935–36). This step involves at least two striking innovations and consequences so far as the traditional outlook on these topics goes. First, a formal ordering is said to struggle with but *not* overcome and master a material order and the true relation between them not being mere agent versus patient, formal shaper versus material stuff. In this case earth is an active force and power that demands to be experienced in its own right. And second, a key position is assigned to the work of art, and such other

works as take part in and contribute to working out the historical relations between world and earth, within which men dwell, protected and exposed.

3. In the writings after the mid-1930s, in those increasingly devoted to Hölderlin and the Greek sources, another dimension becomes explicitly registered: that of being under the heavens (see, especially, "Poetically Man Dwells," 1950). Thus could we say that human existence is defined by its relations of being in the world, being on the earth, and being under the heavens. And lastly,

4. These various formulations get woven together in a last formulation as the gathering of the Fourfold (*das Geviert*), which opens and holds, earth and heavens, mortals and immortals, in face-to-face relationship. In this step Heidegger's most advanced statement appears to coincide with a common archaic and traditional cultural matrix, one that is not widely questioned until early modernity, at the dawn of the scientific and technological age.

I do not enter full rehearsals of each of these steps but only remind us of these now fairly familiar moves in Heidegger's thought, and instead raise the question whether any significant steps have been taken with respect to the concept of world *since* Heidegger's work. Having presented some appreciative and critical remarks on the post-Heidegger efforts, I try to propose a new version of the concept of world that makes use of key strands in the tradition, that preserves what is interesting and suggestive about Heidegger's view, but which also critically revises that view to make better sense of our own specifically late modern, barely post-modern historical place.

II

I can summarize the subsequent philosophical history by saying that while Heidegger gave an ample and experimental treatment of world, his most obvious successors associated with post-phenomenological hermeneutics make some use of the concept but contribute little significant development. Hans-Georg Gadamer, for example, first introduces it in an important discussion at the end of the Third and final Part of *Truth and Method*.[8] Thanks to language, he says, man has a world and distinguishes himself from living creatures with their habitats. Unlike these creatures, man attains a certain distance and freedom with respect to his world and experiences it as expansible and alterable. Moreover, the linguistically constructed world of men actualizes itself in conversation, in which the social life of the community is lived out and tradition formed. Learning to speak a foreign language, for example, is entering into the world of its community, not merely acquiring a facility for speaking.

An ambiguity in Gadamer's account arises because he sees the world in this sense not only formally but also substantively in terms of a content. He puts this by saying that our experience of the world is always perspectival and relative, but also that these perspectives are tied to or implicate being in itself, yet which we are never in a position to compare with the perspective. While I admire his desire to avoid simpleminded solutions, Gadamer runs together several different ideas in his discussion of world. At one point he asserts, "No one questions that the world exists without man and perhaps will do so."[9] Insofar as the existential world is linguistically constituted, that amounts to saying there could be language without man, which won't do even if one subordinates the speaker to language, as Heidegger wants. The term might then rather refer to beings or reality that might precede or continue apart from the linguistically constituted world, but it could not be world that is independent. This shows how slippery is the term and how world has not been carefully and specifically thought through. Perhaps this ambiguity is deliberate and reflects how Gadamer does not set the same store on the creative moments of language and art that Heidegger does, and that for him the constitution occurs in the course of the conversation. Elsewhere I have argued that this difference is due to Gadamer's remaining bound by the humanistic and aesthetic conception of literature, his critique of aesthetics notwithstanding.[10] Looking at the other apparent successor, Paul Ricoeur, one notices that although world defines a key moment in Ricoeur's more recent writings on hermeneutics, the concept itself remains rather undeveloped.[11] This might be explained by the fact that Ricoeur does not intend to add a new concept of world so much as to resituate the Heideggerian notion of *Welt* in the context of contemporary hermeneutics and other analytic resources.[12]

In the same period during which the concept of world seemed to reach a certain plateau among Continental philosophers, there sprang up a new interest among analytic philosophers in the topic of possible worlds and possible world semantics. This returned to fashion a problematic familiar since Leibniz, now restated in the terms of recent modal logic and the debate about its interpretation. Then a second shape in which concern with a concept of world emerges is found in Nelson Goodman's *Ways of Worldmaking*.[13] For our purpose, consider the following two observations:

First, these treatments employ a rather undefined understanding of world, or at least undefined with respect to the essential structure of world as distinguished from the definedness of its variant world members or items. Indeed, there is a certain willingness to call almost anything a world or possible world. In these discussions, world remains an undernourished, vague idea. Alternatively, we could say, it is taken for granted without considering that a world is *no more than a set*: a set of things, features, sentences, and so forth.[14] But such a determination cannot capture that conjuncture in the historical tradition we pointed out between the ontological and the human, and by itself cannot attain a specifically philosophical level or angle of concern. It could at most become philosophical only if tied to a transcendental placement or some appropriate successor project. My point is somewhat like Kant's distinction between what is required for a general logic of thought and what is required for a philosophical transcendental logic. An analogy between this distinction and the possible successor discourse might be to distinguish between language in general with its conversational structure and poetic language in particular with its power of inaugural naming, provided this relation be grasped dialectically rather than foundationally.

Second, Heidegger's own notion of world might well seem indefinable, not merely undefined. Since Heidegger's *Welt* has no essence independent of existence, it's been argued, it does not and could not possess an essence in any traditionally recognizable sense.[15] If anything, we could say this inseparability of essence from existence is more pronounced in the later Heidegger than in *Being and Time*. Nonetheless, this does not prevent either Heidegger or us from discussing the structure of world; rather, it means that the essence of world is to be thought in a contextual, relational, and historical fashion. We are asked to recognize the verbal-temporal essencing that goes on in the language – conversational and poetic – of the West. Recognizing such an "existential essence" leads us to think it not in universal and necessary terms, but in local, regional, transcendental terms that may strike up relations with other transcendental neighborhoods, yet without requiring any imperial universal meta-logic.

Unavoidably the analytic discourse on variable features or variable worlds operates in terms of some sense of world, else they simply could not be possible *world* talk. Goodman argues against a more dramatic and possibly incoherent version in his *Ways of Worldmaking*. This freewheeling opponent might be called the "Now For Something Completely Different School of Monty Python Ontology" or "Goodman's tamer Disneyland" comparison.[16] This brings us to consider Goodman's own theory as offering something appealing to hermeneutics, though also something deeply unsatisfactory.

Goodman offers a refreshing versatility in the range of his attention, in his studied inclusion of artistic symbolization on a par with
scientific invention, and in his useful inventory of major operations of
fabrication — composition and decomposition, ordering, deletion, supplementation, and deformation.[17] Ostensibly he discusses these operations in the context of a theory of construction worlds. On the other
hand, Goodman says remarkably little of what world means across the
variegated applications, or even within each of the various domains.
It seems to mean something more than merely a set and yet apparently
less than the hermeneutic sense of world. Goodman thinks of himself
as a pluralist because of his insistence on the variety of symbolic forms.
He is like Cassirer in this regard; however he is unlike Cassirer in
rejecting the hierarchicalization that the theory imposes. Nonetheless,
he remains in the positivist tradition in that he restricts truth to statement and to scientific symbols, although he devises substitutes and
analogues such as rightness and fit for the others. In Goodman's view,
we find minimal characterization of the world(s) men inhabit. Goodman differs from Heidegger (in these last two respects) because he does
not go as far.

Finally, I agree with Ricoeur that in Goodman's account of
worldmaking "the factor of otherness is overshadowed by the factor
of fabulation."[18] Goodman describes his orientation as situated in the
mainstream of modern philosophy read as a sequence of substitutions,
wherein world is replaced by mind, mind by concepts, and then, finally,
concepts by symbol systems.[19] Yet an ambiguity marks Goodman's own
presentation: at the start of the sequence, world is a name for the *Ding
an sich*, pure *Vorhandensein*, namely, that which passes away with the
"world well lost." Yet the worlds that are made in the process of symbolic fabrication cannot be world in the same sense, and thus a quite
different sense of world must appear at the end of the sequence. In
this respect, Heidegger's thought is both more daring and more satisfactory; more daring because it breaks with the mainstream of modern
philosophy rather than adding to it, and more satisfactory because it
tries to combine the factor of otherness with the factor of construction.
World fabrication in Heidegger's sense is what makes possible the
discovery of things, others, the experience of earth and heaven, and
that which displays the moving whole of what Heidegger calls Being.
We gain access to these kinds of otherness through the various instituted
relationships. Yet this access is different from a mere possession
because we do not stand outside them manipulating them and owning
them. Furthermore, it is different because disclosure and bringing out
of hiddenness is thought against the resiliant opacity and pull of con-

cealment. To this pull, the disclosive thrust is never equal or exhaustive, and we always lack an Archimedian point from which to dominate it. As a consequence there is a constant process of making and remaking the world, and never a final state or revelation. This is why Heidegger stresses its living, dwelling, inhabitative character. A world defines a form of life, a way of being according to the concealments and revelations afforded by our languages and works and the supporting history of effects. This means that fabulation opens up possibilities, summons latent potentials, and affords new departures, but also, for the time being, it seals off, closes down, and silences others.

III

This section advances a particular hermeneutics of the world, a particular conception of the frame of reference of habitation and encounter. This conception builds upon the work of Heidegger but also criticizes and seeks to move beyond certain of its disadvantages. The compass of this presentation will not allow for more than a stating of theses, with some sketching in and explanation of reasons for preferring this scheme over others. The essential traits of a world, which distinguish it from a mere collection or set, are that it affords a *ground* on which men dwell, a *horizon* in terms of which they move and understand their place, and a *measure* in the light of which they live out their lives. I want to argue that this approach allows us to overcome certain deficiencies in Heidegger's formulation, among which I identify two:

The four of Heidegger's fourfold is only oddly four since these are not four in the same sense or on the same plane of being − two are places, two are beings. Really they divide into a twosome that stand in relation rather statically, overpowered by a certain verticalism and sometimes by an incantatory holism. My tri-part distinction identifies three dimensions that retain their differences and comparability, but shows the horizon functioning as the moving mediation in the play of relationships. The mediative function of horizoning needs to be asserted against the overshadowing of the horizontal by the vertical in Heidegger's later thought. To do justice to the horizon of the world we need to recuperate the notions that appear in *Being and Time*, the earlier Hölderlin lectures, and associate them with that of the region of region (*Gegnet*) in *Gelassenheit*. In the second place, our version assumes the task of specifying criteria for distinguishing between authentic and inauthentic modalities of these three world relations. While some clues can be discerned in Heidegger's texts, these are never carefully explicitly developed by him.

The first essential trait of a world is that it affords a ground on which to dwell, which means that dwelling involves a form of dependence and need for support. Because man is not the sole sustaining cause of himself he stands grounded by something other than himself. Ground is that upon which men and women stand, rest, work, play, build, struggle, wander, settle, journey, perish. Correspondingly we can say that ground supports (standing), accommodates (resting and playing), yields the stuffs for making and construction and the fruits for nourishment; it affords the scene of struggle between men, that against which and sometimes for which they struggle to establish or maintain sites of dwelling. The ground further provides the expanse that we traverse for the aimless as well as purposive journey, and lastly the ground is the receptive bosom in which mortal remains are laid. But equally important and indigenous to ground in these aspects is that the ground can upset, overturn and cause us to lose our balance; that it also harbors the possibility of withholding and unfruitfulness, and of scarcity in the face of want. The ground can turn inhospitable to us and, obstructing passage, pose obstacles to our pathmaking and our voyaging out. These are all genuine aspects of the ground as well.

By these tokens it should be clear that ground is meant here not in the sense of a philosophical first principle or a theoretical foundation. Indeed philosophy has tended to ignore or only to try to circumvent ground in the special sense we are using, which it has done by characteristically trying to locate something absolutely below or absolutely beyond this meaning of ground as its ideal substitute. Although ground in the sense we are speaking of it must always be given, ground is not simply 'given' but must 'be given.' Ground names a function and relationship, a function and relation that needs to be established and instituted. Ground denotes a relationship between the Earth and men, and this relational ground is something opened up and instituted primarily through language. The ground as said represents the saying response to the Earth that clears a place for habitation and encounter. If language is essentially poetic, that means that the Earth becomes for us a ground insofar as it is poetically spoken — through poems, novels, songs, inaugural speeches. Poetic works are thus essentially involved in our having and finding a place for home and homeland.

As earlier indicated, each dimension of world-making must be understood as susceptible to authentic and inauthentic tendencies from which liability there is no escape. We can express the difference by broadly drawn criteria; in the case of the ground we can say it is petrification that marks the pseudo-version of ground. In this attempted condition the ground is made solely in order to secure and guarantee men; in this fashion the inhabitant of the world wants only to master and possess the ground. This deformation contravenes the fact that it's only (in part) because of the ground that man's being in the world becomes possible, as well as the fact that a relationship of response, which is what the grounding of the ground establishes, cannot be an object of possession. In this pseudo-version the sense of earthly otherness is shut out, along with what is mysterious and unsettling about it.

In the array of world dimensions that we are considering none enjoys a logical or ontological priority over another, though none is equivalent or exchangeable. In the order of my exposition I shall next turn to the dimension of the measure, while reserving what I call the middle dimension of the horizon for the last part of our discussion. By measure in the present context I mean the notion of a higher than human reality, that is, a domain in some fashion transcendent and more enduring than mortals. The measure functions to gather men into an ensemble wherein they recognize themselves, to give them a sense of scale and proportion, and to provide an exceptional affirmation of life. The saying of the measure is a speech that responds to the claims of the Divine, a measure-taking that seeks to establish the due proportion between Divine and human. Such speech brings men under the vault of the heavens, but also brings them on to the earth in a new sense. (We may say that the true measure is holy but not strictly Divine.[20] This formulation of the meaning of measure does not decide the question of whether at a given time the Divine is experienced, measured, as plural or singular, as impersonal or personal, as absent or present, or other qualities of its manifestation. Clearly the measure has been variously taken at different times and places – and partly defines such differences. In a positive sense the measure is finitely bound and variable with circumstance, if we are talking of actual manifestations.

What corresponds in this case with respect to the differentation between authentic and inauthentic, or true and pseudo-measure, we could say, is one that conceals or suppresses its status as a particular historic saying response, *and* one that conflates with the Divine. In this manner taking the measure pretends to a possession and certainty about the Divine, and arrogates to itself a sense of authority founded on this certainty. In this way it promotes what in traditional terms would be called idolatry. The greatest danger and temptation arises when the Divine withdraws itself, and the gods flee, leaving a vacuum. That gods by their essence truly appear and disappear, that absence also can be holy, is an unreassuring truth. From this vantage the so-called god of the philosophers, of metaphysics, is inauthentic, and its demise as a vital philosophical concern need not be lamented. Ecclesiastical institutions, as the authorities on the Divine, are always in tension with the polymorphous power of the religious and poetic texts they seek to command. This shows up in the way they always seek to substitute the textbook for the text and the way they seek to control the proliferation of interpretation.

Besides a ground and measure, a world must have its *horizon*, and while there are many relations among the dimensions, the horizon enjoys a special importance in world formation and so in our account. Although the notion of horizon has somewhat declined in fortune in recent times, it should be remembered how an entire philosophical movement once associated itself with it, so that Levinas could justly remark "Since Husserl the whole of phenomenology is the promotion of the idea of horizon. . ."[21] Now of course arguably this idea finally led to the *dissolution* rather than the promotion of phenomenology conceived as a certain enterprise. I shall mark the steps as succinctly as I can.

The first form of horizon discovered by Husserl is the perceptual horizon of the perceived object, that includes the internal horizon of the possible perception of the object and the external horizon of the object within a field of objects.[22] Derrida remarks about the status of horizon, that "In phenomenology there is never a constitution of horizons, but [only] the horizon of constitution."[23] This is true because the horizon is the necessary accompanying background of the object seen, that is to say, "the unobjectifiable wellspring of every object in general." Consequently horizon cannot be constituted or objectified, nor is it obvious that it can be unified and mastered by an absolute originating subject of the kind Husserl asserts.

With Heidegger's *Being and Time* the concept of horizon undergoes critical revision, in several key respects. First, horizon is not the horizon of perception or of perceived objects. Heidegger shifts his thinking away from the Cartesian ocular model and its skeletal intentionality to the pragmatic context and practice model of Dasein's care for things. As such, and in the second place, horizon is not the conscious unfolding now sequence of object profiles. Rather it is the ecstatically horizontal process of a life, the temporalizing standing outside itself in terms of constant historical having-been and being toward its mortal end. Thirdly, not only is horizon the structure of Dasein's worldly being as an historical happening, as temporal field or clearing, but also horizon must be understood as a finite openness, the essential finitude of the human horizon, and not as Husserl claimed infinitely open. This finite horizon of Dasein is always also a co-horizon and co-happening derived from our everyday being with one another in the world.[24] And finally, the fourth meaning itself is alleged to have a temporal structure rather than a timeless eidetic structure, and this assertion refers not only to human being but to the meaning of Being as such, of which "time is the horizon."[25]

In the late writings after the *Kehre*, when world gets thought as the fourfold, there is the tendency I pointed out to stress the vertical at the expense of the horizontal. This shows up in those discussions explicitly oriented toward the vertical: "The upward glance passes aloft toward the sky and yet it remains below on earth,"[26] a span that the poet is said to measure according to the measure of an unseen godhead.[27] Yet it is also affected by all those figures of ring and "circling compliancy"[28] which emphasize unity: "In the gift of the outpouring earth and sky, divinities and mortals dwell together *all at once*" (Heidegger's italics).[29] Each of the four is said to enfold and betroth the other. While there is a movement spoken of in this gathering-encircling talk, the dynamic is rather static. It is least historical when the archaic quality of this picture rather than its futurism is unacknowledged. (Note the difference in shift when Heidegger writes to a student about the Thing lecture, where he sets the discourse about the divine into an historical horizon with respect to "the divine in the world of the Greeks, in prophetic Judaism, in the preaching of Jesus,"[30] and the other references to Plato, Kant, and Hegel.) Whatever their enchantment, these unitarian and holist figures diminish the horizon and depreciate the historical-temporal.

This feature is much less true of Heidegger's *earlier* lectures on Hölderlin, where the world talk is not as developed. They tend to emphasize Hölderlin as poet of a special time and historical place, such as in "Hölderlin and the Essence of Poetry" (1936). Furthermore, they differ dramatically from the perspective presented in the recently published 1934– lectures *Hölderlins Hymnen 'Germanien' und 'Der Rhein'* (Vol. 39, 1980).[31] Heidegger strikingly insists on the historical character of poetry over and over in *Hölderlins Hymnen*, as can be readily gauged from the sectional titles of that work: "The Historical Time of the People as the Time of the Creative" (p. 51), "Poetry and Language as the Basic Structure of Historical Dasein" (p. 67), "Historical Time and the Basic Attunement (*Grundstimmung*)" (p. 104), "Temporalizing of Original Time as the Basic Event of Basic Attunement (p. 109), "Decision for the Authentic Time of Poetry as Decision for Entering into the Basic Attunement" and others announcing Hölderlin not merely as a German poet but as the poet of the Germans: "The 'Fatherland' as the Historical Being of a People" (p. 120); "Poetry and Historical Dasein" (p. 213), "Hölderlin as Poet of Future German Being" (p. 220), and "The Historical Determination of the Germans" (p. 287). Temporal horizoning in the sense under discussion is pronounced in this interpretation of Hölderlin, as when Heidegger glosses that while we can reckon the time of an individual life in terms of birth dates and death dates, we cannot so easily determine the *time within which* this life transpires. The meaning of the epochal time in which each individual lives is not accessible to him; the time that we live through may *both* be determinative of us and yet be concealed from us. What Heidegger learns, and says, of the German situation may be extended to the situation of other peoples as well. "(T)he time of the Year of the People is hidden from us . . . The world-hour of our people is hidden from us. If we ask concerning our authentic temporal being," we are forced to conclude that "we do not (really) know who we are" (p. 50). Nevertheless, it is just such a questioning and answering that creative minds seek to provide. The great poet and the thinker strive to disclose that which is concealed from us, to bring it to language for the first time and to inaugurate a new period. It is well known that Heidegger claims such a poetic disclosure on the behalf of Hölderlin. But it could be argued that the same process is at work in cultures that Heidegger largely ignores, for instance, as in Vergil's *Aeneid* and Dante's *Divine Comedy* or, nearer home, in Whitman's *Leaves of Grass* and Stevens' late poems *Notes toward a Supreme Fiction* and *An Ordinary Evening.*

While Heidegger began to think the historical-poetical horizon, it then appears to lose importance. Yet the later text called *Gelassenheit* is nonetheless deeply thoughtful about horizon. In the most familiar form we first regard horizon in terms of the horizon of the object perceived or represented and then in terms of the horizon of the world whose subject perceives and represents. When thinking in this fashion we think in terms of the side turned toward us according to our attention and movement. On the other hand, we could think in a quite different, less familiar direction and consider the horizon not as the side turned toward us, operating in terms of our intentional activities and tracing everything to the subject and its performances. This other way would try to regard the surrounding horizon as coming from beyond us, as a grant or gift, that permits our viewings, takings, and standings to occur, endows them with their potentials and leeways, without which we could have no relations at all. Heidegger calls this empowering opening the region that is not just a region but 'the region of regions,' a distinction that Heidegger designates by the word *Gegnet* (from the old German dialect) instead of the more usual *Gegend*.[32] This special sense and direction of region involves several related functions. According to Heidegger, men do not stand outside and opposite this region, unlike some other regions, but rather dwell, live out their lives, within this region; it gathers and shelters things together in relations of belonging. In such circumstance men do not exercise power over the region and its truth but rather they are called to the service of its disclosure. And lastly region in this sense is a region*ing* with its character of event and historical happening, not a fixed framework or boundary. In this respect, we can appreciate a certain primacy of the region or horizon in this fuller sense as a granting of men and things and a sending of destiny.

Despite some difficulties with his general treatment of the world concept, Gadamer has made a significant contribution to thinking about horizontality, through his seminal notion of the fusion of horizons (*Horizontverschmelzung*). This notion expresses the process relating the horizon of the interpreter with the horizon of the interpreted work and the dialectic of familiar and strange. Such a notion allies itself with an emphasis upon the historicity of the horizon, underplayed in Heidegger's later work, and can be fruitful for contemporary refection on intertextuality. What is missing, from our vantage point, is precisely the linkage of horizontality with the dimensions of ground and measure. This in turn requires developing *a poetic rather than literary* conception of horizon formation. If this is done, we would set greater accent on the elements of fracture, discontinuity, and innovation than Gadamer does, and we would also sharpen the distinction between authentic and inauthentic conflict in the account of horizon and inter-horizon.

What distinguishes *inauthentic* horizoning in its *nationalistic form* is that the horizon gets objectified and asserted as possesion rather than as the endowment of an enabling region, and that the meaning of time gets reduced to the selective horizon, and so neighboring gets ruled out. In its opposite *cosmopolitan form* the horizon is abstracted into the totality and universality that subverts the sense of place and claims of belonging, and so, in a different way, excludes the possibility of neighboring. The authentic horizon is always established with respect to a previous horizon. Every genuine projecting and sending involves some encounter with and appropriation of the antecedent form. So, similarly, every allocating of the ground takes place with respect to an already established ground, just as every taking of a measure involves relation to the prior and already familiar measure. Every new beginning starts from the middle and necessarily involves the dialectic of familiar and strange. This means every genuine instauration exhibits an aspect of strangeness. Yet even a highly accustomed world cannot be reduced to sheer familiarity, or else it would cease to function as responsive to the forms of otherness, to their transcendence as well as their presence.

The importance of horizon is, firstly, that through which it is founded and mediated in the relation between the grounding of the earth and the measuring of the heavens. Secondly, horizon makes clear the inter-saying or intertextual character of the three dimensions, and of the world itself. There is an agonistic history of the meaning of the Earth and the forms of grounding, just as there is of measures. The horizon which comes our way as the epoch in which we find ourselves, and which poetic saying limns and discloses, always displaces an existing horizon. Temporally speaking, placement always involves displacement and signifies its in-betweenness. Inauthentic instituting, on the other hand, wants to repress the poetic-historic character of the world, to conceal its tracks, to secure itself against intrusion from the past and future.

In ever more eliptical formulae, the account that we have been exploring asks for the conjuncture and counterpointing of three different dimensions. It pivots on the conception of horizon. Horizon determines the ground as a particular region, a lived geography, a native land, and it brings together an experience of earth with an experience of the divine. In the world, there is a tendency of ground toward groundlessness, of horizon toward horizonlessness, and of measure toward measurelessness, or together, of world toward worldlessness, of which pseudo-world is a spectre. We must recognize that all world formation takes place against a tendency toward worldlessness. In conceiving a world as a fabrication that is a response to earth, time, and the divine, as well as the site of human dwelling, we can understand the vital link between the ontological and human aspects that show up in the history of the world concept.

Part IV.
Narrative Discourse
and History

10. Life and the Narrator's Art

David Carr

Among the types of discourse that have attracted the attention of philosophers, literary theorists and linguists in recent years, narrative discourse seems to have been the object of more intense scrutiny than all the others. Here the historians have also joined the ranks of those interested, since narration has traditionally played an important role in their discipline.

That role has of course recently been attacked by some historians, and narrative history has been eclipsed in some quarters by concern for the social and economic aspects of the past, for which causal and structural explanations are thought to be more appropriate than stories. The historians' attack on narrative in the interest of rendering history more scientific is reminiscent of a concurrent debate among analytic philosophers. There narrative history has had a more vigourous and successful defence. But it is indicative of the aloofness of the philosophical debate, and its lack of effect on the historians' work, that what seemed won at the theoretical level was lost at the practical level of the historian's terrain. In any case, the battle over narrative history continues at various levels.

In literary theory, the discussion has had less the character of a debate than that of introducing and evaluating new techniques proposed for old jobs. To a certain extent the analysis of narrative and plot in drama and literature, from Aristotle on, has always concerned its structure, and it is not so much the structuralist approach to narrative as it is the structuralist approach to other features of literature that has occasioned violent and hostile reactions.

In any case, on all sides of these issues, the amount of ink spilled and theoretical discourse engendered is remarkable. Also remarkable, given the wide diversity of approaches, interests and opinions of whose who write about narrative, is a curious consensus on one important point. It concerns, broadly speaking, the relationship between narrative and the real world. Simply put, it is the view that real events do not have the character of those we find in stories, and if we treat them as if they did have such a character, we are not being true to them.

Among literary theorists we find this view expressed by structuralists and non-structuralists alike. Frank Kermode, in his influential 1966 study *The Sense of An Ending*, puts it this way: "In 'making sense' of the world we . . . feel a need . . . to experience that concordance of beginning, middle and end which is the essence of our explanatory fictions . . . "[1] But such fictions "degenerate," he says, into "myths" whenever we actually believe them or ascribe their narrative properties to the real, that is, "whenever they are not consciously held to be fictive."[2] And in his useful recent presentation of structuralist theories of narrative, Seymour Chatman, also speaking of the beginning-middle-end structure, insists that it applies "to the narrative, to story-events as narrated, rather than to . . . actions themselves, simply because such terms are meaningless in the real world."[3] In this he echos his mentor Roland Barthes. In his famous introduction to structural analysis of narrative, Barthes says that "art knows no static," i.e. in a story everything has its place in a structure while the extraneous has been eliminated, and that in this it differs from "life," in which everything is "scrambled messages" (communications brouillées).[4]

As for history, whose concern is presumably with the real world, one might expect such a view from those who believe narrative history has always contained elements of fiction that must now be exorcised by scientific history. But if we turn to Louis Mink, who above all has championed narrative history as a mode of cognition in its own right, we find him invoking, in one article, the same distinction between art and life that we find in Barthes. "Stories are not lived but told," he says. "Life has no beginnings, middles and ends . . . Narrative qualities are transferred from art to life."[5] And who, among historians, has devoted more attention to the narrative features of historiography than Hayden White? But when White seeks, in a recent article, what he calls "The Value of Narrativity in The Representation of Reality,"[6] it is clear that he finds no cognitive or scientific value in narrative.

White's view is conveyed in a series of loaded questions. "What wish is enacted, what desire is gratified," he asks, "by the fantasy that *real* events are properly represented when they can be shown to display the formal coherency of a story?"[7] "Does the world really present itself to perception in the form of wellmade stories . . . ? Or does it present itself more in the way that the annals and chronicles suggest, either as a mere sequence without beginning or end or as sequences of beginnings that only terminate and never conclude?"[8] For White the answer is clear: "The notion that sequences of real events possess the formal attributes of the stories we tell about imaginary events could only have its origin in wishes, daydreams, reveries." It is precisely annals and chronicles that offer us the "paradigms of ways that reality offers itself to perception."[9]

Many more representatives could doubtless be found of this view, so wide-spread that we can call it, for purposes of this paper, the standard view. Fictional stories are distinct from "reality" or "real life" not just because they are fictional, i.e. because they tell of events that never happened, but also because of the way those events are interrelated as fictionally presented. As for any discourse-like history, but also including biography, journalism or even anecdote — which claims to represent the real: to the extent that it does so in narrative form, that form must alienate it from the reality of the events it relates. Such form is "imposed upon" reality, to use the most frequent expression. It distorts life. At best it constitutes an escape, a consolation, at worst an opiate, either as self-delusion or — and this is a thought White shares with Foucault and Deleuze — imposed from without by some authoritative narrative voice in the interest of manipulation and power. In either case it is an act of violence, a betrayal, an imposition on reality or life and ourselves.

I have taken the trouble to present this "standard view" because, for all that it may have a surface plausibility, I think it is quite wrong, and itself a distortion and confusion or a special sort. In fact, I think of this view what H. White thinks of narrative history, namely that it is tendentious; that is, its real purpose is to express and persuade others of a certain "moral" view of the world without actually stating what that view is. In particular, what is being expressed in this view is marked pessimism about life and a skepticism about certain forms of knowledge. Such pessimism and skepticism can be explained, and even sympathetically understood, and they may even be justified. But they are not in my view supported by the supposed contrast between narrative and the real world that makes up the standard view. Before coming back to the explanation of the hidden moralizing behind it, then, I must turn to the standard view itself and show what is wrong with it.

Its error lies not so much in what is said about narrative itself as in its rather offhand characterization of "reality," "life," or in White's phrase, "the way reality presents itself to perception." It is these that are collectively contrasted with "art" — in this case narrative art — to the effect that the latter is supposed to be a gross distortion of the former. But for all the analysis expended on art, very little is devoted to life.

The study of "life" in this sense used to be the province of *Lebens-philosophie*, phenomenology and existentialism, and as these currents have been eclipsed by the attention to forms of discourse so their insights, I fear, have been forgotten. But if present-day theory of narrative accepts at all the distinction between life and art — a distinction precisely presupposed in the view outlined above — and then makes pronouncements about the relation between them, it had better pay as much attention to the one as to the other. I shall contend that narration, far from being a distortion of, denial of, or escape from "reality," is in fact an extension and confirmation of its primary features.

Returning now to the standard view, what is it that narrative is supposed to distort? "Reality" is one of the terms used by the authors we quoted. But clearly it is not reality as a whole that is being contrasted with its depiction in narrative; nor is it physical reality. It is human reality that is portrayed in stories, plays and histories, and it is against this reality that narrative must be measured if we are to judge the validity of the standard view. This would seem an obvious point, hardly in need of mention, if it were not for the fact that the standard view seems often to draw some of its force from an equivocation whereby anything worthy of the name "reality" must be physical reality. To be sure, this is not a deliberate obfuscation but the expression of long-standing philosophical prejudice. In any case, here reality is the random activity and collision of blind forces, devoid of order and significance; or alternatively, reality is totally ordered along rigorous causal lines without a flaw or gap in its mechanism. What makes these two versions compatible is the notion that in either case reality is utterly indifferent to human concern. Things simply happen, one after the other, randomly or according to their own laws. Any significance, meaning or value ascribed to events is projected onto them by *our* concerns, prejudices and interests, and in no way attaches to the events themselves.

Now all this may be true, but it is of course irrelevant. What stories and histories portray is not physical reality as such but human activity, including the very activities of projecting meaning onto, or finding meaning in, physical events. The physical world does find its way into stories, of course, but always as backdrop and sphere of operations for human activity. It is human concerns and projections, along with the actions, thoughts and emotions with which they are intertwined, that constitute the "reality" depicted in stories and histories. Hence the talk of the relation between art and life. Life — not biological but human — is the reality of narrative, and it is of this reality that we must ask whether it is indeed so devoid as the standard view claims of the characters ascribed to it in stories.

We can best begin this interrogation by considering the sequential character of events. In physical reality, we said, things just happen, one after the other. H. White, in one of the passages quoted, suggests that human events do too. But is this really so, indeed *can* it be so? As Husserl's description of time-consciousness reminds us, even the most passive experience involves anticipation, or what he calls protention, as well as retention. His point is not that we have the capacity to project and to remember, capacities which we occasionally exercise. His conception of retention-protention is much stronger; it means that we cannot even experience anything as happening, as present, except against a background that has a double aspect: it is experienced as succeeding something else and *as* leading to something further. Thus our very capacity to experience is a consciousness which spans future and past, whether we turn our attention to these or not. And the notion of protention is especially important. It means that everything we encounter is experienced as expected or unexpected, as confirming or disconfirming our anticipation.

Husserl, as is often the case in his phenomenological descriptions, considers the most passive of experiences; in this case his example is the hearing of tones and simple melodic lines. What his analysis shows is that even at this level there is no such thing as a mere sequence, with things simply happening one after the other. Whatever events are considered – physical events, human events, even experiences themselves considered as events – : in so far as they enter human experience at all they become entwined in the temporal span of protention and retention.

Husserl's analysis of time-experience is in this respect the counterpart of Merleau-Ponty's critique of the notion of sensation in classical empiricism and his claim that the figure-background scheme is basic in spatial perception. The supposedly punctual and distinct units of sensation must be grasped as a configuration to be experienced at all. Merleau-Ponty conludes that, far from being basic units of experience, sensations are highly abstract products of analysis. On the basis of Husserl's analysis of time-experience, one would have to say the same of the idea of a "mere" or "pure" sequence of isolated events. Perhaps we can think it, but we cannot experience it. As we encounter them, even at the most passive level, events are charged with the signficance they derive from our retentions and protentions.

And if this is true of our passive experience, it is all the more true of our active and practical lives. Here we actively and consciously envisage the future, not as something merely expected but as a sphere we can partly determine. The present, including the objects and persons we encounter, the events we live through, the actions we undertake and those of others that affect us, all derive their sense to a large degree from the envisaged future: they are instruments or obstacles, they further or interfere with our plans, and so on. The past consists of capacities and accomplishments on which we build our present and future, disappointments and mistakes from which we learn, and the like.

These elements are the commonplaces of philosophical accounts of everyday life, from Heidegger and Schutz to analytic theories of action. We invoke them here with reference to the distinction between "art" and "life" in order to make the point that the latter is anything but a "mere" series of isolated events. But we have hardly made our case. One might be convinced of this very limited point about sequence and still deny that life has what White calls the "formal coherency of a story." It is one thing for temporal experience to have a structure, another for it to have a narrative structure.

But what is that structure? The most obvious thing that comes to mind is Aristotle's notion of beginning, middle and end, as invoked by some of the defenders of the standard view quoted above. Life, they say, has no such things. But we are always engaged in actions and projects. We get up, eat breakfast, go to work. We take care of this, accomplish that. To be engaged in an action is to envisage an *end* which for the most part (though not always) lies in the future. Its accomplishment is thus the end of the action in the temporal as well as the teleological sense. The *means* to that end, with which we are involved as we undertake the action, are the temporal intermediaries between the accomplishment of the end and the time before we undertook the action. Beginnings, it is true, may not be as clear-cut as ends. But there is no doubt that we are always in the midst of something by virtue of the teleological structure of action.

What can the proponents of the standard view possibly mean, then, when they say that life has no beginnings, middles and ends? I fear that they are taking these to be merely temporal notions, and that they are lapsing into a highly abstract, and again perhaps non-human conception of events. Are they saying that a moment in which, say, an action is inaugurated is no real beginning, simply because it has other moments before it, and that after the action is accomplished time (or life) goes on and other things happen? Perhaps they are contrasting this with the absoluteness of the beginning and end of a novel, which begins on page one and ends on the first page with "the end."

But surely it is the interrelation of the events portrayed, not the story as a sequence of utterances or sentences, that is relevant here. And what I am saying is that the means-end structure of action displays some of the features of the beginning-middle-end structure which the standard view says is absent in "real life." Aristotle himself, of course, says that a play imitates actions, and the plot, with its beginning-middle-end structure, is the means by which it does this.

Ordinary action exhibits another feature, related to the beginning-end or means-end structure, which gives it a narrative character. I mean that its contingency gives it some measure of suspense and its accomplishment provides the resolution to that suspense. If the action accomplished itself, if the goal were already attained, one would not have to act. If the garbage took itself out, I wouldn't have to do it. Its achievement depends on me, and there's no guarantee I will succeed. Until I do I can never know whether my own inadequacy or the intervention of outside forces will block the action. Reaching my goal is thus not only the *realization* of the projected end and the *justification* of the means, it is also the *resolution* of the suspense engendered in the undertaking.

Now all this may be true, but it still may be objected that we have not succeeded in attributing important narrative properties to everday life. Stories, after all, deal with longer sequences of actions, not just with one action. Any supposed isomorphism between the structure of stories and that of individual actions – beginning-end, means-end, suspension-resolution – is of no use if these properties cannot be carried over to longer-term and more complicated series of actions of the sort found in stories.

Yet surely, no more in "life" than in "art" do actions line up in a mere sequence of unrelated items. Just as there are no punctual, isolated instants in time – except perhaps in theory – so, at a higher level, there are no isolated actions in our conscious, active lives. Even a very small-scale action like closing the door can be composed of several sub-actions: getting up, crossing the room, reaching for the knob, etc. Action theory has long recognized that such an action does not break down into, is not composed of, a series of building-blocks which are non-actions – physical movements of the legs, the feet, the arm. This would instead be to shift to a different kind of description of the same events, with a corresponding difference in the conception of the relations between them: in the one case causal or "external" relations, in the other teleological. And clearly the same thing is true when, instead of moving to smaller-scale or sub-actions we move to a larger scale. Actions relate to other actions as means to ends, and actions of the same "scale" – whatever that may mean: duration, level of complexity, etc. – together subserve larger-scale actions as their component sub-actions. Opening the door is part of taking out the garbage, which is part of doing the house-work, and so on. We describe as actions some long-term and extremely complex endeavors: getting an education, conducting a love-affair, raising a child, fighting a war. We are always engaged in such projects, and we are always acting – which is not to say we are only acting. We suffer too, things befall us. But these too derive their sense from our actions and projects, great and small. Such projects involve sub-actions and sub-plots, diversions and frustrations, reversals of fortune, interminable delays, bitter disappointments, successful completions, dismal failures. Just like a novel!

Not so fast, stammers the beleaguered proponent of the standard view, hastily assembling the tattered remanants of his argument. It may be that many actions and sufferings arrange themselves into larger actions or projects, rather than being lined up in a row. But in a good story, to use Barthes' image, all the extraneous noise or static is cut out. That is, in a story we are told just what is necessary to "further the plot." A selection is made of all the events and actions a person may engage in, and only a small minority find their way into the story. In fact, if actions and events that don't further the plot are included in a story, we consider the story cluttered and its presentation inefficient. But life differs from stories just because such a selection is not made; all the static is there.

Now in one sense this objection to my view resembles another one so naive that it is not worth taking seriously. This is the objection that our lives are not like stories because, after all, stories are so much more *interesting*. To a person who raised such an objection one would of course say *either* that he read only adventure or murder stories, and equated the interesting with the extraordinary; *or* that he led a very dull life; or both. In any case the objection would not prove that lives do not resemble stories, but only that they resemble dull stories. And the same thing is true of the objection that stories eliminate extraneous details and avoid clutter. It does not prove that our lives are unlike stories; perhaps our lives resemble novels, but bad ones, cluttered and undisciplined ones. Our point is not that lives are like the best novels, but only that the structure of narration is drawn from and thus resembles the structure of life.

There is more to this objection than we have thus far admitted, however, and it deserves a better hearing. In one sense it is necessary to concede its truth. If our point is that narrative structure imitates and resembles life, this is not to say that there is no difference between the two; and this objection points to a major ground of distinction. Narratives do select; and life is what they select from. If the knight speeds to his lover's side, we know that he has had to saddle his horse, see that it is fed and watered, adjust his armor, make sure it was sufficiently shining and the like. And he may have been interrupted in a dispute with his serfs over the gathering of the harvest. In a story we are not told such details; in life they are unavoidable.

This is not to say, of course, that these things fall altogether outside the project-structure we have been describing. The best way to put it is that in life we are engaged in many projects at once, not all of which interlock into larger projects, And these often interfere with one another. An event may be extraneous and irrelevant to one project but belong to another. Stories, by contrast, follow certain courses of action and events that make up a plot; they follow the lives of persons insofar they concern these events; and they select out whatever aspects of these lives are irrelevant to the plot.[10]

There is another way of putting this point about selection which leads us into a new domain. As readers of a story or spectators at a play we are told or we are shown only what is essential to the action; the selection is made for us. By whom? Behind every story, sometimes in it, is the author or narrator. (These are not always identical, but let's leave this point aside.) Every story requires a story-teller. The narrative voice, as Hayden White likes to point out, is the voice of authority. Though White says this, I think, for the wrong reasons, it is certainly true in the important sense that the narrator knows the story and we (if we are first-time readers or hearers) do not. He/she knows how it will end before it ends, and we have to wait. The narrator makes the selection, indeed partly on the basis of this foreknowledge. Being a reader or spectator is a form of voluntary servitude. To follow a story is voluntarily to submit ourselves to this authority. It decides what and how much we shall know and when we shall know it.

Now it is here, perhaps, that the advocate of the standard view may wish to retrench. He may have conceded our point that life does indeed have beginnings, middles and ends; but it is here, he now says, that life and the narrator's art really diverge. Life admits no selection process; everything is left in; and this is *because* there is no narrator in command, no narrative which does the selecting. One further point may be added. Our discussion so far has tacitly assumed that narration requires not only a story and a story-teller but also an audience − the reader, hearer or spectator to whom the story is told.

One might counter that the standard view has shifted ground from the content of stories, which it originally compared with real life, to their form. But this would be a petty rejoinder. No, the point is well taken. There is no doubt that in life that sovereign guide and authority, the story-teller, seems to be missing. In the case of fiction, of course, he is not so much selecting as creating *ex nihilo*; or, more precisely, creating the very materials which are to be formed, the very persons from whose lives the events of the plot are to be selected. And even the teller of true stories, like the historian, is sovereign, directing our gaze to this and that, deciding what and how much to reveal and when.

But while this is a good point, it must not be taken too far. It is true that in life, almost by definition, everything is "left in," but it is not true that no selection takes place. Our very capacity for attention, and for following through more or less long-term and complex endeavours, *is* our capacity for selection. Extraneous details are not left out, but they are pushed into the background, saved for later, ranked in importance. And whose narrative voice is accomplishing all this? None but our own, of course. In planning our days and our lives we are composing the stories or the dramas we will act out and which will determine the focus of our attention and our endeavors, which will provide the prinicples for distinguishing foreground from background. Now this may be story-planning or plotting, but is it story-telling? More assuredly it is, quite literally, since we are constantly explaining ourselves to others. And finally each of us must count himself among his own audience since in explaining ourselves to others we are often trying to convince ourselves as well.

But this last remark stands as a warning not to take *this* point — The self as teller of his own story — too far, and gives us a clue as to how much we differ from that imperious autocrat, the narrative voice. Unlike the author of fiction we do not create the materials we are to form: we are stuck with what we have in the way of characters, capacities and circumstances. Unlike the historian we are not describing events already completed but are in the middle of our stories and cannot be sure how they will end. We are constantly having to revise the plot, scrambling to intercept the slings and arrows of fortune and the stupidity or stubbornness of our uncooperative fellows, who *will* insist on coming up with their own stories instead of docilely accommodating themselves to ours. We are ourselves sometimes among that recalcitrant audience, and each of us has his own self to convince and cajole into line. We must then give up any pretentions we might have to anything like being the authors of our own lives: not only do we not control the circumstances, which could conform to our plans, we do not control our own plans. Even very identity of the self who plans is threatened in the internal dialogue whereby we become our own worst enemies.

At the limit we are, as Wilhelm Schapp has so brilliantly observed, caught up (*verstrickt*) in stories already under way, stories in which we seem merely to play roles already assigned to us by some anonymous and indifferent playwright or director. How difficult it is to take over or even figure out the end of the story when its author is nowhere to be found.

Yet, in all these struggles, we are not entirely without resources. We can, after all, exercise some effective control over the circumstances around us; we do manage to get along with other people, usually not by controlling them but by compromising with them; and finally, the warring factions of our own souls do achieve some measure of *entente cordiale*, at least for specific purposes. And these purposes, these projects do, after all, with some luck, occasionally achieve success. Or so it is with most of us most of the time. All of us, of course, experience those moments and times when we are beaten by circumstances or by the hostility of others, and when not only our plans but our very selves seem to fall apart at the seams.

It is these moments and times, I believe, that are given expression by the standard view. And here I come to the moral message which is being covertly conveyed in this view. It is not an edifying message, but it must be admitted that there is something very healthy and realistic about it. It is saying that stories have something definitive and satisfying about them that life never has. They do not just end; they give us what Kermode calls the sense of an ending − closure or wholeness − in which, whether happily or sadly, all the threads of the plot are tied up neatly and everything is explained. Life, to be sure, is never like that. Stories, of course, are not always like either. There may be some primitive story-structure still found in fairy tales, detectives stories, Harlequin romances and adventures, which neatly begin once upon a time and end with eveyone living happily ever after. Perhaps all stories trade on this primitive structure, but some of the best leave us unsettled because the sense of an ending, and perhaps even a beginning, and a middle, are lacking. But our point here is not − nor are we qualified − to discuss the literary structure of stories. It is to evaluate the standard view on the relation between stories and life. And our point is that while life is not altogether like stories in its structure, it is not altogether unlike them either. The standard view errs by the sort of exaggeration that results from frustrated expectations. Because the events of our lives do not fit together quite as neatly as do the events that make up a plot, it is said they occur randomly, one after the other, as in annals and chronicles. Because we are engaged in different projects at once, not all of which are compatible with the others, it is said that our lives are scrambled messages, a hubbub of static interference and noise. Because we experience no neat, absolute beginnings, and no ultimately satisfying and all-explaining endings, we are said to have none at all.

Our lives may tend toward this kind of chaos but why speak as if it were the norm? Perhaps it is something about the times. Perhaps the central problem is that of the narrative voice, which seems to be hoarse and cracking or to have fallen silent altogether. That imperious autocrat we were speaking of before, who creates the very materials he then shapes, who arranges things to make them come out right in the end — where is he? When the great Author of our lives was perceived to be falling down on the job, for whatever reason — such as sheer lack of existence — we were supposed to take over from him, each of us, presumedly for himself or herself. In our shock and dismay at how poorly equipped we are at this task, is it any wonder that we should doubt not only our competence as self-authors but our very existence as integrated selves — which may be the same thing? *Creatio ex nihilo* is a difficult act to follow, even if it is only a self, rather than the whole universe, which is being created.

So the standard view turns out to be another version of the cry of modern man in face of the Death of God. I have always been suspicious of such talk, partly because of its windy generalization, and partly because it seems just another case of making God — dead or alive — responsible for what is, after all, our problem. If we are going to indulge in *ad hominem*, why not try it where the shoe fits? Why not say that the standard view is the cry of a few professors of philosophy and literature who spend too much time reading stories, who have trouble organizing their research, and who are bitterly frustrated at what little effect they and their work have on the world around them?

But this form of dismissal is probably itself an exaggeration. There is no doubt that the feeling is more wide-spread than just the academic community that things are conforming to nobody's plan, whether God's or ours. And this in spite of the control made possible by advancing technology. Or perhaps because of it, since it raises too high our expectations of what can be done and how much we can do. One of my favorite passages in Kermode's *The Sense of an Ending* is his brief discussion of the notion of crisis.[11] It has become such a deadening cliché to behold that we are faced with some kind of crisis — technological, military, cultural — that we can only groan. Indeed, so meaningless has this sort of wolf-crying become that one wonders what will become of the very term, whether, in our use of language we are not being led to a brink, a turning point, to some kind of . . . The point of course, is that things are getting out of hand, the center will not hold, confusion reigns, chaos abounds.

Perhaps there is something genuinely modern about this. But then Shakespeare's Macbeth uttered a very similar view when he complained that life was a tale told by an idiot, full of sound and fury, signifying nothing. There is a deep and ageless truth in this sentiment, but it is an indirect truth, I would say, about human expectations and their bitter disappointment, and indeed the falseness of both, not a simple and direct truth that one utters prosaically in the pages of an academic essay. All of us want to shout Macbeth's complaint from time to time. But to believe and act on it would be to become that idiot or to renounce life. Most of us just get on with it and continue muddling through as before.

But all this is by way of explaining, and perhaps even sympathetically understanding the standard view, which has not been our primary purpose in this essay. Our point rather has been to show what's wrong about that view, and it is to this argument that we must return in conclusion.

Shakespeare expressed it in his way. It may seem to be told by an idiot and to signify nothing, but life is a tale nonetheless. And Kermode's insight is that the very idea of crisis is a way of making a story out of this very lack of our sense of an ending. We deal with chaos by placing ourselves in the midst of it, at a turning point, faced with crucial alternatives. By giving it a middle we give it a narrative structure, something at least resembling a middle and an end. Life that is not some kind of story is unthinkable – or more precisely, unlivable.

I said that the standard view erred by exaggeration, that it finds less or less tidy structure in life than in art and confuses this with no structure at all. But in the end its error is more serious, because this exageration leads to a deep confusion, to putting the cart before the horse. Having decided that the events of real life have, in themselves, no structures at all, the standard view concludes that if any is found in or attributed to them it must come from without, imposed from above, from an alien source. Narrative history or any other attempt to tell true stories as stories is then seen, as by H. White, as wishful thinking or worse, the product of dreams and fantasies. One is also led by this path to one of the more absurd versions of the claim that life imitates art, namely that insofar as we perceive structure, significance or – if you will permit – meaning in our lives it must be because we are pretending to be characters in novels we have read – or bedtime stories we have been told, or myths inscribed in the deep structure of our brains, or whatever. All this is very structuralist and post-structuralist, of course. Above we have the free floating world of language, composed of texts – one does not ask who composed them or otherwise where they came from – which consort only with other texts and have no real reference, in spite of appearances, to anything beyond themselves. Below is what used to be called the real world, life, existence, now banished to outer darkness, the *Urschleim*, without form, and void.

By attempting to revive a sense of the structuredness of life and action I hope to have shown the exaggerated character of the "standard view" of life, and also to have made possible a sounder view of the relation between life and the story-teller's art. One way to put it is that life *already* has the quality of telling stories — to oneself and to others — and of acting them out. Usually, though not always, one is oneself the central character in these stories, and one has a character or achieves a character — and self-hood itself — in virtue of one's role in them. Life has this quality, I am claiming, in itself, and does not have to borrow it from literature. If anything, it is the other way around, and yet I am not simply asserting that art imitates life, either. The art of narrative is not the mirror of life but its confirmation and in some cases its completion and perfection. In fiction it can make things come out right, it can produce a wholeness and closure that life, it is true, never achieves. In history and other truth-telling genres it has the advantage of hindsight, it tells stories that are finished and can see in them and relate contours and significance unavailable to those who participated in them. The products of the narrator's art neither simply imitate nor distort life but confirm it and enrich it. But they do so by borrowing the structure, indeed the narrative structure, from their source.

11. The Sound of Songs: the Voice in the Text

Marc E. Blanchard

The inspiration for the present paper came from a previous paper in which I had called for a discussion of the issues raised in narrative theory by recent developments in deconstructive practice.[1] The model for my reflection then had been Gerard Genette's last chapter "Voice [or] Voices" in his book *Figures III*, a study of Proust's narrative techniques and a consideration of the levels of involvement of the narrator with his story.[2] Most of Genette's study is occupied with distinctions of forms of discourse designed to refine what Genette considers an autonomous narrative system. All these distinctions serve Genette in the same way previous distinctions have served other students of narrative like Booth and Barthes.[3] They enable him to suggest a closed rhetorical system guaranteeing that the interpretation of the narrative, while informed by various symbolisms, is still oriented by a single goal, a narrative *telos*. It is presumably to tie all possible interpretations of the *Recherche* that Genette gives us his last chapter entitled "Voice"(or is it "voices"? in French "voix" can be either singular or plural: "The Narrating Instance"). This chapter represents a last ditch attempt to synthesize the analysis of the various parts of the Proustian discourse in order to give it unity and meaning by referring it to the voice of the narrator articulating that discourse. In a few years since the heydays of structuralism, narratology has thus moved from a position of pseudo-scientific objectivity in reaction against the psychologisms of the old school of literary aesthetics, to a search for the subject making all narrative models operative. That this search ends with the trace of the subject a linguistic narratology had sworn to extirpate from literary studies is not one of the lesser paradoxes of the history of literary criticism.[4] The chapter "Voices" is modelled on Jakobson's description of the functions of communication.[5] Somewhat dissatisfied with his model, however, Genette suggests that the importance of the *"intradiegetic* function" which regulate the narrator's discourse, keeps the time of discourse distinct from the time of the story and account for what is generally known as aesthetic distance, pales in comparison with what he calls the *"extradiegetic* function," which allows a narrator to present his own opinion through the mediation of his characters.[6] One of the uncanny aspects of this metaphysics of the voice is that it invokes a voice more powerful and deeper than the narrator's own. The text resonates with a voice which seems to transcend the persona of the narrator and vouch for the narrative's authenticity. This is where Genette's book ends — and my paper begins: I am puzzled by this recourse to the aboriginal voice of an elusive pretextual subject.

The archeological reference to an anonymous voice in the prehistory of texts can be seen as a response to the need to justify a reference to a subject, the actual person articulating the written words of a particular text.[7] And in this sense Genette's concept of an anonymous voice is heuristic: it provides a theoretical, an "objective" cover for the reference to a real person, a subject, which structuralism prefers to avoid. However, this reference to a voice can also be viewed in the context of a strategy — *deconstruction* — which seeks to pin down the closure of a tradition of narrative on precisely the play and concealment of a subject, a voice articulating this narrative. Since to investigate this concealment cannot be done without returning to the sources of our Western tradition, I have decided to collect proofs or *traces* of the inscription of this voice through the ages. I have selected six texts, four from Antiquity and two from the present. There are, first, the two passages in the *Odyssey* where Ulysses confronts the Sirens and the one where he starts crying at Demodokos' song about the Trojan war and Ulysses' own exploits. Then there is a passage in Herodotus' *Histories* about the god Pan's admonition to the Athenians before the battle of Marathon and a passage in Livy *Roman History* about a voice warning of an impending invasion by the Gauls and remaining unheeded. My two modern selections are from Elias Canetti's *The Voices of Marrakesh*, where an unsuspecting Bulgarian Jew living in England and writing in German writes a "record" of his visit to Arab Morocco.

Retracing my steps to the putative origins, even the mythical prehistory of our culture, I am, like Ulysses, fascinated by the Sirens' song, and asking myself with Kafka whether the Sirens did sing or whether they remained silent throughout the whole episode.[8] The problem with Kafka's interpretation is that it does not have much to do with the Greek text. Kafka claims that Ulysses stuffed his ears with wax, while the Greek text insists – and it is one of the main points of the story – that Ulysses did not stuff his own ears but only those of his companions who, oblivious to the Sirens' temptation, continued to row.[9] If Kafka's interpretation is thus erroneous from a philological point of view, one can still ask what could have led the author of *Parables* to think that it was the Sirens' silence, not their singing which captivated Ulysses. Not only does the noise of the wind and the sea abate, as Ulysses' ship nears the island and "there was/A windless calm, and some god put the waves to sleep,"[10] but the strange mixture of hearing (Ulysses') and the deafness (his companions') which accompanies the Sirens' song indicates that the voice is almost too pure and too beautiful to be heard. It resonates on the edges of the world – the Western Mediterranean which still caused great anxiety to tenth century B.C. navigators – in a space between life and death. It sings a song of tenuous difference, one for ever remembered by the poets.

What *is* the difference? As Homer takes Ulysses past the island of the Sirens to the point where their voice is no longer audible, he mentions that Ulysses decides to remove the wax from the ears of his companions. The Greek uses two words to refer to what the translator routinely translates by "voices." One is the word *"phtongos,"* which refers to the sound of the voice proper, and the other is *"aoiden,"* which refers to the melody, the chant which this voice can sing. While both words are used in a formulaic pattern to refer to the bard's voice, one ("phtongos") designates the physical articulation of the larynx which produces the sound which, in turn, enables the listener to distinguish sounds from noises and to understand messages, and the other (*"aoiden"*) refers, more specifically to the song which this voice articulates, and which is the object of the listener's artistic appreciation.[11] The Greek text specifies that Ulysses removes the wax, as soon as "we could hear neither the sound nor the song of the Sirens" (12,197). Although none of the translations stresses the difference between "sound" and "song,"[12], it would be interesting to find out what it was that Ulysses stopped hearing first. Was it the sound or the song? Was he able to distinguish between the sounds coming from the Sirens' island and the song of divine knowledge which those sounds make up? Homer lets us believe that *both* (*"pthongos"* and *"aoiden"*) were "mellifluous" (*"meligerun"*) or "clear-toned" (*"liguren"*) and "harmonious" (*"kallimon"*).[13] Perhaps, it is this inextricable collusion of sound and song which causes Homer to remain silent on what Ulysses has learned. It is this silence, then, to which Kafka refers when he explains that the Sirens "no longer had any desire to allure; all that they wanted was to hold as long as they could to the radiance that fell from Ulysses' great eyes. . . . If the Sirens had possessed consciousness they would have been annihilated at that moment. But they remained as they had been; all that had happened was that Ulysses had escaped them."

If we now follow Ulysses to the Pheacians, we'll see how the man who longed to hear the Sirens' voice and did it without injury to himself or to his companions, breaks down at the sound of Demodokos' voice. After jousting with the Cyclops, Ulysses "nobody,"[14] entranced by the voice of the bard, regains his identity by confronting the image of his own self in the voice of someone else. Demodokos' performance is so stunning that Ulysses, who had challenged him to give an accurate account of the Trojan war and of his own exploits, breaks down, and confronted by Alkinoos, has no recourse but to finally identify himself. There are many ways to explain the Demodokos episode. But let me concentrate on this one. The revelation (*apocalypse*) through which Homer confronts both the narrator with his own image in Demodokos, and Ulysses in the image of the hero sung by Demodokos, is central to the *Odyssey*. It brings to an end the sequence of travels of a hero in search of himself and paves the way for his reinstatement at Ithaca, the very next and last stop in the *Odyssey*. Ulysses' recognition comes at a point in the story of the return, the *nostos*, where fiction turns into diary and the narrative voice becomes the voice of autobiography. With this song *en abysme* where the first and the third person take on each other's existence, we the listeners and readers are confronted with a new experience. We watch Ulysses break down and drop his guard. But the breakdown of his defenses is also an experience for us, as we associate with the bard, the hero, the whole audience in this cathartic denouement. It is as though the narrative had changed its course and become more than the perfunctory medium of a formulaic story. It is the catalyst through which the story comes to life, not simply as what Booth, then Structuralists have described as the *implied author's* or *diegetic* narrative but as a chant emanating from the text and where the voice moves us all with its ring of truth.

Moving from the epic to history and according to Lukacs, to a type of literature where the magic style of an oral tradition is replaced with the sense of an irretrievable past and an intractable present,[15] let us now study Herodotus' description of the battle of Marathon between the Athenians and the Persians. There is a passage in the *Histories* (VI, 102) where the *Father of History* recalls the story of Phidippides. Phidippides, the "hemerodrome," a man whose job it is to act as a courier and herald between officials and thus to articulate, to voice the concerns of one head of state or agency to another, was confronted, on his way to Sparta, by the voice of the god Pan, who wanted to know why he had fallen out of favor with the Athenians. Although Phidippides was unable to convince the Spartans to come to Athens' help and to enter into battle with them against the Persians, the Athenians decided upon Phidippides' return to heed Pan's voice and to make up for their inadequate concern with the Panic cult in the past. This served them well in the end, since history has it later that Pan successfully helped the Athenians overcome their atavistic fear of the awesome Persians and even to instill what is now known as *Panic* fear in their ranks.[16]

Having learned from Herodotus that history is possible if attention is paid to the voice which is alone capable of articulating those events into history, let us move to another instance of history in the making. In Book 5 of his *Roman History*, Livy recounts an episode whose significance is fundamentally the same as in Herodotus, although the point is made in the negative mode. While Rome was still in the process of establishing itself as the central power in Italy, an obscure plebeian one day heard a voice which told him of the impending invasion of the Gauls, and presumably, of the calamities which would be visited upon Rome, should it ignore the warning. This warning Rome did ignore. It chose to ban from its midst the only man who could have saved her. After the sack of Rome by the Gauls an unexpected malaria decimated the ranks of the Gauls, the Roman Senate recalled, albeit too late, Camillus who convinced his fellow-citizen not to move to Veies and they in turn, recognizing that they had lent a deaf ear to the voice of history, erected a chapel to the *unknown voice*.[17]

In the Judaeo-Christian tradition references to a voice of history are frequent. They include the story of Abraham hearing Yahwe's voice in the Bible, of Constantine hearing the voice telling him that the sign of the cross would ensure his victory, and of Joan of Arc hearing voices urging her to save France from the English. But those instances are different. With Constantine, for example, the voice is accompanied by a sign: the sign of Cross. To be a Christian and to win are for Constantine one and the same thing. The voice of God and the sign of the Crucifixion are symbols of victory and history unfolds, not as a matter of reason, but as a matter of faith. In this tradition, the voice is clearly defined. Its function is to authenticate a monotheist history. In the Livy story, however, the voice is undefined. First, it makes itself heard to Caecides "the man of the accident" or the "man of destiny."[18] As a matter fact, since the man is a plebeian, someone who, at the beginning of Roman history, would have had no weight against the patriciate, he wears his name very well: fate used him, so that, being who he is, he would not be recognized and the Romans would thus have to pay for their banishment of Camillus. Second, in Greek and Roman culture, neither fate (*Tyche*) nor destiny (*fortuna*) have a clearly defined status. If there are many temples to the goddess Fortuna, there is really no representation of her. Fortuna is a later representation of the Fates, passed on from antiquity to the Middle Ages and the Renaissance.[19] There is, to be sure, a tradition of the three sisters of fate, the three *moires*, but the tradition is more mythological and allegorical than plastic and representational. The sisters of fate are mostly silent. When Plato describes them performing their work at the end of the *Republic*, he has them work to the rhythms of an ethereal music, but they have nothing to say about the fates they apportion to man.[20] Likewise, when the time comes to decide the fate of Achilles and Hektor, Zeus holds up the scales of fate, without saying anything; nor is he told anything. Hektor's fate is decided silently as death now awaits him.[21] In truth, destiny has no face and no body.

What is also intriguing is the oblique way in which either Fortune or Fate, or Pan — one of the more obscure and mysterious deities of the pantheon — is made to take charge of *a* story. That a reference to Pan is made in the story of the battle of Marathon is logical, since the name of the game was to terrify and rout the Persians and to free Attica. And yet, when we look at it again, this whole business of instilling fear in the hearts of the Persians and with it the whole story of Pan's involvement, may have been nothing else than the consequence of Herodotus' desire to glorify the Greek army — just as the story of Brutus against Tarquinus and of the exploits of the young Roman republicans after the downfall of the patriciate are for Livy essential to his reconstruction of a history which may have been far less glorious than he claimed. This is the sense in which Duby and many of the historians of the *Annales* school claim that some of the most famous battles in Western history and the narratives that go with them are in fact a reconstruction *ex post facto* of the various circumstances in which the original narrative was elaborated and adjusted.[22] What we have then with this introduction of the voice into an original story might be nothing else than a narrative in reverse, viz. a narrative seeking to reestablish its beginnings, and with those beginnings, the authority which it lacks. We are very close here to the interpretation offered by Derrida that writing is forever indebted to the authority of a voice. The fictitious product of this writing, only *appears* to precede writing as narratives recreate their past and reestablish their origin every time circumstances demand that the course of the story be modified. "Representation mingles with what it represents, to the point where one speaks as one thinks, as if the representer were nothing more than the shadow or reflection of the representer."[23]

We do not know too much about the real scope of Marathon. But what is clear is that the battle's fame was enhanced by the reference to Pan. We know that the Athenians had good reasons to mistrust the Persians, whose huge Asiatic empire they saw as all too ready to engulf them. In fact Herodotus and others report that the Greeks were generally terrified of the Persians.[24] This reconstruction of the whole Panic story was only recently authenticated when a chapel to Pan was discovered near the Acropolis, whose remaining fragments were transported to the Fitzwilliams Museum in Cambridge. On one statue one can see an inscription which invokes directly Pan, as the guarantor of historical thruth: "Miltiades [the Greek *strategos* at Marathon] is the one who erected me, Pan, the one of the goat feet, who took part in the battle against the Medes at the side of the Athenians."[25] That a stone is now made to voice in reverse (no longer from Pan, but to Pan) the story of the Panic which culminated in the victory of Marathon, that this stone is part of the chapel honoring the real winner at Marathon, is a testimony to the circular destiny of all narratives. When a chapel has been erected to Pan, the reconstruction of, literally, the *voice* narrative is complete. The reference to the voice imports into the narrative a syndrome of repetition as the search for a cause, an origin, causes the historian to look for an outside agency whose influence on the course of the story is later shown to have been authenticated by written evidence – and the written evidence, in turn, refers to the original voice which authorizes the story in the first place. In the circular process of establishing the historicity of narratives, the modern reader no longer knows which is the cause and which is the effect: either the desire of the people to glorify their heroic forebearers with a flattering circumstance or the fact that a particular circumstance is actually the occasion for such glorification. History has become a monad whose unity is ensured by an utterance which, while marginal to it (neither Pan nor the voice that speaks to Caecides were originally supposed to be included in the course of events), ensures that the adventitious and the unexpected remain under control. In the Pan episode, the best way to guarantee that the Greeks will not freeze before the Persians is to assure oneself of Pan's good will, according to the classical religious contract: do to your god what he requires and he will do for you what you require. By inserting the Caecides episode, Livy in fact explains why the Romans were defeated by the Gauls.

In both cases the recourse to the voice helps explain the unexplainable: why a tiny Greek army managed to overcome the huge Persian force and provides retribution or punishment for unreasonable behavior, why the Romans had to get rid of Camillus in the very moment when his services were so badly needed. Before and after the fact, the voice reestablishes the context missing in the story. By making reference to a voice, instead of giving what would today be considered an historical explanation, i.e. that the Athenians knew how to engage their enemy and that the Romans had simply no idea that the Gauls would be invading, the Ancient historians chose to emphasize, in what was to become the Polybean model for all histories, the nonchanging, nonevolving character of the history they reconstruct. In it, present and past recoup one another as human motivations and needs remain the same and the origin and the end are fully integrated into one monad. The alien voice which is supposed to explain the run of things does not alter any of the facts, since it remains at a distance from those facts: *before* Marathon, Phidippides runs to Sparta and as the Senate deliberates *after* the fact, it finally acknowledges Caecides' report. It is then the use of an extra- or meta-historical reference to point to a missing sequence (how did the Athenians overcome their fear?) which justifies the recourse to the voice. The voice is thus responsible for the inscription, the embedding of a discourse in need of being heard within the larger context of another discourse which supplies the missing narrative sequences, is what gives historical discourse its ongoing recursivity – whence the iterative form used by Livy to describe the voice that repeats *"Aius Locutius."* In the Latin phrase, the adjective *"locutius"* modifies a noun derived from the radical of an archaic verb *"Aio"* which the Romans of Livy's time would have used only in the third person singular (*"ait"*). *"Aius Locutius"* thus refers to a speaking divinity that speaks. Had they listened to it, the Romans would have averted disaster. But had they listened to it, there would have been no invasion and no history and Camillus would not have been able to play the prodigal son. By letting us listen to it now that we are reading his history, Livy confirms the history that is with the history that wasn't.

The last episode I would like to review is a dyptich from Elias Canetti's travelog *The Voices of Marrakesh (Die Stimmen von Marrakesch)*. In two instances in this short book, Canetti is struck by the importance given to the voice in a culture and a language whose sounds he does not understand. At the end of our odyssey through the land of the voiced and the unvoiced, we are confronted by the image of a narrator who grapples with the sounds emanating from bodies who cannot see him or which he cannot see. The first Canetti fragment is titled "The Cries of the Blind." During his stay in Marrakesh, Canetti is surrounded by blind beggars whose language he doesn't understand, and who call the name of Allah, repeating the word ceaselesly, amplifying it: "Repetition of the same cry characterizes the crier. You commit him to memory, you know him, from now on he is there; and he is there in a sharply defined capacity: in his cry. You will learn no more from him; he shields himself, his cry being also his border. In this one place he is precisely what he cries, no more no less: a beggar, blind. But the cry is also a multiplication; the rapid, regular repetition makes of him a group."[26] Quoting someone or referring to someone's words is always unproblematic, because language always allows the possibility to specify through a combination of persons and modes the subject of enunciation in discourse. Communicating the fact of a voice being sounded, however, is something else. This sound, as such, does not mean anything. Language has equipped us only, as Saussure told us in his *Course* with "sound images" (*"des images acoustiques"*).[27] This implies that in using language we not only hear sounds, but that we are also able to visualize them: that we perceive what Jakobson and Waugh define as the "sound shape" of language.[28] The sounds we hear, which constitute the outer envelope of our meaningful communication and whose place in this communication we have, since the advent of phonology, learned to recognize, are only representations, mediated through our larynx, our palates, our whole bodies. Saussure adds that no one knows what constitutes a really pure sound. Much less, shall we say, a voice, except that the voice always belongs to someone and we are used to referring to voices of individuals we can recognize. Sounds are thus representations which engage our body and the body of others we are familiar with. When those sounds are actually parts of a discourse we understand, they become part of the *"parole,"* the speech which is part of language, but which the linguist cannot know, because they lie outside the purview of language. The *"paroles"* of speech we understand to be the property of an individual and yet it is not because of this individuality that we understand them, but rather because they remain universal and anonymous. Words belong to everyone, the voice, one voice only to someone. It is this ambiguity of a body like no other and of this sound like all others, with which Canetti confronts us.

Although Allah will, like the Christian or the Judaeic God, look with favor upon those who have mercy on beggars, the name "Allah," constantly repeated, loses its significance. It becomes an image of pure sound, an illustration of the powers of the Aius Locutius of Livy. Like the Colossi of Memnon, in whose dewy klang Hegel refused to see any form of rational discourse, the beggars overwhelm the passer-by with the force of their voice.[29] In a curious way, the fact that they are blind only amplifies the raw tones of their voice. Having no story to communicate, striking the flaneur with the shock of a Benjaminian encounter, they only emit a call to Allah.[30] The listener finds himself confronted by the group of these blind men, whose presence awes him. He can be certain that they do *not* see him, but he may still wonder whether they do not, in spite of their blindness, feel him, just as they feel the alms deposited in their wooden alms dish. Shortcircuiting the narrative of their own poverty, the blind beggars confront the listener with a piece of their life that cannot be narrated or represented: "Back from Morocco, I once sat down with eyes closed and legs crossed in a corner of my room and tried to say "Allah! Allah! Allah!" over and over again for half an hour at the right speed and volume. I tried to imagine myself going on saying it for a whole day and a large part of the night; taking a short sleep and then beginning again; doing the same thing for days and weeks, months and years; growing old and older and living like that, and clinging tenaciously to that life; flying into a fury if something disturbed me in that life; wanting nothing else, sticking to it utterly."[31] Canetti goes on to say that he understands the seduction of a life reduced to a kind of repetition. The fact is, the beggars' voice cannot be a part of narrative. Only its effects are, and it is those effects which in the Canetti fragment mediate the presence of the beggars to the narrator and the response of the narrator to those cries which mediate the presence of the narrator to the beggars. The question is, then, can one separate the voice from its effects without being always confronted with a presence, unexplicable, unrepresentable? And if the experience of the blind beggars is no doubt well transcribed by Canetti in written terms and with analogies giving us a story we can understand and remember, the repeated cry of the beggars for alms remains fundamentally untranslated, not understood, since it is more than a cry for alms. Continuing, whether they receive the alms or not, it is the most fundamental cry of their existence, something like the first whimpers of a newborn baby crying for release. It is the cry of a life reduced to its most simple image: a sound. And what is a sound that is neither music nor story?

The other Canetti episode drawn from the "Voices of Marrakesh" bears the title "The Unseen." It is the story of a strange failure: Canetti's failure to trace and confront a voice which pierces the air of a Marrakesh square from morning to night. "At twilight I went to the great square in the middle of the city, and what I sought there were not its colour and bustle, those I was familiar with, I sought a small, brown bundle on the ground consisting not even of a voice but of a single sound."[32] The narrator feels ambivalent about this voice. On the one hand, he is content to know the place in the city out of which the voice emerges, and on the other hand, he cannot bring himself to confront the precise origin of the voice. Is the bundle the maimed body of those

child beggars one can see all over Africa and the Middle East, that of
a dwarf, of an invalid? No matter, he is unable to go touch and see this
bundle: "The helplessness was in regard to myself. I sensed that I would
never do anything to discover the bundle's secret."[33] The distance from
ear to mouth, from the place where the voice is emitted to that where
the voice is heard is not only the physical distance over which sound
propagates. It is sacred, and treated as such. As with the Homer of the
Sirens, the distance remains unnegotiated, however. The narrator, or
his hero, remain in awe of a voice whose bodily, personal reference
they do not care to confront. As Ulysses skirts the island of the Sirens,
the narrator of The Voices of Marrakesh makes sure he never comes in
contact with the "creature": "the creature was bound to notice and
perhaps it had a second sound with which it would have responded."[34]
That narratives may not return to their origin with impunity or that
this origin is restricted is a familiar notion in the history of religion and
anthropology.[35] Each narrative asks a question which it seeks to answer
– and as we know since Heidegger and Gadamer, the difference
between narratives is as much in the form of the question as in the
form of the answer.[36] We also know, from the studies of historians of
literature inspired by the advances of phenomenology and Rezepzion-
theorie, that the study of history cannot be limited to the formal techniques of narrating but must include a review of the changing ways
in which the question of the relevance of the narrative is asked.[37]

In this context, much of narrative time appears devoted to telling
the story of a travel to a place which is the narrative's very raison d'être,
its source, but which cannot really be visited. In most narratives, then,
there are two levels to consider. In the first level, that of the narrative
of action, the narrator seeks to develop an approach to a truth which
stands purely outside the story. He is mostly concerned with having
his hero reach a goal, complete an action (the hero must go out and
conquer the monster, retrieve the princess and inherit the kingdom).
But there is another level, on which the narrator is concerned with a
truth inside and not outside the story. That is the level of experience.
On that level, the Odyssey, indeed, asks the question of what it means
to go home. To be sure, the function of any good narrative is to make
its listener wise (gnarus) by teaching him something about the world;
and in this general sense, narratives of experience are not altogether
different from narratives of action. But on the level of experience, the
hero operates in a more restricted framework than on the level of action. Although he may still have a goal, this goal is more than dangerous.
It is problematic, because reaching the goal does put an end to the very
enterprise which it is the business of the narrative to record.[38] Narratives

of experience take the attention of the listener or reader away from the consideration of the end (the *telos*) of the narrative. Such a diversion aims at raising the fundamental questions never raised in the course of a narrative only concerned with completion of its performance. Such questions are intuited rather than made explicit, mainly because to know how to pose the question is to be able to give the answer. For instance, it is obvious that the *Odyssey* is more than a simple story of return, of post-Aegean *nostos*. The question is not how to return, although that too is part of Homer's grand design, but what it means to return — a thought in itself (on the level of an action to be completed) so boring and unbearable that Katzanzakis, in his own 33,333 line *Odyssey*, has Ulysses leave home again the very next day after his return to Ithaca. To return is to ask the question of origin and most narratives of experience, because of their engagement with the voice which gives them birth, are obsessed with the beginning, not the end. As the beginning of the *Odyssey* states: "Tell me, Muse, about the man of many turns . . . ".[39]

Pursuing our investigation we find that there is a hierarchy between our two narrative levels. Narratives of action are usually *subordinated* to narratives of experience. That Athena, the goddess of wisdom should be Ulysses' counsel and that the *Odyssey* should be mostly the story of a man discovering the world and anxious to find out the ways of other people, is significant of Homer's priorities. That each of the hero's exploits is preceded or accompanied by a description of the procedures required to complete the exploit (to harden the tip of the spear with which the Cyclops will be blinded, to put wax in one's companions' ears and to have oneself tied up to be able to survive the Sirens' song) is good indication that the narrative's function is to ask the question of human wisdom while reviewing the narrator's and listener's *common stock of knowledge* (as the social phenomenologists would say).[40] Each time Ulysses demonstrates his skill in some art or craft, the sum total of the cognitive acquisitions of the culture in which his actions are narrated is redefined and readjusted. The narratives of experiences in which parts of action narratives actually correspond to stages in the hero's education constitute the very core of all narratives. Take away from the *Iliad* or the *Odyssey* those endless descriptions of counsel and preparation and you are left with but a barebone plot of the epic. You have lost both the mythic and human dimension of the story. In the texts I have selected, however, the narrator involves the reader or listener in a quest in which preliminary procedures have not yet been reduced to automatisms. Ulysses putting wax in his companions' ears is more than a trick to achieve the goal of reaching the island of the

Sirens. It involves a direct relation with Ulysses' desire to know the song of the Sirens, who, after all, know everything. The Demodokos episode is more than an anthropological reference proving that the Trojan War has, by the time of writing of the Homeric texts, become a motif *oblige* of postfeudal life in the Aegean. It is mostly symbolic of Ulysses' *apocalypse*, his recognition of himself, which is precisely what brings him one step closer to home.

At the end of a meditation on the place and the role of voice in narrative, let me suggest a few possibilities. First, as the voice that tells stories is the source and the resource of all narratives, a narrator can, by finetuning his voice, modify our perception of the mood of the story. By modulating a voice here and now as we read the story or listen to it, he can alter our understanding of characters and places then and there. For the *phonologist*, then, the most urgent task is to delineate this territory of the voice, to mark the points at which it enters the narrative prospect. Booth, Genette and many others have shown us the way. There are now enough categories of self and other, enough codes between those various sublocutors and personas of the great writer to satisfy the most exigent, the most structuralist student of narrative. I am not going to add my grain of salt to this very respectable body of critical work. I mean to suggest a study of the process of inscription of the voice in narratives. On the model of Ulysses listening and recognizing his own voice in the song of Demodokos, I am calling for a study of the processes of the refraction of the voice in narrative texts – the ways in which the consciousness of existence with which fictional characters must always come to grips also affects our *persona*: how the question of the locutor develops into the question of the reader.

Using my previous distinction between levels of action and levels of experience, let me suggest that there are two ways in which we hear this voice. The first way is that of the model listener who always loves a good story, a narrative of action, and whose understanding of the voice is limited to the *acoustic image* defined by Saussure. The voice in the narrative is then articulated as the support for a discourse, a text which is mostly concerned with erasing the traces of its construction, its development, just as Ulysses forgets the reason for his endless travelings. In this perspective, different kinds of voice are seen as stylistic categories in a message which is governed by the completion of a narrative *telos*. But I suspect that the very completion of this telos and the *overall* information we derive from this completion is actually dependent on the use of specific "voices." To take a new example, it could be shown that Flaubert's realist effects in *Madame Bovary*, besides all the things that it has been shown to be (i.e., reaction against the excesses of Romanticism, byproduct of the realization of the closure of the bourgeois world), are produced by the use of a famous reported speech, neither the author's nor Emma's nor, to be sure, the reader's (summarily defined as *"skaz"* by the Russian Formalists) — which ultimately allows the readers to experience Emma's world as though it were totally neutral (I would say orphaned and silent: the implacable mediocre world in which she dies). The second way, already suggested by Baudelaire's "hypocritical reader, my brother!"[41] is the way in which both the listener and the reader behind him seek, in narratives, not the good story with which they can while the time away or forsake their pain, but the experience which the narrator's voice suggests. They hope to find the answer to what Baudelaire used to call "the sorrowful secret"[42] which is, for most of us, still enshrined in *Fleurs du mal* as "the stone's dream"[43] of a silent sphinx. Our task then is to catch the voice, no longer melodious or honeydewed, before it remains forever frozen and silent in the pages of the book.

Part V.
The Deconstruction
Controversy

12. Deconstruction; or, The Mystery of the Mystery of the Text

Joseph Margolis

Many people wonder what deconstruction is, or what it is to deconstruct a text. Of course, to ask the question is to ask, at least initially, what Jacques Derrida means by deconstruction. And to ask *that* threatens to set in motion an anxiety of infinite regress or an infinite anxiety of regress or, for that matter, an infinite anxiety (or an infinite prospect) of infinite progress; for, as everybody knows, Derrida's notion was bound to invite its own deconstruction and every would-be analysis or interpretation of it was bound to be subject to the same sort of development (if that's the right word to use). Will it be worth our while to attempt to answer the question? One can only assume the risk. We cannot even help prefacing our answer thus – which, in effect, confirms at least a part of what Derrida himself has said in laying out his notion.[1] A knowledgeable audience will nod knowingly (even if it yawns), because to begin this way suggests a certain playful seriousness (not to deny a certain serious playfulness) that fits a reasonably perspicuous grasp of Derrida's notion – without of course directly stating the least truth about it. Derrida, we suppose, supposes that we will understand him, that is, understand what he says; but in leading us to understand what he says, he supposes – and we, with at least an inkling of what he has in mind, suppose – that we understand what he says, by understanding what is and must be left unsaid in what he says in order (precisely) to convey his meaning. Apparently, he has succeeded all too well, because here we are playing his game with the greatest of ease. Or is it that he has really failed, because it's still so hard to tell the difference between explaining his notion and only pretending to do so? Or is it that it isn't a notion that *can* be explained, which is quite a different matter from its failing to be a geniune work-

138

ing notion at all? Or is it just a jumble that vibrates somehow with the recollection of concepts past?

Derrida himself says of a notion (or anyway, of something like the notion) *différance* – which he supposes (and we are led to suppose) is very closely linked to deconstruction – that it (*différance*) is "neither a *word* nor a *concept*."[2] He also speaks, it is true, of *différance* as "the nonfull, nonsimple 'origin' [of the structured differences of a language]; it is [he says] the structured and differing origin of differences."[3] But he says this in order, first, to contrast what we distinguish structurally within a system and what cannot be captured within any such system but may be taken to enable any and all such systems to be generated; and second, because he treats the differences within any system as structured *traces both* of some supposed anterior but equally contingent and restrictive system of differences (what may be called deconstruction in the shallow sense – not the real thing at all, something closer to mere deciphering or Freudian analysis) *and* of the unstructurable, unnameable, ultimately inconceivable, nonsignifying power of *différance* (in the deeper sense of the term, the sense in which deconstruction cannot be a form of deciphering at all).

Once the import of these distinctions dawns on us, we realize that *différance* simply *is not*, although, in grasping that, we hardly mean (because Derrida hardly means) that *différance* is nothing. The reason is plain: in a sense, deconstruction addresses everything. Have we then succeeded in deconstructing Derrida so quickly? Who can say? The fellow seems, in his own lifetime, nearly prepared to produce an infinite text, that is, an infintely deconstructed text, that is, an infinite deconstruction of a supposed text – which is what a text *is*. The style, you see, is marvellously energizing, even self-energizing, certainly (without ever saying so) somewhat self-congratulatory. But it is more than that. It marks a necessary beginning, in a certain sense of "necessary" that concerns the rhetoric of taking responsibility for clarifying a difficult notion, and in a certain sense of "beginning" that signifies starting in the middle of things – and possibly even in a certain sense of "necessary beginning" that fixes a serious perception of our own mortality in taking responsibility thus in the middle of things.

Now, then, may we begin again?

The theory of deconstruction can be seen to be the fruit chiefly of Derrida's sustained reflections on the work of Saussure and Heidegger – also, to be accurate, on the work of Nietzsche, Freud, and Husserl; also, one begins to meander, on the work of Hegel, Rousseau, Aristotle . . . Roughly speaking (that is, to state what is essential in the briefest and most potent way), Derrida finds that, in theorizing about human discourse, Saussure immediately turns to construct a more congenial but entirely fictional world of language, which he (Saussure) frankly acknowledges to be such but which he also believes we cannot avoid in talking about discourse (itself apparently incapable of systematic analysis of a purely linguistic sort); and yet, somehow, as he proceeds, he (Saussure) seems to forget that the system of language *is* but a fiction – which is to say, *it is not*. Saussure's candor or naiveté, then, mirrors a more pernicious and ubiquitous tendency in Western philosophy and science, namely, the conviction, declared or implicit, that the world and the human mind have the very same structure, so that we, mere human beings, can justifiably claim to discern immediately or progressively the actual way the actual world is. This is what Heidegger believes he has exposed as the pervasive disorder of nearly all Western thought, what he calls "onto-theology," the belief that reality is present or presented or manifests its presence in a way that is adequately matched by the developing conceptual or categorial distinctions of inquiring man.[4] (Heidegger, on Derrida's view, has observed the endlessly varied forms of that pride, though he himself is tempted by the vision that Being cannot *thus* be captured.) The resulting disorder, intellectual, perhaps even moral, perhaps even tinged with a lapse of natural piety, Derrida terms logocentrism.[5] Deconstruction is its avenging angel and our salvation.

Nevertheless, it is a fact that we cannot avoid language, even when we expose its presumption. We are, therefore, forever threatened by an incipient "philosophy of presence," by a tendency to fall back to the confidence that what we *say* captures the way the world is – once and for all or even approximately. We cannot *say* things differently: we can of course say different things, by favoring this conceptual scheme or that; but we cannot, by such alternatives, undermine (or altogether eliminate) the tendency to look at the world – confidently, trustingly, reliably – in order to find out simply and straightforwardly whether what we have said is true. It isn't even necessary *to* eliminate that way of conducting ourselves; after all, there is in a sense no substitute for it, and the impatience of life encourages us to adopt it. But a deeper understanding corrects the false presumption even as we yield to its seductive routines. Deconstruction is the general strategy that exposes, by a thousand tactics, the myth of the fixed, essential, timeless, and naturally accessible structure of an independent reality that (our) would-be total networks of intelligibility have "found out." Deconstruction permits us to recover the power of *différance*, unnoticed by us in the ongoing and multiple busyness of generating systems of concepts and words with which to net the world – unnoticed because it cannot be noticed, the source of what we generate but not itself a generative process at all, but because *it is not* (in a deeper sense than that in which the would-be intelligible world is not) and because if we say that *it is.* in that sense in which the things of the intelligible world are said or thought to be, then it *could* be designated by terms in the same way *they* are, which is to say in the same way in which (falsely) we suppose reality to be perfectly caught by words.

Thus construed, its mission would be utterly lost. By way, then, of exposing the deforming power *of* what we say, of whatever we *say,* deconstruction enables us to recover what cannot be said, also what makes possible our saying *whatever* we say; and by doing that, we grasp the nameless wisdom — *not* the articulate knowledge — of the unavoidability of no saying. This, Derrida terms "writing," which of course is not the recording of what is uttered ("writing," in the merely dependent, merely conventional sense) but the power of *différance* underlying the joint processes of speech and written language. "Writing" links whatever we thus utter (within what, at least tacitly, we suppose to be the total and timelessly adequate system to which all wellformed, successful communicative utterances belong) *to* whatever we can persuasively induce our readers and auditors (in *that* context) to consider as a richer and ampler source of conceptual distinctions ("differences"). These "differences" could have provided (and now appears to provide, reasonably enough) a source from which the set of distinctions affirmed unspoken in what we have explicitly affirmed may be seen as a merely distorting and confining restriction. This source (therefore), in its turn, we can, now, more than suspect to be similarly subject to being exposed within the as yet undisclosed patterns of ongoing human communication. In *this* sense (if a lengthy ramble may be trusted), to speak of an unperceived "writing" that underlies all explicit speech and "normal" writing is to say that what we interpret are always and only texts; to speak of nature, then, is in effect to speak of nature "texted" — to speak in a way in which we could never separate pristine nature from the textualizing categories that we (must suppose we) must impose upon it. This indeed is Derrida's conception of writing and texts: what we call literary texts are simply special, restricted constellations of these more global texts, that we choose to isolate for particular scrutiny. These texts, then, themselves inviting interpretation, require the provision of suitably enclosing texts interpreting a suitably intertextual world within which to locate them correctly, or at least to locate them convincingly as — reflexively — we "locate" the world, our world, within which we mean to locate them. "Writing" indicates, suggests, recalls, enables us to recover — but does *not* signify — a radical alterity that is the origin of the power of every conceptual scheme; hence, also, of the limited, deconstructible power of every particular such scheme.

We are not, however, to rest with "corrections" merely, which, powered so to say by the very surd *différance* − "itself" not a word or a concept, though 'it" masquerades as a technical neologism or neographism − *does* provide a sort of "internal" correction, in fact a perpetual supplement and displacement within the very play of those alternative schemata by means of which we (logocentrically) first supposed we could capture the world. We need not deny such a gain; we could not if we wanted to. But it runs the risk of being every bit as idolotrous (to trade on Heidegger's idiom) as what it displaces. It is hopeless to think that, by the exercise of deconstruction, our conceptual networks are somehow getting to be more inclusive and more accurate. No, deconstruction signifies the contingent, provisional *supplément* of all such reflexive efforts *within* the movement of human history, deprived of logocentric pretension, and imbued with the unutterable wisdom of *différance*.

Here, a genuine distinction beckons. Dreams, taken in the usual Freudian sense − not in the sense in which Derrida modestly sees his own innovation in certain incipient worries of Freud's own, nor, analogously, in certain extreme, self-defeating possibilities that Husserl nearly acknowledges and then resists, or in Hegel's characteristic irony and superabundant dash, or in Nietzsche's tightrope adoption of whatever he rejects − dreams, then, taken in the usual Freudian sense, *signify* an absent that is present because it is *decipherably* absent, determinately absent, however difficult and approximate our science. In the jargon, dreams signify an alterity that is hidden, obscured, displaced, deformed, censored: it leaves a trace in what is manifest but can be recovered because it *is* present (as absent). But, for Derrida, the alterity that "writing" conveys is utterly radical: there *is* no decipherable, determinate *structure* linking what is present and what is absent (in the manner, say, in which Saussure's signifiers are present and their signifieds, absent); there is a power inherent in human thought and language (as much a limitation as a power) that, in generating what we conventionally depict as relational structures (the manifest and latent content of dreams, for example), generates whatever it does within the ineliminably nameless alterity of so doing. "The structure of alterity (otherness and absence of meaning or self)," Gayatri Spivak says in her admirable Preface to *Grammatology*, "must be operative within the sign for it to operate *as such*."[6]

But this is a mistake − a most profound mistake. Spivak adds rather coyly, quite inexactly, explicating the mysterious mark *"différance"* −

which she says "comes close to becoming Derrida's master-concept" — that *différance* is "the structure (a structure never quite there, never by us perceived, itself deferred and different [in the dual sense of the French verb *différer*]) of our psyche — is also the structure of 'presence,' a term itself under erasure [*sous rature*, that is, protected against being captured by the kind of metaphysics Heidegger and Nietsche inveigh against]."[7] (It is, in fact, the same mistake that treats *différance* as a *concept* and that speaks of the *structure* of alterity, in the Derridean sense of "writing." All these terms — "structure," "presence," "sign," "psyche," "Being," and the rest — are terms that do not *signify* alterity, do not signify a trace of what is determinately absent, the decipherably-signified-absent, relationally linked to what is present within an articulated system; rather, they oblige us to recognize that there is only a nameless alterity to be acknowledged in *any* apparently useful, successful conceptual scheme of ordered differences that we suppose we employ.) To fail to see this is to fall back to onto-theology; to succeed is to perceive the permanent or perceptual inadequacy of structuralism. Deconstruction, therefore, is the enemy of decipherment.[8]

Shall we begin again, again?

Consider the following remark, wonderfully cryptic and wonderfully illuminating:

> Within a language, within the *system* of language, there are only differences . . . If the word "history" did not carry with it the theme of a final repression of differance, we could say that differences alone could be "historical" through and through and from the start.[9]

Notice the silent change from "e" to "a" in shifting from "differences" to "differance." Notice that although differences are historically contexted, the notion of history itself is inimical to *differance* — apparently because it suggests a "start," a first beginning, an origin that is not merely posited but actually discovered once and for all (shall we say, contrary to any deconstructive work?), an origin that is genuinely "originary," a kind of natural First Cause. If Derrida's remark is taken as an oblique reference and criticism of Saussure's *Cours generale*, then, if we equate "differences" with "*relata*," we can recover Saussure's claim and Derrida's deconstruction of it in the service of his exhibiting how deconstruction bears, destructively and therapeutically at once, on the entire movement of Western intellectual history. Whether such a reading, uniting (as was promised) Saussure, Heidegger, and Derrida, would be a deconstructive reading of Derrida himself remains to be seen. Perhaps. But here we are only at the modest beginnings of a start.

Well, then, to begin:

If one considers what it is to be a pawn in a chess game, then it is not unreasonable to characterize it as what it is only within the total system of rules and pieces and purposes and possible moves of the game. Nothing is separately, in isolation, a pawn, a chess piece. A pawn is a *role*, a function within a game that "something" (not otherwise specified) can occupy − at a time, among ourselves, if we wish. It is, therefore, a *relatum*, a "differènce" among a system of differences similarly noted, that thereby form a *system*. Furthermore, a *relatum* is what it is only within the network in which it functions: change the network of concepts and you change its *relata*; admit you are unable to specify the total system of *relata* in which a given *relatum* is identified and you admit you cannot rightly identify that *relatum*; propose an alternative but incomplete network within which you suppose a given *relatum* would function differently and you cannot say for certain whether you are changing that concept or merely explicating it more fully. What Derrida says in the passage cited is that language (on Saussure's view) is an *imposed* system of *relata* (or differences). But nothing *is*, is real, simply as a *relatum*; to treat anything merely as a *relatum* is to deny that it *is* as such, or is real.

Now, Saussure concedes this, insists on it in fact. It is for this reason (in part at least) that he declares: "I propose to retain the word *sign* [*Signe*] to designate the whole and to replace *concept* and *sound-image* respectively by *signified* [*signifié*] and *signifier* [*signifiant*]."[10] So the functional distinctions of "signified" and "signifier," so essential to Saussure's theory of language, are eligible only within the invented (notational) *system* said to be language (*langue*) imposed on the heterogeneous, *apparently* unsystematizable jumble of actual human discourse (*discours*): they are *relata* or differences only. Yet they are also distinctions, as he says, within the *whole*, the *sign*. And what is that? Derrida clarifies, or deconstructs, Saussure's meaning by linking his (Saussure's) thesis to that of Plato and Aristotle: "Let us recall the Aristotelian definition: 'Spoken words are the symbols of mental experience and written words are the symbols of spoken words.' Saussure: 'Language and writing are two distinct systems of signs; the second *exists for the sole purpose of representing* the first.'"[11] So, from Derrida's view, Saussure defines the undertaking of general linguistics as concerned with a *system* in which the "spoken word" alone "*constitutes the object*;" but *that* system, precisely, is presupposed by − not analyzable in terms of (and ultimately, never analyzed or explained at all in any terms) − by the imposed (notational) system of signified and signifier.[12] Hence, Derrida concludes: "The thesis of the *arbitrariness* of the sign (so grossly misnamed, and not only for the reasons Saussure himself recognizes) must forbid a radical distinction between the linguistic and graphic sign."[13]

There is a sense in which a mere notation *is* arbitrary, but that the "graphic sign" *represents* the linguistic (or phonic) sign presupposes a deeper (unanalyzed) ability to fix the latter so that *it can* be thus represented (however arbitrarily). Saussure never satisfactorily addresses that problem. For him, writing, written notation, is *external*, "unrelated to [the] . . . inner system" of language.[14] But "the thing that constitutes language [*l'essentiel de la langue*] is [itself] unrelated to the phonic character of the linguistic sign;" linguistics is, finally, only a part of a more general semiology. As Derrida puts it: "The affirmation of the essential and 'natural' bond between the *phonè* and the sense, the privilege accorded to an order of signifier (which then becomes the major signified of all other signifiers) depend expressly, and in contradiction to the other levels of the Saussurian discourse, upon a psychology of consciousness and of intuitive consciousness."[15]

Saussure's distinction, then, between the exteriority of written notation (its arbitrariness) and the interiority of spoken language (which preserves a "natural bond" or "natural functioning" between sound and sense) betrays an entire armory of errors, inadequacies, and, most important, the systematic delusions about knowledge fancied by the entire Western world. (Here, characteristically, deconstruction works by reversal within an altered and supplementary system — made plausible by its apparent linkage to the system apparently being employed.) On Derrida's view, Saussure must, in privileging the spoken word as he does, assume that there is, ultimately, an unproblematic *cognitive* faculty that human beings manifest in using language naturally in their intercourse with the world: "What Saussure does not question here [Derrida warns] is the essential possibility of nonintuition,"[16] that is, the profound possibility that there are no cognizable structures of the world independent of our cognizing mind, that match the structures of that mind. For if there is no such matching, discourse about the world is already produced *within* the world already texted by a system (or something like a system) of relationally linked differences.[17] Hence, discourse about the world presupposes, and indeed perpetually manifests anew, the radical alterity that is the unsystematizable origin of all systems. (Note that grammatology, in Derrida's sense, is the "science" of "presence" or "writing" — the strange capacity to propose supplementary structures in order to reverse and enrich the force of given structures, precisely when there are none absent [merely] *in the decoder's sense of alterity*, and in order to recover that radical alterity that we cannot capture in any system.[18]) It is the failure to perceive these constraints that the exteriority of writing really betrays; and yet, as Derrida goes on, "my quarry is not primarily Ferdinand de Saussure's intention or motivation, but rather the entire uncritical tradition which he inherits."[19] So Saussure's acknowledgement of the invented (arbitrary) system of language imposed on the seeming heterogeneity of "natural" speech: (1) displaces our attention from such speech to mere notation; (2) leaves as utterly mysterious (Saussure's own term[20]) that deeper and apparently more natural stratum of language; (3) confirms that that deeper stratum does not even fall within the competence of the student of linguistics but only of the one called "psychologist;" (4) nevertheless ventures the undefended view that, at that deeper (in fact, that deepest) level, there is some intuitively and directly accessible similarity or matching at work in virtue of which the arbitrariness of written notation does not even inhibit the proper functioning of such notation. Beyond these considerations, Saussure is also committed to believing: (5) that, at every stratum of functioning language, particular signs serve some total, closed, and finite system within which they are identified as "differences;" and (6) their being ultimately grounded in some natural or intuited way signifies that there *is*, in principle, an "originary" or genuinely first or foundational source insuring the cognitive power of language − which we may progressively approach.[21]

Having said this much, we can return to say again (or is it perhaps for the first time?) that deconstruction primarily directs all would-be (or actual) analyses and interpretations of texts and theories (as texts) *to the recovery* of the unsayable power of *différance*, that "first" enabled even such would-be systems as Saussure's to be generated *and* now "first" permits them to be effectively deconstructed.

It looks as if Derrida himself, however, has not yet been deconstructed. So let us start again.

We may now presume to say that everything we *say* (in presuming to say what is true about the world, or about what is suitably linked to what is true about the world) is and cannot but be deconstructive and deconstructible. Because, in speaking thus, we cannot really suppose that there is a fixed, finite, and adequate conceptual scheme that *we* draw on in so speaking, that *was* drawn on by all who spoke before us, and that, intact through the entire sequence, *will be* drawn on by those who are still to come; or that may be formulated, made explicit once and for all, tested somehow for its adequacy to fit and accommodate (without distortion) whatever, *in fact*, corresponds to whatever is true.[22] No, even in the most naive and unthinking judgment about things, the very act of saying what we take to be true implies some power that (at least in the retrospective speculations of those who care to review such matters) involves a marshalling of concepts that (we suppose) cannot be a mere selection from an accessible, fixed, finite, total, and unified single system or reservoir of such concepts – that is, neither a *system* (in Saussure's sense) nor a *ready and unchanging supply* (say, in Plato's sense). On the best speculation, we work improvisationally, in a way in which we can at least take note of the salient distortions, inadequacies, limitations regarding the use of the key concepts used to organize what we *take* to have gone before – that we mean *now* to add to and correct and change in some convincing way, and that is bound to suffer (or enjoy) the same fate in the future. Deconstruction is simply the power or activity of speaking (now) about the world or about what men have said about the world – ultimately one and the same, since the world and we may be said to be texts open and apt for deconstruction, and since the Derridean notion of writing generates both oral and written discourse and our understanding of the world in the same way. Deconstruction *is* that power or activity, viewed in terms (1) of the relationship between the "system" of concepts we theorize we provide, now, as a supplement to and an adjustment of the "system" we (retrospectively) theorize had been in place before – using which what was once said was said, and displacing and adjusting which what is now said is and can be said – *and* (2) of the deeper, originary power of language and thought (*différance*) that permits the generation of any and all such systems (conceding, always, that there is no original original of such systems, no total, single network to which we can forever expect to return). Furthermore, proceeding thus, both the deconstructive effort and what is deconstructed are risked by our natural incapacity ever to fix the *system* of differences or concepts of the one and of the other, within which alone those putative concepts have – on the structuralist assumption itself – any function at all. The power of *différance* helps no one here: neither Saussure nor Husserl nor Heidegger – nor Derrida.

Once we see this, it becomes relatively easy to see that (what we call) texts and (even more narrowly) literary texts are probably only the salient, convenient foci for the deliberate practice of an improvised and most uncertain deconstruction and the perception of what we construe as the deconstructive activity of every such text with respect to its own intertextual heritage. By *our* deconstructive work, we construct the texts that are themselves the deconstructive work of others with respect to their own intertextual world. But to say that is, in effect, to say that the theory of deconstruction is only a *comment* on whatever way we have of generating and interpreting texts (which remains a mystery). It is emphatically not a methodology of interpretation, not a canon of procedures or criteria for testing the adequacy of procedures

for interpreting texts or for assessing the cognitive fit between interpretation and text or (what comes to the same thing) between interpretive text and the world, or a basis for any measurable confidence
on our part that our sustained inquiries are getting closer to the Truth.
It is not a theory of a new kind of criticism or interpretation; it is a
view of any and all kinds of criticism and interpretation, *without regard
to their respective differences* (but of course without denying that there
are differences among them), except insofar as they deny or fail to grasp
that there is no foundational or originary or "ontotheological" resource
to draw on cognitively, or except insofar as they deny or fail to grasp
that this applies as much to their own work as to what they would say
they are describing or interpreting. So seen, there is no pertinent difference between the world (of which we speak) and our speech (about
the world). But if so, then the deconstructive thesis is *not* a thesis about
what, in any sense, is *internal* to the practice of readings and interpreting
texts, *offered by someone* (Derrida) *comparing the relative merits of alternative reading of given texts or of alternative conceptions of what it is to
read a text* — though that indeed motivates the thesis; it is rather a thesis
about the relationship between doing *anything* of the kind and whatever,
grandiosely put, is the cosmic import of so doing.

Deconstruction *cannot* be a method or, if construed as a strategy
primarily — for instance, as Derrida's own way of reconstituting a particular text painstakingly, step by step, in accord with what may be supposed to have been the purpose of its author, in order to test whether
its deconstruction would be illuminating in accord with Derrida's own
purpose — it could not yet provide a proper setting *for* disclosing
Derrida's purpose. The reason is elementary. The manifest distinctions
of an author's text reveal his provisional system of structures (*relata*),
of which he may himself be partially unaware, and our own "shallow"
deconstruction may be rather like a deciphering of it, or perhaps only
an idiosyncratic alternative system of structures substituted for it. In
either case, disregarding obvious difficulties, such efforts presuppose
some sort of structuralism. But *if* a system, as Derrida never tires of
pointing out, is a system of differences, *not* reducible to an aggregate
of atomic units or items of some sort that merely happen to be organized into relations, then *there is absolutely no theoretical basis for supposing that deconstruction could ever discover in a veridical sense any deeper
system of structures that the system supposed signifies by its decodable
alterities.* Stated in an altogether different idiom, if classical realism and
foundationalism are denied, then extensional programs of science are
themselves, ineluctably, only (but they are at least) functional conve-
niences in the service of an irreducibly intensional and holistic network

of categories. We need not deplore the fact. But it affects in a decisive way our picture of whatever promising results we might have supposed the science of grammatology could unearth. Differences — conceptual distinctions — are only *relata*: they function only within a holistic network of such differences, whether or not we can speak of a finite and total system of such differences. This must affect Derrida's remarks every bit as much as Saussure's, our own, or those of those who will deconstruct us in turn. Derrida's observations can make no sense, *unless* some network of differences is in place, in virtue of exploiting which, including the dialectical relationship between the deconstructed and deconstructing networks, we are led to the radical alterity that defies decoding. Communication, therefore, is invariably modeled in the decoder's way — however provisionally and heuristically; but Derrida's ultimate discovery, which deconstruction somehow indicates (but does not signify), is the very surd from which such networks arise.

This, then, is the unsayable wisdom of *différance*, a kind of terror or perhaps joy or perhaps longing or perhaps misgiving or perhaps grim determination or perhaps indifference or perhaps something even more animal and inattentive caught up in the very busyness of getting on with the business of making texts and commenting on them *ad infinitum.*

Perhaps to say this is to say that Derrida is the theologian of the Text — not of the Word, for the Word is originary in the worst (and best) sense. He is the theologian of the unsayable power of whatever we say — which, once uttered, invites and requires a *supplément* for whatever, within an infinitude of possibilities, is thus uttered.[23] To rhapsodize a bit further, Derrida is the theologian who has escaped the grip of the onto-theological; but who, but a kind of paradox and perverse vengeance, has actually managed to invent an onto-theology that is not a member of the class of such theories just because it is a member, or perhaps is a member because it is not. In any case, Derrida's theory of deconstruction leaves the world as it is and was, as far as the interpretation of particular texts is concerned; but it emphatically does not leave the world as it is and was, as far as our grasp of why it is and must be left as it is and was. Whether we are thereby made sadder or more joyful or more indifferent is a contingent matter that hardly disturbs the thesis. It warns us, makes us more agile, orients us to possibilities we may not have anticipated. But the merit of what we say, of whatever we say, judged *solely within* the practices of so saying and so judging — which, after all, is the only way to speak and judge — remains sublimely indifferent to all that. Derrida's own ("shallow") deconstructions (or decipherings) of particular texts — for instance, of Saussure's — *never require* and *cannot even use* his theory in order to improve or challenge the particular claims he considers. What we are calling shallow deconstruction is utterly unlike deconstruction proper: the first is hermeneutic or psychoanalytic, and supplements what is manifest by reference to what is semiotically present-as-absent; the second is concerned with the surd of human existence, with what cannot be said at all. What misleads readers, here, is simply that *both* Heideggerian de-struction and Derridean deconstruction are opposed to "metaphysical thinking," logocentrism, onto-theology. As Derrida himself remarks, by way of metonymy: "Despite appearances, the deconstruction of logocentrism is not a phychoanalysis of philosophy."[24]

Derrida's own texts, then, like Saussure's and our own, cannot but provide new specimens, *sub specie aeternitatis*, of the threatening presumption of the human species to overtake its natural condition. That, of course, must invoke the zeal of the theologian again. Having attempted a deconstruction of Derrida himself — humanly at least — we should have to acknowledge that, though we may bring it to a close, we cannot hope to bring it to an end. Signs are traces, on the deconstructive view; but there *is nothing* that is present-as-absent that can identify the alterity of which they are traces.

So let us, finally, begin again. Deconstruction exposes, distributively and in detail, the myth that the structures of language and thought are, ultimately, the structures of reality itself. Deconstruction demonstrates that, in any (our own) historical setting, it is always possible to construe any established schemata for analyzing and interpreting familiar phenomena as more restrictive, more distorting, more inadequate than another that can be generated, now, by submitting the one or ones in question to the process of supplementation. Deconstruction opposes the pretentions of totalizing, of the timeless adequacy of any synchronic system of differences imposed on the unending changes of human experience. Deconstruction acknowledges the inescapability of conceptual systems, but requires them to give up the delusion of essentialism, foundationalism, correspondence, cognitive privilege, onto-theology, logocentrism, in the very process of being viable. Deconstruction admits the viability of the conceptual schemes it deconstructs. Deconstruction recognizes that, internal to any conceptual scheme, relative and only relative to that scheme, judgments of comparative value and comparative strength are both unavoidable and convincing, but that no such scheme can insure its own apparent power on grounds external to itself. Deconstruction insists that every conceptual system is a trace of absent systems that cannot be recovered except as conjectured from the vantage of the one in question. Deconstruction reminds us that the infinite regress and progress of such conceptual networks depend on the power to deconstruct them, and that that power, always deployed through some particular network, is not specifiable within any. Deconstruction warns us that even a conceptual network used in accord with its best scruples remains deconstructible, but that it makes no sense to speak of deconstructing deconstruction. Deconstruction cannot deconstruct any schema that is used in the deconstructive spirit, but any such schema can be altered and replaced in precisely the same way as any deconstructed schema. Deconstruction makes a point of the fact that any schema can be used in the deconstructive spirit or in opposition to it. Deconstruction cannot supply in a privileged way criteria or grounds on which the supplementation of any deconstructed system can be justified, and such criteria or grounds can be identically applied in a nondeconstructive manner. Deconstruction favors no conceptual or interpretive schemata, though those we favor it favors deconstructively, and any schema can be favored anti-deconstructively. Deconstruction is exclusively concerned with deconstructing texts, signs, concepts, conceptual networks, that is, with linking whatever it deconstructs, however it does so, with the unnameable surd in the name of which it does so. Deconstruction . . . well, perhaps this is as good a place to stop as any.

13. The Pleasures in Postcards

Alphonso Lingis

S peech bespeaks a world — works out, articulates, extends a world.
Just in speaking, just by vibrating the air between us as we stand
on our narrow islands of sensuous material, a world emerges about us,
takes form, becomes clear and distinct, phosphoresces and differentiates. All of Heidegger's work wonders over this primal event in which
we stand, in which we exist. We exist in speech; it is for us a transparency, and our eyes are absorbed by the world that lights up and takes
form across speech.

We can direct our scrutiny upon the contrasts between the clear
and the obscure, upon the contours between the extended and the contained, so as to study the phrasing and the punctuation of the world.
But we can also refocus our attention, to catch sight of the relations
and the moves internal to the speech that works out the world. The
transparency in which we stand now begins to crystallize into a communication system whose parts and movements are not simply those
of the world. I call it here a communication system, not so much to
say that it serves as a means or an instrument to communicate the world
that takes form about one individual to another individual, but rather
to say that one envisages it as a distinct domain, a distinctive objectivity, when one sees that the units and moves of speech refer to one
another and replace one another systematically, with movements that
are not those of the things of the world.

But one can study the communication system itself in three ways.
One can study the meanings, distinguished from the referents, of the
communication system. One can show that the field of meanings has
its own laws, its own logic, its own dialectical development, its own
history. One can do a Hegelian or Husserlian — metaphysical — study
of this region of ideal objectivity.

But one can, by a shift of attention, or a "reduction," envisage the means of communication – the signs themselves, the signifiers. The signifiers are the constituents of the communication system taken not in their empirical but in their ideal materiality. One envisages the element as a signifier when one takes the material element – word, visual mark or auditory element – not in its here and now facticity, but detached and distinguished, individualized, by its significant, signifying differentiating traits, and universalized, taken as repeatable anywhere, anytime. One takes the word "tree" as the same each time it is pronounced, by male and female voices of different timber and volume, each time it is written, in ink, by carbon ribbons, in different sizes and colors. One learns to see then that the signifiers are systematically organized into a stratum with its own consistency: a signifier is determinate through its differences from the other signifiers; there are paradigms for forming words and expressions in a given tongue, patterns for altering them in significant ways. This stratum and its laws has been scrutinized for a couple of millenia – scientifically explored by the ancient Sanscrit and Greek grammarians. What is contemporary is the structuralist philosophy which has realized that the lines of discrimination, the systems of combination and substitution which operate within the stratum of the signifiers induce certain effects in the field of the significations. The field of the meanings is a zone of ideal objectivity, and is neither caused by nor is a reflection of the layout of the world; Husserl's phenomenology proposed to understand it as constituted by acts of subjectivity. But now we see that if a certain signification exists in a communication system, that does not simply depend on whether or not a transcendental subjectivity actively posited it; it can result from, be induced by, be an effect of, certain conjunctions, certain juxtapositions legislated in the system of the signifiers. A subject is not the agent-source of a significant system, but appropriates language, and does so only when his own position is designated by himself with a signifier, when he identifies himself with a signifier.

Thirdly, one can, by another shift of attention, another "reduction," envisage the means of communication more materially still; one can study the vocal element or the inscription, not physically but as the space of communication. One notices that there are possibilities proper to writing which are not those of vocalization, for example, and that these properties are systematic. Mathematics, for example, is an ideal field of signs which can be constituted with graphics, but which cannot be instituted in the vocal language: one calculates with, but does not converse in trigonometry. Ideal, infinite, space is not, as Kant supposed, an *a priori* of the sensibility; it is by essential necessity constituted through, idealized beyond, the spacing of graphics. Thus writing, or vocalization, can become the object of a scrutiny, an ideal objectivity for itself. And once one has determined the distinctive properties and laws in effect within the ideal sphere of writing, one can then begin to study the effects certain procedures – phonetic, pictographic, rebus – can have on the field of the signifiers, and their after-effects in the order of the signified. Inscription, which is not simply an epiphenom-enon of vocal signifiers, circulates differently: it is transferred or transported from one writer to another through the mail, and between the sending and the receiving there is not the ideal coincidence – that ideal of self-consciousness – that occurs when the speaker hears himself; there is always the eventuality of the message getting lost in the mail. One can do an analysis and also a history of those instituted forms of transference or transport of messages. That what is distinc-tive to our appropriation of writing is not the personal letter, veritable essay one Victorian correspondant wrote to another, Virginia Woolf to Victoria Sackville-West – but postcards: that too has its effect on what gets signified. By the communication field we also mean the trains and the airlines; by their intrinsic and material possibilities they constitute, institute, organize, regulate the circulation of subjects, but also the delivery, and the loss, of the mail, of the writing. One would then have to study the networks, the connections, the circuitry. The psychoanalytic legacy, for example, gets transmitted from one generation to the next by the didactic self-analysis of the future subject-repository of this theoretical practice – and therefore essentially by filial transference.

The interest, the contemporary, the philosophical interest in display-ing the laws that regulate the ideal objectivity of the region of the signified, of the signifiers, of the writing and its modes of transmission, is in discovering how these strata affect one another. One creates philosophy by showing how the form the world takes is constituted in the categories and laws of the signified; one destroys transcendental philosophy by showing that the signified are not posited by acts of sub-jectivity but induced by the operation of the field of the signifiers; one destroys the metaphysics of presence by showing that presence is an ideal induced by the *telos* of coincidence of speaker and listener in con-sciousness, which is intrinsic to and distinctive of the medium of vocal speech.

In fact the various strata could not be studied one by one in isola-tion because they are constituted by one another. The big discovery, which created structuralism, was that units of meaning are constituted not as pure effects of subjective acts, but as surface-effects of conjunc-tures and convergences on the level of the signifiers. But the signifiers themselves cannot even be identified except through their relations with the signified: a word as such is not simply a physical unit of sound; it cannot be physically identified. It is a unit taken as significant, taken as a signifier of a meaning.

Derrida's works explore these constitutive relationships with different emphases. *Voice and Phenomenon* exhibited an ideal system of concepts, called the metaphysics of presence, which gets formulated in Husserl's phenomenology in the imperative of intuitionism, the principle of all principles, the primacy of perception, consciousness as the constitutive source and reduction to subjectivity as transcendental understanding, presence as the *telos* of all consciousness, the living present as the very form of evidence, time as the ideal reproduction of the present. Derrida showed that all these theses form a coherent system of concepts which holds together, and which is metaphysics itself, is what metaphysics means to say. Husserl did not in reality suspend or reduce metaphysics, but formulated its most rigorous and lucid system. But in addition to showing what Husserl's methods and procedures mean to say, Derrida also exhibits the relationship of this structure on the level of the signified with the vocal medium, the living voice, consciousness as the voice that is affected with itself, hears itself.

In other works I have the disagreeable sentiment that Derrida moves in an idealist, that is, dogmatic, fashion; now that he knows that this conceptual system, this idealism of presence, is what metaphysics means, he shows us that texts which seem to signify other things — Levinas' anti-Heideggerian philosophy of alterity, Bataille's anti-Hegelian philosophy of expenditure without return, Artaud's theater of cruelty, Genet's poetry of pornographic effects, Lacan's psychotherapeutic theoretical practice — nonetheless do nothing else than reformulate this metaphysics of presence. Because the signifiers, the essentially Greek and German, the essentially metaphysical language can mean nothing else, because the language is metaphysical, Being inhabits language, Being is present in this language.

Derrida's first book, the *Introduction* to *The Origin of Geometry* explored the relationship between the ideal signifiers, the most ideal signifiers, those of mathematics, with the writing that makes them possible and obscurely constitutes them. And Derrida's last book, *La Carte Postale de Socrate à Freud et au-delà* (*The Postcard from Socrates to Freud and Beyond*) is attentive to the sense of the mail in the sense — the postal zones, the mailmen (who are also male men, phallocrats), the delivery and the loss of the postcards, the post offices, which are also power positions, the trains, telephones, telecommunications, television. The book is of course fragmentary; it is itself, as it is entitled, a postcard, more exactly a 551 page pile of postcards.

I thought it contained some of the most exasperating, and some of the most precious, things Derrida has so far sent our way: The untalented Joycean preciousness of *Enyois*, the sarcasms of *Le facteur de la vérité*, which ever so, ever too neatly exhibit the whole rigorous and indissoluble conceptual system of the metaphysics of presence in Lacan's theory of psychoanalytic cure. But also the splendid text *Spéculer — sur "Freud,"* which I would like to comment on now, so as to appreciate his deconstructive achievement. For the pleasure, then, to share with you the pleasures in Derrida's postcards.

The text in question here is Freud's *Beyond the Pleasure Principle*. Derrida is throughout concerned both with what Freud says and with what he does — both with what the speculation yields and with what it is. And in turn I shall be concerned both with what Derrida says, what he means or what he says Freud means to say, and with what Derrida does.

Beyond the Pleasure Principle is a text of pure speculation. Just what is speculation as a means of research? It is not philosophy — Freud is explicit and insistent to repudiate philosophy, to heap sarcasms on philosophy; he has even painstakingly avoided reading Schopenhauer and Nietzsche, finding painful that what gave psychoanalysis such trouble to reach was given so painlessly to them. The movement of this speculation is not that of speculative dialectics — that is, not that of the culminating form of metaphysical philosophy — ; it is also not science, in the canonical and original Western sense, established by philosophy. Its movement is a-thetical, without a thesis or a position. "What we must do is try to *connect* — precisely through the analysis of the values of connection, *nexum*, *desmos* or stricture — the quest of *life death* with that of *position* (*Setzung*), positionality in general, positional (oppositional or juxtapositional) logic, themes or theses" (277–78) " . . . . [T]he 'logic' of the *beyond*, or rather of the *step beyond*, would exceed the logic of positions . . . " (278).

Why does the Freudian speculation have the form of a movement without theses, without positions? On the one hand, because the central and most celebrated analysis of the text, the reinvention of language as Freud reported it in observing his grandchild Ernst, the constitution of his ooo-aaah system, that is, of the *Fort-Da*, the first present-absent symbolism, offers us a genealogy of the origin of language, and thus of objects — for objects are not the immediate correlates of perception, but terms identified and idealized through a symbolism — the origin of objectivity in general, as well as of labor and seriousness and mastery. One cannot simply then subject to the criteria and procedures of scientific objectivity an account which means to reveal the genesis of objectivity.

On the other hand, there is no thesis because there is no position of a given. The speculation is about pleasure and unpleasure, the pleasure principle, and what goes beyond it – and these are not given in any perception, evidence, presentation. One cannot – Freud cannot, science can not, philosophy can not – say what the pleasure and the unpleasure "which act so imperatively upon us" are. Pleasure differs from unpleasure by its specific quality. But this quality and this essence of pleasure eludes any apprehension. On the last page of his book Freud wonders whether "the feeling of tension is to be related to the absolute magnitude, or perhaps to the level, of the cathexis, while the pleasure and unpleasure series indicates a change in the magnitude of the cathexis within a given unit of time?" (87) By keeping away from philosophy Freud has also, Derrida points out on the last page of his book, kept away from a note in Nietzsche's *Nachlass*, where Nietzsche wrote that pleasure is constituted by the rhythm of excitations in a given unit of time – a given rhythm of excitations of small magnitude, that is of pains. Pain then, he said, is something else than pleasure, but it is not its contrary. If Freud proceeds in the absence of any eidetic formulation of what is this quality that is pleasure given in experience, he even finds himself in the situation of not knowing whether what is given in experience *is* pleasure. Nothing would seen to be more irreducibly phenomenal than pleasure: isn't it true that pleasure is in consciousness, wholly in consciousness, that, for Husserl, it is the first and most obvious instance of apodicticity? And yet all of psychoanalysis is there to tell us that there is repression, that an actual pleasure can be consciously lived as unpleasure. And that what is consciously perceived as pain can very well be an actual pleasure in the subject.

Just as Derrida showed that Husserl's *Logical Investigations* formulates the essence of intentionality as signification in the absence of any eidetic insight into any formulation of the eidos of signs in general – so Freud formulates the pleasure principle and the reality principle about a pleasure of whose quality and whose essence there is no concept. Freud's speculation is set in motion by a decision to privilege the economic point of view: pleasure and unpleasure will be treated as two quantities: unpleasure will be formulated as a quantity of tension, unbound excitation, that is in excess – relative to the stability of the organism – and pleasure as its release. The law of life, which is also the law of death, will be formulated as a relationship between the quantity of something whose essence is unknown to us, whose very qualitative appearance is uncertain, undecidable, since what is phenomenally unpleasure may well be pleasure in the psyche, since pleasure can well be lived through consciously as unpleasure. The speculative law is not possible in science as objective knowledge, which could not formulate an equation of quantitative evaluations of qualitative affects in the subject that evaluates. Nor is it possible in philosophy, for which the criterion for knowing what is pleasure and what unpleasure is experience, consciousness or perception, for which a pleasure that would not be experienced as pleasure could not be what is meant by pleasure.

The speculation is in the same position before the pleasure principle, the reality principle and the death drive. If psychoanalysis never encounters unequivocal evidence of the death instinct, which if it exists works in silence, it also cannot demonstrate the pleasure principle, whose dominance is "unhesitatingly assumed" as a given.

Pure pleasure, as well as pure reality, are ideal limits, or fictions. "Each time one of the 'terms,' the pseudo-terms or pseudopodes, works and goes all the way to its end, thus to its other, holding on to its extreme and pure autarchy, without negotiating, without speculating, without passing through the mediation of a third party, there is death, the lethal torque that puts an end to the twists of the calculation." The pleasure principle is "highly dangerous" to the organism it dominates, but so is the reality principle. "If the reality principle becomes autonomous and functions all alone (a hypothesis by definition absurd and one that covers the field called pathological), it cuts itself off from all pleasure and all desire, from the whole auto-affective relationship without which neither desire nor pleasure can appear"(305).

And the death drive — whether it is suspected in repetition compulsions, traumatic neuroses or sadism — never appears save as voluptuous, compounded with libido. Sadism, whether directed outward or inward, is not simple destructiveness, will for annihilation; it produces orgasm in the annihilator.

The speculation, then, is a demonstration in the absence of a given, an observed or perceived plenitude, anything presented. The demonstration, Derrida says, is a de-monstration, to be understood as deconstruction, undoing of construction that does not yield a display of positive constituents. "The de-monstration makes up the proof without showing, without putting any conclusion in evidence, without giving anything one can take away from it, without making any thesis available" (317). It would be a mistake to imagine that the Freudian speculation has turned the pleasure principle and its beyond, its other, into principles available for subsequent theoretical constructions or deductions. Or that Freud had so used them.

The steps the speculation takes do not form one method, one procedure. *Beyond the Pleasure Principle* contains pieces of cellular biological theory formulated in strategico-military terminology, pieces of neurology transferred to the psychic apparatus, fragmentary reports of psychoanalytic treatments, narrations of domestic scenes, pieces of autobiography, auto-thanatology, and auto-analysis, pieces of heterobiography and heterothanatology composed not out of the narratives of the other but out of transference with him. The speculation was composed the year of the death of Freud's "Sunday's child," Sophia, mother of the grandchild whose repetition compulsion the text analyzes so pregnantly; this connection Freud himself speculated over the Wittels the year Sophia's second son Heinerle died and Freud underwent the first of thirty three operations for cancer. The text also contains pieces of fiction, and is itself splendidly composed in accordance with literary canons. It contains fragments of myths. A piece of Plato's *Symposium* is repeated in the text, a passage from Aristophanes attributed to Plato, whereas in reality Plato identifies Aristophanes as the enemy of Socrates and the first accusor in the trial, principal accomplice, then, in Socrates's suicide. The trenchant force, the dogmatic tone of pieces of the text constitute decisions Freud is taking not only in speculation but in the psychoanalytic cause or movement. The text is a factor in the struggle for investiture and for the position of heir and successor to Freud in the psychoanalytic institution that was then being waged.

Derrida does not set out to organize these different kinds of steps of the speculation into a hierarchical system by establishing relations of founded and founding between them. For him the text, which is about the repetition compulsion, the *Fort-Da*, is itself composed of essentially repetitive moves; it is atelic and athetic. The repetition, however, each time occurs in and produces a displacement in the signifiers. Freud has said this: the passage from an observation to its description is not a depiction, but already a translation (*Übersetzung*). It is then necessary to transfer, by a supplementary estimation (*Überschätzung*), the description into the language of theory. But the schemas with which the psychoanalytic theory is built are themselves transferred from other, already existing, sciences (*Übertragung*). But one cannot divide between proper meaning and figurative meanings in these movements of transference. For when, one day, the present terminology of psychoanalytic theory will be retranslated into physiological or chemical terminology, this will be progress, Freud says, in that the terms will be "more familiar" and "simpler," – not nonmetaphorical, proper or appropriate. In fact we do not have something like an observation, a given, a perception, and then a language that would be appropriate to it or figurative, transferred to it from elsewhere. *For it is the transfer of the terms from elsewhere that makes the perception itself possible.* "Without [the aid of this figurative language] we could not in general describe the corresponding processes, but what is more, we would not even have perceived them" (83). The transferred usage of signifiers to make an observation possible, the translation of the observation into descriptive language, the supplementary estimation that transports the description into the register of theory, the transposition of the signifiers from other sciences that makes a theoretical language possible − all this is the very procedure of the speculation, as transference is the whole procedure of the psychotherapy itself.

In the *Introduction* to *The Origin of Geometry* Derrida had first understood how repetition constitutes the ideal element of the theoretical order: the ideal is not what is to be defined metaphysically as what subsists independent of the differentiation of time and place, but is to be defined phenomenologically as what recurs the same whenever, wherever it appears. The ideal is what can recur, at another time, in another place, the same, but it is also that whose first apparition to me, to us, is not given as its origin. Its first occurence to us is given as a recurrence; the first time I thought of the number 4 it figured as an occurence among others in a series of indefinite recurrences. Now Derrida explains that the elements distinctive to the speculative order recur by displacement, by transference. The speculative element recurs, the speculative movement repeats, returns each time in a new guise, in a new warp and woof of signifiers.

A final trait of what Derrida does, speculating on the Freudian speculation, is the putting it into correspondence with the *Philebus. The Postcard*, as the title of his book reads, is sent *from Socrates to Freud.* Freud cites Plato in his text, cites the *Symposium*, but, Derrida shows, his own text is a citation of the *Philebus*; his own text is an incription of what was sent forth, across the distances of culture, by the one who wrote nothing. This is the part of Derrida's deconstructive practice that has disturbed me throughout his work. Here his connection is made this way; whereas Freud says that we have no idea of what pleasure is, still he does use the term simply in the ordinary way, that is, he appeals to the meaning the term has had in current language. The *Philebus* is the first text that formulates that sense of pleasure, which is destined to be invariant in the text from Plato to Freud. "Plato stands behind Freud," Derrida writes. "Or, if one prefers, Socrates . . . The two bodies of text, Freud's and Plato's, are each a part of the other. They are addressed to one another in a fabulous correspondence" (425). I have never known what to make of this Derridean and first Heideggerean thesis that metaphysics, Platonism, inaugurates the conceptual apparatus which the history of metaphysics is subsequently destined only to elaborate in full and in all its variants, including its inversions.

Particularly since here Freud himself in quoting Plato derives the doctrine from the *Brihadárayakaupanishad*. The most obvious objection is that Derrida can, at most, show that what the *Philebus* meant, by the dialogue on pleasure, turns up again as the implicit and common meaning of the term in ordinary language and in Freud's sense of the term in particular. But to show that would be contrary to the whole deconstructive project with regards to the Freudian speculation: one would have to show not that the signified meaning, but the signifiers, the graphics, and the material means of communication of the Platonic dialogue commands an essential and not only extrinsic correspondence with the signifiers, the graphics, and the material means of communication of the psychoanalytic discursive practice – which seems so manifestly false. This is why the Derridean intent to show the Freudian speculation too as elaborated with the metaphysical closure seems to me to be idealist.

Up to this point I have spoken of what Derrida does with what Freud does; now I would like to say some things about what Derrida says about what Freud says. The differentiation is of course only a deferring of what is not separate. I am only going to say something about the principle of all principles, which in psychoanalysis, unlike in phenomenology, is not intuition, but pleasure. But isn't pleasure, like intuition, presence, plenitude, *ousia*, substance and subject?

"In the theory of psycho-analysis," Freud begins, "we have no hesitation in assuming that the course taken by mental events is automatically regulated by the pleasure principle." But what pleasure is, what is its qualitative essence, neither science nor philosophy nor even psychoanalysis, we have noted, can tell us. In addition what is experienced perceptively as pleasure may in reality be unpleasure; every neurotic unpleasure is a pleasure which cannot be experienced as such. This does not mean that pleasure is a plenitude in itself, but not for us. For although the pleasure principle is absolutely dominant in the physic apparatus, it is also absolutely dangerous; it is then itself indistinguishable from the death drive in that apparatus. In order to maintain itself, and its dominance, the pleasure principle postpones itself; it must delegate the regulation of mental events to the reality principle. The reality principle is different from, but not opposed to the pleasure principle; it serves it precisely by deferring it and opening up a detour, distance, "the long indirect road to pleasure." "The pleasure principle itself persists, however, as the method of working employed by the sexual instincts, which are so hard to 'educate,' and by those instincts . . . it often succeeds in overcoming the reality principle, to the destruction of the organism as a whole" (6). The reality principle only holds in suspense and represents the pleasure principle, deferring its dominance, introducing a delay, a detour, a distance. The reality principle is itself produced by the pleasure principle, which differentiates, defers, distances itself. Between the dominance of the pleasure principle and the ascendancy of its bondsman there is not dialectics, opposition; here difference is not opposition, although the alterity is more irremediable, uncancellable, unsublateable, irreducible still than any opposition. Plenary pleasure, as well as full regulation by reality are ideal limits, the one as destructive and lethal to the organism as the other; they are fictions. The *Wirklichkeit*, the effective operation of mental events, of the physic apparatus, is the differance that works between them and that works them out.

The dominance of the pleasure principle is effective then in a deferring, a detouring, a distancing of its dominance. "The pleasure principle extends its domination (*Herrschaft*) over the psychic, over the psychic *domain*. But since it dominates every living subjectivity, such a mastery is not limited to any region. In other words, we are not here just speaking of domination, mastery, metaphorically. It is out of, on the basis of the mastery exercised over every psychic subject (every conscious or unconscious living being) by what is here called the pleasure principle that one can then determine what any other kind of mastery, figurative or derivative, could be and could mean. From this 'phychic' mastery is derived mastery in the so-called current, usual or literal or proper sense, mastery in the 'domains' of technique or expertise, politics or the struggle between consciousnesses. All these forms of mastery refer to the subject or to consciousness. But since over this subject or this consciousness there first reigns the mastery of the pleasure principle, one has to first refer to it in order to seek any 'proper' meaning, and any meaning for the 'proper,' the 'one's own' " (419).

Yet there is a mastering prior to, and independent of, the pleasure principle. What seemed to contest the domination of the pleasure principle is the repetition compulsion, which compulsively reinstates not only pleasurable events but also unpleasurable ones. In traumatic neuroses the patient compulsively reinstates the traumatizing shock, in psychotherapy the neurotic compulsively repeats the most painful events of childhood, the child Freud watched compulsively reenacts the disappearance of his toys to reenact the painful departure of his mother. Freud interprets the repetition as the principle mechanism of mastery; the event passively undergone is repeated actively: mastery is assured. What is to be mastered is the excess influx of excitation from without or from within, the traumatizing shock or the force of the primary processes of the mental apparatus. Freud conceives this mastering according to the Helmholtzian distinction between freely utilizable and bound energies, which distinction Breuer had transposed into the sphere of psychic energy, translating it into a distinction between freely mobile and bound energy. The freely mobile energies invading the organism in shock, or the freely mobile energies of the organism's own primary processes, have to be bound; of themselves they would immediately destroy the psychic organization. "The binding of an instinctual impulse would be a preliminary function designed to prepare the excitation for its final elimination in the pleasure of discharge" (86).

Before the pleasure principle can enter into its dominion, first this preliminary mastery over the influx or the upsurge of freely mobile excitations must be ensured. But this binding also limits, diminishes, the pleasure as well as the unpleasure that can be produced from excitational processes. ". . . [T]here seems to be no doubt whatever," Freud wrote, "that the unbound or primary processes give rise to far more intense feelings in both directions than the bound or secondary ones" (86). The pleasure principle can become dominant then only once the pleasure possibilities of the primary processes of psychic life have been undermined by the first compulsive mastery. When the pleasure principle takes control of the metal processes, it establishes its domination at the expense of pleasure, over a subject already bound, constrained, whose pleasure possibilities have been sapped. The domination of the pleasure principle is not only a domination of pleasure, it is a domination over pleasure. Yet the first compulsive mastery is at the service of the pleasure principle; it is its delegate and its representative. Pleasure as a principle, an origin, an *archē*, defers itself, precedes itself or lets itself be preceded by itself in the form of the compulsive mastery which is indifferent to pleasure and to unpleasure, and repeats them compulsively in order to bind and therefore undermine them.

There is then a kind of speculation within the psychic apparatus which measures, limits, contains the pleasure possibilities of the mobile energies by binding them in order to make the pleasure principle dominant. What speculates is not the structure of mastery, that is, the pleasure principle itself, but a movement that differentiates, defers and distances the domination of the pleasure principle from the compulsive mastery, as it defers and distances the pleasure principle from the reality principle. This irreducible and originating *differance* is not opposition; in its movement the unpleasure of the bound processes, compulsively repeated in order that they be bound, and the pleasurable processes diminished by being bound, are not opposites, as the pleasure of the release and the death is not the opposite of the mastery of life that binds, as the pleasure is not the opposite of the reality. There is not, within the mastery of life the dialectic of negativity, lack and opposition; there is pleasure that limits and defers itself, pain that limits and discharges itself. The economy of life is not what Bataille, and first Nietzsche, called a solar economy, of expenditure without recompense, without restraint. The pleasure in life is not that godlike feeling Nietzsche called humanity, that "happiness of a god full of power and love, full of tears and laughter, a happiness that, like the sun in the evening, continually bestows its inexhaustible riches, pouring them into the sea, feeling richest, as the sun does, only when even the poorest fisherman rows with golden oars!" (*The Gay Science*, §337)

Every instinct, every compulsion in an organism, Freud says, is conservative, is a compulsion to restore an earlier state of things which the living entity has been forced to abandon under the pressure of external disturbing forces; it is compulsion to restore the quiescence, the death of the inorganic. Notice — and this Derrida does not take note of — this *Todestrieb* is not the Heideggerian *Zum-tode-Sein*, ecstasy by which ex-istence projects itself into nothingness; it is what Le Clézio called material ecstasy — the expulsion of life out of itself into the mineral, into the inorganic inertia. "[T]he instincts of self-preservation, of self-assertion and of mastery . . . are component instincts whose function it is to assure that the organism shall follow its own path to death, and to ward off any possible ways of returning to inorganic existence other than those which are immanent in the organism itself" (51).

The compulsion which is stronger than the compulsion to live, or to die, is the compulsion for one's own. For one's own, the proper, is not given, but is sought in the compulsion to live and the compulsion to die. The one's own is not identity or coincidence, but compulsion for itself, appropriative compulsion. And it is not a compulsion to possess one's own being or one's own life, but to possess one's own dying. The most compulsive compulsion, the master compulsion, is the compulsion to appropriate one's own expropriation. This kind of compulsion for one's own, this exappropriation, is what dominates, is mastery itself.

Part VI.
Heidegger's Critique
of Derrida

14. Quasi-Metaphoricity and the Question of Being

Rodolphe Gasché

Derrida's insistence upon the fact that philosophy, from its beginnings, has conceived of itself as a discourse entirely transparent to Being and free of all figurative use of language, has fostered the mistaken opinion that Derrida's aim would be to challenge or "deconstruct" the *regina scientiarum* by playing literature and its metaphoric use of language off against this discipline that pretends to dominate all other disciplines. Nothing, however, could be more inaccurate than to confound the deconstruction of philosophy with a non-argumentative, literary, and metaphoric play. This belief is incorrect not only because of its reductive understanding of literature, but as we will see, for other, more essential reasons.

Derrida has never left the slightest doubt that metaphor is by nature a metaphysical concept. In spite or rather *because of its negativity* it belongs to the very order and movement of meaning: the provisory loss of meaning that metaphor implies is subordinated to the teleology of meaning as one moment in the process of the self-manifestation of meaning in all its propriety. The philosophical concept of metaphor, and there is no other, makes metaphor depend on the absolute *parousia* of meaning.

Metaphor denotes a reality derivative upon proper meaning whether the metaphoric displacement is seen as a moment of loss anticipating a future recuperation or only as an ornamental and exterior supplement to proper meaning. Instead of uncritically revalorizing metaphor, instead of simply playing it off against philosophy, Derrida's repetition of the question of metaphor is an interrogation of the philosophical concept of metaphor, of its limits, and, as is to be seen in "White Mythology," of philosophy's attempt to systematically ques-

166

tion the metaphorical origins of its concepts.[1] In other words, Derrida's reformulation of the question of metaphor is concerned with the fundamental complicity between the philosophical determination of the concept of metaphor and the apparently subversive attempt to challenge philosophy on the grounds that its concepts are hidden tropes. Rather than participating in this double enterprise, Derrida's efforts involve an analysis of the presuppositions of this problematic, and an attempt to delimit the metaphysical and rhetorical schemes that constitute it. This analysis implies a profound suspicion of the concept of metaphor as a metaphysical concept; consequently, one never finds Derrida flirting with this concept of metaphor as if it possessed within its parameters and all by itself, any decisive properties that would be potentially subversive of logocentricism. Yet, of course, there is no such thing as a purely metaphysical concept. If concepts could be purely metaphysical they would resist all questions concerning them. As a result, Derrida can nonetheless point to a certain irreducibility of metaphor with respect to its possibility, and short of its rhetorical repetition and philosophical conceptualization. Focusing on this specific irreducibility, metaphor appears to be the metaphysical name for something which is "older" than the philosophical distinction between the proper and the metaphoric (*SP*, 103), and which might thus be in a position to upset the conceptual columbarium of philosophy. Consequently, rather than simply attempting to reverse the classical hierarchical opposition of the proper and the figural, of the philosophical and the metaphoric, Derrida aims at something which is only very improperly called metaphoric without, for that matter, being something proper in itself. Being no longer either metaphoric or literal, an allegorical illustration without a concept or a pure concept without a metaphoric scheme, the irreducible in question can not only no longer be referred to by the *name* of metaphor but is properly unnameable. As Derrida has argued in "The *Retrait* of Metaphor," the sort of metaphor in question is in withdrawal — it retires.[2] Being neither of the order of the concept or of metaphor, the irreducible in question escapes the order of the noun in general, within which, as Derrida has shown in his analysis of *Aristotle's Poetics* and *Rhetorics*, the philosophical elaboration of metaphor takes place, an elaboration which links metaphor via a theory of *mimesis*, to the doctrine of being or ontology. It is unnameable not because of some Romantic nostalgia for the ineffable, nor because man's limited faculties as a finite being would be too narrow to express what overpowers them, but because of this irreducible's exorbitant position with regard to the opposition of the proper and the figural, Being and beings, God and men, a position which escapes the logic that ties *logos* and Being together. Derrida refers to it as *quasi-metaphoricity* or, simply, metaphoricity.

Metaphoricity, then, is not a quality presupposing an already constituted and philosphically determined metaphor. Nor is metaphoricity the savage production, unmediated by concepts, of metaphors as a quality attributed to, say, literary language. As that which opens the play between the proper and the metaphoric, and which metaphysics can only name as that which it makes possible, metaphoricity is not endowed with those qualities traditionally attributed to metaphor but rather with attributes which in traditional philosophy would be called constituting or transcendental. Metaphoricity is a transcendental concept of sorts. Yet from this it does not follow that Derrida would simply do away with the so called ornamental and poetic functions of metaphor, reducing them, as does philosophy, to a literary border-phenomenon of philosophy. The absence of such a derogative gesture, however, does not mean, as is often assumed, that Derrida would turn the literary qualities of metaphoricity against the conceptual language of philosophy with its desire for univocity, exactitude, and clarity. In truth, the notion of metaphoricity as advanced by Derrida is neither opposed to the philosphical concept of metaphor (and there can be no other), nor simply identical with what philosophy calls the ornamental poetic function of metaphor, nor does it view metaphor as a moment in the process of meaning. Metaphoricity, in Derrida's sense, refers to something *structurally* phenomenal, i.e. to something of the order of conceptual, the transcendental, but which in spite of its heterogeneity to the so-called real world, also combines with the supplementary and ornamental mode of the rhetorical figure of poetics. As the result of a destruction of metaphor, and *eo ipso* of the proper and the literal, metaphoricity yields a structure that accounts for the difference between the figural and the proper, and which comprises properties that are by right "older" than those traditionally attributed to the transcendental and the empiric. Since, as an "originary" synthesis, metaphoricity is more originary than what one formerly referred to as transcendental, and since it also combines with the most exterior qualities of metaphor, with metaphor's exteriority to the concept, we will hereafter try to define it as a non-phenomenologizable *quasi-transcendental.*

The following analysis of "White Mythology" is an attempt to characterize a bit more fully the status of metaphoricity, by examining the different ways in which Derrida is led to elaborate this notion. We have already stated that metaphoricity is something structurally phenomenal that serves to account for the philosophical difference between the proper and the figural. It already became evident that this notion is altogether different from what either the literary critic or the philosopher designates, or would designate, by such a notion. This gap widens even farther as soon as we explore the problem that this notion of metaphoricity (if one may say ultimately) serves to address in Derrida's work. Such a demonstration, however, requires a detour of sorts.

1. The multiple senses of being

As Heidegger himself points out, his interest in philosophy was awakened by his reading in 1907 of Franz Brentano's dissertation *On the Several Senses of Being in Aristotle* (1862).[3] Studying Brentano's analysis of the multiple ways in which being is expressed (*pollakos legomenon*), Heidegger began to reflect on the primary and fundamental meaning of Being presuppoed by these multiple senses. It is important to recall here that within the problematical horizon of classical philosophy, the question concerning the unity and the manifold of the senses of Being is none other than that of analogy. Indeed, a tradition that starts with Scholastic philosophy has Aristotle determine the relation between being and its multiple senses in terms of this figure of thought. It is within the same tradition, precisely, that Brentano situates his own investigation of the problem. Although Heidegger's fundamental philosophical concern does not take place under the explicit title of "analogy," it is most certain that his investigation into the question of the meaning of Being, or into that of the difference *as* difference, is essentially an attempt to come to grips with the traditional problem of analogy, whether or not that notion is mentioned.[4] In the pages that follow, we will try to substantiate this point with a brief analysis of some paragraphs of *Being and Time*.[5]

Whether or not certain philosophies explicitly reflect on the problem of analogy, all metaphysics, insofar as it is concerned with the unity in difference, would have to understand itself primarily as a philosophy of analogy, as Puntel has most forcefully argued. Although "analogy" acquires the explicit status of a philosophical issue only with Plato, analogy, as the problem of the identity that lets differences (as well as the various linguistic articulations of being) come to the fore is already *a* − if not *the* − major figure of thought in philosophical thinking from its very incipience, as we will briefly outline.[6] Up through Aristotle, analogy had the meaning of mathematical proportion, relation, ratio, correspondence, thus reflecting its origin as a mathematical concept formulated by the Pythagoreans. It did not signify a simple relation or a simple proportion, but a system of relations or proportions. Puntel writes: "Analogy is a relation of relations, a proportion of proportions, in short, a correspondence of relations."[7] According to this originary meaning of analogy, the unity or the identity that difference presupposes, and which mediates between what is different, is one that becomes manifest in the similitude of opposing but back-stretched relations. As a matter of fact, the whole problematic of analogy is one of determining these relations. As mentioned above, Scholastic philosophy extended the problem of analogy to the question of being and made Aristotle the first thinker to have determined being in such a manner. Indeed, the Scholastics contended that Aristotle conceived of the relation between the different senses of being and being itself as one of similarity by analogy. Ever since Ockham's view that there is no analogy of being, this question has been an issue in philosophy. We cannot attempt here to develop in full this most difficult problem, nor can we discuss Aubenque's thesis, in *Le Problème de l'être chez Aristote*, that the Scholastic position does not correspond to Aristotle's thought, and that the doctrine of the analogy of being represents, on the contrary, a platonization of Aristotle.[8] Nor will linger on Ricoeur's contention in *The Rule of Metaphor*, that the entire theory of analogy is no more than a pseudo-science, the result of theological pressure on a specifically philosophical discourse.[9] Suffice it to say that the fundamental reason why these and other authors reject the idea of an analogy of being is that they contend that Aristotle knew only the mathematical notion of analogy as a quantitative proportion which, strictly speaking, could not be applied to the relation between the meanings of being and being itself, for being itself can no longer be posited in relation to an other.

This argument is substantiated it would seem, by the fact that Aristotle never applied the concept of analogy – a concept which he indeed uses on several other occasions in the strict sense of a relation of proportion – when speaking of the multiple meanings of being. When, for instance, at the beginning of Book IV of the *Metaphysics*, he writes that " 'being' has several meanings but that they all have a central reference to some *one* nature (*pros hen kai mian tina physo*) and are not entirely different things that happen to have the same name (*homonymos*)," he does not use the word "analogy."[10] Moreover, the *pros hen* in the proposition, instead of signifying a correspondence of relations, indicates only the simple relation of a manifold to an originary oneness, with respect to which everything else is derivative and dependent. In the aftermath of Trendelenburg's attempt to save the analogy of being by elaborating a qualitative proportionality, hence a concept of analogy more general than its first and original sense as quantitative proportionality, Brentano, following in this scholastic tradition, also assumes a second type of analogy in order to explain the relation in Aristotle between the non-generic concept of being and its different senses. However, this second type of analogy is not one of proportionality (quantitative of qualitative) but, as the Scholastics called it, one of attribution or, to use Brentanos' words, one with respect to one and the same *terminus*. Being, according to Brentano, has the unity of analogy, a unity that grounds the manifold and categorial senses of being, because its different meanings relate to it in an *ad unum* relation. Being's equivocal meanings are connected to the unity of a *non-accidental* name (*homonymos*). Although of different meanings, the categories relate to a common name as to a common origin by virtue of an analogy of attribution. They are indeed not entirely different things that happen (*accidentally*) to have the same name, but refer to one necessary name as the source of their plurality. The unity of this *homonymon* is the non-generic unity of analogy. For Brentano, therefore, being is doubly analogical: its different meanings relate to it according to the analogy with respect to the same terminus, and, as Trendelenberg had shown, they also form an equality of relations. Indeed, although Aristotle in Book IV does not use the term analogy with regard to the question of the multiple senses of being, he nevertheless says in Book V that whatever is related as a certain thing to another, and what "bears to each other the same ratio or relation that another pair has" (*osa ekei os allo pros allo*), is analogical.[11] Yet it is such an equality that Aristotle claimed for his categories, and which, along with *on* and *ousia* are, according to Brentano, the major senses in which being is said.[12]

For what is to follow, it is important to remark that the theory of the analogy of being implies that being is in itself relational. Yet, as Puntel has intimated, this self-relationality of being presupposes that "being is in itself and as itself *difference* i.e. a self-relation that repeats itself in and through itself."[13] Only to the extent that being is difference can it be said to be analogical. Although this conclusion may not have been thematized in the tradition that stretches from Aquinas to Brentano, the critics' objections to the doctrine of the analogy of being may well, in essence, pivot around this issue of difference. In any case, it is as a doctrine of the difference of being that the theory of the analogy of being is of interest to us here. It is only in this perspective that this doctrine is taken up again by both Heidegger and Derrida, as we will now attempt to show.

As an inquiry into the manifold sense of Being from the perspective of *Dasein*, Heidegger's investigation in *Being and Time* continues, at first, the classical problematics of analogy, for it displays a nongeneric conception of Being. As *"the* transcendens *pure and simple,"* to quote *Being and Time,* Being lies beyond what is, beyond all imaginable ontic determinations. Heidegger conceives of his fundamental theme in a genuinely Aristotlian sense as "no sort of genus of beings."[14] But the true reason for seeing Heidegger's philosophy as a continuation, and even as a radicalication of this tradition, is that his investigation of the different modes of *saying* Being is an investigation of Being as the difference which, within Being as a *terminus,* makes it possible for one mode of uttering Being to relate — analogously — to that *terminus,* in the two senses of analogy we have already distinguished. The difference of Being as a difference of the same is the title under which Heidegger engages his debate with the traditional philosophical problem of analogy.

In *Being and Time* this problem takes shape as the *as-structure* of the understanding of Being. After having established that understanding and states-of-mind *(Verstehen* and *Befindlichkeit)* are fundamental *existentialia* of the being of the *Da* — *existentialia* which secure the primordial disclosedness of *Dasein* as Being-in-the-world — Heidegger proceeds to complete the structures of *Dasein* by adding not language but the *possiblity* of language to it. In §32 of *Being and Time,* Heidegger starts out by demonstrating that understanding is made explicit *(ausdrücklich)* through interpretation *(Auslegung).* The analysis of interpretation in the sense of *Auslegung (hermeneuein)* is an intermediary step in the discovery of the third fundamental structure of the *Dasein* which is discourse *(Rede).* Discourse indeed, is the *possibility* of speech.

For what is to follow it is imperative to understand in what way interpretaion is said to make explicit what is implicitly understood or sensed by the *Dasein.* It is important to realize that interpretation of what is understood must take place, according to the *structural* status of *Dasein* (which, we must repeat, is therefore not just another name for subject or for *anthropos),* in an essentially pre-linguistic, non-propositional, pre-predicative, and non-thematic manner. The *Dasein* encounters the things that surround it primarily as things which serve this or that purpose, and not as pure things or objects upon which it subsequently bestows determining attributes. Hence, the interpretation of what is understood circumspectively is characterized by the structure of *something as something.* Heidegger writes:

> That which is disclosed in understanding — that which is understood — is already accessible in such a way that its 'as which' can be made to stand out explicitly. The 'as' makes up the structure of the explicitness of something that is understood. It constitutes the interpretation.[15]

In other words, interpretation is the laying out (*Auslegen*) of the primary articulation of what is understood according to the as-structure which is an *a priori* articulation (*Gliederung, Artikulation*). Interpretation makes explicit that all understanding is primarily articulated according to the structure of "something as something," or in other words "with regard to something" (*auf etwas hin*). Heidegger calls this primary articulation of understanding and interpretation *Rede*, which one may translate by "discourse" if one keeps in mind that it marks a structural level of articulation anterior by right to all possible linguistic utterance. As "the articulation of intelligibility," discourse is coeval with states-of-mind and understanding and precedes all predicative and thematic expression and vocalization of understanding and states-of-mind.[16] As the third fundamental *existentiale* of the *Dasein* it represents the very *possibility* of vocalization, of speech, of speech acts, of language as the mundane or worldly mode of the being of the *logos*. Discourse in the sense of *Rede* is merely a translation of '*logos*.' It signifies the "logical" articulation of *Dasein's* pre-understanding of Being and thus corresponds to the ontologically fundamental structure of the meaning of Being. The meaning of Being hinges on its articulation in terms of the as-structure.

The "existential-*hermeneutical* 'as' " is the name Heidegger gives to the primordial 'as' of all interpretation that understands circumspectively, in other words, "with regard to something."[17] This 'as' is the fundamental structure of the logos as discourse, as the primary articulation of understanding and interpretation and achieves the originary discovering and dis-closure, which Heidegger will later call the primary opening, within which propositional predication may (or may not) come forth. We will not deal here with the leveling modifications that are required to transform the existential-hermeneutical 'as' into the apophantic 'as' which is itself the structure of possibility of assertion.[18] Let us only say that as little as vocalization is an attribute of the logos as *Rede*, so little is it an integral part of assertion. Yet, just as logos as *Rede* contains the *possibility* of language in the form of the structural determination of expressed*ness* (*Hinausgesprochenheit*), it also contains the possibility of assertion in the structural form of what is called *Ausgesprochenheit*, and which ensures that stating *can* become communicative revealing. These structural determinations are structurally phenomenal and belong to an order altogether heterogeneous to that of factual realization and vocalization. We are only concerned, here, with these originary structures of the logos, apart from its factual and contingent vocalization. These structures are not discovered at the expense of the logos' vocalization but inscribe it as a possibility.

Having characterized, with Heidegger, *logos* as discourse, i.e., as constituted by the articulation of intelligibility according to the as-structure, it is important to note that the primary disclosure achieved by the as-structure is at the same time a primary covering-up. Indeed, since the as-structure uncovers "with regard to," it veils *and* reveals in the same gesture. Thus, Heidegger has inscribed an originary falsehood into the very articulation of the *logos*, which will allow him, with one structure, to account for why propositions *can* be wrong. The as-structure as the primary articulation of the understanding of Being, made explicit in interpretation by the logos *as discourse, is thus a structure which makes all understanding of Being by the Dasein* structurally dependent on circumspect inference. Everything, as it were, is primarily understood not by focusing on the thing as such but with regard to something else, say to the *what-for* of the thing. As far as the meaning of Being is concerned, it can only be known *as* its different senses. Since the originary articulation of the understanding of Being – its interpretation – precedes any particular determination of Being, and since each such particular sense of Being is structurally covered-up Being, Being itself is always only in its own deferral. *Being is dif-ference, it is analogical in the sense that it is articulated within itself as the unity of its self-same senses.* Being is nothing *in itself*, but it is the very "logical" articulation of its own understanding within which it appears in a multitude of irreducible senses.

Ricoeur, in *The Rule of Metaphor*, shows a certain awareness of the continuity between the traditional problematic of analogy and the philosophies of Heidegger and Derrida when, in chapter 8, after a discussion of the problem of the analogy of being in Aristotle and of the *analogia entis* in Thomas Aquinas, he proceeds to discuss Heidegger's and Derrida's treatments of metaphor. Yet, because Ricoeur is primarily concerned with warding off the intrusion of poetics into philosophy, he remains blind to the fact that Heidegger's and Derrida's investigations into metaphor and metaphoricity are not simply poetical inquiries but are based on a *philosophical* concept of metaphor, and are thus a debate with that *philosophical* concept. Moreover, he fails to see that this debate is engaged with the classical problem of the analogy of being. One can perceive the real continuity of all these problematics only by recognizing that the concept of metaphor in Heidegger and Derrida is not simply one of poetic resemblance but one which receives a transcendental qualification from the field it is applied to, to use Ricoeur's words – a qualification similar to the one which Ricoeur powerfully demonstrates in the case of the analogy of being as well as with regard to the concept of the *analogia entis*, both of which are said to be nonmetaphorical theories of analogy (supposing that metaphor is one with poetic resemblance).

In the paragraphs ahead, we would like to argue that Derrida's treatment of metaphor is a resumption not of what Heidegger explicitly developed about metaphor, but of the more fundamental structure of the *logos* and of the much older problem of the analogy of being. Consequently, we will attempt to show that Derrida's critique of the philosophy of language or of linguistics opens itself, not unlike Heidegger's critique, to an exploration of ground structures which are to account for the phenomenon of language. Yet, as we will see, the status of these ground structures in Derrida is for essential reasons very different from the immanent or finite transcendental structures in Heidegger, as we will call them.

Since analogy is, according to Aristotle, not only one genre of metaphor, but the metaphor *par excellence* insofar as it is based on an equality of relations, the doctrine of the analogy of being — whatever the meaning of analogy may be — indicates that a certain metaphoricity is constitutive of the very unity of being. The as-structure of understanding unearthed by Heidegger characterizes understanding and the saying of Being as hinging on a movement of transfer. The relation of "with regard to" in the primary mode of the circumspective understanding makes all understanding of something understanding of *something as something*. A movement of *epiphora*, the movement constitutive of metaphor, is present in all understanding of the *as what*. With this, we face a clear continuity between the traditional problem of the analogy of being, Heidegger's investigation into the fundamental structures of the *logos*, and, as we will now see, Derrida's treatment of the problem of metaphor.

2. The generalization of analogy

Before embarking on an analysis of "White Mythology," let us first establish that our linkage of Derrida's treatment of the concept of metaphor with the question of the analogy of being is not an artificial imposition but is supported by the texts. Indeed, Derrida explicitly recognizes that his analysis of metaphor cuts into the problems delineated by the analogy of being. What remains perhaps implicit is that these analyses of metaphor are intrinsically connected with the problem of the analogy of being. After having reminded Benveniste, in "The Supplement of Copula," that the very possibility of a science of language hinges on a knowledge about the essence of what is called "category," Derrida writes:

> The categories are the figures (*skhemata*) according to which the "simple term" being is said in that it is said in several ways, through several tropes. The system of the categories is the system of being's turns of phrase. It brings the problematic of the analogy of Being, its equivocalness or unequivocalness, into communication with the problematic of the metaphor in general. Aristotle explicitly links these problematics in affirming that the best metaphor coordinates itself to the analogy of proportionality. Which would suffice to prove that the question of metaphor is no more to be asked in the margins of metaphysics than metaphorical style and the use of figures is an accessory embellishment or secondary auxiliary of philosophical discourse. (*M*, 183 – 184)

The problem of metaphor is, then, clearly said to encroach upon both the problems of analogy and Being. Any inquiry into metaphor is thus *per se* an investigation into the possibility of the univocity of Being. Yet, Derrida does not explicitly address the problem of the relation of his analysis of metaphor in general to the problem of the analogy of being. Although he claims in "White Mythology" that all the features which distinguish metaphors in the theory of metaphor seem to "belong to the great immobile chain of Aristotelian ontology, with its theory of the analogy of Being" (*M*, 236), and that the privilege which Aristotle attributes to the metaphor by analogy shows that "this privilege articulates Aristotle's entire metaphorology with his general theory of the analogy of Being" (*M*, 242), he refrains from clarifying this relation. "We cannot undertake this problem here," he writes, referring the reader to the studies of Aubenque and Vuillemin (*M*, 244). Still, throughout his work, Derrida has repeatedly linked the problem of analogy and metaphor, and has systematically questioned the relation of these two figures with respect to the problem of Being.

Although in the *Poetics*, Aristotle conceived of analogy as only one species of metaphor – metaphor by analogy – , in his *Rhetoric*, it already becomes *the* paradigm of metaphor. "Analogy is metaphor par excellence. Aristotle emphasizes this point often in the *Rhetoric*," notes Derrida in "White Mythology" (*M*, 242). Such a privilege makes the whole of Aristotle's metaphorology dependent on his general theory concerning the analogy of being. "Metaphor in general, the passage from one existent to another, or from one signified meaning to another, [is] authorized by the initial *submission* of Being to the existent, the *analogical displacement* of Being" (*WD*, 27). Elsewhere, "Metaphor, thus, as an effect of *mimesis* and *homoiosis*, [is] the manifestation of analogy"

(*M*, 238). In other words, analogy is a phenomenally more fundamental mode of transport than the *epiphora* constitutive of metaphor. Metaphor and the movement of *epiphora* are to be thought on the background and with respect to the more general problematic of analogy.

It is in particular in his analyses of Condillac and Kant that Derrida has pointed out that this "fundamental analogism" (*AF*, 83) from which metaphor is derived is not only a principle of methodic and universal linkage for philosophy but a general principle par excellence insofar as it concerns the proper name of being. Indeed, within metaphysics, analogy assures both the continuity of all derivation and the homogeneization of opposite orders (*M*, 311–12) Thus, for instance in Kant, "the recourse to analogy, the concept and the effect of analogy, are or make the *bridge* itself," as and through which the third *Critique* bridges the abyss between the two absolutely heterogeneous worlds of Nature and the Ethical (*VP*, 43). The analogy "brings together without-concept and concept, the universality *without* concept and the universality *with* concept, the *without* and the *with*" (*VP*, 88). It serves to seal up (*cicatriser*) the gap and to think the difference (*VP*, 43).

But the function of analogy is not exhausted by establishing such continuity and homogeneity through a relation of proportionality or of attribution between homologous elements. "The analogical process is also a refluence towards the *logos*. The origin is the *logos*. The origin of analogy, that from which analogy proceeds and towards which it returns, is the *logos*, reason and word."[19] In metaphysics, analogy is suspended upon the non-analogical *logos* as its origin. In "Economimesis" we read, what "regulates all analogy and which itself is not analogical, since it forms the ground of analogy, [is] the *logos* of analogy towards which everything flows back but which itself remains without system, outside of the system that it orients as its end and its origin, its embouchure and its source."[20] As Derrida has demonstrated in "Plato's Pharmacy," a certain dominating and decisive hierarchizing takes place between the terms of the relations that enter into correspondence in a relation of analogy. This hierarchizing authority of logocentric analogy comes from the fact that one term within the relation of relations comes to name the relation itself. Consequently, all the elements that make up the relations find themselves comprised within the structure that names the relation of analogy as a whole. That name, ultimately, is that of the logos. (See *D*, 117.)

Suspended at the non-analogical ground of the *logos*, analogy is dominated by the proper name of the *logos* outside and beyond language, which, according to Derrida, is "analogy through and through" (*SP*, 13). Dependent on the proper saying of Being by the *logos*, the initial submission of Being to what is in the analogical displacement becomes sublated in the non-analogical ground. And yet, what Derrida's analyses consistently show is that the attempt to properly name analogy and consequently, to ground it in the name, only takes place through analogies of analogies. As a result, the "analogy makes itself endlessly abysmal" (*VP*, 43). It continues to belong to language and to the laws of difference, relation and proportionality which characterize it. Thus, although the analogy serves to connect the heterogeneous and to homogenize the differences at the benefit of its allegedly external ground (the *logos*), analogy also engenders, as Condillac knew, a negative product, "the analogue of the analogue, the useless and vain simulacrum of discourse, prattle, nonsense," in short, the frivolous (*AF*, 83). The message of this double of analogy is that the proper or literal meaning of analogy is analogical. Analogy, hence, is the rule, not *logos*.

Considering what we have tried to develop up to this point, the generalized analogism that we have pointed out must serve to account for at least two things:

1. the fundamental analogism in metaphysics which, under the form of the analogy of being secures the univocity and the proper name of Being through an idealization and simultaneous destruction of analogy – by casting metaphor against metaphor in a war of language against itself, in short, through the metaphysical *Aufhebung* of analogy, metaphor, and all other rhetorical figures. Even in Heidegger where it is clear that "Being is nothing outside the existent" and that "it is impossible to avoid the ontic metaphor in order to articulate Being in language," Being itself is still said to be *"alone* in its absolute resistance to *every metaphor"* (*WD,* 138).

2. the ineradicably analogical nature of the proper name of Being and the irreducible plurality, i.e. Nothingness, that separates the different senses of Being and haunts Being's proper name insofar as, precisely, it is a proper name.

One may argue, as Ricoeur does in *The Rule of Metaphor*, that the introduction of the problematics of analogy into the transcendental discourse on being is the result of an exterior pressure of the discourse of theology upon the discourse of philosophy. One may also argue, as he does, that philosophical discourse maintains its sovereignty by stripping the mathematical notion of analogy of its conceptual rigor, a loss through which it acquires the necessary transcendental qualities of the field to which it is applied. One may, in addition, recognize, in this reduction of the notion of analogy, a movement similar to Hegelian *Aufhebung* through which a notion foreign to the philosophical discourse is turned into a truth of being. Yet, however one attempts to explain away the impact of the question of analogy on that of being, the simple fact that the notion of analogy *can* and *must* be brought to bear upon the question of being shows that this notion profoundly affects the very concept of being and cannot be entirely controlled by *Aufhebung*. If the concept of being — the concept of that which is supposed to be the most original, unique, and irreplacable — *can* be affected at all by analogy, then this possibility has to be accounted for and must be inscribed into the concept of being itself. If being *can* be said in different senses, it is because the name of being is *not* a proper name. In that case, however, analogy or metaphor do not surprise being from the outside. The possibliity of being affected by analogy must, then, come to being from the inside. Indeed, it is the very idea of a unity of being, the idea of a being *as such*, of being as thought (*als Gedachtes*), which requires the inner doubling of being in order to appear *as such*. The space of this inner doubling within being is the original space of analogy or metaphor in general. The analogy of being reveals what Derrida calls, in *Of Grammatology*, "a metaphoricity, and elementary transference" (*OG*, 292). This irreducible metaphoricity of the *as such* cannot be sublated in a gesture of idealization because the space of doubling and repetition that it opens, within which being can be related to itself, is the very condition of idealization. Ideation, or the beholding of the general, of the universal, is the intuition of the *as what* of species and singularities. Yet, the generality of the *as what*, that which corresponds to the proper, literal meaning of singularities, is the accomplice of analogy or metaphoricity in general. Indeed, it is "from the trope that we learn about the status of literal, proper meaning, the status of that which *gives itself as* proper meaning" (*M*, 280). Hence generality, universality, that is the "origin in general," is clearly derivative of derivation, of the generality of analogy or metaphoricity.

We will have to discuss in more detail this complicity between the general as the proper, the origin, Being, etc., and a general analogism which at the same time constantly disappropriates and particularizes the general, as we engage in an analysis of "White Mythology."

3. Quasi-Metaphoricity

One would be severely misguided if one took "White Mythology," as Ricoeur does in *The Rule of Metaphor,* as an essay developing some thesis or truth about the concept or reality of metaphor. To do so would be to miss Derrida's whole argument, and to attribute to Derrida one or several of the traditional philosophical or rhetorical positions on metaphor that are critically dealt with in that essay. "White Mythology" is not primarily concerned with metaphor. From the outset, Derrida makes it clear that metaphor is a philosophical concept through and through and that it fosters a continuist (diachronic and symbolic) conception at the expense of the systematic, the syntactic, and the arbitrary. The subordination of the syntactic is inscribed into the most invariable traits of the concept of metaphor to such an extent that a valorization of metaphor, say over concept — a philosophical thesis par excellence — is radically excluded by the premises of Derrida's philosophy. "White Mythology" is a text concerned with the *difference* (and its economy) of metaphor *and* concept. Assuming that both are irreducible to one another, Derrida examines here *the more general analogy that allows metaphor and concept to relate to one another* and that organizes the exchange that takes place between them. Focusing on the regulated play within which this exchange takes place implies the relative autonomy of both metaphor and concept, and precludes any final resumption of the concept by metaphor.

From this perspective, the philosophical positions on metaphor displayed in the essay — the position that philosophy is a white mythology, on the one hand, and on the other that philosophy is free of all metaphors — are not positions on which to capitalize, but whose implicit logic is, rather, to be exhibited. This logic belongs neither to a rhetoric of philosophy nor to a metaphilosophy but represents the larger vista of a discourse on figure no longer restricted to a regional or specific science, linguistics, or philology.

As soon as one reflects on the conditions of possibility of a general metaphorology according to which all philosophical concepts would be hidden, worn out, or dead metaphors, the need for a more embracing discourse on figure becomes evident. Following the presupposition of such a (philosophical) position to its logical end — a position that believes it can demystify the discourse of philosophy by forcing it to deliver the metaphorical credentials of its concepts — Derrida demonstrates that the conditions of possibility of a general philosophical metaphorology are by right its conditions of impossibility. Indeed, if a general metaphorology that systematically investigates the metaphorical credentials of philosophy's conceptuality must presuppose the concept of metaphor, then one concept, at least, the concept of metaphor, necessarily escapes the enterprise of accounting for the metaphoricity of all philosophical concepts. At least one metaphor, the metaphor of the concept of metaphor required to make a philosophical metaphorology possible, escapes the enterprise of classification as well. Thus the metaphor that escapes a general metaphorology, the metaphor of metaphor, the metaphor of the philosophical concept of metaphor, which one presumes in order to reduce all other concepts to the metaphors they conceal, can, of course no longer be a simple metaphor. It cannot merely be identical with the improper figure of a proper concept which, however, is not to say that it would be a more fundamental proper concept. The metaphor of metaphor, since it is no longer derivative upon a concept, or an ultimate signified, signifies a *mise en abime* of the philosophical concept of metaphor. As a relation of figure to figure, of the improper to the improper, it is indicative of a different articulation between metaphor and concept, which Derrida will substitute for the classical opposition.

The larger vista of a discourse on figure to which Derrida refers is primarily concerned with this *other* articulation. It is imperative to see that this articulation is not some common essence of both concept and metaphor, not a truer definition or proposition that would embrace both in a more global concept. As the conditions of impossibility of a general philosophical metaphorology have shown, this different articulation is that of a *general metaphoricity* on which metaphorology's claim to universality is based. This general metaphoricity enables metaphor and concept to enter into a relation in the first place, and thence to indulge in a mutual exchange. It is an articulation that allows a concept to be an idealized counterpart of a sensible image without, however, lending itself to any final reduction to its sensible substrate. The general metaphoricity organizes these exchanges, their generality and universality, without ever having been thematized in traditional philosophy. Let us now try to characterize in more detail the irreducible metaphoricity in question. To sum up the conditions of impossibility of a philosophical metaphorology, let us cite the following lengthy passage:

> Metaphor remains, in all its essential characteristics, a classical philosopheme, a metaphysical concept. It is therefore enveloped in the field that a general metaphorology of philosophy would seek to dominate. Metaphor has been issued from a network of philosophemes which themselves correspond to tropes or to figures, and these philosophemes are contemporaneous to or in a systematic solidarity with these tropes or figures. The stratum of "tutelary" tropes (*tropes "instituteurs"*), the layer of "primary" philosophemes (assuming that the quotation marks will serve as a sufficient precaution here), cannot be dominated. It cannot dominate itself, cannot be dominated by what it itself has engendered, has made to grow on its own soil, supported on its own base. Therefore, it gets "carried away" each time that one of its products — here, the concept of metaphor — attempts in vain to include under its own law the totality of the field to which the product belongs. If one wished to conceive and to class all

the metaphorical possibilities of philosophy, one metaphor, at least, always would remain excluded, outside the system: the metaphor, at the very least, without which the concept of metaphor could not be constructed, or, to syncopate an entire chain of reasoning, the metaphor of metaphor. This extra metaphor, remaining outside the field that it allows to be circumscribed, extracts or abstracts itself from this field, thus subtracting itself as a metaphor less. By virtue of what we might entitle, for economical reasons, tropic supplementarity, since the extra turn of speech becomes the missing turn of speech, the taxonomy or history of philosophical metaphors will never make a profit. The state or status of the complement will always be denied to the interminable *dehiscence* of the supplement . . . The field is never saturated. (*M*, 219–220)

Let us recall that both metaphor and concept are philosophical concepts. If a general metaphorology claims that all concepts are worn out metaphors then the same must be true of the philosophical concept of metaphor. Yet, this metaphor of metaphor must remain unthematized if a general metaphorology is at all to succeed (and thus to fail). The metaphor of metaphor is therefore the "founding" trope of the project of a metaphorology. As a tutelary or instituting trope, as a "first" philosopheme, as a "defining trope" (*M*, 255), as Derrida also calls it, the metaphor of metaphor forms a system with a chain of other such "archaic" tropes, giving the character of a "natural" language to the so-called "founding" concepts of philosophy (*theoria, eidos, logos,* etc.). But, asks Derrida:

can these defining tropes that are prior to all philosophical rhetoric and that produce philosophemes still be called metaphors? (*M*, 255)

A concern with the founding concepts of the entire history of philosophy does not coincide with the work of the philologist, etymologist or classical historian of philosophy, nor with that of the rhetorician of philosophy. In other words, the exhibition of the defining tropes of the founding concepts of philosophy, such as the metaphor of metaphor, neither proclaims the literary or poetic nature of philosophy nor generalizes metaphor as a figure. The Nietzschean "generalization of metaphoricity by putting into *abyme* one determined metaphor," Derrida notes, "is possible only if one takes the risk of a continuity between the metaphor and the concept" (*M*, 262). Indeed, such a generalization of metaphor may well signify the *parousia* of the proper and the concept. Insofar as the investigation into the tropological movements at the basis of the grounding concepts of philosophy lends itself to a generalization, it is one which will deconstitute the borders of the propriety of philosophemes.

Of this generalization, Derrida remarks in *Dissemination*, that "since everything becomes metaphorical, there is no longer any literal meaning and, hence, no longer any metaphor either" (*D*, 258). What is being generalized here is neither the proper nor the improper, neither metaphor nor concept. On the contrary, it is something that explodes "the reassuring opposition of the metaphoric and the proper, the opposition in which the one and the other have never done anything but reflect and refer to each other in their radiance" (*M*, 270–271). The generalization hinted at by the metaphor of metaphor – general metaphoricity – is that of the logic of contamination and of the contamination of the logical distinction between concept and figure. Therefore, what is thus generalized can no longer be designated by the philosophical names of metaphor, trope, or figure, much less by the philosophical name of concept. In short, the metaphor of metaphor, or more generally, the founding tropes of the founding concepts, are not strictly speaking, tropes. As Derrida asks in "Plato's Pharmacy," how could the heart of all metaphoricity be a simple metaphor? Hence, Derrida's recourse to Fontanier's notion of catachresis in order to characterize the instituting tropes or the primary (*de 'premier degré'*) metaphors as the "nontrue metaphors that opened philosophy". (*M*, 259) Indeed, these "forced metaphors" or catachreses are none other than violently creative, tropological movements which, within language, found the values of propriety. For the same reason for which the metaphor of metaphor is a *mise en abime* of the concept of metaphor – the absence of any ultimate concept of which this metaphor would be the metaphor of – the metaphor of metaphor is also a catachrestic production of concepts (and, subsequently, of metaphors of these concepts). Consequently, the metaphor of metaphor is a nontrue metaphor, a "philosophical phantom" of metaphor (*M*, 258) at the basis of the philosophical values of propriety, conceptuality, Being, etc., as well as their negations, impropriety, figurality (metaphor), nothingness, etc.

In the essay "The *Retrait* of Metaphor," Derrida advances his elaboration of the structure of metaphoricity (or rather "quasi-metaphoricity" as he calls it here) by analysing a tropic movement which is complementary to the violent catachrestic production we have outlined. In this essay, the articulation that is said to be more originary than the distinction of metaphor and concept, that splits, intersects and recuts it, is analysed in terms of the Heideggerian notion of trait (*Zug*). The trait, writes Derrida, "is [for the difference between metaphor and concept] their common origin and the seal of their alliance, remaining in this singular and different from them, if a trait could be something, could be properly and fully originary."[21] Yet, the quasi-metaphoricity of the trait through which a relation or reference in general is traced, by which something *can* come to the fore in the first place, also implies an originary withdrawal, a *retrait* or retreat of the trait. Consequently, within the catachrestic production of the instituting nontrue tropes metaphoricity does not reveal itself as such. On the contrary, because the trait is by essence *retrait*, the act of instituting, grounding, and defining inaugurated by the "first" tropes is self-effacing. It is by the *retrait* of the trait that the originary tropic movements of metaphoricity permit something like the proper, the concept, Being, etc., to come forth as the very obliteration of their relations to the trait.

At this point we will reflect upon what Derrida's inquiries into the question of metaphor aim at. As is well known, the problematic of the trait for Heidegger is linked to the question of Being. The trait of Being reveals itself in its very withdrawal. Now we have seen that the question of metaphoricity is that of the generalization of something anterior to what is traditionally considered to be general and universal. It concerns the general conditions (and limits) of generalization. By tying the problem of this more "originary" general to the problematic of the trait as *retrait*, Derrida makes it clear that this more "primary" general – beyond and at the root of the distinction of the proper and the improper, the concept and metaphor, the literal and the figural – cannot be a more proper general. It cannot be exhibited as such. Moreover, by linking the problematic of this anterior generality to the Heideggerian notion of the *Zug* as *Entzug*, Derrida shows that his exploration of metaphoricity is also an attempt to come to grips with the question of Being. More precisely, it is an undertaking that inquires into the generality of that which is most general and proper – the generality of Being. It is an attempt to link in one non-phenomenologizable synthesis, the general or universal and Being. From everything that has thus far been said, it should be clear that the linking of Being to the no-longer-metaphysical concept of quasi-metaphoricity does not promulgate, in a Nietzschean or Renanean fashion, a metaphorical origin of Being. The latter enterprise is grounded in etymological empiricism. What we are dealing with here is, on the contrary, a *sort of* transcendental undertaking. To show this, let us briefly comment on the following passage from *Writing and Difference*:

> Every philology which allegedly reduces the *meaning* of Being to the mataphorical origin of the *word* "Being," whatever the historical (scientific) value of its hypothesis, misses the history of the meaning of Being. This history is to such an extent the history of a liberation of being as concerns the determined existent, that one may come to think of the eponymous existent of Being, for example, *respiration*, as one existent among others.

Renan and Nietzsche, for example, refer to respiration as the etymological origin of the word *Being* when they wish to reduce the meaning of what they take to be a concept – the indeterminate generality of Being – to its modest metaphorical origin . . . Thus is explained all of empirical history, except precisely for the essential, that is, the thought that respiration and *non-respiration are*, for example. And are in a determined way, among other ontic determinations. Etymological empiricism, the hidden root of all empiricism, explains everything except that at a given moment the metaphor has been thought *as* metaphor, that is, has been ripped apart as the veil of Being. This moment is the emergence of the thought of Being itself, the very movement of metaphoricity. For this emergence still, and always, occurs beneath an *other* metaphor. As Hegel says somewhere, empiricism always forgets, at the very least, that it employs the words to be. Empiricism is thinking *by* metaphor without thinking the metaphor *as such*. (*WD*, 138–139, slightly modified translation)

The fallacy of empiricism as outlined here affects both the general project of the philosophical metaphorology and the attempt to explain philosophy (and the question of Being) by its linguistic, literary, or metaphorical origins. The enterprise of reducing philosophical concepts to figures of speech, tropes, and other particular rhetorical operations amounts to a facto-genetic description, with the help of available empirical tools, of what by right absolutely resists these empirical linguistic roots. Without denying the utility and legitimacy of such reductions, "such attempts, however, would have their full value only insofar as they would be conducted with the certainty that everything is spoken of then *except* the reduction *itself, except* the origin of philosophy and history *themselves* and as such," writes Derrida (*OG*, 132). Indeed, what the empirical etymologism and/or tropologism cannot account for is the rift in the finite linguistic and tropological figure through which it designates nothing less than Being. In *Writing and Difference* we read: "Supposing that the word 'Being' is derived from a word meaning 'respiration' (or any other determined thing), no etymology or philology – as such, and as determined sciences – will be able to account for the thought for which 'respiration' (or any other determined thing) becomes a determination of Being among others" (*WD*, 139). What all these empirical approaches cannot hope to account for is the interruption of metaphor by the thought of metaphor as such, by which rift metaphor *as such*, or metaphoricity, becomes thinkable as the movement of Being itself. Without the thinking of metaphor *as* metaphor, one particular metaphor could not be raised to the status of naming Being as that which renders metaphors mere existents. Being, then, is absolutely resistant to metaphor, as Heidegger claimed, because (as the ontico-ontological difference) it corresponds to the very moment of metaphoricity itself. Consequently, to investigate metaphoricity as Derrida does is to continue, in a certain way, the Heideggerian questioning of Being. As we have already explained, both Heidegger's exploration of the fundamental structure of the logos, the as-structure, and Derrida's exploration of the irreducible metaphoricity of the founding tropes, represent debates with the much older problem of the analogy of being, and are thus related to the question of Being as such, and particularly insofar as this question pertains to the being of language. For Heidegger, the being of language resides in the as-structure characteristic of the logos; for Derrida, it coincides within the context of this given problematics, with metaphoricity as previously outlined.

But to the extent that Heidegger's notion of Being, according to Derrida, is also a proper name, a proper unified meaning outside the system of differences and metaphors that it makes possible – in other words, still a metaphysical concept – Derrida's inquiry into quasi-metaphoricity is an attempt to more radically displace the question of Being. Derrida achieves this displacement by (1) demonstrating that Being, the proper, etc., does not escape the chain and system of differences (*Il n'y a pas de hors-texte*) and (2) by "deepening" the question of Being through a systematic exploration of the movements of quasi-metaphoricity that it designates. Schematically speaking, the first demonstration takes place in "White Mythology," whereas "The *Retrait* of Metaphor" addresses the second aspect of the displacement. In "White Mythology" everything developed with respect to the proper name of the sun as implicated within the general law of metaphorical value also applies to Being. If the proper name of the sun *can* give rise to heliotropic metaphors, if the sun, this "nonmetaphorical prime mover of metaphor, the father of all figures" (*M*, 243) can be said to "'sow,' then its name is inscribed in a system of relations that constitute it. This name is no longer the proper name of a unique thing which metaphor would *overtake*; it already has begun to say the multiple, divided origin of all seed" (*M*, 244). Similarly, the proper and the essence of Being can, as seen, be said analogously Being is not One or unique: "the determination of the truth of Being in presence passes through the detour of . . . [a] tropic system" (*M*, 254). Although the concept in its universality is irreducible to metaphor, figure, or trope, its status *as* concept (its intelligibility and universality) hinges on its possibility of lending itself to metaphorization. General metaphoricity, or quasi-metaphoricity is the name for that possibility that inaugurates the concept's universality. At the same time it limits this universality by virtue of its generality, a generality that cannot be subsumed under universality inasmuch as the latter has grown on its soil.

The displacement of the question of Being is thus twofold. On the one hand, it appears to be inscribed in a system of differences; on the other, it appears to be a function of quasi-metaphoricity. In withdrawing, the forthcoming trait makes it possible for something such as Being to come forth as the proper name *hors-texte* for a non-metaphorical origin of metaphors. Metaphoricity names the "origin" of an unavoidable illusion, the illusion of an origin. Obviously enough, the "origin" of what has always been construed as origin can no longer be understood in terms of origin. The concept of origin (*archē*) is a founding concept of philosophy. The instituting tropes which, in a catachrestic movement, give birth to that concept cannot be original, first, or elementary in the sense of origin, nor derivative of the founding trope's act of founding. To cite again:

> Supposing that we might reach it (touch it, see it, comprehend it?) this tropic and prephilosophical resource could not have the archeological simplicity of a proper origin, the virginity of a history of beginnings. (*M*, 229)

Yet, there is still one more reason why the instituting tropes cannot have the simplicity of an origin, a reason which may be coeval with the founding trope's production of the concept of origin. This reason concerns the plurality of the tutelary tropes:

> . . . Metaphors. The word is written only in the plural. If there were only one possible metaphor, the dream at the heart of philosophy, if one could reduce their play to the circle of a family or a group of metaphors, that is, to one "central," "fundamental," "principal" metaphor, there would be no more true metaphor, but only, through the one true metaphor, the assured legibility of the proper. (*M*, 268)

This plurality of the defining tropes, of the irreducible metaphoricity, contributes to characterize in depth the sort of transcendental status of this pre-philosophical resource. The irreducible metaphoricity of the instituting tropes, of tropes which are not preceded by any proper sense or meaning, but which are the "origin" of sense or meaning, is essentially of the order of syntax. The last chapter of "White Mythology," which demonstrates that an exploration of the founding tropes of philosophy cannot be a meta-philosophical enterprise comparable to Bachelard's meta-poetics, opposes this value of syntax to the primarily *thematic* and semantic understanding of metaphor in traditional philosophy and poetics:

> Now, it is because the metaphoric is plural from the outset that it does not escape syntax. (*M*, 268)

The inextricable plurality and residuary syntax of the metaphoricity of the founding tropes leads to a dissemination of the metaphorical in the pre-logical, within which metaphor destroys itself. It is a destruction which "passes through a supplement of syntactic resistance, through everything (for example in modern linguistics) that disrupts the opposition of the semantic and the syntactic, and especially the philosophical hierarchy that submits the latter to the former" (M, 270). How, then are we to characterize the irreducible metaphoricity to which a destruction of the philosophical discourses on metaphor gives rise, i.e., an operation which follows a certain logic of these discourses to its necessary conclusion, and which recognizes the necessity of marking off that result from its homonym within the discourse of philosophy? The irreducible metaphoricity of the instituting tropes of philosophy is to be characterized as a *structure* of instituting, of grounding, of defining, which *qua* structure, and by virtue of its plural and residuary syntax, eliminates itself as origin. This self-destruction of metaphor, although similar in so many ways to the Hegelian *Aufhebung* of metaphor in the parousia of meaning, is totally different from it, if for nothing other than the absence of all teleology. This self-destruction of metaphor allows Derrida to write: "Metaphor, then, always carries its death within itself." (M, 271). This death within metaphor reaches beyond the traditional opposition of dead or living metaphors, that is to say, beyond the grid within which Ricoeur attempted to corner Derrida.

Metaphoricity, because of its structure and the problems it accounts for, is thus not to be confused with its empirical (philosophic or literary) homologue. In Derrida's sense, metaphoricity is a structure of referral that accounts for the possibility and impossibility of the philosophical discourse, yet not insofar as this discourse may be construed as literary (sensible, fictional, etc.) because of its inevitable recourse to metaphor and poetic devices, but *insofar as it is a general discourse on the universal*. The literary dimension of the philosophical text is by nature, incapable of pointing to, let alone accounting for, this constituting nonorigin of philosophy.

Seen in this perspective, metaphoricity is a transcendental concept, *of sorts*. Although it is likely that the term we shall propose will meet with a good bit of disapproval, we will call metaphoricity a *quasi-transcendental*. By calling it *quasi-* we wish to indicate that metaphoricity has a structure and a function similar to the transcendental without actually being one.

In order to conclude, let us briefly elaborate on what we understand by such a notion. It certainly makes sense here to define the quasi-transcental by demarcating it from that to which it seems to correspond in Heidegger's philosophy, from what we would like to call *finite or immanent transcendentals*. Until further systematic and technical clarification of the notion of a finite transcendental and its difference from Kant's *a priori* forms of objective knowledge — forms which characterize the finite subjectivity and reason of the human subject of cognition — we shall call finite those structures in Heidegger's fundamental ontology that characterize *Dasein*. Since *Dasein* is, according to the Heidegger of *Being and Time*, the exemplary locus of the understanding of the meaning of Being, i.e. of the *transcendens* pure and simple, the finite transcendentals are those existential structures which constitute Being as understood and interpreted Being. It is clear that such a determination of the transcendental in Heidegger's thought hinges upon Heidegger's concept of finitude (insofar as it pertains to *Dasein* or man (*Mensch*)) and in particular, after the so called *Kehre*, upon Being itself, although the term "finitude" is, as Birault has shown in his excellent study on Heidegger, no longer mentioned after Heidegger's *Kant and the Problem of Metaphysics*.[22] It is a concept which has little or no relation to the Judeo-Christian idea of finitude. As Birault has demonstrated, Heidegger's concept of finitude does not coincide with the ontico-ontological idea of a *summun ne-ens* in its difference from a *summen ens*. Nor can it be conceived of in terms of the classical or modern forms of the *ouk on* or the *me on*. Rather, Heidegger's finite concept of the transcendental is a function of his investigation into the structures of the *logos of* Being, whether this investigation be pursued through the analytic of *Dasein* or, as after the *Kehre*, through Being itself.

Whereas Heidegger's discovery of the finite transcendentals is the result of his philosophizing logic — the *logos* of Being, Derrida's quasi-transcendentals are a function of his inquiry into the conditions of the possibility and impossibility of the logic of philosophy as a discursive enterprise. (Discursive is meant here to include the conceptual, rhetorical, argumentative and textual order of philosophy as the thought of unity.) The quasi-transcendentals — metaphoricity, for instance, upon which philosophy's universality is grounded are no longer *simply* transcendentals because they represent neither *a priori* structures of the subjective cognition of objects, nor the structures of *Dasein*'s understanding of Being. The quasi-transcendentals are, on the contrary, the conditions of possibility and impossibility concerning the very conceptual difference between subject and object and even between *Dasein* and Being. Nor are quasi-transcendentals finite, as one could prove by pointing to Derrida's persistent critique of the notion of finitude. Instead of being situated within the traditional conceptual space that stretches from the pole of the finite to that of the infinite, quasi-transcendentals,

more importantly, are at the border of the space of the organized contamination which they open up. Unlike the finite transcendental structures which preserve the difference between the *a priori* and the
empirical order (though for Heidegger, Being is clearly nothing exterior
to the existent) because they represent answers to *fundamental* questions (onto-phenomenological or not) concerning the *essence* of Being,
the quasi-transcendentals are situated at the margin of the distinction
of the transcendental and the empirical. They reinscribe "the opposition of fact and principle, which, in all its metaphysical, ontological,
and transcendental forms, has always functioned within the system of
the question *what is*" (*OG*, 75). Therefore, the quasi-transcendentals
cannot be said to account by more *radically* fundamental concepts, say,
by a more radical concept of presence (*Anwesen*), for the presence
(*Präsenz*) of metaphysics. By dislocating the opposition of fact and principle, that is by accounting for this conceptual difference *as* difference,
the quasi-transcendentals, instead of being more radical, seem to be
characterized by a certain irreducible erratic contingency. This contingency of the Derridean transcendentals, their aleatory heterogenity,
is, however, nothing less than that of the structural constraints that
simultaneously open up and close philosophy's argumentative discur-
sivity. The question of the quasi-transcendental, of quasi-metaphoricity
in this case, is a judiciary question in a new sense. Instead of inquiring
into the *a priori* and logical credentials of philosophical discourse,
Derrida's heterology is the exhibition of a law that is written on the
tinfoil of the mirrors between which thought can either maintain the
separation of fact and principle in the endless reflection of each other,
or else sublate them into a finite synthesis.

15. From the Primordiality of Absence to the Absence of Primordiality: Heidegger's Critique of Derrida

John D. Caputo

The task which Professor Silverman has set for this session — Heidegger's critique of Derrida — is itself something of a reversal and requires a certain violence. We are asked to take up the matter of Derrida from the standpoint of Heidegger. The movement is not the historical one, from Heidegger to Derrida, but a critical-philosophical one, from Derrida to Heidegger.

This is a task of the treatest importance, but one that I do not engage without a certain hesitation. For I admire Derrida's attitude towards Heidegger, which is at once critical yet appreciative, productive not merely reproductive. Derrida maintains the momentum of Heidegger's critique of metaphysics. His "exorbitant" method (G, 227/158),[1] as he himself requires of method, opens up a reading of the Heideggerian text. It is at a far remove from the epigonism and bad repetitions of the Heidegger literati who talk like Heidegger talks, who repeat what Heidegger says, and who regard every criticism of Heidegger as a misunderstanding. Derrida's reading is not a mere doubling of the Heideggerian text but a thoughtful exercise in its own right which stands in relationship to Heidegger as Heidegger himself stood in relation to his own masters and antecedents. The violence which Derrida lays on Heidegger is precisely like Heidegger's own violence towards the pseudo-Scotus, Kant, Parmenides, Hölderlin and the rest.

What Heidegger and Derrida have in common above all is a great destructive unrest, an enourmous energy for breaking through the commonplace and the familiar, the received interpretations, the common wisdom. They each know how to open up a text so that we can hear – or read – it anew. Together they direct a tremendous critical energy on the encrusted dogmas of Western metaphysics. They expose the strategems by which metaphysics seeks to comfort itself with dreams of presence and plenitude, and the various devices it employs to insulate itself from limit, negativity, impermanence, death and difference. They disagree in an important and, to my mind, decisive way about the place of Nietzsche in this history (G, 206/143), but they otherwise agree that the history of metaphysics holds sway from Heraclitus to Husserl.

I particularly admire the works which lead up to and include what Barbara Johnson calls the great "biblioblitz"[2] of 1967 (*Husserl's "Origin of Geometry;" Writing and Difference; Speech and Phenomena; Of Grammatology*), and it is this early framework of Derrida's thinking that I will discuss. My focus in these remarks is upon the dialogue of Husserl, Heidegger and Derrida, and in particular upon the issue of what Derrida calls the "transcendental signified" (G, 33/20). I regard Derrida's critique of Husserl to be among his most important achievements, and I want in a sense to join the momentum of Derrida's critique of Husserl, to rejoin it in such a way as to find in Husserl the suggestion of a rejoinder, a suggestion which is acted upon by Heidegger himself.

Husserl provides Derrida with a paradigm case for the application of his deconstructive method. If Husserl talks of first-hand seeing, the things themselves, presence in the flesh, fulfilled meanings and the like, Derrida sees in this a host of promises which cannot be kept. The metaphysics of presence for Derrida is always a hollow vow, a claim upon which metaphysics cannot deliver. Even when metaphysics boasts the loudest about the presence of Being, or rather precisely then, Derrida finds that it resorts to a substitute for presence, an *Ersatz*, a supplement which must do duty at some critical point where presence fails. Husserl illustrates this so perfectly that the critique of Husserl appears to have been the birthplace of Derrida's method. For the principle of principles is precisely a promissory note upon which Husserl cannot make good. The perceptual object, contrary to Husserl's repeated claims, is not a pure presence, not primordially and corporeally present in person (*leiblich*), but precisely a complex interplay of presence and absence. The perceptual object is a presence which has been thoroughly patched up by protention and retention in order to be rendered suitable for sensory presentation. For Derrida's Husserl the perceptual present must first be made presentable. And indeed as Husserl himself explicitly points out, there is *more* to the intentional object than what is present.[3]

Now this more, since it is not given, must be supplied (*supplié* is the Derridean-Rousseauean term). What is present must be supplemented lest it fail to appear. Husserl says this in so many words, which is why Derrida's critique illustrates so well what deconstruction is supposed to be. The supplementing of presence is at work in the Husserlian text, contrary to Husserl's stated wishes, his *vouloir-dire*, his declared intentions; but it nonetheless gets said – or written. As Prof. Spivak says in the "Introduction" to the English translation of *De la grammatologie*, Husserl seems to be an unusually astute grammatologist and an unusually resolute suppressor of his own suggestions (G, 1i).

And what is true of Husserl's analysis of perception is no less true of the analysis of intersubjectivity. The other person is not present in person but is precisely absent, and his absence must be compensated for by an act of empathetic supplementation, by constituting the other as other via a kind of transcendental transference from the sphere of ownness. The other is not encountered but is absent, not perceived but ap-perceived, not overtly present but a concealed absence. Presence is always infiltrated and undermined by absence, and perception must always be supplemented by ap-perception. Intentionality must make up the difference by always already intending more – for not enough is originally delivered.[4]

This superlative critique of Husserl which I have only sketched here is one which any Heideggerian could embrace, were it not for the *direction* in which it is taken by Derrida. For Derrida concludes from it that there is no phenomenon, that the principle of principles is an illusion, that "experience" is a dream of presence (G, 72/49). But I want to argue that this deconstruction needs itself to be deconstructed, that what Derrida would have shown, although this is not what he wishes to say, is that there is indeed a primordial phenomenon, but it is not, as Husserl mistakenly supposed, sheer effulgence and self-showing but rather an interplay of presence and absence. Derrida would have shown, although he declares the opposite, that there is a primordial phenomenon, but that it is not merely given *simpliciter* but is rather a giving which is equiprimordially a withholding. Derrida would have shown that beneath the giving of presence there is always a play of withdrawal. But according to Derrida's own declared intentions the result of this deconstruction is only the breakdown of all notions of primordiality and phenomenality.

Derrida has isolated the failure of presence which belongs in a more radical phenomenology, but he has mistaken its import. Instead of being led by this analysis to a more radical, that is, a more merciless and comfortless sense of the phenomenon and primordiality than was possible for classical phenomenology, he is led only to the conclusion of the death of primordial experience. Instead of finding in his analysis a break-through to a more essential realm, he consigns every "more essential realm" to the metaphysics of presence. Instead of being drawn beyond phenomenology to a more radical alethiology, in the manner of Heidegger's radical deconstruction of phenomenology, he is led instead to deny *aletheia* (G, 405 – 6/286). Thus the debate which I am posing here between Heidegger and Derrida has to do with their competing decon-structions of Husserlian phenomenology.

Let us return then to the critique of Husserl, but let us not lose Derrida's momentum. Let us hold fast to the failure of presence at work in phenomenology which Derrida isolates, but let us repeat this analysis by retrieving it (*wiederholen*) and making it say what Derrida does not mean to say. To this end, I propose that we draw upon another Husserlian theme, one which bears directly upon the texts which Derrida wants to deconstruct, and that is the issue of what Husserl calls "transcendence." By this route we will be led to the question of the transcendental signified.

In Husserl, the absence which infiltrates the phenomenon, and which Derrida has so pitilessly flushed out, is testimony to its transcendence, that is, to that otherness which is irreducible to con-stitutive consciousness. Transcendence is the limit of philosophy for Husserl, the stone wall which philosophy cannot surpass, question or put in doubt. The task of phenomenology is to serve transcendence: not to put it on trial but to supply it with an account of itself. It is not the belief in transcendence which divides the natural attitude from transcendental phenomenology, but rather the naïveté and unreflec-tive spontaneity with which that belief is embraced in the natural atti-tude. The transcendental philosopher knows that transcendence is not some kind of miracle, some extraordinary explosion on the perceptual screen; it is rather the correlate of carefully and harmoniously enacted acts of conscious life, the details of which he is prepared to give an account. Husserl had no intention of reducing the real thing to the con-tents of consciousness, of making it into a mere being of reason, but rather of explicating its constitution.[5]

And the way in which Husserl went about showing the transcen-dence of the real thing, given the limits of his metaphysical presup-positions, is penetrating. For he says that it is precisely insofar as consciousness is unable to encompass the phenomenon, to get it within the full grasp of intuitive life, that the phenomenon shows its transcen-dence. The conscious correlate of the thing itself, insofar as the latter is real and other than consciousness, is precisely the impotence of consciousness in the face of it. It is precisely insofar as the thing itself eludes and shatters the aspirations of intuitive consciousness that it is taken to be real. In other words, absence is the indicator, the transcendental clue to reality, transcendence. Transcendence is disclosed by absence. The transcendent is defined negatively, privatively, differentially, absentially: as that which is not present, not given up to the eye of intuition. The real is what resists the grasp of intuition, which refuses to give itself up to its omnivorousness. This very breakdown of presence necessitates on the noetic side having recourse to protention and retention, and it is that necessity which bears witness to the thing's transcendence. It is precisely because the object cannot be seized by intuition that it is taken for real, precisely because it exceeds and transcends the reach of intuition that it is taken to be other. Were it possible to make it fully present, we would not believe that it exists, except of course as a part of my own conscious stream. The complete transparency of a phenomenon, the total domination of it by consciousness, is the defining characteristic of its immanence for Husserl. The only things which have such immanence and transparency are my own *Erlebnisse*; transcendent things do not.[6]

You see now how we are going to try to make Derrida say what he does not want to say, to make him own up to something transcendent, to direct the bite of his critique of Husserl into his own hide. For as I see it Heidegger's rival deconstruction of Husserlian phenomenology in fact followed up this clue of the "transcendence" of the phenomenon. The irreducibility of the phenomenon to intuitive consciousness in Husserl becomes in Heidegger the interplay of concealment and un-concealment. The failure of presence which in Husserl is the clue to the transcendence of the real becomes in Heidegger the withdrawal of Being. The concealment of Being in Heidegger is its withdrawal from presence or manifestness, and that is the basis of Heidegger's assertion of its primacy over thought. The task of thought is to wait upon and heed the hidden movements of Being, to serve its needs and be at its disposal, to serve and preserve, to shelter and shepherd. Thus the failure of presence which Derrida flushes out in Husserl is for Husserl himself testimony to the transcendence of the phenomenon, and for Heidegger it is the clue to the primacy of Being over thought. Now I want to show how Heidegger and Derrida are led in opposite directions by their respective deconstructions of Husserl's phenomenology. To do this I want to contrast the import of the notion of withdrawal in Heidegger's later writings with the theory of the supplement and the denial of the transcendental signified in Derrida.

In Heidegger's later writings, as is well known by now, the history of metaphysics is more fundamentally the history of Being in which the various senses of Being that have emerged across the epochs are made possible by a sending in which Being itself withdraws. Metaphysical thinking is a certain preoccupation with present entities to the neglect of Being itself. It seeks to map out their dominant characteristics which Heidegger calls variously beingness (*Seîendheît*) as opposed to Being, or Being as opposed to Being, or Being as opposed to *Ereignis*. But however it is articulated, the point is that metaphysics remains oblivious of the essential withdrawal in virtue of which presence is made present. Metaphysics preoccupies itself with what is given to the neglect of the withholding in virtue of which and *as* which this giving takes place.

If metaphysics itself occurs as a certain stepping back from beings to being-ness (or Being-as-presence), the "overcoming" of metaphysics consists in a second, more radical step back from being-ness (or Being-as-presence) to Being or *Ereignis*. But the troublesome question is, what sense can an "overcoming" of metaphysics have in a doctrine of the radical withdrawal of Being? Obviously this cannot consist in some kind of breakthrough into a sphere of pure presence, as if the step back were in fact a kind of Platonic ascent − a step *up* instead of a step *back*. On the contrary, it is described in the minutes of the "Seminar" on "Time and Being" as an awakening *to* the withdrawal of Being *as* a withdrawal, as a matter of taking up one's stand *in* this absence. But the withdrawal of Being does not cease in this moment of "awakening."[7]

Human Dasein is drawn along by this withdrawal, drawn out into it, rather the way one is drawn out by a receding tide. Dasein is swept along by, caught up in, this receding movement. But there are two different senses or levels in Heidegger's writings in which this withdrawal takes place. On the one level, this being-drawn means that Dasein is "taken in" by the withdrawal, caught up within the network of manifest entities, tinkers with the toys of the micro-electronic revolution, in oblivion of the deeper destiny which is at work in Western history. On this level, the withdrawal means Dasein's own oblivion of the withdrawal. That is what can be overcome, and it is overcome by awakening *to* the withdrawal *as* a withdrawal. Dasein understands that the history of metaphysics is a revelation which is made possible only by a more essential concealment. But the withdrawal itself, the withdrawal in the second and more radical sense of self-concealment of Being (Being, *Ereignis*) persists; it is not somehow extirpated or erased. Thus, far from being an entry into an upper world or an intuition of pure presence, Dasein's awakening consists in entering into that withdrawal all the more primordially. Metaphysical thinking is overcome but the withdrawal of Being persists. It is recognized for what it is. We stand in it and acknowledge its sway. What has been overcome is the naîveté, the obliviousness of metaphysical thought. The point of what Heidegger calls thought is not to overcome or lay aside this withdrawal but to enter into it in a more radical way. When Dasein is "awakened" it is not "enlightened," suffused with light, but rather alerted to the bottomless depths of the darkness and the withdrawal.

The withdrawal of Being is a drawing out of Dasein which, if its lead is followed cautiously and discerningly, leads Dasein out of the illusions of representational thought. Dasein is drawn out beyond its own representations into the self-withdrawing movement of Being or *Ereignis*. And it is here that the shattering of subjectivity takes place. Dasein experiences that its manifold representation are so many ways that it has been taken in by the withdrawal or holding back of Being. It experiences that it is caught up in a movement which does not dominate and in which everything depends upon the movement of the matter itself (*Sache*), the depth movement which moves across the epochs, concealing itself as it sends forth its emmisaries.

The response of Dasein to the transcendence/withdrawal of Being is what Heidegger calls *Gelassenheit*: letting go, letting be: that movement in which Dasein, having let go of its own representations, releases itself into the essential movement which is at work in Western history. *Gelassenheit* is the experience of the power which overpowers Dasein, not by its violence, but by its retreat and withdrawal. That is why Heidegger calls *Gelassenheit* "openness to the Mystery."[8] It lets the mystery be *as* a mystery, experiences it *in* its mysteriousness, lets it hold sway precisely as a withdrawal. And it is this moment of *Gelassenheit* that I locate the most extreme divergence of Derrida from Heidegger. In *Gelassenheit*, man is de-centered in favor of a centering on Being or *Ereignis* as the gentle power which withdraws. Drawn out of himself by the withdrawal of Being, Dasein under-stands – stands under, stands open to – the more profound recesses and inexhaustible depths from which things emerge. The illusion of human mastery is dispelled and the rule of the abyss, of *Ab-wesen* and *Ab-grund*, is established. Dasein learns in *Gelassenheit* that it belongs to something which exceeds (which "transcends") Dasein. The exceeding of Dasein by Being is the receding of Being from Dasein. The deconstructed meaning of transcendence is withdrawal, and of constitution is *Gelassenheit*.

But in Derrida's hands, the whole import and significance of the failure of presence first established in the Husserl-critique undergoes a sea change, the end result of which is an almost total metaphoric reversal focussing precisely on the denial of the *Sache selbst* under the name of the transcendental signified.[9] For Derrida the failure of metaphysics to keep the promise of presence means that we are left holding a kind of grammatological bag, a shell, a web of signs, a differential system. The absential dimension is not the withdrawal *of* Being but the simple failure of Being to make itself felt. Absence is not the gentle power of withdrawal, the mystery concealed within things, but the vacuity of signs, the systematic displacement of things with their place-holders, the necessity of the supplement, the substitute, writings. Derrida moves from the failure of presence, not into the transcendence and recessive mystery of things, but into the indefinite play of differential systems, of infinitely interchangeable interpretations. He proposes not the gentle openness of *Gelassenheit* which accedes to the mystery within things, but the violence of language. It is of course true that all representations are violent, a will to subdue things to our own proportions, but that only points to non-representational language which surrenders and yields itself up to the movement of withdrawal. This is not the language of man but of language itself, of *Sprache, la langue,* and it is not made possible by violence but by letting be.

But if the recognition of the *Sache selbst* does not belong to Derrida's *vouloir-dire,* one place where it gets itself said in spite of "Jacques" is the section in the *Grammatology* where he writes of the *"surprise"* of Rousseau. There is a logic of the supplement which overtakes Rousseau, which plays itself out in his discourse against Rousseau's wishes, so that, having degraded writing and supplementarity, Rousseau finds himself endorsing its essential necessity (G, 226−7/158). But is not this *sur-prise* the *Eingenommenheit* of language and Being of which Heidegger speaks?[10] Is this not the way that man is taken in by, taken under the control of, language and Being, which hold sway over human discourse? For Derrida himself Rousseau's surprise means that all discourse is caught up within a system of differences, that one sign defines another, that the whole plays itself out according to a logic which Rousseau cannot dominate. In this way Derrida thinks that things, that the matter itself, are indefinitely put off, de-ferred, and there remains only a network of signs in which we are all caught. But is not this *sur-prise* something more? Is not the *sur-prise* the way we are taken-in, or drawn-out, by the movement of with-drawal? Is not this *sur-prise* the way Being makes its mark on human discourse and makes light of human intentions? Is not this play the play of Being, of the abyss, the world-play which plays without why across the epochs?[11]

I would pinpoint the essential divergence of Derrida from Heidegger, and hence from the standpoint of Heidegger, the essential fault of Derrida, to lie in this metaphoric reversal and upheaval by means of which the Heideggerian theme of Dasein's belonging to and heeding

of the matter to be thought is overturned in favor of the play of substitutes and supplements, of masturbation and the hymen, of signs and
writings. In Derrida the matter itself has become, not an illusion, but
a supplement. But that is to mistake the import of ab-sence. For the
essential force of absence is to be an experience of Being. Absence
means *ab-esse*, being-away-from, Being itself in the mode of withdrawing. Absence, *Ab-wesen* belongs equiprimordially to *Wesen* itself as its
concealed depths, even as *lethe*, concealment, *Verborgenheit* belong to
the heart and core of *a-letheia*. Absence is Being's own withdrawal,
drawing us out of ourselves, beyond the comforting plenitude of the
world and into the abyss, into the power which overpowers us, by which
we are delivered over to a movement over which we have no lordship.
Far from delivering us over to signs and supplements and substitutes,
the movement of absence is an initiation into a sphere of primordiality
and aboriginality. And if it is true that such an origin is likewise a nonorigin, this is not because we have always and already to do with
derivatives, but because, in a genuine alethiology, the origin is always
already concealed and withdrawn. Instead of the substitute, Derrida
should speak of the aboriginal abyss; instead of the supplement, the
hidden depths; instead of masturbation, the primal birth of things in
lethe.

In the end, for Derrida, the Saussurean analysis of signs controls
the Heideggerian thought of withdrawal, and the Nietzschean play of
interpretations controls the philosophy of signs.[12] There is a wildness
to Derrida's play, a Dionysian frenzy. Derrida's "thought of the trace"
(G, 142/93) lacks the piety of thinking, for it is no longer in the service
of anything. Like a Kierkegaardian aestheticism it refuses to be bound
by anything but wants only to enjoy the play of differences (G, 62/42).
Like the "rotation method" described by Kierkegaard it wants to avoid
at all costs being bound, to deny all genuine "contact" and "experience,"
in order to savor indefinite substitution and interchangeability. For it
fears that anything else is the metaphysics of presence. Here the piety
of thought is overturned by a wild play of supplements. The nostalgia
for presence is countered, not by a readiness for anxiety and an openness to the mystery, but by the wholesale refusal of the matter for
thought.

In the end, for Derrida, the *Sache selbst*, the matter for thought,
the matter of withdrawal and drawing out, has become a version of
the fallacy of the transcendental signified. Thought lacks piety because
it lacks anything to serve — for what is there to serve, Derrida thinks,
but presence? But what if thought were to serve the withdrawal which
draws us out with it? Heidegger has broken the spell of the metaphysics

of presence precisely in order to hearken to the mystery within things, the recessive, withdrawn dimension within them in virtue of which things elude every scheme which representational thought can draw up. Heidegger has deconstructed metaphysics in order to make room for Being, for ~~Being~~, for *Ereignis*, for the matter to be thought. His deconstruction has all along been meant to free up the mystery of *aletheia*, to shatter the obstables in the way of our openness to the mystery.

When Heidegger still used the word *Wahrheit*, he liked to say that *Wahr-heit* meant *verwahren, wahren*, preserving or sheltering.[13] The task of thought is to preserve the matter itself from the destructive gaze of metaphysics, from the idols of conceptual thought: *eidos, ousia*, and the rest. He attacks the idolatry of metaphysics whose substitutes and supplements for the *Sache selbst* are counterfeits which representational thinking inevitably mints. In Heidegger's view it is presence itself which is the substitute devised by metaphysics to fill up the hollow, to cover over the withdrawal. Heidegger wants nothing to do with substitutes, not because of some Schwarzwaldian nostalgia for presence, but because he has always taught readiness for anxiety. He wants nothing to do with a violent language, not because of a longing for innocence, but because he wants to let the mystery be. His "readiness for anxiety" and "openness to the mystery" are meant to cultivate the withdrawal as a withdrawal so as to protect and shelter it from the supplements and illusions with which metaphysics seeks to cover it over. The whole point of Heidegger's thought has been to keep the wound of mortality and withdrawal open, and to keep open to it. But if in Derrida the ruses of metaphysics are exposed for what they are, nothing is thereby served or preserved. Instead, the experience of loss has become the loss of experience and the primordiality of absence and has been turned into the absence of primordiality.

16. Derrida and Heidegger

Thomas Sheehan

One might be tempted to engage in a Heideggerian critique of Derrida, if for no other reason than that there has long been a Derridian critique of Heidegger. From his early essays up through his more recent publications. Jacques Derrida has not ceased to take on Martin Heidegger, worrying his texts, unraveling and deconstructing them. The question in all of this might be: Has Derrida gotten Heidegger right?[1]

To be sure, Derrida's later discussions of Heidegger seem more muted and less polemical. In his 1980 Cérisy lecture published under the title *"D'un ton apocalyptique adopté naguère en philosophie,"* Derrida takes Heidegger less as an adversary and more as a silent partner-in-dialogue throughout a forty-page discussion of the themes of apocalypse and the end of philosophy. And in discussing Heidegger in the interview "Choreographies," published in *Diacritics* in 1982, Derrida seems to retract the charges he laid against Heidegger with regard to feminism and sexuality in *Éperons: Les styles de Nietzsche* and in *La vérité en peinture.*[2]

But even though the tone is more muted, what remains unchanged in these later discussions is Derrida's fundamental claim: that while he may not have replaced Heidegger, he has in some sense surpassed him insofar as his own thought of *différance* is anterior to Heidegger's ontological difference and the truth of being. In short, from beginning to end Heidegger remains not his model but his target, for, as Derrida has said, "How can one model oneself after what one deconstructs?"[3]

It seems time, then, to take a look at Derrida from Heidegger's viewpoint and to evaluate the results of what, up to now, has been a very one-sided dialogue. In attempting to do that, I will focus not on Derrida's work as a whole, for given the volume of his output, that would be altogether too immense a task. Rather I will concentrate only on his interpretations of Heidegger and, more narrowly still, on the one central theme of the relation of Dasein and being. First, I shall review Derrida's critique of Heidegger on that issue and make a brief reply. Secondly, I shall argue that in this confrontation – whether it be a question of Derrida's critique of Heidegger or a supposed Heideggerian critique of Derrida – anything like "criticism" in the usual sense of that term is very problematic, perhaps impossible and almost certainly beside the point. In that second part I shall remark on what reading is and how it relates to deconstruction, retrieval and what Derrida calls undecidability.

In all, I hope to show that despite all of his tendentious readings, and even misreadings, of Heidegger, Derrida has finally gotten it right on the major topics – for example, *différance*, trace, the abolition of the transcendental signifier – and that he has opened up one of the few viable roads for those who, having learned something from Heidegger, want to think after and beyond him.

But there is a paradox in all of this. On the one hand, there is the clear evidence that Derrida, at least in his early work, simply misunderstood the central issue of Heidegger's thought, the relation of being and Dasein. And on the other hand, there is the strong suspicion, for this reader at least, that when Derrida does get matters right and proposes some truly interesting issues for philosophical reflection, he does so in large measure by reinventing what is already to be found in Heidegger's thought.

That last assertion might sound like a peevish attempt to show that Heidegger "said everything already," but such is not my purpose at all. Things are much more complicated than that, and a simple comparison of texts in Heidegger and Derrida does not get to the point. In order to frame my reading of these two thinkers, I will propose, by way of an "exergue," a political tale about Heideggerians and Hegelians, and in particular about how, after the deaths of their respective masters, the disciples broke up into rival groups. Let me start with the Heideggerians.

It seems that for some time now, in fact beginning before Heidegger's death in 1976, his followers have tended to divide into two fairly definable groups over the issue of how to understand being (*das Sein*). One group emphasizes the presential dimension of being, even if it be a deferred presence, a future "new advent" of being-as-presence after the period of technology and the *Gestell*. The other group emphasizes the absential dimension of being: its receding character, its mysteriousness, the primacy of difference over any form of presential identity – in short, the primordiality of the abyss that Heidegger, using the Greek word, entitled *Lethe*. I call these groups, insofar as they are recognizable as such, the Right Heideggerians (those of being-as-presence) and the Left Heideggerians (those of being-as-absence), on a very rough analogy with the division that separated the Hegelians after Hegel's death in 1831. As regards the Heideggerians, both the Right and the Left seem to lay valid claims to being correct interpretations of Heidegger insofar as both discourses, the primacy of presence and the primacy of absence, appear to be found in Heidegger's texts. Or to put it another way: it may be impossible to decide whether Heidegger himself was a Right or a Left Heideggerian.

An analogous problem troubled Hegelians after Hegel died. Was Hegel essentially a Christian thinker, was his thought the speculative fulfillment of the core idea of Christianity, as many Right Hegelians maintained? Or was his thought, as Left Hegelians like Friedrich Richter held, fundamentally independent of Christianity – perhaps even atheistic – and thus in need of purification of its residual Christian elements so that it could fulfill itself in social praxis? Which of the two groups could rightly claim Hegel for themselves?

In an attempt to resolve the question Bruno Bauer in 1841 resorted to a crude subterfuge. Bauer himself had begun as a Right Hegelian but had moved to the Left after being swayed by David Strauss' arguments in his *Life of Jesus* (1835) that Christianity was based on myth. Bauer came around to the position that philosophical knowledge itself was the incarnation of the Absolute and therefore that Hegel had been, or should have been, an atheist. But instead of presenting his conviction directly, he pulled off a ruse, and a fairly complicated one at that. He wrote and circulated a tract that he passed off as the work of a pietist critic of Hegel. The booklet argued that Hegel was indeed an atheist, and it substantiated the charge with ample quotations from the published works. It bore the title *The Trumpet of the Last Judgment Against Hegel the Atheist and Anti-Christ: An Ultimatum*, and we imagine that among the philosophically unwashed it had some of the effect that Bauer intended. In any case the pamphlet made it appear that a pious soul, having seen through the Christian sheepskin in which the Right Hegelians clothed their atheistic master, was now banishing Hegel from the Christian fold, leaving him, as Bauer desired, to the Left Hegelians.[4]

Is it conceivable that Jacques Derrida has done something similar to Heidegger – no, not similar but much more audacious? If we study Derrida's early interpretations of Heidegger in *Marges de la philosophie* and *De la grammatologie*, we find him attributing to Heidegger positions that simply cannot be found on Heidegger's page. Deconstructionists, of course, might reply that what Heidegger explicitly intended and wrote is not the issue. The point, rather, is to reveal the unspoken secret that lies hidden within his texts, much as Heidegger himself did with any number of metaphysical thinkers. Be that as it may, Derrida claims to have discovered that Heidegger *malgré soi* is a victim of the very tradition he tried to overturn, that he is a hidden metaphysician replete with logocentrism and a teleology of being as pure presence. To put it succinctly, Derrida has exposed Heidegger to be a Right Heideggerian.

But let us imagine that Derrida, somewhat like Bruno Bauer, is pulling our philosophical leg. Allow for a moment that he is intentionally misrepresenting Heidegger as a Right Heideggerian, one who directly or indirectly reduces all absence to presence, precisely in order to rescue him from that camp and save him for an extreme Left position of being-as-absence under Derrida's own rubric of *différance*. Regardless of whether that was his intention, Derrida, I believe, has made such a convincing case for the ineluctability of asymptotic difference over against all systems of identity that he has destroyed the metaphysics of being-as-presence, including the Right Heideggerians' "new advent of being," once and for all. And in fact who except the most fervent and discalced of Heideggerians ever really believed in the mythical metaphysics of history starring that mysterious power called "Being," which, like a secular Yahweh, oversees the drama of the forgetfulness and recollection of Itself, mostly hiding Itself but occasionally revealing and salvifically sending Itself to select prophetic thinkers (posthumously canonized by Heidegger) as It leads the Qahal of the Chosen through the desert of technology to the New Jerusalem of pure present Being?

Derrida as Heidegger's Bruno Bauer? As improbable as this scenario seems, it does present itself as one way to make sense of the gross misreading of Heidegger that we find in Derrida's early work, a reading which Derrida has never recanted. Otherwise, with all due respect for the legitimate subversiveness of deconstructionist method, we would be constrained to charge him with the same critique that Sartre leveled against Georg Lukacs: that for all his brilliance Derrida, like Lukacs, had failed "to read [Heidegger], to grasp the meaning of the sentences one by one."[5]

I am quite sure that Derrida does not see his work in this light, and in fact, in good deconstructionist fashion, I am presenting this tale for a particular strategy of my own. But for a moment allow the analogy, improbable as it seems, to stand, and then take it a step further.

Bruno Bauer, we know, was hardly the last word among Left Hegelians. Once he had claimed Hegel for the Left, the real work began: that of showing that Absolute Spirit had not yet come into its own in the concrete order of social praxis, in fact, that Absolute Spirit was the human essence in alienated form. After Bauer, then, Feuerbach. And here too Derrida might fit the analogy. First Derrida, alias Bauer, lays the ghost of Right Heideggerianism with his "differential" critique of logocentrism and its transcendental signified. But then, just as the Left Heideggerians are arriving on the scene to claim Heidegger's remains for themselves by allegedly demonstrating the primordiality of absence over presence, Derrida ambushes them too by blurring even that distinction in the name of "undecidability," the inability to know where presence leaves off and absence supposedly begins. Hence, neither the positive theology of the Right nor the negative theology of the Left. Derrida, as Heidegger's Feuerbach, leaves more philosophical corpses on stage than in the last act of *Hamlet*.

I have presented this tale in order, first, to contextualize the problem of reading Heidegger at all, and secondly to raise the question of how one might interpret Derrida's reading of Heidegger. The import of this framework will emerge, I hope, at the end. But the task for now is to review Derrida's critique of Heidegger on its own terms.

1. Derrida's Reading of Heidegger

Derrida's critique of Heidegger is unique for at least two reasons. On the one hand, it comes from within. By that I do not mean to say that Derrida is a Heideggerian. In fact, he expressly denies filiation and says that all his essays constitute "a *departure* from the Heideggerian problematic." No, not that he is a disciple, but only that, unlike many other critics of Heidegger, he has studied the Heideggerian corpus at some length and readily acknowledges his debt to it. He has said that "Heidegger's text is extremely important to me" and "constitutes a novel, irreversible advance." But on the other hand, this reading from within is, or intends to be, utterly devastating. It accuses Heidegger of being an unwitting co-conspirator in the very metaphysics of presence that he claimed to have overcome. Derrida asserts that "the Heideggerian problematic is the most 'profound' and 'powerful' defense of what I try to call into question under the rubric of the *thought of presence*." Derrida, burrowing from within, attempts to hoist Heidegger on his own petard.[6]

Derrida tells us that the place where he began to see through Heidegger's surface to the concealed theme of presence was the question of authenticity (*Eigentlichkeit*) in *Being and Time*. To be sure, he could not have chosen a more central point, not only because authenticity is the heart of the existential analytic of Dasein but also and above all because, as Derrida correctly notes, the topic of *das Eigene* (roughly, the "own") is "the most continuous . . . thread of Heidegger's thought," weaving its way right up to the apex of his later writings, *Ereignis*, "appropriation" or "enownment."[7]

Let us leave Derrida aside for a moment and ask how Heidegger himself, speaking *in propria persona*, seems to understand the issue of *Eigentlichkeit* and *Ereignis*. To state matters briefly and no doubt inadequately, Heidegger claimed that the "topic of thought," *die Sache des Denkens*, was neither the human essence taken as some kind of encapsulated subjectivity, nor "being" taken as a heteronomous power, but rather the kinetic bond that holds these "two" (which are not two at all) together. This bond is the movement of finite disclosure which issues in accessible, intelligible entities and which happens only in the disclosive movement of the human essence. Thus the topic of Heidegger's thought is the movement whereby the finite being/intelligibility of entities happens (or "comes into its own": *Ereignis*) insofar as the human person comes into his or her own finitude (*Eigentlichkeit*). Let us look at each of these in turn.

Ereignis: Insofar as movement always comports a dimension of absentiality as well as presentiality, the happening of intelligibility is always circumscribed by an outstanding and ungraspable limit (*Ende*, *Grenze*), an unpresential but nonetheless experienceable dimension that rules within any present world of sense. Heidegger expressed this point by saying that the "coming into its own of a finite world of sense" (*Er-eignis* or *aletheia*) is scored in the key of "never fully coming into its own" (*Ent-eignis* or *Lethe*). This happening of sense is always an asymptotic or differential pres-ab-sentiality about which one can say little more than "it happens."

Eigentlichkeit: The limit-situation of sense is likewise the defining term of the human essence. Human beings come into their own precisely by being eccentrically dis-owned, by being self-transcendent towards the differential pres-ab-sential happening of sense. To be authentic or one's proper "own" (*Eigentlichkeit*) is to live in the coming-into-its-own of sense (*Ereignis*) which never fully comes into its own (*Enteignis*). In short, the ownness of Dasein and of being is "dis-owned-ness," the finitude of movement and difference.

Obviously, then, by linking *Eigentlichkeit* and *Ereignis*, Derrida has zeroed in on the center of Heidegger's thought. But it is equally clear that if he got it wrong there, the chances are he has gotten it wrong on the entire Heideggerian enterprise.

Derrida's critique of the phenomenon of being-Dasein proceeds not straight-on but by the indirection of a quasi-etymological analysis of the family of words surrounding the German adjective *eigen*. And there we find a startling concatenation of equations:

$$das\ Eigentliche\ =\ le\ propre$$
$$le\ propre\ =\ le\ proche$$
$$le\ proche\ =\ la\ présence\ à\ soi.$$

That is, Derrida takes Heidegger to be saying that to be authentic, to become in resolve the finitude that one already is, means to become self-present in absolute proximity to oneself, in fact, to be identical with oneself. And not only is Dasein ontically present to itself; it is also absolutely close to, and in fact identical with, being itself.[8]

What governs the relation of being and Dasein, Derrida asserts, is the guiding vision of phenomenology, which he interprets as "the principle of presence and of presence within self-presence, such as this shows up in and to the entities *we* are." Thus, when man attends to the voice of being in what Heidegger calls the "call of conscience," Derrida will assert that this voice speaks at the point "nearest to oneself" (*au plus proche de soi*) in a pure self-affection which borrows nothing from outside and is untouched by otherness. This monadic self-affection is what Derrida takes to be Heidegger's "temporality." No matter that the early Heidegger clearly asserted, and presumed to show by a phenomenology of lived experience, that temporality, as man's relatedness to being, is constituted by negativity and in fact is the very inscription of otherness at the heart of human being. "Man," Derrida claims for Heidegger, "is the near of being, and being speaks to him from very close, speaks into his ear." In the 1975 "Economimesis" essay the organ changes: being for Dasein "passes through the mouth." But whether ear or mouth, whether hearing a voice or eating being, it is all the same. At the heart of the analysis of Dasein — which means: at the heart of everything that can be said about being — there lurks "*le poids de la métaphysique*," the weight of a metaphysics of presence.[9]

This is extraordinary. Heidegger's texts, taken at their word, clearly say that authenticity means living in one's thrownness and self-absence and that what is proper to Da-sein lies precisely in its condition of being "*Fort-sein*," self-transcendent in the direction of the finite delimitation of any present world of sense. But to the contrary Derrida claims to have shown by deconstruction that being is immediate presence to Dasein which in turn is defined as presence to itself.[10]

From this startling and, let us say, original reading of the being-and-Dasein relation, Derrida moves to the question of language and to his charge that Heidegger is caught in logocentrism.[11] In order to follow this radical critique we need to understand the presuppositions that underlie Derrida's use of *logos*. His appeals to Plato with regard to this phenomenon are well enough known. But when we scratch the surface of his usage of this central term of Western metaphysics, we find lurking underneath it certain Aristotelian and even classical medieval elements which have not been sufficiently brought to light.

Derrida uses the word *logos* in its classical fourth-century meaning (already found in Plato but systematically worked out by Aristotle) as apophantic speech, rather than in the pre-Socratic sense of pre-verbal "revelation" or disclosure that Heidegger, at least after *Being and Time*, tended to favor. Derrida, following that classical tradition, correctly interprets *logos* as a supplement for and as an anticipation of the pure self-coincidence and presence-to-itself that defined the ontological and epistemological apex of the Aristotelian cosmos: *nous* in its perfect form of intellectual intuition of itself as intuition. *Logos* for Derrida is the discursive dream of *nous*, which in turn is the normative instance of being: the perfect interiority of the soul in living presence with itself.[12]

Logos, therefore, must be read from *nous*, and *nous*, perhaps more than any other term, defines the ontological ideal of classical Greece and the philosophical culture that followed from it. Ruling this vision is the ontological and epistemological identity-principle which holds that knowing follows being in a descending hierarchy of analogical levels of connaturality between the ontic self-presence of the knower (*nous*) and the epistemic penetrability of the known (*nooumenon*). In the classical Greek vision, being in its ideal state is transparency and perfect identity, clarity and stability. Because to be means to be translucent (first of all to oneself), then to the degree of one's own self-clarity, all else is correspondingly clear.

Classical metaphysics, whether Greek or medieval, establishes its viewpoint as the apex of the perfect − light and repose, *nous* as self-identity − and reads everything backwards, as it were, from those Olympian heights. It reads the imperfect from the viewpoint of the perfect, and movement from the standpoint of repose. Anaxagoras had already expressed this identity-principle in his *Panton nous kratei*, "Nous empowers everything" (Frag. 12). Aristotle continued this theme, but his genius consisted in envisioning, as did the Neo-Platonists after him, the analogical levels of this ruling identity, from its perfect state of luminosity and repose down through lower levels of imperfection. In God, where there is no obscurity, *nous* and *nooumenon* are one and the same. But in human beings, where obscurity is admixed with clarity because of the diminution of noetic power, *nous* is tarnished with the imperfection of having to move through (*dia*) the interconnections of things in discursive progress towards clarity. Thus it is bound up with *dia-noia*, that is, with *logos* taken as the faculty of differential *synthesis* and *diairesis* and thus as the basis of apophantic speech.[13]

But even in its imperfect human knowledge, *logos* is still ruled by *nous* in the specific form of *nous poietikos* or "agent intellect." This is the power of "making all things [intelligible]." Here *poiein* does not mean mere making or doing in the ordinary sense. Rather, as already in Plato, it is the bringing of something from non-being into being, from non-presence into present and therefore knowable reality. Dianoetic *logos* can know things only because, according to Aristotle's metaphor, the *nous poietikos* first "brings them to light." And agent intellect *can* illumine the world only because it participates in and indeed anticipates the perfect noetic self-luminosity and repose of God. Aristotle saw *nous*, when it operates with diminished intensity in man, as either divine or "the most divine element in us." Clearly, then, the logocentric world of discursive metaphysics is a noocentrism *manqué*, a dream of theologic self-presence.[14]

Medieval Scholastic thinkers continued and advanced the classical theme of *logos* as deficient nous under the rubric of the tension between *ratio (=dianoia)* and *intellectus (=nous)*. On the one hand, man's "intellectualism," represented by both his faculty of agent intellect and even, as in Eckart, by mystical intuition, makes him like unto God and the separated angelic substances; but on the other hand, his rational, discursive faculties measure his distance from those ontically-epistemically normative spirits. The specifically kinetic and differential — that is, synthetic-diairetic — character of *logos* precludes it from being an end in itself, for *non enim habet rationem termini motus*: motion in itself has no grounds for being a *telos*.[15]

Therefore, a metaphysical gap or *chorismos* separates the imperfect and the perfect, the posterior and the prior, and everything comes down to the *methexis*, the participation of the imperfect in the perfect, the appropriation of the posterior by the prior. From man's side of the gap, this means that the agent intellect or *lumen naturale*, insofar as it is "the most divine element in us," allows us to illumine and know the finite world only because it participates in, indeed anticipates, the full luminosity of God: "*In lumine tuo videbimus lumen.*" Thus man's nature is to be a kinetic *pros ti*, a self-transcending analogical referral to the divine.

In carrying out this reference of himself to God, man likewise enacts the teleology of the cosmos and brings the entire created world back to the divine. This principle of the teleology of cognition as a supplement of noetic self-identity runs through the whole of classical metaphysics.

We see it in the (Platonic-) Aristotelian idea of God as mimetically drawing the world onward to perfection (*kinei hos eromenon*: *Meta.* L, 7, 1072
b 3) and in the Augustinian vision of consciousness as a *mens secreta*
which knows itself to be privy to the divine mind through illumination.
It is found as well in Leibniz' notion of the world as a rational system
which the philospher can analyze back (*via inventionis*) to God's causative
and creative idea or "adequate notion," from which all the properties
of the notion can be deduced (*via demonstrationis*). It reaches its climax
in Hegel, who regains for speculative knowledge the thing-in-itself
which Kant had denied it, but at the expense of sublating finite subjectivity into the infinite spirit which expresses itself in a teleologically
exfoliated history that has finally come to self-possession.

The Ariadne's thread of this metaphysics of identity is the thesis
that all knowing, all *logos* as a prolepsis of *nous*, is a "*krisis*" or "*krinein:*"
a "critical" measuring of the finite objects of one's cognition, on the basis
of a prior "critical" measuring of the distention of dianoetic *logos* as an
anticipation of full noetic self-presence. The human knower is *panta
pos*, able to be present to all things, only because he or she is *theos pos*,
able to be present to God. Logocentric cognition, which follows ontology, teleologically intends a noocentric theology.

One of Derrida's major contributions consisted in finding this constitutive core of traditional metaphysics – noetic identity and its supplement in logocentric teleology – still operative in Edmund Husserl's
Logical Investigations. From his reading of the First Investigation in *La
voix et le phénomène*, he discovered the Husserlian ideal of the relation
of man and meaning to be, at one pole, meaning as an absolute self-
identity, which is present, at the other pole, within the self presence
of transcendental life. Derrida then generalized this position backwards
to the entire metaphysical tradition, which he found to be ruled by the
same ideal of "full language," of "speech dreaming its full self-presence"
and believing "itself to be its own father." This, as we have seen, is the
dream of pure self-affection uncorrupted by any otherness or "outside."
Derrida cites Rousseau: "Nothing external to oneself, nothing but oneself
and one's own existence; so long as this state lasts, one suffices to oneself,
like God." And the deconstructionist *j'accuse* that Derrida hurls against
this tradition is that it is fundamentally the desire to exclude writing,
taken not primarily as "putting words on paper" (although that is the
major symptom) but rather as *archi-écriture*: exteriority, mediation, irreducible difference.[16]

What is extraordinary is that Derrida presumes to discover this same
extreme model of *logos* in Heidegger's own position on the structure
of Dasein and being. Derrida is correct, of course, that the underlying

issue in the Dasein-being phenomenon is *logos*, but he fails to see that in both the early and the later Heidegger this term functions as asymptotic difference.

What informs the Dasein-analysis in *Being and Time*, for example, is not at all the phenomenological principle of presence but rather Heidegger's deconstruction of the Aristotelian analysis of *logos* as both apophantic and practical disclosure. In his early Freiburg and Marburg lecture courses on *Peri Hermeneias* and *Nicomachean Ethics VI*, Heidegger found that both the apophantic and practical modes of disclosure have in common the differentiality of *synthesis* and *diairesis*: the joining and distinguishing of entities and their being-dimension, whether that be apophantic or practical (the *Wozu* for which tools are useful). The radicalness of Heidegger's deconstruction of Aristotle consisted in showing, first, that the practical hermeneutical as-factor — the unthematic and prepredicative lived understanding of what an entity *is for* — has priority over the apophantic as-factor, and, secondly, that the meaning of the hermeneutical as-factor is temporality: correspondence with the factical asymptosis of the finite happening of sense. Hence we must say that, yes, Heidegger *is* logocentric from beginning to end. But *logos*, as he used it, had already awakened from the dream of *nous* and subverted it in the name of the irreducible differentiality that rules in the inseparable structure of Dasein and *Ereignis*.[17]

Derrida's failure to see this state of affairs is evidenced by his interpretation of Heidegger's later position on being-as-*logos*. Apart from his use of the word "transcendental" in the following sentence, Derrida starts off on the right foot. According to Heidegger, he says, being is the *Urwort*, "the transcendental word guaranteeing to all other words their possiblity of being-words." That is, being-as-*logos* "is tied, if not to a particular word or to a particular language-system, at least to the possibility of the word in general" — but then here comes the twist — "and to its irreducible simplicity." That last phrase means: the abolition of difference. Here Derrida shows himself to be so captured by the traditional report on *logos* as the desire for *noesis noeseos* that he fails to see that Heidegger had already undone that position. Perhaps Derrida was disadvantaged by not having at hand Heidegger's early lecture courses on Aristotle, but I do not think so. For, even a cursory reading of *Identität und Differenz* or *Zeit und Sein*, both of which were available to the early Derrida, reveal the persistence of the synthetic-diairetic character of *logos* within being itself taken as *Unter-schied, Austrag* and *Differenz*. Derrida has quite simply missed Heidegger's point.[18]

And that is why, for Derrida, Heidegger is a theologian who dares not speak his name and in fact is unaware of his own genealogy. It does not matter to Derrida whether Dasein's self-presence be finite or full, or whether being-as-presence be ontically possessed or teleologically promised as the ultimate signified. A delayed presence, that is, a teleologically desired presence, is presence nonetheless. It is the Aristotelian god at the end of a long history of Augustinian desire. *"Le désir est désir de la présence."*[19]

It would be unfair to end this preliminary reading of Derrida's critique of Heidegger without noting that Derrida admits to being uncertain about whether he can legitimately lay all these charges at Heidegger's doorstep. He ends up declaring that Heidegger's position vis-à-vis the metaphysics of presence and logocentrism is "ambiguous." He is reluctant to accuse Heidegger of being entirely caught within metaphysics, so he charges him with only "a little bit of Platonism" (*"quelque platonisme"*). But let's face it: when it comes to metaphysics, a little bit of Platonism is like a little bit of pregnancy. The hymen is gone, the undecidability dissolved. Heidegger is an onto-theologian.[20]

This "critique" of Derrida's reading of Heidegger is not only provisional but also fundamentally unsatisfying insofar as it merely lays two texts side by side and compares them, as it were, line by line. To a certain extent such an approach is necessary and perhaps helpful. In fact, Derrida himself frequently demands that kind of close textual comparison when it comes to what he thinks are misunderstandings of his own work by, for example, Paul Ricoeur, Christine Glucksmann, Jacques Lacan or John R. Searle. But if we do lay *Being and Time* or *Letter on Humanism* or *Holzwege* alongside the corresponding pages in *Marges de la philosophie* or *De la grammatologie*, we find Derrida proposing readings that, quite frankly, we would not accept from our own graduate students.

Nonetheless, I find this approach unsatisfying. It not only misses the unquestionable brilliance of Derrida but also fails to raise the question of the principles guiding deconstruction. Above all it does not get to what Heidegger called *die Sache selbst*, the topic of post-metaphysical thinking. Deconstruction, after all, is a way of *reading texts critically*, presumably with the purpose of getting to that topic. Therefore I propose another approach. Let us look at *reading* and *criticism* to see what these reveal about the issues that seem to divide, but may unite, both Derrida and Heidegger.

2. Reading, criticism and the undecidable

I will argue that "critique" in the usual sense – whether Derrida's critique of Heidegger or an alleged Heideggerian critique of Derrida – is very problematic, perhaps impossible, and almost certainly beside the point. I shall do this by reflecting on what reading is and what it effects. Derrida usually talks about writing rather than reading, but from what follows, I believe it will become clear that they are the same.

We can begin with the obvious: to read is to interpret. It is never just to run one's eyes over signs but to follow their movement and to draw out and articulate their sense, whether those signs be words on a page or persons we meet or other entities in the world. I believe that, in a certain sense, Maurice Blanchot is right when he says, "The act of reading does not change anything, nor does it add anything to what was already there."[21] The word "change" might imply that things are first one way, of and by themselves, and that when we interpreters contact them, we make them out to be some other way. No, as soon as we see or meet entities, we have already read them, already found them in a schema of interpretation. Italo Calvino puts it exactly: "We live in a world where everything is already read even before it starts to exist."[22]

If we can find no origin, no presuppositionless beginning outside of reading, that is because we are the living entities who have *logos*: *ta zoia ton logon echonta*. We cannot step outside the circle of *logos* and move about as *zoia* in the blissful innocence of animal immediacy. We are always worrying things, splitting and mediating them, reading them in terms of this and that or *as for* such and such a purpose. The notion of empirical immediacy, as Derrida says, is a dream that "vanishes *at daybreak*, as soon as language awakens."[23]

"Reading" is what is meant by *hermeneia*, interpretation; that is, it translates what the early Heidegger (but not Derrida) meant by *logos*. And all three — reading, *hermeneia* and *logos* — name the same thing: the human way of being, the first-order activity of Dasein that makes it possible for us to perform such concrete activities as interpreting texts and other entities. And further, because the human being *is* interpretation (*logos*), all entities available to us are *texts* (*legomena*). This state of affairs is the phenomenological correlation in the form of the hermeneutical circle.

To sort out what reading is and does, I shall resort to a spatial metaphor. Reading means living "on the other side" of things, that is, on the other side of a supposed subject-object encounter. If, from our first meeting with them, things are *already* interpreted through the network of the "in terms of" and the "as-for," then we already live over there in that movement of the "as-factor." Before it is ever an act done *by* a subject, reading is the act of *displacing* the subject; or better, reading *is* the displaced subject — which, of course, we can no longer call a "subject" but might better call an "eject" or a "project" (*geworfener Ent-*

wurf). We do not "have" *logos* so much as we "are" or even "are had by" *logos*. It rules us, constitutes us, speaks when we open our mouths. It is our insubstantial essence, in and by which we live and move and have our being.

Furthermore, living on the other side of those things which may appear (= *ta physika*) by living in the movement of the as-factor which lets them appear (= *meta*) means being meta-physical. Or again, living on the other side of entities (*ta onta*) by living with their boundness into schemata of possibility and purpose (*legein*) means being onto-logical. Reading is intrinsically metaphysical and ontological, but in the "good" sense of those terms, that is, without any referral of entities to presence as transcendental signified in that onto-theo-archeo-teleo-logical scheme that both Heidegger and Derrida call into court. Reading is indeed the referral of *ta onta* beyond themselves, but it is a referral to no-presence; hence, always a referral of entities as traces-of-no-presence.

This notion of reading escapes the charge of the "bad" metaphysics of presence in two ways. In the first place it undoes the traditional metaphysical schema of potency and act, *dynamis* and *energeia*, the *ateles* and the *teleion*. Primacy no longer rests with *energeia* and *telos*; but neither, by a simplistic binary reversal, does it rest simply with *dynamis* and the atelic, as if these could be substantialized into things in themselves. Rather, there is no more primacy at all. At best we can speak only of a relative priority of open-endedness over closure in an on-going movement in which there is no advance to a *telos*, no *Aufhebung* unto a terminus that would tranquilize and end the chain of referrals, substitutions, and traces of no-presence. Insofar as no *arche* or *telos* – no identity of sense outside of interpretation – is available, reading is thrown back on a positive affirmation of the classical axiom that motion has no grounds for being a *telos*. What Derrida calls *le supplément d'origine* translates into a virtue what medieval metaphysics saw as a defect. *Quod non potest fieri per unum, aliqualiter saltem fiat per plura*: In the absence of unity, one lives and acts in unending plurality. Our condition as readers condemns us to the movement of "ever approaching" (*anchibasie*), to what James Joyce called "almosting it."[24]

Secondly, this notion of reading escapes "bad" metaphysics by effecting a transcendental reduction of entities from their supposed independent status of "already-out-there-now-real" – but without reducing them either to some constituting subject (because reading is the displacement of the subject) or to any form of *ousia*, whether present presence or deferred presence or, if it be possible, absent presence. Reading reduces entities to the status of "traces of . . . ," but traces of what? Entities read as traces are not (or not primarily) referred to some thing "on the other side" of *logos*, let us say, to a substantial predicate in such a way that the "S" and the "P" would be two *differands* that refer to each other. Rather, in reducing the entity to a trace, reading refers that trace to the differentiating process itself, to the non-teleological, ever splitting-and-mediating movement that is *logos*, the referring that refers to no-presence. Entities are traces of the movement of reading itself, of *hermeneuein* or *legein*. In Heidegger's terms, they reveal-for-a-while the revelation process (*das Jeweilige*). In Derrida's terms, they "make an economy of the abyss."[25]

Under the title of "to read is to interpret," I have been attempting to substantiate concretely what I only hinted at in the first section: that Derrida misses the point of Heidegger's use of *logos*. *Logos*, like *hermeneia*, names the unique movement of differentiation and reduction-to-trace that the early Heidegger retrieved from the phenomena of *synthesis* and *diairesis* in the sentential logic of the *Peri Hermeneias* and that the later Heidegger, beginning around 1944, called *Austrag* – literally, dif-ference – in his halting attempt to translate the Greek *diaphora*. This seems, then, to be a critique of Derrida. But paradoxically it is not that so much as it is a demonstration that both Derrida and Heidegger are concerned with the same post-metaphysical topic.

Above we noted that deconstruction is a way of *reading texts critically*. What, then, does reading have to do with criticism? Derrida, as we know, shies away from the term "criticism," or at least from its usual meaning. In the *"Double Séance"* he says that "criticism . . . , as the name indicates, is linked to the possibility of decidability, *krinein*," whereas the *"Double Séance"* is precisely a "deconstructive 'critique' of the notion of criticism" *qua* decidability and a demonstration of the inevitability of *un*decidability. What, then, is the relation between decidability and undecidability on the one hand and criticism on the other?[26]

Heidegger takes the word *krinein* to mean the separating out of the *proteron* from the *hysteron*, the prior from the posterior. That seems to be a "metaphysical" act and a "metaphysical" distinction, and it is – but in the "good" sense. The posterior is the entity as trace; and the prior is not some first origin but the act of *legein* itself, the non-teleological movement of the referring of traces. *Krinein*, Heidegger says, means "the 'critical' ability for differentiating [*Unterscheidung*] which in turn is always a deciding [*Entscheidung*: resolve]." *Krinein* does not mean making a decision which settles matters by choosing between binary opposites. Derrida notwithstanding, the decisiveness of resolve does not move us out of the state of inauthenticity into pure authenticity as self-presence. Rather, it always lands us precisely in differentiating, that is, in the movement of *Eigentlichkeit-Ereignis* which is the undecidable itself, neither presence nor absence, neither inside nor outside. The crisis of resolve does indeed give us what is proper to us, but that turns out to be undecidable *kinesis*, the dislocation that never arrives at a new locus, the effacement of entities by reducing them to traces which in turn are not reducible to any *telos*. Undecidability is at one and the same time the *act* of critical reading and the *outcome* of that act. *Criticism enacts undecidability.*[27]

We may arrive at this same point by another route: retrieval. Yes, insofar as reading is an interpretation, it is always a retrieval. But what gets retrieved in this retrieving? That upon which the retrieval works (*das Befragte*) is always some thing, but what gets retrieved (*das Erfragte*) is not a thing at all. That is most clear when the act of reading turns on itself, not only so as to understand, through a quasi-phenomenological-eidetic reduction, how it interprets entities other than itself, but also and above all so as to interpret itself as interpreter through a quasi-transcendental reduction (Heidegger's analysis of conscience, resolve and temporality). In this latter move we find that no reduction is possible at all, insofar as reading is always a displaced *in*-duction: Dasein's self-transcendence to the undecidable, differential pres-absentiality that is the happening of sense at all.[28]

This, in fact, is what literary criticism is really about when it gets beyond academic preening and hazards "the thing itself." It is not the critique of a text as object (*to on*) but of the text as read or readable (*to on legomenon*), and therefore ultimately a critique of *reading itself* (*to legein*) as an unending semiosis which retrieves itself in its situated confrontation with this particular text. To read reading, to interpret ourselves, to turn *logos* critically back on itself, is to retrieve nothing stable and substantial but only the very movement of reading itself. To criticize means to retrieve the inevitability of first-order *hermeneia* as our way of being – and that means: to retrieve the ineluctability of undecidability.

Therefore, when criticism does its work rightly, it does not place one thinker over here and another thinker over there. It does not exhaust itself in comparing texts, as we did above, or in making decisions between themes or positions ("thematic criticism"). Criticism is the retrieval of undecidability right down to the undecidability of what makes sense come about. In Heidegger's formulation it lands us in the unrepresentable *Es gibt*, the fact of "there-is-finite-historical-interpretation." This place of reading which is no place, this being-at-work which never comes to an end (cf. *energeia ateles*), is what Derrida and Heidegger are talking about.

It is at this point — Derrida's insistence that deconstruction is "play" and that it is "not the most assured of exercises" — that scholars stiffen a bit. Isn't this arbitrariness? When Jean Hippolyte in a 1966 conference at Johns Hopkins, asked Derrida in what direction he was going, Derrida answered, " . . . I am trying, precisely, to put myself at a point so that I do not know any longer where I am going." That may sound arbitrary, relativistic and simply not serious, but it also may be the most serious statement he has uttered and indeed one that Heidegger himself might heartily affirm. Recall Heidegger's imaginary "Conversation on a Country Path." Three men are walking through the forest as night begins to fall. After their long deconstructive dialogue, one of them is moved to say, "I hardly know anymore who and what I am." And his friend, who presumably speaks for Heidegger, answers: "None of us knows that, as soon as we stop fooling ourselves."[29]

Are we, then, really at the end of philosophy? Does reading as the retrieval of difference and the engendering of uncertainty leave philosophy with nothing to do? It does seem that reading is what Heidegger called *die Sache selbst*. It names the condition of *Fort-Da-sein*: living with, and indeed as, difference, the asymptosis which issues in, but is not reducable to, all the asymptoses or differences that we call, as a whole, meaningfulness or language. Reading is thus an on-going subversion of all stability and of all attempts to divide up the undecidability of the coming-into-its-own-of-sense into presence and absence. It is never a complete revolution — that would be decidability — but more like an earthquake fault that "sollicits," that is, shakes all forms of certitude and keeps them in constant uncertainty.

Derrida's name for that subversion is "the end of eschatology" and "the denunciation of false apocalypses."[30] If he does make an advance beyond Heidegger, or the Heideggerians, that step might well consist in his indictment of eschatology as the final form of decidability. Derrida is remarking not only the closure of the metaphysics of presence from Plato to Husserl, so that we might then begin to meditate on absence; that is, he is not exchanging Right Heideggerianism for Left Heideggerianism. Rather, the Left too seems to be shot through with the urge to decidability insofar as it opposes the *Geviert* to the *Gestell*, or Being-itself to *Seiendheit*, or meditative thinking to calculation. Rather, Derrida is remarking the closure of eschatology in *all* its forms, from Zoroaster, where the notion seems to emerge, down through Daniel and Jesus and Augustine and Hegel and perhaps even Heidegger. Eschatology always draws a line — for example, between the metaphysics of presence and the no-longer-metaphysics of heeding the primordiality of absence. Derrida blurs the line between these supposed "two," between the positive theology of the Right Heideggerians and the negative theology of the Left, so that one no longer knows what is sacred and what is profane, or what is metaphysics and what is not. The distinction between the Left Heideggerians and Derrida is subtle but important. Perhaps it is like the difference between walking on the edge of the parapet of the Empire State Building — one eye on the terrace, one eye on the abyss — and walking blindfolded anywhere, on any ground, such that you do not know where your next step will fall.

This is what I was alluding to when I proposed Derrida as Heidegger's Feuerbach. He is a brook of fire, a purgatory for any who would consider toying with apocalyptic fire. He purifies not only those who hope to read their way through to some eventual full presence — *Sein* in the sky by and by — but also those who, without sharing that chiliastic expectation, nonetheless hope to read to the end of the text, to the point where reading ends and reverence begins, even if there is nothing to revere but absence. For, even if there were such absence, would not Left Heideggerians be condemned to silence about it, or as Heidegger once said, even to silence about their silence?[31]

Here is the final paradox of undecidability: we cannot tell the difference between the silent and discalced initiates of the *Lethe* and the very verbal Brook of Fire who would purge us with the experience of *différance*. The end of philosophy indeed. The utter silencing of theology — not only of revealed theology but also of philosophical ontotheology and even of negative ontotheology — might well be a contemporary echo of the suggestion made in 1843 that "the critique of religion is the premise of all [other] critique." The deconstruction of *Lethe* in the name of the undecidability of presence and absence might be the prelude to a new critique of the earth.[32]

I have suggested Derrida as Heidegger's Feuerbach for two reasons. First, because the point is to get the other side of this fiery brook and not to stand in mid-stream; Feuerbach is finally dispensable. And secondly, because getting to the other side entails raising the real important question: How to be Heidegger's Marx?

17. Heidegger and Derrida Redux: A Close Reading

Nancy J. Holland

At last year's SPEP meeting, John Caputo and Thomas Sheehan addressed the topic of "Heidegger's Critique of Derrida." Caputo put forward the basic proposition that Derrida's supposed critique of Heidegger failed because, in effect, Derrida was not Heidegger and Heidegger was right. Sheehan, on the other hand, reproached Derrida for not being enough unlike Heidegger, that is, for merely being his Feuerbach rather than being his Marx. Sheehan said that Derrida created a left-leaning Heidegger and a right-leaning Heidegger and attacked both of them, albeit with something of bad faith in the first case, since Heidegger is clearly not a right-leaning Heideggerian.

In the past, Hugh Silverman and Richard Rorty have also addressed the relationship between Derrida's work and its admittedly Heideggerian antecedent(s). In the 1978 volume of *Research in Phenomenology*, Silverman notes an argument in Derrida's discussions of Heidegger which makes a link between the concept of Authenticity and a supposed continuing primacy of the Subject in Heidegger's thought. The claim could be traced out in English through the chain Authentic-Author-Authority, and a similar move could also be made from *eigentlich* to *Ereignis*.[1] In his article for the November, 1977 issue of *The Journal of Philosophy*, Rorty suggests that Derrida's definitive move against Heidegger is the rejection of the ability to say anything positive at all, about Being for instance, without immediately falling back into the metaphysical, because language itself is always already metaphysical.[2]

Rather than challenge any or all of these general claims, what I hope to do in this paper through a careful reading of Derrida's "Restitutions" is to show how Derrida does display at least this many attitudes toward Heidegger and comments explicity on the short-comings of each. I will

then try to provide, dare I say, a unified reading of at lest one strain
in Derrida's commentary which is consistently maintained throughout
"Restitutions" (and, I would propose, all of Derrida's work). Such a
"unified" reading might provide a way of addressing the similarities and
differences between Heidegger and Derrida which would lead to a
deeper understanding of both points of view. Whether this approach
to reading Heidegger constitutes a valid critique of Heidegger's thought
is a separate question which I will address only briefly at the end of
my paper.

Derrida is clearly ambivalent about any critique of Heidegger, and
not least of all his own, as is shown by his constant statements that
whatever he says has already always been circumscribed, said, delim-
ited, etc., by Heidegger. Thus, like Caputo, he has a side which believes
that Heidegger cannot be exceeded in whatever direction one may like
to go. In "Restitutions," for instance, he says that

> I always have the impression that while commenting on Heidegger, while
> restoring him in an apparently rigorous fashion, he's made to say something
> completely different (*tout autre chose*); all the accents are changed, and his
> language is no longer recognizable. The commentary becomes obscene and
> to think differently becomes thinking differently than he who wants to
> think the remnant 'properly.'[3]

In a sense, that quotation provides a variant on Sheehan's point as
well, but in the part of "Restitutions" which was added after the initial
French publication and hence does not appear in the English translation in the 1978 volume of *Research in Phenomenology*, Derrida traces
out both a left-leaning and a right-leaning Heidegger, makes the link
more or less explicitly a political one, and then proceeds to criticize
the left-leaning Heidegger, just as Sheehan's analysis indicates. Here,
the right-leaning Heidegger, who comes first of course, appears in the
possibility of a pre-critical reading of the Heideggerian text, in this case
"The Origin of the Work of Art."

> It is that the step back from a truth of adequation toward a truth of uncon-
> cealment, whatever its necessity and its "critical" force may be, can also
> easily be left practically disarmed in the face of the ingenuous, the pre-
> critical, the dogmatic, in the face of any (in-)vested interest ("*pré-
> investissement*") . . .[4]

Clearly, however, this is not Heidegger's own position.

And in this case, even if there is an error of attribution or projection of
peasantry, the margin of aberration would be very narrow. It is the truth

of the being as product that is important. If there is projection, the handle is small for the painting police, for this discourse of order and propriety in painting.[5]

Note, moreover, that the "true," left-leaning Heidegger must be protected from his right-leaning *Doppelgänger's* police mentality. Finally, however, even the left-leaning Heidegger is, at base, insufficiently radical because, to take one example,

> When one is assured of the thing as a pair, when one forgets that detachment also goes from one shoe to the other and divides the pair, one represses all these questions, one makes them re-enter the order.[6]

The point suggested by Silverman clearly appears in the English translation of "Restitutions", when Derrida says that

> Let's suppose as an axiom that the desire for attribution is a desire for appropriation. In matters of art as everywhere else. To say this (this painting or these shoes) returns to X, that amounts to saying: *ça me revient*, it comes back to me through the detour of the '*ça revient à (un) moi*,' the 'it comes back to me (to a self)'.[7]

He sees its limitations and refutes the point later on, however, by saying that

> Clearly Heidegger's text opened this debate. Now doesn't it leave far behind all problems of subjectivity? In fact, subjectivity supposes what is here de-sedimented by him, among others, the determination of the thing as '*hupo-keimenon*,' support, substratum, substance, etc.[8]

Rorty's argument is stated as such only in the full French version of "Restitutions." There Derrida asserts, with regard to the "reliability" of the Earth in Heidegger, that

> . . . the whole problematic of the subject, of the law, and of the fetish, in their 'forms' available today, all of this would first be based on such a reliability. But to say that it is the earth or the sub-soil (sub-stratum) on which marches a discourse on the earth, the march, the sole, the shoes, the feet, etc., wouldn't this be already to translate it, this reliability, into the marks of that which it makes possible?[9]

Still, it is not at all clear that he accepts this line of argument either, because of passages where he says things like

'We name it *reliability*.' This nomination, this giving of the name is also a complex 'act': it supposes, in its very performance, a reliability of language and discourse; but it produces it at the same time, it engages itself there.[10]

This suggests a performative way of understanding the Heideggerian text which might escape the trap of metaphysical language.

If Derrida himself indicates that each of these ways of criticizing Heidegger is inadequate for the reasons given, is there any way in which he thinks a valid criticism of Heidegger can be made? I would like to propose that there is at least one such critique implicit throughout Derrida's writings, a criticism of the metaphysical tradition as a whole which he seems to think applies at least in part to Heidegger as well. Since it makes little sense to criticize Derrida for doing something he already describes as inadequate, this more general level of analysis might provide a way of revealing something about the relationship between Derrida and Heidegger which does not yet already appear in one, or both, texts.

It is important to understanding what I take to be a consistent way of reading the metaphysical tradition in Derrida and its application to Heidegger that you realize that the English translation of "Restitutions" omits a vital introductory note that appears on the inverse of the title page for that article in *La Verité en Peinture*. There it is clearly stated that "Restitutions" is a "polylogue (for n + 1 voices – feminine)."[11] What I hope to establish here is that Derrida carries on an implicitly "feminist" critique of Heidegger which is based on a basically "feminist" critique of the metaphysical tradition as a whole. Obviously, within the confines of this paper I will have to limit my comments to Heidegger, but the general form of the same argument can be found in Derrida's work on Plato, Rousseau, Nietzsche, Freud, etc. – in short, in every deconstruction of the metaphysical tradition in which Derrida engages.

Moreover, this "feminist" line of criticism extends to all aspects of Heidegger's work. That Derrida intends for this implied criticism to be carried beyond the immediate confines of "The Origin of the Work of Art" is clear when he says

Elsewhere I'll also propose to put in a series, in a gallery, all the figures of woman which punctuate with their discreet, furtive, and nearly unnoticed apparitions Heidegger's discourse on the thing: the peasant woman, the Thracian servant woman, the woman museum attendant, the "young girl" as a "a young thing, still too young" in the locution cited at the beginning of our chapter . . . .[12]

What Heidegger says or does not say about women, on this view, is a more telling critique of his work than whether he is insufficiently "radical" or still trapped within "subjectivism" or merely says too much in a language which is still "metaphysical." In fact, it is just because, Derrida suggests, Heidegger does not depart from the metaphysical tradition in his treatment of women that he in some ways still remains within that tradition.

This is where the close reading comes in. As Sheehan indicated, one way of seeing the relationship between Derrida and Heidegger is through the concept of undecidability. It becomes clear in "Restitutions," however, that this undecidability is, at least in part, a sexual undecidability, an ambiguous sexuality in the metaphysical or Heideggerian text. One facet of Derrida's approach to "The Origin of the Work of Art" is the consideration of the Van Gogh painting of the shoes as a study in fetishism. "All this happens as if the truth about the fetish is meant, is what one wants to tell. Shall we risk doing that ourselves right now?"[13] Just as *La Verité en Peinture* as a whole is about the three ways in which the title might be interpreted in French, so "Restitutions" is about the truth represented in the fetish, the truth represented by the fetish, and the truth about the fetish, but never forgetting that the fetish is always sexually ambiguous: "In any case, for Freud *the* shoe *is* no more *the* penis than *the* vagina."[14]

This fetishism, furthermore, has its roots in castration anxiety. On this view, whether or not one is willing to see the attempt on Heidegger's part to reappropriate the unattached shoes in the painting on behalf of the peasant (who is sometimes a woman) as an attempt to return to some primacy of the Subject, it would at least or also be an attempt to flee from the manifest detachment of the shoes. "One hurries to resume relations with the subject. The detachment is unbearable."[15] None of this is accidental or idiosyncratic in Heidegger. The desire for the supremacy of the Subject is, on this reading of Derrida, identical with the desire to avoid the anxiety generated by an awareness of the female's lack of a penis: it is the same move as the supposed supremacy of the Subject which has allowed no place in philosophy for the castrated male that the female represents.

Toward the end of the English version of "Restitutions," however, Derrida deepens the analysis considerably from what may appear to be an over-extended Freudianism. Here, he leaves the question of the truth of the fetish for the question of the fetish of truth.

To what sex do these shoes return? This isn't exactly the same question as before, when we asked ourselves if there was or was not a symbolic equivalence between the supposed "symbol" shoes and such and such a genital organ. Or if a differential and idiomatic syntax alone could impede bisexuality, conferring on it such a seductive or dominant value, etc. This isn't the same question, and yet the attribution of the shoes (as painting) to a subject-bearer-wearer

– of the shoes and of a sex

– masculine or feminine, this attribution is not without resonance with the first question. Let's not forget that the *Origin* treats the essence of truth, the truth of essence and of the abyss (*Abgrund*), which plays the role there of some "veiled" fate (*fatum*) paralyzing Being.

Grafting sex on the shoes. This isn't impeded by the *Origin* . . . .[16]

In a sense, as is always the case with Heidegger, the question of the fetish is already a move within "The Origin of the Work of Art," rather than an exorbitant move that would exceed it, and yet it is no clearer than ever that this is a move that Heidegger made.

The shoes are a fetish, the more so because they are taken in isolation from the feet which would bind them to some human subject and render them useful. Their status as fetish is their inutility, but is precisely their inutility which is central for Heidegger's own investigation of the truth of the painting: " . . . that which resembles a process of fetishization (the inutility of the work and of the product, the inutility of the product at work in the work) is described by Heidegger as a strange movement of *alétheia*."[17] So it is exactly that which makes the shoes a fetish, their status as representations cut off from reality, that makes them revelatory of truth. Their inutility, hence their truth, is based on their status as castrated, cut off. So, if the truth of the fetish is castration, the fetish of truth is likewise a castration.

Of course, truth is no more simply a castration than it is simply an adequacy of intactness. The undecidability of the fetish requires that the truth also be a veil, the veil of *alétheia*, and that the veil of *alétheia* be a hymen, a hymen between the fetish and its bearer:

> . . . the figure of veiling, of linen veiling as the over-underwear (*dessus-dessous*) won't be long in appearing, and the hyman which involves it in the undecidable won't be unrelated to the sock, the bobby sock (*soquette*) or the stocking, between foot and shoe. . . "[18]

As fetish, the truth is undecidable, sexually ambiguous, the ambiguity which gives rise to (sexual) desire. Thus the argument I have traced out above is only one strand in a braid that would refer us backward and forward, to the uterus,[19] to marriage,[20] to the Mother,[21] and to the very possibility of the pair, as in a pair of shoes, or socks. Each of these strands, in turn, refers to others, both within and beyond "Restitutions," none decidably male or female, pro- or anti-Heideggerian.

So, how do these shoes stand as a criticism of Heidegger? If one were to take the history of metaphysics to be motivated, at least in part, by a castration anxiety and fetishism which requires that the truth about women be in all ways excluded from the metaphysical realm and another truth erected in its place, then one would have, in place of Heidegger's unmotivated *Seinsgeschick,* a motivated history of the tradition. Whether this way of looking at the metaphysical tradition constitutes a criticism of Heidegger, or is a better way of understanding that tradition, remains an open question. David Allison, for instance, has developed a related but more limited line of argument in "Destruction/Deconstruction in the Text of Nietzsche,"[22] but does not present it is a criticism of Heidegger. In commenting on a related paper by the speaker, Hubert Dreyfus noted that such a motivated history of metaphysics would constitute a regression to the Heidegger of Division Two of *Being and Time,* where man's anxiety is based on his awareness of being the null basis of a nullity (an interesting phrase for castration anxiety, at least). If one wanted to maintain that, nevertheless, Derrida does develop such a motivated history of the tradition and does see it as a possible criticism of Heidegger, it is interesting to note that in "The Ends of Man," Derrida questions the validity of the distinction between an "earlier" and a "later" Heidegger.[23] From this point of view, therefore, Derrida would at least challenge any question here of "regression."

However, I hope I have made it sufficiently clear in general that, as always with Derrida's work on Heidegger, one can never be certain that Derrida himself sees what he says here, or elsewhere, as a criticism of Heidegger rather than an amplification or radicalization of what is already present in the Heideggerian text. To say that Heidegger recognizes the significance of undecidability but does not understand that its primary forms (or one of them) are sexually ambiguous seems, if not naive, at least not demonstrable. On the other hand, the subordinate status of women in the Heideggerian text is clear, and it is not at all certain that his overt "masculinism" is merely a veneer over a truly deep understanding of how the exclusion of women is definitive of the metaphysical tradition. One never wants to be "fooled again," in philosophy as elsewhere.

What has been accomplished here, therefore, is not any kind of resolution of the question of Heidegger and Derrida, but, I hope, a deepening of our understanding of both philosophers, and especially of the form which Derrida's supposed critique of Heidegger takes in one of its most recent and most telling forms. The strongest argument that can be made for the truth of this "feminist" critique, which cannot, of course, be made here, is the similarity between Derrida's reading of Heidegger on this point and his readings of other philosophers within the metaphysical tradition. At the very least, I hope to have laid to rest various overly simple ways of seeing what Derrida is about when he discusses Heidegger and to have struck a blow for the kind of close reading of the Derridian texts that he is usually generous enough to grant to other writers.

Part VII.
Post-Derridean Reading

18. Abysses

Stephen H. Watson

Kant had proceeded some six hundred pages into the first *Kritik* before he reached the problem of abysses. He had faithfully followed out the Enlightenment's search for foundations, its peculiar form of the *recherche de la verite*, as it was called. He had deployed the schemata of the Enlightenment's beliefs. Transcendental arguments, always, at least in Kant, were regressive. *"If knowledge is to be possible"* — it postulated a complete picture of knowledge as well as possibility. And, no one doubted it — let alone Kant, for whom Newton, Galileo, and Euclid provided the texts for an archive of pure reason. The systems, the *principiae* were introjected: the schemata for synthesis — the bringing of the manifold of sensation into a unity, the necessary unity of knowledge, of concepts, of judgment, and thereby of objects. And consistently, self-critically, and the anathema to all neo-Kantianism, Kant's Dialectic would not allow these grounds to go themselves ungrounded. "Reason" seeks the conditions of the conditions, a higher unity, which might ground even the certainty of the understanding. The search for grounds, for justification, for legitimation, for necessity is not tangential to what had gone before; it is necessary. A final grounding is requisite that can satisfy the search, providing a complete determination or ground for logical and ontological possibility such that it might be affirmed, finally and ultimately that "everything which exists is completely determined."[1] Being would be both rational, i.e., orderly, *and* intelligible.

It was Kant's peculiar twist, 'trope' would be adequate here, to have recognized that this project, the project of all *metaphysica rationalis*, was part and parcel theological. The foundation which would found logic and ontology must also be inherently theo-logical. In short, as he put it, the project of rationality was 'onto-theo-logical.' The object of this search would contain by *implicatio*, the sum total of all possibility. It would be the *omnitudo realititis*. Since all particularity (manifoldness) would be a limitation of it, it would be the primordial being (*ens originarium*). As the condition of the conditions it would be the highest being (*ens summum*). And since everything that is conditioned is subject to it, it would be the being of all beings (*ens entium*).[2] With this ultimate grounding *metaphysica rationalis* would have found completeness. Bacon's foundations would have finally hit bedrock. Transcendental logic as a logic of truth would have been vindicated. Objectivity would have finally been assured in accordance with a necessity which had driven the search after truth since Plato's dialectic.

Kant recognized this was fundamental to the project of pure reason, unavoidable to the problem of certainty; implicit to the problem of bringing the dispersion (the manifoldness, the divided being) of a finite knower to certainty. It was, consequently, fundamental and insurpassable. 'Natural' was Kant's word for it[3] and it would bring Hegel's response that it still smacked of an indefensible psychology.[4] And yet, equally unavoidable was the 'fact' that this search implicitly contained, as well, a certain *delirium*. Its search involved an illusion (that transcendental ideas could receive the *'Sinn und Bedeutung'* as Kant was the first to call it,[5] of what he also called 'experience'). Such a Being, albeit necessary and inevitable to Reason's search, was merely a *focus imaginarius*. But it wasn't merely a necessary delusion, in the sense of the *postulates* of practical reason, somehow. It was a delusion that struck at the heart of Reason itself. This was the delusion of the project, the failure of the foundation which ultimately justified what had gone before. It was, after all, the ground of all grounds. And, Kant, despite all his commitments to philosphical modernism and the heroes of the Enlightment, did not fail at least to blink, to use a Nietzschean phrase, at what he had wrought:

> Unconditioned necessity, which we so indispensable require as the last bearer of all things, is for human reason the veritable abyss.[6]

"Der wahre Abgrund," the combination expresses the paradox, the undecidable of German Idealism. *Wahre Abgrund*. True abyss. The truth of grounding, to be *without* grounds. A truth which arises *from* grounds: to be without, to be *Abgrund*. It is a peculiarity of German, Hegel believed a "delight to speculative thought," and he referred in fact in this context to this word, to have a "twofold meaning," and it must be kept in mind throughout.[7] Heidegger appealed to it as well, saying at the same time that "we must avoid uninhibited word-mysticism."[8] And yet, while it does not occur in English (abyss) or French (*l'abîme*), it is there in their etymological past (*a byssos*).

Notwithstanding the circumflex's and peculiarities of 'those who come after' Kant, he does not merely mention this word with two-folded meaning, but bends it, again, fully cognizant of what had transpired. It involves, he says, a thought that "(w)e cannot put aside, and yet cannot endure . . . ." Namely, that

> All support here fails us (*Hier sinkt alles unter uns*); and the *greatest* perfection, no less than the *least* perfection, is unsubstantial and baseless for the merely speculative reason, which makes not the least effort to retain either the one or the other and feels indeed no loss in allowing them to vanish entirely.[9]

It is a curious passage; a thought which cannot be put aside, namely, that of the ultimate ground, the ultimate truth, the true *Abgrund*, and at the same time cannot be endured. And yet, the speculative reason "makes not the least effort" to retain the order that it implies! Kant's whole effort in the succeeding pages will be to reinstate the shell of *metaphysica rationalis* as a *hypothesis* — what cannot be determined will be regulated, reflected, understood 'as if' it were so.

The end result circles back upon one of the axioms of Kant's position, but in this text it is stated in a form whose anticipations are overdetermined.

> The thing itself (*die Sache selbst*) is indeed given, but we can have no insight into its nature.[10]

That is, we are barred from its essence in a radical split between the phenomenal and the noumenal, between the *a priori* and the *a posteriori*, divided by the appearance of the sensation, that event which both 'gives' the thing and withdraws it. And this sensation, consequently, just is that "element in the appearances . . . which can never be known *a priori*, and which therefore constitutes the distinctive difference between empirical and *a priori* knowledge" and which "cannot be anticipated."[11] The thing itself 'ist gegeben' but as divided and screened beyond, as appearance and its other which is given without appearing, just as the positivity of the appearance itself remains divided already between the *a priori* and the *a posteriori*, as effect in the distinctive difference that constitutes it, that divides, ultimately, the thing itself from our grasp, that divides all presence from within, and finally, which divides the finite subject internally, interminably.

And yet in the above passage, where all support fails, speculative reason seems content to let the play of imagination loose. Speculative reason, for just a moment, in blinking before this opening, seems content, as he put it in the *Anthropology*, to have that state of affairs in which the "imagination runs riot," since it is "richer and more fertile in ideas than sense."[12] And the corresponding state, the noesis, if you will, might be characterized by what Kant calls "amentia *(Unsinnigkeit)* . . . the inability to bring one's idea into even the coherence that is necessary to make experience possible."[13]

Kant's abyss did not sink from sight in those who come after. Schelling was perhaps right that this "abyss" that "all men are warned of" is a consequence of "mechanistic philosophy . . . in its highest expression."[14] There is a sense in which *metaphysica rationalis* and the postulate of complete determination could only be systematically (if not successfully) completed under the hypothesis of mechanism, as e.g., Laplace and those who come after him understood. Consequently, Schelling attempted to do away with the hypothesis, which did not make his metaphysics any more successful *or* rational. Kant's mechanistic schemata were after all just his interpretation, his proviso on *finitude*, on what would provide *finite* experience with *Sinn und Bedeutung*. And the point was that others were possible, and that no finite cognitive act could ultimately determine or ground.

Hegel, on the other hand, overcame the problem of the *abyss*, as is usual in his work, by regulating it in the economics of *Aufhebung*, that other German word whose polysemia is to bespeak a speculative truth. In the *Science of Logic*, recounting the end of the chapter on Grounds, Hegel states:

> (T)his end itself, *this falling to the ground (Zugrundegehen)* of the mediation, is at the same time the *ground* from which the immediate proceeds. Language . . . combines the meaning of this *downfall (Untergang)* and of ground; the essence of God, it is said, is the *abyss (Abgrund)* for finite reason. This it is, indeed, in so far as finite reason surrenders its finitude and sinks its mediating movement therein; but this *abyss*, the negative ground, is also the *positive* ground of the emergence of simply affirmative being, of essence which is in its own self immediate; mediation is an *essential movement*.[15]

Hegel's *Abgrund* is as usual controlled. An economics of truth with its own economics of signs. The negative is implicitly the positive, the negative and positive in the economics of *Aufhebung*. One always buys the whole package in Hegel. On the basis of it in the *Lectures on the Philosophy of Religion*, with Kant clearly in mind, Hegel was content to reinstate the ontological argument.[16] In a sense, however, the *Logic* had always already presupposed it, the function of Kant's onto-theo-logy. It was after all "the exposition of God as he is in his eternal essence before the creation of the world."[17] And within it the same economics which regulates positive and negative mediates the inner and the outer, the sensible and the intelligible, the phenomenal and the noumenal.

II

For Nietzsche, on the other hand, Kant is "a delayer *par excellence,*" who sees but does not see "what stands at the door."[18] Only recently, perhaps, have we begun to see Nietzsche as the post-Kantian, notwithstanding all that he himself states. If Hegel was able to transform Kant's abyss into finite self-affirmation, Nietzsche intended to cut loose all intention to *ground.* He is indeed post-Kantian, in the words of Kant, making "not the lease effort to retain either the least or the greatest perfection." Nietzsche enters the abyss, neither to despair nor simply to nihilate (it is, after all, nihilism which stands at the door), but to affirm infinitely its groundlessness, its heterogeneity, to use a Kantian word.

Just like those others that are normally called 'post-Kantian,' Nietzsche had little use for the notion of the *Ding-an-sich:*

> The sore spot of Kant's critical philosophy has gradually become visible even to dull eyes: Kant no longer has a right to his distinction "appearance" and "thing-in-itself."[19]

The thing in itself involves "the scientific prejudice," the last of the prejudices of the Enlightenment to be dissolved (which began precisely as an attempt to dissolve prejudice):

> Against the scientific prejudice. – The biggest fable of all is the fable of knowledge. One would like to know what things in themselves are; but behold, there are no thing-in-themselves! But even supposing there were an in-itself, an unconditioned thing, it would for that very reason be unknowable! Something unconditioned cannot be known; otherwise it would not be unconditioned![20]

The scientific prejudice is precisely this belief in unconditioned facts, unconditioned grounds. But as a consequence of Kant's *Abgrund,* there are no such unconditioned grounds. And the grounds that buttress Kant's architectonic are no less implicated in this failure:

> The categories are "truths" only in the sense that they are conditions of life for us: as Euclidean space is a conditional "truth."[21]

What arises then is a play of conditions from which one cannot escape. This itself, in fact, is identified by Nietzsche as the new "infinite," namely that the perspectival character of existence extends indeterminately, *in indefinitum*, as Kant would say.[22] Whether existence without interpretation makes any sense, cannot be decided, for to decide it we would have to get around our own perspectives, interpretations, etc. But "(w)e cannot look around our own corner."[23]

Truth then must be put in scare quotes and is variously characterized as a 'reduction,' a 'fiction,' a 'lie,' as 'ugly,' an 'inertia,' an 'error,' 'falsification,' a 'schema,' the 'greatest error ever committed,' 'nonsensical,' a 'seduction,' but in any case a failure, one which accompanies a belief in knowledge-in-itself, and a world-in-itself, and especially an it-itself which might be set over against a 'for-us,' a fiction, falsity, etc. Furthermore, it is not a question of positing appearance over against the in-itself or the real, a positive over against its negative limit, the dissolution of the positive and the negative into some third more real thing, removing the screen between accident and essence. Abolishing the system of exclusion which constituted the element that differentiated the 'real' dissolves its opposite, the 'positivity' of the apparent as well.[24] What results, then, is another infinite play of affirmations.

Nietzsche's affirmation, however, stands outside the affirmation of Hegel, or even that of the tradition which precedes him. Hegel had himself blinked at this chasm precisely before introducing its dissolution before his *Aufhebung*. Speaking of the problem of grounding he declared:

> In fact one finds oneself in a kind of witches circle (*Hexenkreis*) in which determinations of reflection, ground and grounded, phenomena and phantoms, run riot in indiscriminate company and enjoy equal rank with one another.[25]

Nietzsche instead refuses to reduce the Other to the Same. It is, rather, the affirmation of difference, of chance, of the irrational that must be faced (for reason is simply unquestioned belief). There is a refusal to reduce all attributes to an univocity. A refusal, therefore, of ontology, of 'Being,' all is interpretation and exegesis. The world is, in short, an abyss, an *Ab-grund*. Nietzsche's abyss, however, is neither a negative ground for a positive emergence (as was Hegel's) nor one which can countenence a philosophy that proceeds as if it had not been met (as did Kant, whose regulative employments following the failure of foundations makes him a 'scarecrow' as Nietzsche depicts him). It is a chasm of infinite alterity, the infinite return of this Other without a Same. It is the return of the Other, of becoming, of difference. "That everything recurs is the closest approximation of the world of becoming to a world of being."[26] The confrontation of all this is in fact Zarathustra's mission. Facing this perfect circle, this eternal return which refuses all reduction, Zarathustra proclaims at the decisive conclusion of part III, "I call you my most abysmal thought!" (*Dich rufe Ich meinen abgrundlichsten Gedanken!*)[27]

What remains then, Nietzsche proclaims, is the infinite play of life itself, this play of alterity.[28] Otherwise stated, what remains, or rather becomes without being, is precisely the will to power. It is the will to power which infinitely interprets. In this sense, nature, as well as 'the problem of its synthesis,' to speak Kantian, becomes a play of forces, one which, again to borrow from Kant's characterization of the moral law, 'possesses us rather than we possess it.'

III

Just as Schelling and Hegel had transformed the material into the spiritual within, Nietzsche transforms the paradigm of mechanism from within arriving at the will to power, a monadalogy without a center:

> The victorious concept "force" by means of which our physicists have created God and the world, still needs to be completed: an inner will must be ascribed to it, which I designate as "will to power," i.e., as an insatiable desire to manifest power; or as the employment and exercise of power, as a creative drive, etc.[29]

Still, it is not the case, certainly, that Nietzsche is to be taken as a physicist. This thought which concerns the will to power is not a new *Naturphilosophie*. Drawing upon the distinction between explanation and interpretation, Nietzsche becomes one of the first philosphers to consider (or fear) that far from reserving a justified domain of enquiry for the *Geisteswissenschaften*, the problem that emerges with interpretation is one regarding the 'universality' of interpretation itself. Neither domain, consequently, functions as a grounded domain of enquiry. Physics, too, might turn into interpretation.

> It is perhaps just dawning on five or six minds that physics, too, is only an interpretation and exegesis of the world (to suit us, if I may say so!) and *not* a world-explanation . . . .[30]

Physics, then, becomes an interpretaton rather than the paradigm of certainty and justification, an interpretation of the infinite affirmation of the eternal return. It posits a sign for the process in which it participates without, again being able to look beyond its own corner:

> The mechanistic concept of "motion" is already a translation of the original process into the sign language of sight and touch.[31]

Scientific discourse is part of the infinite series of translations and interpretations of the 'original process' in which language tropes the world
of becoming. And, 'truth' persists only as the rigidified effect in this
'mobile army of metaphors.'[32]

Will to power is itself original assertion, a force which Nietzsche
himself was willing to trope, belonged to every body in that each "strives
to become master over all space and to extend its force (− its will
to power) and to thrust back all that resists its extension."[33] But all
in any case shared in what underlie the force of interpretation (again
which is attributed synonymously to all bodies): "the essential priority of the spontaneous, expansive, form-giving forces that give new
directions . . . ."[34]

And all evaluations here must proceed accordingly, affirming what
enhances, liberates, breaks-down, experiments, enjoys uncertainty, all
in short that refuses to confine the will to power within the myth of
knowledge and its correlate which would similarly bifurcate the world
into good and evil. Indeed, in one of those loaded statements which
perhaps overcomes the tradition by twisting it, which ruptures truth
while connecting it to the moral or the immoral, which denounces logic
by connecting it to force, which delivers all justification to its practice,
Nietzsche proclaimed:

> The criterion of truth resides in the enhancement of the feeling of
> power.[35]

IV

This shift haunts the legacy of the Nietzschean (and perhaps
Kantian) text, dividing it from within. But what is its status? Does this
Wahre Ab-grund, this deflected truth which enjoins force in Nietzsche,
which defies logic for practice, which exchanges the timeless for the
contextual, does it form a correction for truth or its dissolution? Does
it mark a limit, a transformation, or a simple substitution?

Ordinarily, as Martin Heidegger notes, such a question would be
'perverse.'[36] There is a whole archive in Western thought for dealing
with the skeptic, the sophist, the misologist who would give up truth
for rhetoric, for persuasion, in short, for force. Even so, it may be argued
that even Heidegger himself did not face the issue seriously enough.
"Truth" in any case, and in more than one domain, has become a problematic marker. And faced with recent events in these post-Kantian
fortresses of certainty, e.g. in philosophy of science and epistemology,
not to mention metaphysics itself, it may appear that the question of
truth now just needs to be forgotten − for the sake of the artist's faith,
Nietzsche himself would say, but as well, because we simply cannot

escape our practices or paradigms. We cannot, consequently, get around the issue of certainty, but maybe we can just get rid of it, because *we* at least seemingly can always straighten out our references, if not truth; our assertibility conditions, if not justification. Beyond this scope, the problem of truth or Being simply seems to make no sense. And, all of this seems to substitute, in some fashion, *Pragmata* for truth and reminds us as well that the history in which Nietzsche participates still needs to be written along with those others which claim that truth is expansive or 'expedient' as James put it.[37]

What haunts the interpretation of post-Kantian thought in this regard is just the *primat* it grants to the practical. It is a primacy which marks the limits of speculative thought and unleashes the scepter of nihilism. It occurs perhaps for the first time in that conflict between classical science and classical metaphysics outlined above which issues in Schelling's proclamation that would resound in the nineteenth century's commitment to practice, namely, that "Will is primordial being."[38] In any case, this *primat* marks as well the end of metaphysics and the need for its overcoming. *'Ueberwindung'*, the word is Nietzschean, but is to be found at the center of later thought as well, explicitly in Heidegger or Derrida, certainly, but also in Wittgenstein and Carnap, who used it in 'overcoming' Heidegger,[39] and implicitly in any number of thinkers who have felt of late the effect of history and conditioning, becoming worried once more that physics, just as much as what came 'before' it, meta-physics, may be a form of *eisegesis*.

V

Nietzsche had overcome the scientific prejudice, the prejudice of foundations and, ultimately, metaphysics itself by an appeal to that which underlies it, the force that it constrains, the will to power. Enhancement, like efficacity or expediency, was seen to underlie truth, and thus 'truth' and 'truths' were seen as transferences, to use a Freudian metaphor, rigidified effects, to use a Derridean metaphor, or petrifications, to use a Wittgensteinian one, of the forces or practices from which they merge. Hence, Nietzsche claimed in 1885 "logic does not stem from the will to truth,"[40] but from a fundamental falsification that stems itself from will to power.

But what sense can this claim that denies claims, this assertion which denies 'assertion' make? Martin Heidegger who has perhaps faced this issue in Nietzsche's text as strongly as anyone provides an exacting comment for this passage:

That is surprising. According to Nietzsche's own conception, truth is indeed what is firm and fixed; but should not logic emerge from this will to fixate and make permanent? According to Nietzsche's own conception, it can only derive from the will to *truth*. If Nietzsche nontheless says, "Logic does not stem from the will to truth," then he must unwittingly mean "truth" in another sense here: not in *his* sense, according to which truth means error, but in the traditional sense, according to which truth means agreement of knowledge with things and with realty. This concept of truth is the presupposition and principal standard of measure for the interpretation of truth as semblence and error.[41]

In what sense is this 'truth' to be understood in Nietzsche? Is it to be understood as what 'truly' is, or as what is valid in all judgments or life? In calling truth a lie what must be presupposed? Nietzsche himself had claimed that logic was, at best, an organon, or, within the problematic of force or of willing, an imperative. And consistent with this, in a move not unheard of *vis à vis* the collapse of correspondence theories, he turned to coherence, and once again to practice, what was 'taken' as true. The claim that the axioms of logic are *adequate* to reality therefore "contains no criterion of *truth*, but an imperative concerning what *should* count as true."[42] Still, Nietzsche reminds us that such a world is not the *real* world but the apparent one, the one that must also be abolished if we are to surpass Kant.

"Truth" then is to be seen as the attempt to master the multiplicity (that of 'sensations', but the will to power, and ultimately the eternal return). "The character of the world in a state of becoming" Nietzsche states is "incapable of formulation" is "false," and "self-contradictory." Knowledge and becoming exclude one another.

> Consequently, "knowledge" must be something else: there must first of all be a will to make knowable, a kind of becoming itself must itself create the deception of beings.[43]

Truth becomes "truth," knowledge becomes "knowledge." And the will to power becomes. But here Heidegger grows uneasy. Why are there no scare quotes around this 'will to power', this marker for becoming that "creates reality" through the axioms of logic? And, what in the end is the relationship between the signs of Nietzsche's metaphors and the becoming they indicate? What in the end is the relationship between this becoming and these 'lies' these falsehoods which are, terribly, Nietzsche's truth? What voice speaks from *Ecce Homo* to proclaim with the same deflection

> (T)he truth speaks out of me — but my truth is *terrible* for so far one has called *lies* truth.[44]

What Sphinx proclaims three years earlier all the while that there is
no truth, that

(t)here are many kinds of eyes. Even the spinx has eyes – and consequently
there are many kinds of "truths," and consequently there is no truth."[45]

VI

Nietzsche nihilates Being for the sake of what becomes. He turns
the truth of Being to a fable, its verification into falsification. Heidegger,
however, has refused this simple transformation that would exchange
one side of the polarity for the other, Becoming for Being. Kant had
similarly bifurcated the world into the sensible and the intelligible, the
real and the apparent, a dichotomy that Nietzsche had attempted to
overcome. Yet, at the same time, Kant himself was unable to simply
limit reason to the apparent, to the sensible, to the experience of physics.
No more, nontheless, could the bifurcation hold in Kant's own text.
Human reason was inherently, 'naturally' metaphysical. It inherently
surpassed the limitations which reason placed upon its own endeavors.
What is thought inherently transcended what reason might be certain
about. "Being," which Kant attempted to confine to mere position, to
mere positing,[46] even within the Kantian text problematically and yet
indeterminately extended always further than any possible conceptualization or schematization. Inherent to Kant's position, then, as
Heidegger points out in his work on Nietzsche, is precisely a notion
of Being that eludes that classical determination which would grasp
it as *ground*, as *stasis*, as receptacle of all predicates. In this regard, in
this overcoming which lies beyond but within metaphysics itself, Kant's
abyss is likewise the abyss of Being itself.

But the celebrated "universal" significance of "Being" is not the reified emptiness of a huge container into which everything capable of transformation
can be thrown. What misleads us in the direction of this notion is our long-
accustomed way of thinking that thinks "Being" as the most universal determination of all and therefore can admit the manifold only as the sort of
thing that fills the vast empty shell of the most universal concept.[47]

Consequently, rather than seeing Being as the set of all predicates
in terms of which all entities would receive complete determination,
as did *metaphysica rationalis*, metaphysics at its end would be forced
to face the indeterminacy or under-determination of Being with respect
to all positing, but *also* the overdetermination of Being in an abundance
which transcends all predication. What becomes 'imperative' for
Heidegger, then, is precisely to grasp this janus head (*Doppel-gesicht*)

of Being[48] and the discord it initiates between representing and understanding, between using and relying on, between retaining and forgetting, and saying.

The overcoming of metaphysics is consequently not to be found in the creativity of the will to power that would make manifest the becoming of beings. Rather in the thought of ontological difference between Being and the emergence of beings is that ontological differentiation which was for Kant a natural disposition, the differentiation of categorization and what always eludes any and all presentation.

Surpassing the failure of metaphysics, then, means precisely remaining open to the surpassing in Being itself, remaining open to the otherness which Being itself grants. Moreover, what constitutes human authenticity in its ownmost or most proper possibility involves remaining open to what is disclosed in the encounter with Being. Truth becomes then not a fable, an entity without time, a being in itself. Rather, it involves remaining free in the revelation of Being, a freedom which is itself the letting-be of Being in its Otherness.[49] And, it is precisely this freedom before Being, this surpassing which calls upon human response, this difference which beckons human freedom that constitutes Heidegger's own abyss. Freedom must itself be ungrounded beforehand, and yet (the paradox retains a certain Hegelian overtone) it is grounded precisely in what withdraws from its grasp. In *Vom Wesen Des Grundes* which concerns the problem of foundations, of grounding, Heidegger states:

> Freedom is not a ground in any *one* of the ways of grounding, as we are always inclined to think, but is the grounding unity of the transcendental dispersion of grounding. As *this* kind of ground, however, freedom is the abyss (*Ab-grund*) of Dasein, its groundless (*grundlos*) or absent ground. It is not as though the only kind of free behavior were groundless (unmotivated) behavior. Instead as transcendence, freedom provides Dasein, as "potentially for being" with possibilities which gape open before its finite choice, i.e., in its density.[50]

Heidegger's abyss is the event of Dasein's freedom, an event which it receives in transcendence. This freedom is as much receptivity as spontaneity. Human Dasein is 'thrown' into it, a word still with Nietzschean overtones.

And yet, this thrownness belies Nietzsche. This Being which perpetually escapes is not created, not simply 'effect,' nor is its force simply one form of Becoming. There is Being. '*Es gibt Sein*,' Heidegger points out, is again another fortuitous idiom ('There is Being,' 'It gives Being') whose twofold meaning portends the necessary overdetermination of speculative thought – and Being itself, as has been seen. And it opposed all that Nietzsche stood for. As the latter proclaims clearly and consistently in *Thus Spoke Zarathustra*:

> "It is given" (*Es gibt sich*) – that is also a doctrine of submission. But I tell you, you comfortable people: *it is taken* (*es nimmt sich*) and will be taken more and more from you.[51]

VII

While it is true that no one has more forcefully faced the challenge of what has been limited here to Nietzsche's question, Heidegger's treatment is not uncontroversial. Jacques Derrida, for example, despite his differences with Heidegger's Nietzsche books, using words he employs sparingly, characterized it as "that mighty tome."[52] Gilles Deleuze, on the other hand, claimed that "Heidegger gives an interpretaion of Nietzschean philosophy closer to his own thought than to Nietzsche's."[53] Both may be true, even though they might still disagree.

Derrida's interrogations of the Heideggerean reading of Nietzsche have centered around the machinations of authenticity in the Nietzschean abyss. He has, certainly, affirmed the problematic of the Heideggerean question. For example, commenting upon Nietzsche's claim that the truths of his books remain *his* truths, Derrida states:

> The very fact that "*Meine Wahrheiten*" is so underlined that they are multiple, variegated, contradictory even can only imply that these are not *truths*. Indeed there is no such thing as a truth in itself. But only a surfeit of it. Even if it should be for me, above me, truth is plural.[54]

There can be no decidability in the exchange between the true and the false. But again, Derrida queries, what sense can be made of 'truth' if there are no 'truths-in-themselves.' This means, moreover, that once this abyss has become pluralized, all oppositions become in a sense indefensible. And, for Derrida, this includes the opposition of an 'authentic' or 'inauthentic' response, reading, or hearing of 'Being.' 'Being' and 'beings,' what exceeds and what erupts, presence and absence become lost in an infinite labyrinth of exchanges. Still, the gift of Heideggers *Es gibt* is, seemingly, precisely that proper, that standard, that origin in terms of which one may still in accord with the scientific prejudice adjudicate between the authentic and the inauthentic, the true and the false, between what gets revealed and what gets covered up.

Heidegger hoped to restore the authenticity of the origin, of Being by a recourse to a proper-ty of the abyss of Being itself: "The noble or the worthy Appropriation of the origin is the unique release as Appropriation of freedom, which is unconcealment of concealment, because it belongs to the abyss, *das Eignethum des Abgrundes*."[55] Derrida aptly questions whether Heidegger's whole understanding of Being, of its withdrawal of the abyss itself does not have built into it a privilege, a proper, a bifurcation which is itself indefensible, positive in line with its speculative (Hegelian) ancestry. In all this it remains, Derrida charges, despite all the critical resources of the ontological question, pre-critical: "in its relation to the signified, in the return to the presence of the spoken word, to a natural language, to perception, to consciousness, and its phenomenological system."[56]

One must tread carefully on this site, given the Derridean choice of markers here. The very meanings of 'critical' and 'pre-critical' themselves emerge only from the history of transcendentalism. However, this history is being dissolved. And if it is to be overcome, as is evident from a text in *Of Grammatology*

> (I) believe that there is a short of and a beyond of transcendental criticism. To see to it that the beyond does not return to the within is to recognize in the contortion the necessity of a pathway. Without that track, abandoned to the simple content of its conclusions, the ultra-transcendental text will so closely resemble the precritical text as to be indistinguishable from it . . . .[57]

And yet, for Derrida this uneffaceable within of the transcendental text already contains its beyond in what exceeds it. Like Kant's own unconditioned necessity, indispensably required as the last bearer of all things, the first ground of transcendentalism, too, becomes the veritable abyss. Speaking of the event of freedom's appropriation – an event which Heidegger himself describes as Being's expropriation of itself in its withdrawal – Derrida states:

> Finally, then, once the question of production, doing, machination, the question of the event (which is one meaning of *Ereignis*) has been uprooted from ontology, the proper-ty or propriation is named as exactly that which is proper to nothing and no one. Truth, unveiling, illumination are no longer decided in the appropriation of the truth of being, but are cast into its bottomless abyss as non-truth, veiling and dissimulation . . . . The proper-ty of the abyss (*das Eigentum des Abgrundes*)is necessarily the abyss of proper-ty, the violence of an event which befalls without being.
>
> Perhaps truth's abyss as non-truth, propriation as appropriation/ a-propriation, the declaration become parodying dissimulation . . . .[58]

The truth of grounds here as well becomes the abyss of truth. The abyss of truth as non-truth, the dissolution of all truth, of all immediacy, of all origins. In a sense Derrida has forsaken the Heideggerean text for its Nietzschean ancestry — but perhaps wholly on Heideggerean grounds. But, by defining truth as revealment, as *aletheia*, even if no final interpretation renders a sign complete, didn't Heidegger himself *guarantee* truth, since there is nothing more primordial to being Da-sein — as revealing, disclosing?

And yet, Heidegger himself wavered before this abyss. It was, he relates in his 1964 Unesco address, and Derrida's above text depends on it, "inadequate and misleading to call *aletheia* in the sense of opening, truth."[59] In this hasty identification, truth and Being are still too much thought together thought too much within the coupling which links together the opening of presence with the simple *correctness* of statements and judgments, too much abstracted from the event itself. Being, after all, withdraws without fully presencing, without, therefore being fully 'adequatable.' In this regard, Derrida's abyss is seemingly Heidegger's as well. Where is truth to be placed in this event which appropriates and de-propriates at the same time? Heidegger's own query following his own deconstruction and retrieval of the Greek origins of the tradition takes us to this limit itself:

> *Aletheia*, unconcealment thought as the opening of presence, is not yet truth. Is *aletheia* less than truth? Or is it more because it first grants truth as *adequatio* and *certitudo*, because there can be no presence and presenting outside of the realm of the opening.
> This question we leave to thinking as a task.[60]

VIII

But then what is to be made of the belonging-together of Being and Truth? What is it that remains undecidable in *aletheia*? And what is it that remains insurpassable, that leads this abyss, the *Ab-grund* to be connected time and again with the problem of truth or its loss?

In 1927 Heidegger seemed sure of all this:

> *Why must we presuppose that there is truth?* What is 'presupposing'? What do we have in mind with the 'must' and the 'we'? What does it mean to say 'there is truth' ("*es gibt Wahrheit*")? 'We' presuppose truth because 'we' being in the kind of Being which Dasein possesses, are 'in the truth' . . . .
> It is not we who presuppose 'truth'; but it is 'truth' that makes it all possible ontologically for us to be able to be such that we 'presuppose' anything at all. Truth is what first makes possible anything like presupposing.[61]

A strange passage. One which marks again the passage of truth to 'truth,' fully cognizant that this truth as well cannot be the truth of *certitudo* or *adequatio*. And it enframes, also, the same appeal to transcendentalism and its *conditio sine qua non* with which Heidegger had met Nietzsche's own quotation on truth (*supra*, p. 13).

But then why is it not classical, this appeal to the *'es gibt'* once again. Is this not an appeal to grounds, the 'presupposing' that 'subject' and 'object' are always already in harmony? Shouldn't we hear Nietzsche's roar that the appeal to a subjective necessity does not prove 'truth,' that roar that was to shake Kant's faculties and synthetic *a priori* judgment to the ground?[62] Isn't Dasein's "presupposing" to be taken, after all, *as* Dasein's? After all, it was Heidegger, too, who was quite willing to say that "'There is' truth only in so far as Dasein is and so long as Dasein is?"[63] *Es gibt or es nimmt*? Constituted or revealed? The problem remains, it might be said, assuming the Heideggerean genre once more, "undecided," the legacy of the undecidable transcendental ideal.

What remains true, however, is that this 'truth' which always already includes its own deferment cannot ground this abyss, but derives from it. Similarly, it cannot solve the problem of modernism and its search for unequivocal grounds or foundations. Rationality exists in the end without foundations, as not only Kant, Nietzsche, and Derrida *et al* came to realize, but as have Kant, Kuhn, Feyerabend *et al* as well. All judgments are conditional, 'presuppose' a prior framework and the ensuing 'truths' are by no means commennsurable. There is clearly no truth in itself, any more than there could be knowledge in itself.

And these other, remaining 'truths,' this labyrinth without decidability? Here, as Heidegger consistently claimed, "A skeptic can no more be refuted than the Being of truth can be 'proved.' "[64] Scare quotes again: 1927 again. Notwithstanding his later, perhaps hasty characterization, Heidegger's 'truth' never was the truth of modernism, the truth of proof, of certainty, of adequation. If his story then sometimes looked neo-Kantian in its search for the *conditio sine qua non* of truth, the resulting quoted, troped 'truth' was in this respect already Nietzschean. And he gave up on *Fundamentalontologie* faced with the abyss at which it unavoidably arrived. Fourteen years later in "Recollection in Metaphysics" he would claim little else in stating that the truth of Being cannot be proven and "is inaccessible to every explanation,"[65] — at least not from the perspective of beings, of totalization, of completeness. One must look rather to that thought of what exceeds:

> What "is" Being? May we inquire into Being: as to *what* it *is*? Being remains unquestioned and a matter of course, and thus unthought. It holds itself in a truth which has long since been forgotten and is without ground.[66]

The question is whether this is enough, and what sense is to be made of it. Isn't one person's abyss another's ground, one person's listening another's response, one person's authenticity another's inauthenticity, and even one person's *es gibt* another's *es nimmt*? Hasn't Heidegger simply exchanged reason for taste, philosophy for poetry? Recall that Carnap, too, praised Nietzsche in his *Ueberwindung*, precisely for having realized that metaphysicians were bad artists who masked their emotional commitments.[67] Now finally we were in a position to clarify science and send the metaphysicians to art school. A modernist concern, certainly, retaining its commitment to the purity of reason and the univocity of its methodology but also one that stands at the center of something like a 'post-modern' understanding of 'rationality'.

IX

Heidegger's response is first a claim about the modernist project itself and its commitment to a "technical scientistic view of language"[68] which reduces it to a frame, a metalanguage — one that would either present the ultimate picture of reality, or, under the guise of the latter's failure, in an appeal to relativism, claim that as Quine put it, 'to be is to be the value of a bounded variable.' It forgets, thereby the ontological difference in an antimony, to speak Kantian, which grants either too much or too little, "both" sides claiming "more than it knows."[69] Further, it thereby functions on the ground of nihilism, as Heidegger would say, since, "the essence of nihilism is the history in which there is nothing to Being itself,"[70] Being here either having been dissolved or totalized.

Still the other side of what Heidegger called philosophy's "most extreme counter-positions," what he termed "the speculative-hermeneutical experience of language" with all its overtones to what has gone before cannot provide a simple or easy alternate. If language here is the 'house of Being' the place of the occurrence of the *'es gibt'*, it must still be anything but the simple Absolute of the Idealist tradition *it* stands upon. Heidegger, certainly, had learned the failure of that event of Will, of realization that would get around Kant's dilemma. There is no final proof in all this for Heidegger, not even the proof of practice. That recognition seems to override his rejection of reason as in, for example, a paper on Nietzsche's proclamation that God is dead, in which reason is described as "the most stiff-necked adversary of thought."[71]

Rather, it is thought and thinking that are to prevail now. "Thought," is a speculative mark that may still descent from the machinations of German Idealism, however. It is, as Phillipe Lacoue-Labarthe has said, "the word of greatest proximity to Hegel," and consequently, "the word of greatest danger."[72] For if Being is to be authentically disclosed and divided it is to be received in thought[73] – speculative hermeneutical thought, two words which in other arenas Heidegger might have rejected. If nonetheless, Heidegger dissolves the proof of this Being, if he forces the recognition that there is no final foundation, no final proof for the matter of thought, this does not deny that there is a strictness to thought. Using characterizations which hark back to Husserl's notion of *Strenge Wissenschaft*, and a text which Heidegger claims is "much too neglected today"[74] he states:

> The multiplicity of possible interpretations does not discredit the strictness of the thought content. For all true thought remains open to more than one interpretation and this by reason of its nature. Nor is the multiplicity of possible interpretation merely the residue of a still unachieved formal-logical univocity which we properly ought to strive for but did not attain. Rather multiplicity of meanings is the element in which all thought must move in order to be strict thought.[75]

And, ultimately, this strict thought, overdetermined, incomplete, groping, interpretative, remains 'true' thought precisely to the extent that it responds to this Being without proof. Notwithstanding the failure of science or the failure of metaphysics, then, Heidegger remains committed to "thought," to *strictness*, to the matter of thinking every bit as much as Hegel with his own "element of thought" (*Elemente des Denkens*)[76] and all the baggage of its metaphysical commitments – to the intelligible or the spiritual versus the sensible, the inner versus the outer, the essential versus the accidental.

Yet this 'strict' thought cannot remove itself from its own contingency, presuppositions, possibility, and historicity – which is why *aletheia*, as Heidegger ultimately realized, must mean more than truth (*Wahrheit*), must mean more than the safeguard of Being as he sometimes allowed. There remains the problem of abysses. There remains the problem of the Other, that risk which turns all perception, all *Wahrnehmung*, as Heidegger ironically liked to hyphenate it, into a mere phantasm. Perhaps this is what haunts phenomenology, like all commitments to the immediacy of the given, namely, in a fundamental repetition of Kant once more, that "the thing itself (*die Sache selbst*) . . . is and remains inscrutable." In this respect there remains the Nietzschean question, overdetermined in its reference, and unavoidable in its force:

> Is seeing itself – not seeing abysses?[77]

And, what holds for the pure seeing of the given must stand perhaps, as well, for Heidegger's 'matter of thinking,' which he believes can remain in the former's disappearance. Certainly this is why the Heideggerean text for all its strength seems problematic, and, as no one knows better than Jacques Derrida, a bit comic in the 'strictness' of the disclosure of its *magnum mysterium*.

Still, it is not a question of alternatives, of oppositions: the logic itself has become overdetermined. A simple dismissal here would be fallacious in its implicit appeal to a story about certainty and the sure progress of knowledge that has been put in question. We should not, consequently, dismiss the Heideggerean text too fast. Heidegger perhaps does not say it often enough; often enough, he says the opposite. But he too knew the theoreticians's dilemma:

> Whether the realm of the truth of Being is a blind alley or whether it is the free space in which freedom conserves its essence is something each one may judge after he himself has tried to go the designated way, or even better, after he has gone a better way, that is, a way befitting the question.[78]

19. Binding Withdrawal

Gayle L. Ormiston

I would like to stake out and reiterate, in advance, two of Jacques Derrida's remarks. The remarks are cited to supply a framework within which the comments *I* advance and the questions *I* pose (indeed, the strategies *I* enact and embrace) can be comprehended.

La Carte Postale announces the following:

> Repetition is bequeathed; the legacy repeated.[1]

Here Derrida's writing traces a motif unraveled and reinscribed in *Writing and Difference*:

> What is tragic is not the impossibility but the necessity of repetition. ("The Theater of Cruelty and the Closure of Representation", *WD* 248)

Derrida's writing becomes the medium and the condition for speculation on that proper name, that signature, "Jacques Derrida" – and the possibilities, the openings and closures, indicated for reading and writing post-Derrida.

I will address a certain thematic preoccupation capitalized and punctuated in the writing of Jacques Derrida.

One might identify this theme, tantamount to a thematic web *and* a problematic matrix, as a desire or a tendency or a drifting that prefigures Derrida's text and is affirmed in that writing. Grossly stated, the thematic preoccupation to subvert and to invert, to pervert, and to go beyond apparently dominant philosophic, literary, political, and pedagogical concepts, frameworks, and structures of authority is the "desire" in question.

Derrida's writing engenders and demands a desire to go beyond *itself* as an identity of self-sameness, a sovereign source, i.e. as sovereign text, sovereign subject, sovereign signature, or authorial anchor and presence. Derrida's writing enacts and requires engagement of a *text without sovereignty*. So, the desire to read and to write post-Derrida, Derrida *et au-delà*, to post a reading/a writing that *is* one's own(?) is self-menacing.

And yet, the desire can be articulated as the attempt to enact a vague (historical) consciousness − an "unhappy consciousness." It is a consciousness or, for the lack of a better term, an attentiveness drawn out by a dissatisfaction with the dialogue between Derrida's text and its critics and expositors, detractors and disciples. It is indeed, as Hegel notes in *The Phenomenology of Mind*, "the consciousness of self as a divided nature, a doubled and merely[?] contradictory being."[2] The spirit of reading post-Derrida is torn between the dissatisfaction of a mere repetition of Derrida's voice(s) and comprehending the necessity of repetition *to betray* that writing in order to voice my own concerns, to expose my-self.

The desire is thwarted and disarmed, and yet the dissatisfaction is transformed into the desire to go on . . . to live on . . . .

As such, my remarks can be seen as auto-biographical, a feint moment of auto-analysis appropriated in and through an encounter with a text that throws into question sensibilities and values that orient and order contemporary conceptions of literacy and (schemes for) pedagogical practices − reading and writing. Derrida's writing requires a turn toward and on the law(s) that dictate and structure the problems of reading, and the opposition of naive and critical reading. In effect, Derrida's text demands "that reading should free itself, at least in its axis, from the classical categories of history − not only from the categories of the history of ideas and the history of literature but also, and perhaps above all, from the categories of the history of philosophy" (*OG* lxxxix). Here the desire of Derrida's writing is pronounced: Derrida is betrayed, i.e., pointed out, identified, unmasked, delivered to the tradition of Western metaphysics, to repeat a certain *uni-verse* of discourse.

Derrida's desire is the desire of reading post-Derrida − only once re-moved, reiterated always in a certain way. To recite and to reinscribe the thematic and problematic matrix of the history of philosophy is a delivery of one-self − there is a masquerading of figures, a mixing of voices. With the repetition of names and concepts there is the appearance of speaking in unison with the other, the tradition. Moreover, to repeat and reiterate the desires, the strategies, the motifs of Derrida's text is to deploy them according to an economy that takes into account and takes account of the ways in which one inhabits these structures.

The text of the history of philosophy or Derrida's writing, as one more such fragment of that history, is engaged and inhabited always *in a certain way,* "because one always inhabits, and all the more when one does not expect it" (*OG* 24, emphasis added).

I am interested in the different ways to inhabit the textual structuration of Derrida's writing: the ways to inhabit the structure of Western metaphysics. I am interested in the necessity of repetition, the *tragedy* of repetition where the character's voices are fused — mixed, where identity is muddled and of questionable significance. I am interested in *how* repetition, and the chain of substitutions in which it is inscribed, is the possibility or the condition for the formation of "a new combination of ideas concerning the combination of ideas" (*AF* 62). Repetition, reiteration, . . . must generate a different logic, a logic or an economy that breaks with the recomposition of fundamental philosophic themes through the very reinscription of these words and concepts. So, to reiterate:

> the philosopher must form a new combination of ideas concerning the combination of ideas. He must produce another concept of the order and the generation of ideas. (*AF* 71)

To be certain, the question of style interests me. Derrida's writing folds in on itself: the medium and condition for its pursuits is always the history of philosophy, literature, politics, the history of language. With that in mind, the overriding demand "to form a new combination of ideas concerning the combination of ideas" is an overriding demand of post-Derridean reading: to generate, to produce dialogue — with others, with one-self — that *traverses and reaches beyond,* but which can never transcend, the displaced erotic obsession with truth, *aletheia,* interpretive correctness, the interpretation (the explication, the understanding) of interpretation. To read after Derrida is to read, to write, in light of, in spite of Derrida's insights and oversights, but surely never to imitate slavishly. It is a desire that moves to register the question concerning how to generate or to force a breach in a text in order to penetrate its apparent density and, thus, to locate a space that affords some movement within the structure of Derrida's writing. To generate such a breach is to display a style of reading and writing that "has the bearing of re-presentation." However:

> What one cannot represent is the relationship of representation to so-called originary presence. The re-presentation is also a de-presentation. It is tied to the work of spacing. (*OG* 203)

> In this play of representation, the point of origin becomes ungraspable.
> There are things like reflecting pools, and images, an infinite reference from
> one to the other, but no longer a source, a spring. (*OG* 36)

Derrida becomes an analogue, and all the writing underwritten by that
signature becomes so many apologues, for the writing that discreetly
moves toward and against the closure − "I do not say the *end*" (*OG* 4)
− of philosophy's history.

   To continue . . . should one speak of Jacques Derrida as one speaks
of so many other discourses? As the passing of an age? The end of an
era? *The passage of an epoch?* Going beyond? Is this what comprises
reading after Derrida? Perhaps. But how so?
   Allow me to suggest that one speak of Derrida in terms of
possibilities, possibilities for realizing the desires of reading, writing,
critical inquiry. Indeed, what is required here is that one ponder
everything for which that *proper name* − "Jacques Derrida" − is an *index*,
everything that overflows the boundaries and sponges off that *signature*.
   1. Still *différance* requires thinking through. *Différance: the irreducible systematic play and dis-play of differences, the assemblage and scribble
of what has become a legend* in the philosophic market requires a
re-thinking. The economy and logic of *différance* animates, conditions,
permeates Derrida's text as an incessant and strategic movement of supplementarity precisely because "it is the most general structure of
economy" (*Pos* 8). There is no economy without *différance*, without supplementation, without division, without effacement − doubling that
splits what it doubles, what it reproduces. The line from *Of Grammatology* is quite familiar, but do we hear what it announces? The supplement is *already* a supplement of a supplement, always and already
"the supplement of (at) the origin" (*Le supplément d'origine, OG* 313 and
SP 88).

> The supplement is neither a presence nor an absence. No ontology can
> think its operation. (*OG* 314)

The play of *différance* and the seminal dissemination which *is* this play
cannot be comprehended as such: "differance remains a metaphysical
name; and all the names that it receives from our language are still,
so far as they are names, metaphysical" ("Differance," *SP* 158). *Différance*
cannot be consumed by or exhausted in the rubric of metaphysical or
ontological categories. With the presentation of *"différance"* under that
name, according to *that* certain representation, *différance* is effaced,
withdrawn, over taken by the play of infinite redoubling.

To say with Derrida that no ontology can think the seminal production of *différance* is to say that *différance* operates in and through
the dissimulation, the re-iteration of the categories, concepts, and
themes of philosophy . . . but *always and already in a certain way*. The
mark of *différance* (that legend) becomes the mark of self-effacement.

The mark of *"différance"* (that legend) becomes the mark of self-
effacement. The mark of *différance* is that it frames the play of dissimulation as it turns to supplement, subvert, and pervert the production of
differences, possibilities. Derrida's signature renders *itself* legible as a
scribble (*crible*, cf., "Scribble [writing/power]," *YFS*, 58, 116–147; *CP*
7–10). The scribble — of *différance* — *marks out* a general system of
possibilities: overwhelmingly full of holes, overwhelmingly in debt to
a certain intellectual tradition. "Scribble" translates the "assemblage" of
"différance." As Derrida writes:

> the word "assemblage" seems more apt for suggesting that the kind of bring-
> ing together proposed here has the structure of an interlacing, a weaving,
> or a web, which would allow the different threads and different lines of
> sense and force to separate again, as well as being ready to bind others
> together. ("Differance," *SP* 132)

The scribble of *différance* enframes: the scribble screens, sifts and girds
selection, the discrimination, discernment and ordering of various lines
and levels of representation that comprise the legend. The scribble
frames the play but it is always a double frame, a double exposure,
always an over exposure: the detail is not yet dis-played. The scribble
frames the legend marginally, or according to the double pretext,
pretense, and prefiguration of the *parergon*: the fiction of the frame,
the already fractured frame pictured in *La vérité en peinture* ("Parergon,"
19–168).

2. Derrida's signature remains, the already fractured frame for a
marginally legible legend — *différance*. Derrida's *signature*, the very concept of the signature on which Derrida has dwelled so often, remains
to be thought through, especially as it pertains to a discourse about *différance*, especially in its relation to *différance*. It is a signature, a name,
and now a legend that underwrites so many different moves toward
the boundaries of metaphysical discourse and sub-scribes to and supports, i.e., gives *substance* to, so many other texts, discourses, and
metaphysical thematics. As an enframing, the signature endures, it continues to hold (in place) the refuse or the deposits of the metaphysical
tradition, its own legend, legacy, or heritage, all the while obstructing
the order of that placement. The signature that binds Derrida to a
legend, to a legacy, deposits or posts that "name" in an infinite chain

of supplementation as nothing more than a "fold," a *trope*, – a trick, a turn, within an elaborate relay system: *"différance"* is "a relay to mark that there is never anything but, relays" ["Envois," *CP* 206]. Derrida incorporates into his signature or text the sign of its own forgery. Derrida writes in "Signsponge 1":

> Hence the signature has to remain and disappear at the same time, remain in order to disappear, or disappear in order to remain. *It has to do so, it is lacking*, this is what matters. It has to, it fails to, remain by disappearing, *it has to have to disappear*, a simultaneous and double demand, a double and contradictory postulation, a double obligation, a double bind which I have translated as the *double band* of the signature, the double band, the double band(s), hence the double(s) band (*la double band, le double bande, donc les double(s) bandent*). There has to be a signature so that it can remain-to-disappear. It is lacking, which is why there has to be one, but it is necessary that it be lacking, which is why there does not have to be one. (*OLR*, vol 5: 1–2, 105)

The signature rests on and supports, advances toward, inserts itself and withdraws into the assemblage of *différance*, the legend and discourse of historical texts. The signature is a *stitching*, an "interpretive sewing" (*la couture*) – indeed a baste line – that "happens already with an artifact" (*Glas* 233 b; *cf. WD* 342). That is to say, *with* Derrida, "it is the stitching which is in movement here" (*Glas* 234b).

3. Furthermore, one needs to consider the strategies or *strategem* deployed necessarily, but not only in Derrida's text, to announce and to question those norms or laws that regulate the reproductive performance of any text. That is to say, one needs to ponder the laws, to reflect on the prejudices passed over blindly and in silence, that stage the inscription of a text's "heritage" and the *writing* of its self-authorization. Derrida is attentive to these concerns, i.e., the economy of *différance*, iteration, binding repetition, and his writing requires reading to maintain this attention, indeed to maintain the tension of traversing a certain line of thought. What is required is a certain "mindfulness," if you will, of the relationships one bears to a problematic matrix. In other words, what is required is a simultaneous turning, a turn toward and a turn away from an un-mindfulness of how these relationships are framed and inscribed, and how the thematic ligature with such a matrix *prompts and prohibits* criticism.

Deconstruction is one such strategy, one such strategem. Yet, deconstruction has become a monument. It is a memorial in which the once subversive laughter affirming the life of philosophical inquiry, envisioned by Derrida as "the operations of childbearing," is now hushed by the cacphony of so many detractors and disciples. Deconstruction — a word, Derrida writes, "I have never liked and one whose fortune has disagreeably surprised me" ("The Time of a Thesis: Punctuations," PFT 44) is

> not primarily a matter of philosophical contents, themes or theses, philosophemes, poems, theologemes or ideologemes, but especially and inseparably meaningful frames, institutional structures, pedagogical or rhetorical norms, the possibilities of law, of authority, of evaluation, and of representation in terms of its very market. (*PFT* 45)

In *La vérité en peinture* Derrida remarks that deconstruction — as a strategy — provides a means, a way, for a certain style of "critique" ("Parergon," *VP* 24) — not a "master key" or a "frame" within which the "more or less visible framework structures" can be comprehended. To reiterate: Derrida's strategy is to engage critically not only "the internal — at once the semantic and formal — edification (or alignment) of philosophemes" with certain extrinsic conditions that determine their practice and repetition in different discourses. Criticism must turn to engage and embrace the conditions, the historical forces of teaching philosophy, "the social, economic, and political structures of that pedagogical institution," and the "discourse or significant representations" that legislate pedagogical authority. The logic of such a critique rests on and remains "a structure moveable in its depth" (*une structure à fond mobile*, "Passe-Partout," *VP* 17): the *mise-en-abyme*.

To read after Derrida is to produce, to put into practice, a strategy that concurrently works with the flow of Derrida's writing (with any scene of writing) and yet thwarts the desire to be consumed in the reading along with Derrida's script. After all, in this respect, Derrida is not unlike René Descartes. I will advance the claim that Derrida and Descartes are each simulacra — multiple and doubling copies — of the other. With respect to the strategies and stratagems deployed in their discourses, one doubles (as) the other.

In the "Preface to the Reader" of the *Meditations on First Philosophy*, Descartes announces that he is an author to none who merely "read" or desire, by design, to decipher his writing.

> On the contrary, I would never recommend that a person read these things except one who will meditate seriously with me . . . .[3]

A strategy for reading that hopes to reproduce "the conscious, voluntary, intentional relationship the writer institutes in his exchange with history" (*OG* 158) is grounded in the desire to insure the translation of the text, according to laws (protocols) constructed to resist the ambiguous threats imposed by the discourse itself. Critical reading cannot be happy, is not content with this strategy. That is so much like assigning philosophy the task to watch over hermeneutical extravagence. Philosophy would become a police force, a regulatory agency. It would, however, provide a sanguine moment to ponder a rather promising life expectancy for philosophers!

Rather, to read after Derrida is to thwart the desire of analysis to be satisfied, to satisfy itself, to feel as though it had arrived at its anticipated destination as master of the text. In lieu of proffering a strategy designed to conquer, to provide a means so that one can look ahead to a particular destination, or as a way to bring to a close a certain exchange, reading post-Derrida engages and enacts a strategy that is strategically without finality – what Derrida has termed "the aleatory strategy of someone who admits that he does not know where he is going" ("The Time of a Thesis: punctuations," *PFT* 50). Strategies and strategems are necessary to critical reading because it seeks confrontation with opposing textual forces. Critical reading seeks to generate conflict. Strategies are required, and require that they be abused, in order to advance along and traverse so many lines or pathways exposed in a discourse.

So many strategies, stratagems, and cunning maneuvers are required in the reach beyond one's engagement with a text (Derrida's writing), the straining of textual boundaries. The strategy of a strategy without finality must be mindful of the following: "A text always has several epochs and reading must resign itself to that fact" (*OG* 102).

Indeed, a text's binding or stitching withdraws. A text is bound by artifice, dissimulation, deceit, and so many epochs. But here an *epoch* is not a sequence of events, nor is it the passing of time, a particular span of time or stage of development. Instead, as Heidegger notes in the lecture on "Time and Being" (as well as so many other places), it is akin to *epoché* in the Greek: to holding back. Epoch designates withdrawal, the holding back that defers to the *presentation* or the gift of being. Being gives itself only to withdraw itself in "the truth of its own coming to presence with oblivion."[4]

So to speak of Jacques Derrida as the *passage of an epoch* is to speak neither of the end of an era, the passing of a fad, nor of the death of metaphysics, nor of the overcoming of logo-phono-phallo-centric discourse and thought. It is, rather, to be mindful of, and attentive to, what is passed over in silence as one traverses certain pathways, assembled and bound in and through the discourse of an historical problematic.

It is to be attentive to how a multitude of familiar paths lead away from the passages traced. More directly: a multitude of familar paths under-write and undercut each of these passages. There is an endless coiling, turning, and re-routing of trails and tracks as they furrow into one another, rendering the "bush" and the "forest" all the more indistinguishable. On these pathways, these passages that withdraw into the "text," one finds oneself lost — abandoned, overwhelmed. The strategy of a strategy without finality turns against itself, menaces its every step. Further, such a strategy requires that one ponder abandonment — finding oneself — on a trail, bound by it as it withdraws in every direction. A strategy for reading post-Derrida must be to bethink itself with respect to *a priori* withdrawal, the play between tracing, the track, and the holding back — the already not being-there of the already-being behind/being-ahead of the passage. The strategy turns back and in on itself. "It is a question here of the path again, of what passes there, of what passes the path by, of what happens there, or not" (*Il y va ici du chemin, encore, de ce qui y passe, le passe, s'y passe, ou pas* — "The *Retrait* of Metaphor" *EN* 33).

"Jacques Derrida" — that proper name, that signature, that text — is resplendent with artifice. As a proper name, as a signature that names the *propre*, the property, a garbled sign that authorizes reproduction and repetition, Jacques Derrida is an artifact. As such, Derrida's text indicates a certain spacing, a drifting, a "skidding" (*EN* 7) — not a space nor a place it should be remarked, but a spacing — that invites, allows, and summons the surreptitious transformation and translation of speech. To embrace and to enact a strategy without finality necessitates that each step be read as or seen as a feint, hesitant and insecure: one step following in another already there, always under a certain pretense. Each step announces, posts if you will, alerts along the way: Stop! Look out! Beware! Take care!

Every step, each epoch constitutes the text in its theoretical and practical dimensions or rhetorical allusions as *trompe d'oeil*. Every feint is a mask that inaugurates metamorphosis. The surreptitious passage from one voice to another — the passage of a legacy, a tradition perhaps — is a transformation of Derrida's voice into my voice.

To reiterate the line from *La Carte Postale*: "Repetition is bequeathed; the legacy repeated" (357). Repetition is a grounding peg, it allows the passage from one epoch to another to work. Repetiton, iteration of an idiom is translation; it places reading and writing *between* epochs "along all sorts of passages, with intersections, red lights, one way streets, crossroads or crossings, patrolled zones and speed limits" ("The *Retrait* of Metaphor," *EN* 6). In short, repetition forces a turn toward the Heideg-

gerian "neighborhood": a turn toward "the very nearness of that neighborhood in which we already reside" (*nur das Nächste jenes Nahen
unmittlebar zuspricht, darin wir uns schon aufhalten*).[5]
   Repetition of a certain discourse or textual idiom, or what is tantamount to carrying over one voice into another

> is at the same time an example and essence, an event and a rule. *Traditio*
> [delivery, surrender, handing down; instruction and doctrine delivered, the
> incarnate word; the word made flesh] is an example of the *traditio* of
> language, it gives the gift and betrays the betrayal [*trahison*: treachery,
> breach, perfidy]. Lo! And behold the word. (*C'est ainsi que mot est un mot
> Glas* 259b)

To read after Derrida is to translate the idiom of Derrida's text and
discourse into *my own idiom, my own terms and tropes*. It would be an
idiom that would situate me beside myself as my (the) other: it would
be an idiom marked by displacement, dissimulation, *differance*.
   Translation betrays the *authority* and sovereignty of the text. Derrida
is exposed as I withdraw to speak through him; Derrida is denied,
handed over to a legacy as an artifact, as artifice. I am . . . exposed and
I recognize myself as such only as I withdraw into the complex labyrinth
of Derrida's textual analogues. Derrida's writing – indeed, the legacy
of philosophy – is given substance. I find myself uttering Derrida's
words, involved in the attacks his discourse registers on the tradition
of Western metaphysics. However, I am unable to recognize my-self.
I have never seen myself because I identify myself with the other,
because there is no external access to his authority.
   "Jacques Derrida" is a substitution for *me*. Third person reference
supplements self-reference, auto-reference. He is me become no-one,
no-thing. I am no-thing but my *own proper* meditation, my own proper
silent dialogue with myself once removed. I am unable to be my own
self, properly speaking. But what is the idiom of this silent dialogue,
what would be the idiom of my own language, other than the idiom,
the language of Derrida's text, his strategies, or the discourse of Western
metaphysics? It would be an idiom that would prompt me to speak in
a unreserved fashion. It would solicit one from a "natural" anonymity
where I am identified always with and by someone else. The generation of a differant idiom would allow me to come into my own, as it
were.
   To be sure, I remain bound by the desire of an unhappy consciousness. But this desire of reading post-Derrida presupposes so many
epochs, so much that remains unannounced, implicity, withdrawn. So
many themes and motifs that comprise the "more or less visible struc-

tures" of traditional discourse are passed over in silence. Even the need to generate a critical reading of certain texts and discourses maintains silence. Here one must ponder the emptiness of that index "Jacques Derrida." It is an emptiness, a breach, *I* dive or withdraw into that forces a turn on my part, a turn toward a self-reflexive stance. That is to say, I advance toward the enactment of a certain play between unveiling and oblivion, exposure and protection. My discourse is ordered by an economy that necessitates inversion, dissemblance, and dissimulation; it necessitates a turning-out from and a turning-in on my self, my own idiom. It is not, however, an economy governed by the Hegelian *Aufhebung*. As Derrida remarks in *Glas*:

> It constitutes an economy of the undecidable: not that the undecidable here interrupts or suspends [*interrompe*] the efficacy of the economic principle. It places it in the service of a general economy which it requires, then, to break open the field. There is an economic *speculation* on the undecidable. It is not dialectical but plays with the dialectic. (235a)

What remains to be comprehended is what Maurice Blanchot notes in *The Space of Literature*:

> There is no longer concealed Being but the very being of *this concealment*: dissimulation itself.[6]

With dissimulation, with translation, with the passage from one idiom (voice) to another, dialogue breaks off — at least ostensibly. The points of opposition are disengaged and withdrawn in and through the enactment of certain textual themes and motifs. I am brought to a *meta-phase*, an-other epoch in-between epochs. "Meta-phase" is another "name" for that play between epochs, the *différance* in-between before/after, the play and spacing between differences in between clarity/confusion. Meta-phase is another name for the double binding of which Derrida speaks, the binding that carries over the "idea" of a text — the logic of communication. *Meta-phase* marks the in-between, the spacing of differences between *meta-phrasis* — a "literal" word-to-word translation — and *meta-stasis* — the passing over to another place, another way, by way of abrupt change. Meta-phase marks a withholding, the *a priori* withdrawal of extremes. *Meta-phase* marks out "what, without being there, will *have been* there" (*AF* 71). Moreover, "*meta-phase*" translates Derrida's notion of the *already, déjà*:

> Already [*Déjà*], such is the name for what has been effaced or subtracted [*soustraite*] beforehand, but which has nevertheless left behind a mark, a

signature, which is retracted [*soustraite*] in that very thing from which it is withdrawn [*se retire*]. Withdrawn from the hear and now, the hear and now which must be accounted for. (*Spurs* 39)

I am already, already affirmed in the epoch of the meta-phase.

The translation is never literal nor does it pass over the discourse in question in mere paraphrase. Rather, the translation remains some where in-between and necessarily so, always mindful of the divergent paths the extremes sometimes dictate. Translation always involves detours. Detail is to be determined, announced, and animated later.

Further, meta-phasic withdrawal marks the intersection of paths once removed but already traversed. It is the chiastic ligature or joint at which the overriding demand of reading post-Derrida is articulated most clearly: to generate dialogue with oneself and others by producing, putting into practice those themes and motifs always already withdrawn, but always and already at play silently. To say dialogue breaks off is to say dialogue engenders breach, perfidy, betrayal. But dialogue is never arrested. More directly, it is a hiatus at only a certain level of representation, a certain level of abstraction.

I withdraw silently to myself; I withdraw in solitude to meditate, to carry on a silent dialogue with myself so I may occupy the position of Derrida, i.e., so that I may write. In the epoch of meditation rendered as the meta-phase, I speak and belong to a discourse for which no one else has ears, that no one else speaks, a discourse which is addressed to no one in particular, like so many post cards, so many philosophic dispatches or telegrams. It is discourse which has no center, it is ex-centric indeed, and reveals no-thing. For, I am no-thing . . . . Self-reflexive engagement is not a return to the complacent isolation of the subject, a return to "subjectivism": it is not a "one sidedly subjectivistic" desire for self-evidence. It is, however, incited by a realization expressed by Heidegger in *The Basic Problems of Phenomenology* and understood, dare I say with such *clarity* by Descartes. Heidegger writes:

> . . . it is equally necessary not to start simply from the subject alone but to ask whether and how the *being* of the subject must be determined as an entrance into the problems of philosophy, and in fact in such a way that orientation toward it is *not one-sidedly subjectivistic*. Philosophy must perhaps start from the "subject" and return to the "subject" in its ultimate questions, and yet for all that it may not pose its questions in a one-sidedly subjectivistic manner.[7]

Moreover, to broach the question of translation — *as* the passage from one idiom or voice to another — is to pose the question Derrida identifies in his reading of Georges Bataille:

... how after having exhausted the discourse of philosphy can one inscribe in the lexicon and syntax of a language, our language, which was the language of philosophy, that which nevertheless exceeds the opposition of concepts governed by . . . .

the logic of identity and *logos* of presence? ("From Restricted to General Economy," *WD* 252–253)

The question of translation remains textual. It is a question of textual economy, textual binding, binding withdrawal. Furthermore, translation introduces the question of comprehension, comprehension of *how* dialogue breaks off and what that rupture engenders. Because my discourse is ordered and configured by a certain historical problematic or matrix, I do not have a voice of my own to articulate my demands, my questions, desires, insights. If I do, *I* cannot be heard — my voice is sequestered. It feigns authority. — Do I need a hearing aid? — The idiom I use arises in and through the discourse of philosophy — and the passage *through the word*, this dialogue with so many forebearers and bairn, effaces the idiom. I am caught in Derrida's double-bind where a certain idiom — a certain way of writing — or text

presents itself, then, as the commentary on the absent word [*mot*: thing] that it delimits, envelops, overwhelms [*entour*: surrounds] with its solicitude. The text *presents* itself as the metalanguage of the language which does not present itself. But it is merely a question of display. And the one [text] which follows to produce the unfolding abyss [*les creux actifs*: the bottomlessness of infinite redoubly] of the other and pronounce the unpronounced — displayed anew as a metalanguage —, forces [*simuli*: feigns, simulates, fakes] the presentation, ... The anguish of the metalanguage (the metatext, the meta-phase] is, then, structurally interminable. But as effort [strain, rupture], as effect, the metalanguage is the life of the language: always it flutters like a bird caught in a *subtle* glue. (*Glas* 147b–148b)

Withdrawn and effaced already, the subtlety of the glue amounts to this: it draws on the dialogue comprised in the exchange (the economy) of meta-languages *to bind* "internal" textual analysis and criticism. It is a profound resource and demonstrative limit: the cunning of the glue provokes the coming out of solitude to speak once more so that I can be heard. It allows for and promotes this slippage, this slidding, or this drifting rom one mood to another. The glue binds and structures discourse discreetly, as an inarticulable support. What requires re-thinking here, then, is just the effacement of support and structure. Still, what remains to be thought through is *différance*. For one's critical relation, being bound, to a certain tradition can be comprehended through the silence of its inscription, the subtle graphic shift and difference which "differance" institutes.

As the sign unfastens itself [*se détacher*: to detach oneself; to come undone; to break away or off], *that* signifies beyond the cut, beyond the place of its emission [or putting into circulation] or its natural appurtenance; but the separation is never perfect, the difference is never consumed. The sutting detachment [*le détachement sanglant*: the biting or bloody cut] is always – repetition – delegation, mandate, delay, reprieve, relay. Attachment [*Adhérence*]. The detached remnants fit or stick together that way [*par là*], by the [*par la*] glue of *différance*, by the *a* [*par l'a*]. The *a* of gl/binding [*agglutine*] the detached differences. The structure of the *A* is glutinous, adhesive, sticky, gluey [*gluant*]. (*Glas* 188b)

Auto-analysis of translation – the pasage of an epoch and the epoch of a passage – works on (founders on) the following insight or prejudice: meditation on or dialogue with "Jacques Derrida" (signature, proper name, scribble) cannot sustain, nor does it desire to sustain, any resolution to the questions addressed by and generated in the writing that falls under *that* sign (J.D.). What one must be attentive to or mindful of is how the different modes of expression dominant in different textual epochs intrude upon and redirect other expressive modes. The structure of sub-terranean conflict remains unclear. In this regard, *we* need to ponder, incessantly, the heuristic force of a strategy without finality.

Our (and here I speak in the third person plural to designate an ensemble of *others*) encounter with Derrida takes us on a voyage of discovery already enjoyed. In this voyage we are forced to return and to consider our desires to master nature, to understand nature, and to understand the nature of understanding and figures of speech. We are forced to contemplate the very nature or character of thought. But the artifice of Jacques Derrida's writing doubles the journey. The issues are confounded, the questions bound, and answers banned. Even as he writes and speaks a epoch of inquiry is pursued. The turning point or epoch that binds these various meditations is the identification of my reading with Derrida's script.

Here thought remains at the meta-phase.

And the drama remains textual.

Here I turn to enact another's apologue, I turn to embrace another textual epoch: René Descartes' meditations. I disguise myself, I listen in silence as Descartes announces the design for his discourse, the *Discourse on the Method for Rightly Conducting Reason and Seeking for Truth in the Sciences*

Thus my design is not here to teach the Method which everyone should follow in order to promote the good conduct of his Reason, but only to show in what way I have endeavoured to conduct my own. Those who set about giving precepts must esteem themselves more skillful than those to whom they advance them, and if they fall short in the smallest matter they must of course take the blame for it. But, *recommending this writing as a history, or, if you prefer, a fable, in which, among many examples one can imitate, perhaps one will find as man other as you will have reason not to follow,* I hope that it will be of use to some without being harmful to any, *and that all will than me for my frankness.*[8]

Descartes' "narrating narration" announces itself, identifies itself as a fable. But in doing so it effaces itself. The articulated dissimulation of Descartes' discourse, the fable itself, is hidden. The fable is successful. Descartes' pronouncements are read as so many self-evident truths, as if there is a necessary link between Descartes and the truthfulness of his writings, as if narration were a session for truth-telling, a confession. This situation arises out of our obsession with the presentation of some-thing lying hidden behind or beyond the demonstration or the performance. What is required here is an understanding of the "narrating narration" as its own double, its own simularcrum. The naration of Descartes' *Discourse* and *Meditations*, of Derrida's *texts*, can be recast or dispersed as a scene where

> . . . whatever its content exemplifies, it is always describing in advance, with a different posting [*en rapporté différé*], the scene of its own description . . . . It is an abyss of more than one generation . . . . (*CP* 342)

And I withdraw once more to read this line, thinking that "one can never conceive a thing and render it his own so well when one learns it from another, as when one discovers it oneself [*l'invent soi même*].[9] And I shall add, as when one finds it, contrives it, forges it, fakes it, fabricates it, and so on.

20. If the Shoe Fits — Derrida and the Orientation of Thought

Dorothea Olkowski

1. The Correspondence Between Heidegger and Schapiro

What is of interest in the correspondence between Martin Heidegger and art historian Meyer Schapiro; that is, what is of interest to Jacques Derrida, is not the public exchange of letters between the two professors.[1] What is of interest to Derrida, is a secret correspondence.

This other correspondence is guided by the "phantoms" in Van Gogh's paintings and by the phantoms in a particular painting bearing the signature "Vincent." The subject of this painting is identified by Heidegger as being a pair of peasant shoes, and by Schapiro, as the shoes of the artist who is a man of the town and the city. These counter-claims involve the shoes in a "legal process" to establish the rights of ownership and restore the shoes to a standing subject, "the authentic wearer or owner restored to his rights and reinstated in his standing being."[2]

Each of the litigants owes the shoes to whom they belong. Heidegger, in what appears to be a projection of his "pathetico-phantismico-ideologico-political investments"[3] wants to replace the shoes on the feet of a peasant and landsman. Schapiro, for his part, owes a debt to and for Kurt Goldstein. It was Goldstein who first brought Heidegger's essay to Schapiro's attention. Thus it seems that personal biography will influence both the manner and direction of the attempted reappropriations.

The spot around which Derrida begins to turn his questions is that of knowing what phantom returns to the shoes both Heidegger and Schapiro carelessly and before all questions assume to be a pair. Derrida notes that the untied and loosened shoe laces (*lacet* being also a trap) indicate that the shoes are at least temporarily *detached*. The shoes belong to no feet; they are detached both in themselves and from each other, since nothing in their title, "Old Boots with Laces" or in Schapiro's title "Old Shoes" indicates that they form a pair. Therefore we must consider the possibility that the shoes are "unpaired," at least as an outer horizon for our thought. It is the untied laces which trap both Heidegger and Schapiro into restitution. Heidegger and Schapiro are interested in identifying the *subject* who wears the shoes. They want to tie the laces around the right feet, to determine whose shoes they are and whose feet they belong to. Herein lies the significance of assuming that they are a pair.

If they are a pair, we search for their right size (*pointure*). We search for the proper subject, the proper owner; the one whom the shoes fit. The common aim of restitution of the unlaced pair to a rightful owner constitutes a tacit agreement between Heidegger and Schapiro, and the shoes must be attached to the feet of a subject. If they are not a pair, if they remain unlaced and abandoned, the shoes belong to no subject. From this Derrida concludes that there is strong resistance on the part of both Heidegger and Schapiro to give up the subject and thus, to take up what is detachable.

The shoes, if they are a pair, have a certain value. Derrida sees that Heidegger and Schapiro are eager to fill the lace-trap with a subject most valued by each. To appropriate the shoes to the country dweller or to the city dweller is to attempt to return the shoes to themselves through an identification with the rightful wearer of the shoes. However, if the shoes are abandoned, they are detached from a subject; if unlaced they are detached in themselves. If the shoes are detached in both senses, of what value are they; in what *sense* or *direction* do they lead us? The problem is that if we encounter the shoes as detached and unpaired, we do not know how to "orient" our thought.[4] What do abandoned shoes tell us about anything?

This is the same dilemma Heidegger faces in a related context at the beginning of his essay, "The Origin of the Work of Art."[5] Heidegger's investigation of the nature of the relationship between art and nature, seems to involve him in a *circular* pattern of thinking. The question guiding both Heidegger's and Derrida's texts is, where and how do we break into thought? Where does the path of thinking begin?

Detached, unpaired shoes are the empty support of an absent subject who "returns to haunt their open form."[6] But of what *use*, of what *value* are abandoned shoes? Derrida admits confusion. When presented with the shoes, he does not know whether to speak or write. Yet it appears that even Derrida, master of detachment, must do something. The shoes cannot simply be returned to abandonment, for as we shall see, even abandonment is never absolute; the path of thought is always guided by some law of a given context or framework, and within that framework, some discourse must address itself to the shoes.

The correspondence between Heidegger and Schapiro stipulates that the pair and all that is associated with pairing will be the guide or the law for thinking about the shoes. What follows from the assumption that they are a pair, is that as a pair they are no longer detached. abandoned or unlaced; they are reappropriated for *use*, for being used in a proper manner. Therefore, the *usefulness* of the pair becomes their most important sense. Because the shoes are no longer detached but have been made useful, discussion – or dispute – concerning them can take place. Thought can now be oriented in the proper direction, i.e. in the direction of their *use*. This means that their value becomes that of a product; they assume the value of equipment. And yet –

2. The Shoes are Divided

"To commemorate mutual agreement (of the pair), the shoes are divided, each one keeping a piece of the symbolon . . . or rather the piece resembling and different from the same whole."[7] The piece each disputant takes resembles but is different from the same whole. They agree, but remain in dispute; they do not settle the case. They each proceed from the orientation given to them by the law of the pair-product, but in totally different ways.

At this point, Derrida cautions us to take another look at Heidegger's text. Reappropriation is an identification with the proper subject, the user of the shoes. Yet, in "The Origin of the Work of Art," is not the whole point of Heidegger's effort to leave behind all determinations centering around subjectivity? The de-sedimentation of the thing as *hupokeimenon* and *sumbebekos*, as underside and its characteristics, its transformation into *subjectum* and *accidens*, then matter and form, open up a path of thought which does not simply allow us to return to the space of the subject.

If Heidegger "claims to lead back to a point short, upstream or on the verge of the constitution of the *'subjectum'* in the apprehension of the thing, . . . then to ask the *Origin* the question of the 'subject,' . . . that perhaps would be to begin with a mistake."[8] But then, what is it that we are to address ourselves to? We have to remind ourselves that the entire question of the old shoes is related to that of a work of art and to the truth of a work of art; a subject whose subject is, according to Heidegger, a *pair* of peasant shoes.

To make sense of this seeming incongruity, Heidegger's text must be opened somewhat more carefully than Schapiro has opened it. We must go to the context which "frames" the allusion to the well-known painting. The shoes are *detached*, as such they cannot be reappropriated. They are not functional and are useless in two ways: (1) visibly as painted, (2) as disconnected through the detachment of an "emissary," that is, by *substituting* feet or something associated with the shoes for the shoes themselves.[9] It is in this context of detachment and overdetermination of meaning that Derrida makes reference to the fetish. The shoes, the feet, anything *detachable* in the same manner have the same structure as the fetish. These associations or "emmissaries" must be traced carefully. The relationships Derrida sees here between detachment, reattachment and the fetish, should tell us something about Derrida's own presuppositions and interests in this matter. First however, it will help not to digress too far, but to step carefully along Heidegger's path of thinking in search of the sense of his lingering. "And yet —."

3. The Schema of the Work of Art

The fundamental experience of Greek speech, Heidegger tells us, has been lost in the translation of *hupokeimenon*. Because of this, Western thought remains rootless or groundless. Western thought understands a "thing" in terms of form and matter. Matter is what provides things with constancy and, as such, is thought to be the substrate and field for the action of an artist. Form as shape determines the arrangement of matter. Form and matter are gounded in usefulness insofar as the purpose or *use* of a thing controls the interfusion of its form and matter. This structure places the product between works and mere things and presents it as the paradigm for our encounters with both things and works.[10]

But can we approach the character of the "mere thing" by subtracting the usefulness of the product, and say that the thing-being of things is merely the remainder — what is left over? Is not this "nudity," as Heidegger calls it, an assault on the thingly character of the thing? Matter and form are not the original determinations of the thingness of the mere being. This familiar mode of thought, the result of the translation of *hupokeimenon*, obstructs our way to the thingly character and shackles thought. We must therefore take care to distance all preconceptions and assaults on beings. We must leave the being of things to rest in its thing-being and not try to force our way into it.

For this reason, Heidegger takes a few steps backward. To discover the thing-being of the thing, the product-being of the product, the work-being of the work, and so the truth of each, we must lay aside all familiar interpretations which will cover over or which have "fallen-over" the being of things.[11] Yet, if we start our thinking by identifying the shoes as a pair belonging to either a peasant or a city dweller, this is exactly what happens. Any search for the truth of a work, if it starts from the notion of a "restored pair," a useful product, is already determined by the traditional structure of matter and form. It seems that thought might be unavoidably trapped within this schematism.

Heidegger, after exposing the encroachment of the product on thought, goes on to describe a pair of peasant shoes. He does this without the benefit of any theory in order to reveal the equipment-being of equipment. Has Heidegger fallen into the trap? It seems not. Heidegger turns to the pair of peasant shoes, not as Schapiro would suggest, to return to the norm of usefully formed-matter, but to think being-product before and outside of the matter-form determination.[12] The allusion to the "well-known painting" is made in Heidegger's text first in reference to uncovering the truth of a being-product and not the truth of a work. For Heidegger's purposes at this point, any of Van Gogh's canvases would be suitable, even a mere sketch or some old shoes would do, because the painting serves only as a "helpful accessory."[13]

Yet, when Heidegger turns our attention to the painting and we look at the shoes, "There is nothing surrounding this pair of peasant shoes in or to which they might belong — only an undefined space."[14] If we "simply look at the empty, unused shoes as they stand there in the picture, we shall never discover what the equipmental being of the equipment in truth is."[15] This is because there is no *distinction* between the three modes of being Heidegger has concerned himself with. Contrary to Schapiro's claim, they are, if anything, tightly interlaced. Like a lace, each mode of being passes inside then outside of the other again. The movement follows a path similar to that formed by the nexus of art and nature in Heidegger's essay. The pattern moves from thing to product, to work, to thing.

Here, the lace becomes the law; it is the structure of the schema. It shows itself and disappears in the regular crossing of the eyelet-thing. As Heidegger says, the work is more thing than product; the painting of shoes is a product of art yet like a thing, through presenting a product.[16] And yet — this structure may not be exactly as Heidegger suggests because it is only by letting the interlaced work speak that the equipment-being of equipment, the thing-being of things and the work-being of works might be revealed. Yet, says Heidegger, we stand before the work and it says none of these things to us.

4. The Work Speaks

What does happen as we stand in front of the work? There are shoes; they are of the genre clothing and are clothing which is not being used. This is a reference leading us outside the work. It outlines a movement of return to "nudity"; to the thing called, . . . "bare; as unuseful product, currently unused, abandoned, unlaced, offered as thing and as product in a kind of out-of-workness."[17] However, as product, it is able to be used. As a clothing product, it is invested, inhabited, informed, haunted, one might say, by the form of some other *bare* thing (feet?) from which it is detached (and which as bare are also detachable).

There seems to be a double line of detachment. First, the usable product must be waiting to be reattached; the line formed by the untied laces waits to be tightened around something. Second, there is the line of the painting in its frame which detaches the shoes as painted from any subject.[18] These lines refer us both outside to reattachment and inside to the canvas. They follow the movement of the laces in the eyelets, passing in and out of the canvas, perforating both canvas and painted shoe, moving in and out of the painting's internal and external worlds in a play of appearing and disappearing.[19]

The laying bare of the character of usefulness does not give us access to the thing-being of the thing. The product "undressed," merely stripped off, does not restore to us the abandoned "remainder" as "bare thing."[20] For this reason, Heidegger on his path, does not start from the usefulness of products in his quest for the thing-being of things. Some other path must be taken. At this juncture, Derrida mysteriously writes, "within this movement, Heidegger's action speaks at times of the painting in itself, at other times of every other thing outside the painting."[21]

Heidegger refers to a work as that which lets us know what shoes are in truth. Yet, nowhere in the preceeding analysis of the equipmental-being of equipment has he made any reference to any painting, except as helpful (but unnecessary) accessory. In fact, by standing before the painting, merely looking at the detached shoes, we shall never learn anything about product-being. What we learned could have come from *any* product, as this truth is the truth of the proprietary relation of any product to any subject and to any world.[22] But, is it the truth of this painting?

In the painting, the shoes are in an undefined space; they are detached; they are groundless. In the translation of *hupokeimenon*, the Greek experience of the ground has been lost. This ground is the fundamental experience of the Greeks or of their speech which apprehends the thing as *hupokeimenon*, as being-underneath the *hupokeimenon*; being underneath what is underneath.[23] Heidegger sees the *hupokeimenon* as what was spoken of in the basic Greek experience of the Being of beings, in the sense of presence. The *hupokeimenon* must then already cover over something.

Western speech is groundless; its "ground" is always covered over by language. Heidegger is seeking the essence of truth, the truth of the essence and of the veiled, always already hidden by language's *abyss* which is a "veiled fate paralyzing Being."[24] Language and the shoes are both detached. This detachment has led to conceptualizing mere things on the basis of products. Heidegger seeks a deeper origin to avoid the covering over of the truth of work, product and thing.

But what if, asks Derrida, this covering over is the rule, the law? What if it is no accident and at the same time not a necessity of translation which we must try to get under or around? What if the work, the product and the thing cannot determine themselves properly and directly, but are always imposed upon? What if the lace, whose movement thought follows has the same structure of detachment as the shoes and the painting?

Thought *starts*, gets its *orientation* from neither product nor work, yet it cannot think without them either. The subject of the painting of shoes with laces is not a pair of shoes restored but an outside with no product-being or work-being. Thought about the truth of the painting does not take its orientation from a useful pair, but rather from a bare supplement with nothing to supplement. What it supplants in turn becomes its own supplement. The pure supplement, the shoes as detached remainder trace a return to the thing as bare and are supplemented as unuseful product, as abandoned, unlaced, offered as thing and as out-of-work product. The old shoes are interlaced, that is, they are supplemented as clothing, as invested, inhabited, informed, haunted by the form of bare feet from which they are detached. There is a phantom in this painting; Van Gogh's painting if full of phantoms.

The trail of thought regarding detachment in both senses (detached from a subject and detached as painted) is no straight path, nor is it a simple circle. It is pure digression, pure supplement. The detachment is groundlessness. Detachment is what both Heidegger and Schapiro cannot stand. It is here they are both trapped. Does not the "undefined space" surrounding the shoes and their being unlaced suspend all experience of the ground upon which a subject with feet walks? Does not the shoes as painted, hanging on a wall, limited by canvas and frame, provoke, define, translate, signify groundlessness? What then can we make of the desire for the "soil of fundamental experience," the deeper origin? Can the work possibly attain to unconcealedness?

Schapiro has moved precisely in the opposite direction from Heidegger. Criticizing Heidegger for not respecting the particularity of the painting, Schapiro appeals to real shoes which are represented in a painting and belong to a real subject, and so are expressly not detachable. For Schapiro, there are no phantoms in this painting by Vincent Van Gogh.

Heidegger at least does not make this appeal to the reproduction of reality. The work is instead the reproduction of the thing's general essence. But, for lack of seeing this particular painting and these detached shoes, Heidegger has, according to Derrida, fallen into a trap. If we stand in front of this painting, what is there to see?

Leather and canvas are two thicknesses passed through by a single lace and are *indiscernible*; product and work pass through the eyelet-thing and are indiscernible.[25] Thought follows the lace supplement through supplement. Heidegger's path of thinking as well as Schapiro's are without these digressions. Heidegger moves steadily toward the abyss, Schapiro toward reality; each is guided by the law of the pair. What this means is that we cannot think the remainder differently as mere thing, nor the work as pure work and product as pure product. There is only the supplement with nothing to supplement. Because thought has no *place*, the shoehorn becomes a weapon. Heidegger and Schapiro arm themselves with it in order to secure the thing in its proper place.

Derrida associates detachment of shoes and paintings and the desire to reattach with the fetish, a sexual substitute, and with the structure of shoes as detachable. The fetish provides a certain *security* or *reliability*. Heidegger's vivid imagery and the sexual overtones of his descriptions no doubt cover over a great deal, especially, as Derrida points out, because Heidegger's references to mere things and to the deeper origin are always feminine. Exploring these tangents, Derrida notes, would constitute yet another long digression.

What we can realize out of these digressions is the structure Derrida seems to suggest thought might have. Like the fetish, the meaning is a question not of form but of orientation. Thought gets oriented — how? This is precisely the problem we first encounterd. The orientation depends on a particular framework, a syntax.[26] There are only divergences and no essential norms in this structure, a network of differential traces. Thus there is no idiomatic reading of a painting or of anything else. The shoe may have a form which leads us to a subject, but more important, its meaning is constantly supplemented and supplanted. It is convex and concave, with two different surfaces. The lace is the figure of thought in this movement inside and outside, hidden and revealed among the different surfaces, detached and speechless.

Contributors

MARC E. BLANCHARD (Professor of French and Comparative Literature, University of California at Davis) is author of *Le Moyen Age* (with S. Gavronsky) (1972); *Sign, Self, Desire: Critical Theory in the wake of Semiotics* (1980); *Saint-Just & Cie (1980); In Search of the City: Engels, Baudelaire, Rimbaud (1984)*. He has also published widely in semiotics, comparative literature, and the history of art.

JOHN D. CAPUTO (Professor of Philosophy, Villanova University) has published *the Mystical Element in Heidegger's Thought* (1978) and *Heidegger and Aquinas (1982)*. He is currently preparing a book to be entitled *Radical Hermeneutics*.

DAVID CARR (Professor Philosophy, University of Ottawa) is translator of Husserl's *Crisis of the European Sciences and Transcendental Phenomenology* and author of *Phenomenology and the Problem of History* and of articles on Phenomenology, History, and Narrative.

VINCENT DESCOMBES (Professor of Philosophy, Unviersity of Paris-I and Professor of French, The Johns Hopkins University) is author of *Le Platonisme* (1971), *L'Inconscient malgré lui* (1977), *Modern French Philosophy* (1979), and *Grammaire d'objets en tous genres* (1983).

RODOLPHE GASCHÉ (Professor of Comparative Literature, State University of New York at Buffalo) is author of *Die hybride Wissenschaft* and *System und Metaphorik in der Philosophie von Georges Bataille*. His forthcoming book will be entitled *The Tain of the Mirror: Deconstruction and Reflexivity*.

PATRICK A. HEELAN (Professor of Philosophy, State University of New York at Stony Brook) is author of *Quantum Mechanics and Objectivity: A Study of the Physical Philosophy of Werner Heisenberg* (1965), *Space-Perception and the Philosophy of Science* (1983) and numerous articles in the Philosophy of the Natural Sciences.

NANCY J. HOLLAND (Assistant Professor of Philosophy, Hamline University) specializes in current French philosophy, Heidegger, and the philosophy of mind. Her articles include: "Two as an Odd Number: On Cumming on Derrida on Schapiro on Heidegger on Van Gogh" (1982) and "The Treble Clef/t: Jacques Derrida and the Female Voice" (forthcoming).

ALPHONSO LINGIS (Professor of Philosophy, Pennsylvania State University) has translated Merleau-Ponty's *The Visible and the Invisible*, Lévinas' *Totality and Infinity*, and numerous other writings from the French. He is author of *Excesses: Eros and Culture* (1983) and many articles in continental philosophy.

BERND MAGNUS (Professor of Philosophy, University of California at Riverside) is author of *Heidegger's Metahistory of Philosophy* (1970) and *Nietzsche's Existential Imperative* (1978). He has also published many articles, chiefly on Nietzsche and Heidegger.

JOSEPH MARGOLIS (Professor of Philosophy, Temple University) is author of many books, including *The Language of Art and Art Criticism* (1965), *Psychotherapy and Morality* (1966), *Values and Conduct* (1971), *Knowledge and Existence* (1973), *Negatives: The Limits of Life* (1975), *Persons and Minds* (1977), *Art and Philosophy* (1978), *Philosophy of Psychology* (1984), and *Culture and Cultural Entities* (1984).

WERNER MARX (Professor Emeritus and Director of the Husserl Archives at the University of Freiburg, W. Germany) is author of many publications including *The Meaning of Aristotle's "Ontology"* (1954), *Heidegger and the Tradition (1971)*, *Reason and World* (1971), *Hegel's Phenomenology of Spirit* (1975), *The Philosophy of F.W.J. Schelling: History, System, Freedom* (1984), and *Gibt es auf Erden ein Maß* (1983).

MICHAEL MURRAY (Professor of Philosophy, Vassar College) has published *Modern Philosophy of History* (1970), *Modern Critical Philosophy* (1975), and *Heidegger and Modern Philosophy* (ed. 1978). His recent papers included "Time in Hegel's *Phenomenology of Spirit*" (1981), "Heidegger's Hermeneutic Reading of Hölderlin" (1981), and "The Conflict between Poetry and Literature" (1984).

GRAEME NICHOLSON (Professor of Philosophy, Trinity College, University of Toronto) is author of *Seeing and Reading* (1984) and of articles in phenomenology and political philosophy.

DOROTHEA OLKOWSKI (Lecturer, University of Nevada at Reno) is author of "Merleau-Ponty's Freudianism" (1985).

GAYLE L. ORMISTON (Assistant Professor, University of Colorado, Colorado Springs) has co-edited *Hermeneutics and Post-Modern Theories of Interpretation* and has authored articles on topics such as "Nietzsche's Image of Woman: Traces of Derrida," "The Economy of Duplicity: *Differance*", "Epochal Torsion: Remarks on Heidegger's Being," and "Sartre's *Critique* Dialectical Imagination."

FRITHJOF RODI (Professor of Philosophy, Ruhr-Universität, Bochum, W. Germany) is author of *Morphologie und Hermeneutik* (1969), *Provokation – Affirmation. Das Dilemma des kritischen Humanismus* (1970), and editor of the Collected Writings of Wilhelm Dilthey (vols 18 & 19), and the *Dilthey-Jahrbuch für Philosophie und Geschichte der Geisteswissenschaften* (vols. 1 & 2).

CALVIN O. SCHRAG (Professor of Philosophy, Purdue University) has published a number of books including *Existence and Freedom: Towards an Ontology of Human Finitude* (1961), *Experience and Being: Prolegomena to a Future Ontology* (1969), and *Radical Reflection and the Origin of the Human Sciences* (1980).

THOMAS M. SEEBOHM (Professor of Philosophy, University of Mainz, W. Germany) was formerly Professor of Philosophy at the Pennsylvania State University. He has published *Die Bedingungen der Möglichkeit der Transcendental Philosophie* (1962), *Zur Kritik der Hermenetischen Vernunft* (1972), *Ratio und Charisma* (1977), *Philosophie der Logik* (1984), and articles on Kant, German Idealism, phenomenology, and hermeneutics.

THOMAS SHEEHAN (Professor of Philosophy, Loyola University of Chicago) is editor of *Heidegger: The Man and the Thinker* (1981), author of *Karl Rahner: The Philosophical Foundations* (1982), and is preparing *The End of Theology: A Philosophical Critique*.

STEPHEN H. WATSON (Assistant Professor of Philosophy, Notre Dame University) has written a number of articles on topics varying from "The Closure of Modernism" to "Merleau-Ponty's Involvement with Saussure," to studies of Lyotard, Kant, Heidegger, Foucault, Derrida, and Searle.

Notes

Chapter 1

1. This is not quite the sense intended by Heidegger in his influential essay, *The End of Philosophy*. All available metaphysical options in the history of Being have, in effect, been played out for Heidegger. My use of *Vollendung* does not carry this requirement with it.

2. Wilfrid Sellars, *Science, Perception and Reality* (London: Routledge and Kegan Paul, 1967).

3. Richard Rorty, *Philosophy and the Mirror of Nature* (Princeton: Princeton University Press, 1979) and *Consequences of Pragmatism* (Minneapolis: University of Minnesota Press, 1982).

4. Hilary Putnam, *Reason, Truth and History* (Cambridge: Harvard University Press, 1982).

5. I am thinking here more of A.J. Ayer's *Language, Truth and Logic* and the Circle's manifesto than of Wittgenstein's *Tractatus Logico-Philosophicus*.

6. Recent attempts have been made to de-emphasize this "perpetual beginner's" exaggerated hopes for phenomenology as strict science. But to this reader the author of *Ideas* and *Cartesian Meditations* still seems convinced that there is only one secure path for the consummation of philosophy − his way.

7. I am aware that the object of devotion or ultimate concern would also differ. What I wish to stress, however, is the fact that philosophy begins with no pregiven canonical text (in a wide sense), whereas religions do.

8. I shall use masculine gender pronoun references throughout this paper, not for sexist reasons but out of aesthetic deference to the spoken and written word. I should like such references to be understood in their intended gender-neutral sense.

9. It is sometimes suggested, especially by Nietzsche and by Rorty, that the self-deceptive hope that it can be gotten right forevermore functions as a principal motive in doing philosophy. It is as if we could not philosophize (in the traditional sense?) without the hope that among

all the competing world and self descriptions only one will tell us who we truly are.

10. It seems to me that Michel Foucault sometimes suggests that such an unbridled will to power is the hidden spring of the God's eye view.

11. This is true not only of earlier academic skepticism but today. Consider, for example, Lehrer's *Knowledge,* Unger's *Ignorance* and O.A. Johnson's *Skepticism and Cognitivism.*

12. I do not mention cultures in which philosophy as we know it has not arisen – early native Americans, for example – because there can be no end to philosophy where there was no beginning of it.

13. This formulation is distilled from many sources, chiefly deconstructionist, and in particular it owes much to the work of Derrida and Rorty.

14. This reminds one of Aristotle's protreptic dilemma.

15. That is one reason why I have shied away from the hermeneutic label. Therapists are decidedly Kuhnian in their interpretation of science. At the extreme end, they view science as a literary genre. Hermeneutics may leave too much room for a methodological space between the sciences of nature and the sciences of man. But I would not wish to insist on this.

16. This is the path – following James and Dewey – urged upon us by Rorty in his *Consequences of Pragmatism.*

17. *Consequences of Pragmatism,* p. 33.

Chapter 2

1. *"Zur Kritik de Hegelschen Rechtsphilosophie,"* Deutsch-Französische Jahrbücher, 1843/44.

2. Cf. the response of the German Idealists: G.J. Fichte, *Recension des Aesnesidemus, Saemmtliche Werke,* ed. J.H. Fichte, 1845/46, Walter de Gruyter, Berlin, 1971, Vol. I; G.W.F. Hegel, *Verhaeltnis des Skeptizismus zur Philosophie, Gesammelte Werke,* Meiner, Hamburg, 1968, Vol. 4. The conclusion of that debate for Hegel can be found in the Introduction to *Phenomenology of Mind,* cf. *Phenomenology* in Baillie's translation New York and Evanston: Harper and Row, 1967 136 ff.

3. Contrary to modern myth, theory and practice were never separated in the courses of traditional philosophy. In a certain sense they were united always under the primacy of the practical. That Descartes postponed the treatment of ethics does not exclude that ethics is the final goal. Already the title of Spinoza's main work: *Ethica, ordine*

geometrico demonstrata indicates the goal again. No word has to be lost about the 'final cause' of Thomas Hobbes' thought in this respect.

4. Contrary to the German Idealists Kant did not try to "deduce the necessity of his system of categories. His stand in the *Critique of Pure Reason* in this question is most interesting for the problem of the "end of metaphysics." Cf. my: *"Die Kantische Beweistheorie und die Beweise der Kritik der reinen Vernunft", Akten des 5. Internationalen Kant-Kongresses 1981, II. Vortraege*, Bouvier, Bonn, 1981, 127 f.

5. Kant's treatment of scepticism in the *Critique of Pure Reason* A ix, A 388 f, B 513 f, B884 prepares the further development mentioned in footnote 2.

6. Sextus Empiricus, *Outlines of Phyrronism*, Loeb, Harvard U.P. Cambridge Mass. 1967, 122/3 (Bekker 206).

7. Eichte, J.G. Ueber den Begriff der Wissenschaftslehre, Saemmtliche Werke, l.c. I, 54. (My translation).

8. Sextus Empiricus, l.c. 19 (Bekker 25 ff).

9. Abû Hâmid Mohammed Ibn Mohammed Ibn Ahmed Al Gâzali (latin: Algazel) 1059−741, member of the mystic sect of the Sufi. His work known to the Western tradition is the *Intentions of the Philosophers (Makâsid al Falâsifa)*. Within the Islam his *Tahâfut al Falâsifa*, the *Deconstruction of the Philosophers*, is of much greater historical significance.

10. The sources are here the *logoi asketikoi* of e.g. Abba Neilos, Evagrios Pontikos, Isaac of Niniveh (or Isaac the Syrian). Isaac of Niniveh has influence on even the development in the Islam, mentioned above, cf. Burkitt, F.C. Isaac of Niniveh, *Journal of Theological Studies* XXVI, no. 101, 1924. Concerning his and the others influence on the orthodox monastic tradition cf. Seebohm, *Ratio and Charisma*, Bonn, *Bouvier* 1977, 421 ff and according to index. Further literature is mentioned there.

11. Petrus Damiani, 1007−1072, among others, taught that God is even capable of violating the principle of noncontradiction in his deeds if he wills to do so. *De divina omnipotentia*, Migne PL 145, c.5, 603 B; c. 11, 612 A/B.

12. c.f. in this respect H. Kuch, *Philologus, Untersuchung eines Wortes von seinen ersten Anfaengen in der Tradition bis zur ersten ueberlieferten lexikalischen Festlegung*, Akademieverlag Berlin (Ost) DAdW, Sektion Altertumswissenschaft, vol. 48, 1965. For a brief but nevertheless more explicit treatment of the difference between the philological-rhetorical syndrome and the modern philological-historical syndrome cf. my *Zur Genese des Historismus, bewusst sein, Gerhard Funke zu eigen*, ed. Bucher, Drue, Seebohm, Bonn, Bouvier, 1975, 112 ff. With respect to the concept of history within the "philological-rhetorical syndrome" (my term) cf.

Gerald A. Press, *The Development of the Idea of History in Antiquity*, McGill-Queen's U.P., Kingston and Montreal, 1982.

13. e.g. Erasmus of Rotterdam and Michel de Montaigne.

14. Such *topoi* surface also in the presentation of the new philosophy by Professor Magnus and Professor Schrag.

15. Such a program is already sketched out by Hegel in the first part of the *Differenz des Fichte'schen und Schelling' schen Systems der Philosophie* 1801, and the *Phaenomenologie des Geistes*, 1807, claims to have fulfilled this program.

16. Husserl, E. *"Philosophie als strenge Wissenschaft"*, *Logos* vol. I, 1910/11, cf. the letter to Roman Ingraden of July 1935, *"Briefe an Roman Ingarden,"* ed. R. Ingarden, *Phaenomanologica* 25, Nijhoff, den Haag, 1968, 92/93 and *Krisis* Hua VI, Nijhoff, den Haag 1954, Beilage XXVII 508 ff.

17. I mean the turn inaugurated by Thomas S. Kuhn, *The Structure of Scientific Revolutions* (Chicago 1962: The University of Chicago Press).

18. *Differenzschrift*, l.c. section 1.

Chapter 3

1. *The Order of Things: An Archaeology of the Human Sciences* (New York: Random House, 1979), p. 387.

2. *Image Music Text*, trans. Stephen Heath (New York: Hill and Wang, 1977), pp. 142–148.

3. *The Savage Mind* (Chicago: University of Chicago Press, 1966), p. 247.

4. Already in *Being and Time* (trans. J. Macquarrie and E. Robinson; New York: Harper & Row, 1962) Heidegger outlined what he called "the task of destroying the history of ontology" (Sec. 6, pp. 41–49). In *The Basic Problems of Phenomenology* (trans. A. Hofstadter; Bloomington: Indiana University Press, 1982) Heidegger sees deconstruction *(Abbau)* as a critical moment in the more general task of destruction *(Destrucktion)*. "It is for this reason that there necessarily belongs to the conceptual interpretation of being and its structures, that is, to the reductive construction of being a *destruction* – a critical process in which the traditional concepts, which at first must necessarily be employed, are deconstructed down to the sources form which they are drawn," pp. 22–23.

5. *The Languages of Criticism and the Sciences of Man: The Structuralist Controversy*, eds. Richard Macksey and Eugenio Donato (Baltimore: The Johns Hopkins Press, 1970), p. 271.

6. *The Rule of Metaphor: Multidisciplinary Studies of the Creation of Meaning in Language*, trans. Robert Czerny (Toronto: University of Toronto Press, 1977); see particularly chapter 7: "Metaphor and Reference."

7. *Language, Counter-Memory, Practice: Selected Essays and Interviews*, ed. D.F. Bouchard; trans. D.F. Bouchard and Sherry Simon (Ithaca: Cornell University Press, 1977), p. 137.

8. *Freedom and Nature: The Voluntary and the Involuntary*, trans. Frazim V. Kohak (Evanston: Northwestern University Press, 1966), p. 58.

9. "Thus it is clear that the entire initial implication of myself is not a conscious relation or an observation. I behave actively in relation to myself, I determine *myself*. Once again French usage throws light on the situation: to determine my conduct is to determine myself — *se déterminer*. Prereflexive self-imputation is active not observational," Freedom and Nature, p. 59.

10. *Many Dimensional Man: Decentralizing Self, Society, and the Sacred* (New York: Oxford University Press, 1977), p. 105.

11. See particularly his book, *Philosophy and the Mirror of Nature* (Princeton University Press, 1979), pp. 35ff.

12. *Role Playing and Identity: The Limits of Theatre as Metaphor* (Bloomington: Indiana University Press, 1982).

13. John D. Caputo, in his recent article, "Hermeneutics as the Recovery of Man" (*Man and World*, Vol. 15, No. 4, 1982), has sketched a project of restorative hermeneutics informed by Kierkegaard's notion of existential repetition and Heidegger's notion of the retrieval of the sense (*Sinn*) and truth (*Wahrheit*) of Being. He argues that Heidegger's notion of retrieval needs to be understood against the background of Kierkegaard's concrete existential reflections on repetition, and that this entails a consequential difference between the Heideggerian project and Husserl's notion of representation (*Vergegenwärtigung*), which continues to buy into a "nostalgia for presence." Now it is the latter, according to Caputo, that is properly placed under erasure by Derrida's deconstructionist strategy but in such a way that Derrida is misled by mistaking the Husserlian program for that of Heidegger, failing to recognize the restorative posture of hermeneutics as a recovery of man.

Chapter 5

1. *Space-Perception and the Philosophy of Science* (Berkeley and Los Angeles: University of California Press, 1983); hereafter referred to as SPPS. The principal argument of this paper is developed, particularly,

in chapters 9, 10, and 11 of SPPS. A preview of the argument will be found in the writer's "Toward a new analysis of the pictorial space of Vincent van Gogh," *Art bulletin*, liv (1972), pp. 478–492.

2. For hermeneutic phenomenology and natural science, see J.J. Kockelmans and T. Kisiel, *Phenomenology and the Natural Sciences* (Evanston, Ill.: Northwestern University Press 1970), and the writer's "Natural science as a hermeneutic of instrumentation," in *Philosophy of Science* (June 1983), and "Natural science and Being-in-the-World," *Man and World*, vol. 16 (1983), pp. 207–16.

3. H.-G. Gadamer, *Truth and Method* (New York: Seabury Press, 1975). For an excellent survey of the topic, see J. Bleicher, *Contemporary Hermeneutics: Hermeneutics as Method, Philosophy, and Critique* (London and Boston: Routledge and Kegan Paul, 1980).

4. Cf. Gadamer's discussion of the *hermeneutical circle* in *Truth and Method*, pp. 241–253, and M. Heidegger, *Being and Time* (New York: Harper and Row, 1962), p. 194.

5. See, for example, D. Marr, *Vision* (San Francisco: Freeman, 1982), and J. Frisby, *Seeing* (Oxford and New York: Oxford University Press, 1980).

6. The notions *World* and *Body* are taken in a phenomenological sense. *Body, embodied knower* or *subject*, etc. denote the intentional knower or subject, and connote both physical aspects (neurophysiological and somatic aspects, as well as energy fields, instrumental technologies, etc.) and intentional aspects (related to the giving of meaning). See M. Merleau-Ponty for the notion of *Body*, particularly the notion *Body as Flesh* in *The Visible and the Invisible* (Evanston, Ill.: Northwestern University Press, 1964), "Work Notes."

7. The ability to read has to be learnt, and the ability to read difficult and unusual texts is learnt only with difficulty. When I speak of *reading*, I mean to refer only to the easy exercise of an acquired facility. See SPPS, chapter 11. For a brilliant analysis of the hermeneutical role of a *text*, see P. Ricoeur, *Hermeneutics and the Human Sciences* (Cambridge and New York: Cambridge University Press, 1981).

8. M. Polanyi, *Personal Knowledge* (New York: Harper and Row, 1964), chapter 4.

9. See Graeme Nicholson, "Seeing and reading: aspects of their connection," paper presented to meeting of SPEP, 29 October 1982, from which the concept of affinity is taken, and his *Seeing and Reading* (New York: Humanities Press 1984).

10. For Heidegger, perception is hermeneutical in a secondary and derivative sense, and depends on a certain impoverishment of what is given in the circumspective attitude that reduces ready-to-hand to

present-at-hand; see *Being and Time*, pp. 88–89, 190–203. In (2), I am no longer concerned with the defining or articulating aspect of perception – this belongs to (1) – but with acts of perception as acts of recognition, naming, etc, of individual objects, and with the existential-hermeneutical analysis of such acts.

11. Cf. H. Dreyfus, *Husserl: Intentionality and Cognitive Science* (Cambridge, Mass.: MIT Press, 1982) where the introduction by Dreyfus has a good discussion of this point.

12. Heidegger recognized the limitation of this kind of eidos when it is presumed to be complete, and he regarded the activity of articulating such an eidos as a secondary and deficient hermeneutical act, which he took to be characteristic of perception; see n. 10 above.

13. E. Ballard, "The visual perception of distance," in F.J. Smith (ed.), *Phenomenology in Perspective* (The Hague: Nijhoff, 1970). See SPPS, chapter 2, where it is shown that the elements of Ballard's description borrow from different visual spaces, Euclidean and hyperbolic, that these spaces depend on the existence of two different 'texts' in the World, one for Euclidean visual space, and the other for the family of hyperbolic visual spaces. Actual vision fills in the indeterminate clues, according to the dominant interest of the moment.

14. The following responds to an objection raised by Gary Madison to the original version of my paper.

15. See *Being and Time*, p. 191.

16. See above, n. 10.

17. Any process designed to detect empirically the presence or absence of a scientifically described entity or state is a measurement process. See also the writer's "Natural science as a hermeneutic or instrumentation."

18. See SPPS, chapter 11.

19. See P. Heelan, "Hermeneutics of experimental science in the context of the Life-World," *Interdisciplinary Phenomenology*, ed. by D. Ihde and R. Zaner (The Hague: Nijhoff, 1975), pp. 7–50; "Hermeneutical realism and scientific observation," in *PSA 1982* (East Lansing, Mich.: Philosophy of Science Association, 1982), pp. 77–87; and SPPS, chapter 11.

20. A point suggested by Joseph J. Kockelmans.

21. The notion of *complementarity* can be linked to the embodied character of perceptual knowledge, and refers to an in principle inability (of individual perceivers) simultaneously to *perform* without mutual interference perceptual acts of complementary kinds. Complementarity arises out of the contextual character of embodiments; it can account for the peculiar property of quantum mechanics which N. Bohr and

W. Heisenberg called "complementarity," and which provides the rationale for quantum logic; see P. Heelan, "Quantum logic and classical logic: their respective roles," *Synthese*, xxii (1970), pp. 3 – 33; and SPPS, chapters 10 and 13.

22. That perception has a history exhibited in and at the same time influenced by pictorial art is a theme of Wartofsky's writing; see M. Wartofsky, *Models: Representation and Scientific Understanding* (Dordrecht and Boston: Reidel, 1979), pp. 175 – 210. The history of pictorial art is addressed in chapter 6 of SPPS, the history of scientific observation is treated in chapter 13. That even scientific *facts* are social-historical constructions is a theme of the work of T.S. Kuhn, L. Fleck, and many contemporary sociologists of science; see T.S. Kuhn, *Structure of Scientific Revolutions* (Chicago: University of Chicago Press, 2nd ed. 1970), L. Fleck, *Genesis and Development of a Scientific Fact* (Chicago: University of Chicago Press, 1979), and B. Latour and S. Woolgar, *Laboratory Life* (Beverly Hills and London: Sage Publ. 1979).

Chapter 8

1. H.-G. Gadamer, *Wahrheit und Methode. Grundzüge einer philosophischen Hermeneutik*. 4th ed. Tübingen 1975, p. 245.

2. *Ibid.*, p. 246.

3. *Ibid.*, p. 246, 293.

4. Gadamer, *Ibid.*, p. 246; vgl. E. Betti, *Allgemeine Auslegungslehre als Methodik der Geisteswissenschaften*, Tübingen 1967; Betti, *Die Hermeneutik als allgemeine Methodik der Geisteswissenschaften*, 2nd ed. Tübingen, 1972.

5. Gadamer, *Ibid.*, p. 246 f.

6. *Ibid.*, p. XXIV.

7. E.D. Hirsch, *Prinzipien der Interpretation*, München 1972.

8. Th.H. Seebohm, *Zur Kritik der hermeneutischen Vernunft*, Bonn 1972.

9. Gadamer, *op. cit.*, p. XVI.

10. *Ibid.*, p. 517 f.

11. *Ibid.*, p. 513.

12. *Ibid.*, p. 229.

13. *Ibid.*, p. 514.

14. R. Bubner, *Uber die wissenschaftstheoretische Rolle der Hermeneutik. Ein Diskussionsbeitrag*, in: *Dialektik und Wissenschaft*, Frankfurt, 2nd ed. 1974, p. 89 – 111.

15. Bubner, p. 91ff.

16. J. Habermas, *Zur Logik der Sozialwissenschaften. Materialien,* Frankfurt, 4th ed. 1977, p. 265.

17. J. Hauff, A. Heller, B. Hüppauf, L. Köhn, K.-P. Philippi, *Methodendiskussion. Arbeitsbuch zur Literaturwissenschaft,* vol. 2, Frankfurt, 2nd ed. 1972, p. 18.

18. K.-O. Apel, *Transformation der Philosophie,* vol. I: *Sprachanalytik, Semiotik, Hermeneutik,* Frankfurt 1973, p. 51.

19. K.-O. Apel, *Transformation de Philosophie,* vol. II: *Das Apriori der Kommunikationsgemeinschaft,* Frankfurt 1973, p. 206.

20. *Ibid.,* p. 117.

21. H.-G. Gadamer, *Das Erbe Hegels,* in: Gadamer and Habermas, *Das Erbe Hegels. Zwei Reden aus Anlab des Hegel Preises,* Frankfurt 1979, p. 33−84, p. 84.

22. Gadamer, *Hermeneutik,* in: *Historisches Wörterbuch der Philosophie,* ed. by J. Ritter, vol. 3, Basel 1974, columns 1061−1073.

23. Gadamer, *Wahrheit und Methode,* pp. 526−529.

24. *Ibid.,* pp. 205−228.

25. *Ibid.,* p. 223.

26. *Ibid.,* p. 226.

27. *Ibid.,* p. 226.

28. *Ibid.,* p. 228.

29. G. Misch, *Vorbericht des Herausgebers,* in: W. Dilthey, Ges. Schr., V, pp. cxv f. − See also fn. 37.

30. W. Dilthey, Ges. Schr. XIX, ed. by H. Johach and F. Rodi. Göttingen 1982, pp. 296−332.

31. *Ibid.,* p. 304.

32. *Ibid.,* p. 306.

33. *Ibid.*

34. *Ibid.,* p. 307.

35. *Ibid.,* p. 329. Cf. p. 347, 357. − By a printing mistake the last sentence "Life is . . . " has been omitted in vol. XIX.

36. There is no question that Dilthey's concept of *Wissenschaft* contains a number of ambiguities. This, however, has nothing to do with his conviction that life as a whole is unfathomable and that thinking can never get behind life.

37. G. Misch, *Lebensphilosophie und Phänomenologie.* 3rd. ed. Darmstadt 1967, pp. 51, 233. − See also F. Rodi, *Dilthey, die Phänomenologie und Georg Misch* in E.W. Orth (Ed.), *Dilthey und die Phänomenologie,* Freiburg, 1985.

38. Dilthey, Ges. Schr. XIX, p. 307. Misch has quoted this passage from the then unpublished manuscript in Ges. Schr. V, p. cxvi.

39. *Ibid.,* p. 330.

40. See fn. 15.

41. M. Frank *Das individuelle Allgemeine. Textstrukturierung und -interpretation nach Schleiermacher.* Frankfurt 1977, p. 310.

42. Gadamer, p. 179.

43. *Ibid.,* p. 227.

44. W. Dilthey, *Leben Schleiermachers,* Berlin 1870. Introduction to the first edition, p. v (not contained in Ges. Schr. XIII).

45. W. Dilthey, Ges Schr. XIII/1, pp. 229, 292. – See also F. Rodi, *Die Romantiker in der Sicht Hegels, Hayms und Diltheys,* in O. Pöggeler and A. Gethmann-Siefert (eds.), *Kunsterfahrung und Kulturpolitik im Berlin Hegels,* Bonn, 1983, pp. 177–197.

46. Gadamer, pp. 157–161.

Chapter 9

1. One of the early studies of Heidegger is Walter Biemel's *Le Concept du monde chez Heidegger* (Vrin: Paris, 1950); a major journal sympathetic to the trend is *Man and World.* A major topic in the discussion of Husserl has been how, when, and how far a concept of world appears in his thought; the best account is Ludwig Landgribe, "World as Phenomenological Problem," *The Phenomenology of Edmund Husserl: Six Essays,* ed. D. Welton (Cornell University Press, 1983).

2. See *Being and Time,* "The Worldhood of the World," sec. 14f. I don't take up the four senses discussed therein.

3. See *The Essence of Reasons* (bi-lingual ed.) (Evanston: Northwestern University Press, 1969). The following is a simplified version of the world discussion. See also Werner Marx, *Heidegger and the Tradition* (Northwestern Univ. Press, 1971), esp. Part III.

4. Heidegger, *Basic Problems,* cited from Kant, p. 50.

5. *The Essence of Reasons.*

6. *Basic Problems,* p. 165.

7. *Basic Problems,* pp. 171–73.

8. See "Language as Experience of the World," *Truth and Method,* pp. 397–414.

9. *Truth and Method,* pp. 405–06.

10. See my paper, "The Conflict Between Poetry and Literature," forthcoming.

11. For other criticism and appreciation, see my "Text and Reference: The World of the Work," *Papers on Language and Literature* (Winter, 1981).

12. The fullest version is found in *Interpretation Theory* (1976). For

the comment that Ricoeur does not claim to add a new concept of world, see Mary Gerhardt, *The Problem of Belief.*

13. (Hackett: Indianapolis, 1978). See the important "Critical Discussion of *Ways of Worldmaking*" by Ricoeur in *Philosophy and Literature* (Spring, 1980), pp. 107–120, and also Catherine Elgin, *With Reference to Reference* (Hackett: Indianapolis, 1982).

14. Thus "A possible world is a set of basic particular situations" occupying space-time points (M.J. Cresswell, "The World is Everything that is the Case," in *The Possible and the Actual: Readings in the Metaphysics of Modality*, ed. Michael Loux (Cornell University Press, Ithaca, p. 136; or worlds are "sets of intensional objects," constructed out of propositions, with objects belonging to a world seen as set membership (William Lycon, "The Trouble with Possible Worlds," ibid., p. 312).

15. Hubert Dreyfus and John Haugeland, "Philosophy's Last Stand: A Husserl-Heidegger Dialogue," *Heidegger and Modern Philosophy*, ed. Murray (New Haven: Yale Univ. Press., 1978), pp. 225–27.

16. Nelson Goodman, *The Ways of Worldmaking*: "the question . . . is not of the possible worlds that many of my contemporaries especially those near Disneyland, are busy making . . . . We are not speaking in terms of multiple possible alternatives to a single world but of multiple actual worlds" (p. 2). Of course, from a vantage that Stanley Rosen would like to occupy, Goodman appears to be Walt Disney. See *The Limits of Analysis* (New York: Basic Books, 1981), p. 269.

17. *Ways of Worldmaking.*

18. "Critical Discussion . . .".

19. See his Foreword to *Ways of Worldmaking.*

20. See Heidegger, *Erläuterungen zur Hölderlins Dichtung* (4th ed.) and *The Letter on Humanism* in *Basic Writings*, ed. D. Krell. Harper & Row; New York, 1976.

21. Emmanuel Levinas, *Totality and Infinity*, trans. Alphonso Lingis (Duquesne Univ.Press: Pittsburgh, 1969), pp. 44–45.

22. This is a conception expressed as late as *The Crisis of European Philosophy and Transcendental Phenomenology*, trans. David Carr (Evanston: Northwestern Univ. Press, 1970), p. 162; cf. pp. 157–58; Husserl goes on to discuss the temporal modes of horizon that he expresses in "intentional language as a continuum of retentions and protentions" (p. 168). The model of horizon of perception field goes back to the 1913 *Ideen zu einer reinen Phänomenologie* I (Martinus Nijhoff, 1950), pp. 48–49; other characteristic formulae are those of "indeterminate as horizon of determinability"(pp. 80, 99) and "the unknown as horizon of the known" (p. 120). In the text, "The Origin of Geometry," Husserl also speaks of horizon of our fellow man and of our civilization as open and infinite (*Crisis*, p. 358).

23. Derrida, "Violence and Metaphysics," *Writing and Difference*, trans. Alan Bass (Chicago: Univ. of Chicago Press, 1978), p. 120.

24. Heidegger, *Being and Time*, trans. Macquarrie and Robinson (New York: Harper and Row, 1962), pp. 156–81, 264, 384–85.

25. *Being and Time*, p. 488.

26. "Poetically Man Dwells," *Poetry, Language, Thought*, trans. Albert Hofstadter (New York: Harper & Row, 1971), p. 220.

27. "Poetically Man Dwells," p. 221.

28. "The Thing," *Poetry, Language, Thought*, p. 180.

29. "The Thing," p. 173.

30. "The Thing," p. 184.

31. About the first discussion of these lectures is Otto Pöggeler's *Der Denkweg Martin Heideggers* (Neske: Pfullingen, 1963). See chap. VII on "Der Andere Anfang" and the section "Hölderlin und der Andere Anfang," pp. 215f.

32. *Gelassenheit* is trans. as *Discourse on Thinking*, trans. John Anderson & E. Hans Freund (New York: Harper & Row, 1966); see pp. 64f. Compare the discussion of region in *Being and Time*. See also the useful discussion of horizon by Reiner Schürmann, *Meister Eckhardt: Mystic and Philosopher* (Bloomington: Indiana Univ. Press, 1978), pp. 194–202, and the Landgrebe paper previously cited. On notion of region (*Gegend*) in *Being and Time*, see pp. 108 and 186.

Chapter 10

1. *The Sense of An Ending*. Studies in the Theory of Fiction. London, Oxford University Press, 1966, pp. 35f.

2. *Ibid.* p. 39.

3. *Story and Discourse*. Narrative Structure in Fiction and Film. Ithaca and London, Cornell University Press, 1978, p. 47.

4. "Introduction à l'analyse structurale des récits" in *Communications* vol. 8 1966, p. 7.

5. "History and Fiction as Modes of Comprehension" in *New Literary History*, 1979, pp. 557f.

6. In *On Narrative*, ed. W.J.T. Mitchell. Chicago and London, University of Chicago Press 1981.

7. *Ibid.* p. 4

8. *Ibid.* p. 23

9. *Ibid.*

10. This is what Aristotle meant when he said: "The Unity of a Plot does not consist, as some suppose, in its having one man as its subject.

An infinity of things befall that one man, some of which it is impossible to reduce to a unity; and in like manner there are many actions of one man which cannot be made to form one action." Details may help present character, of course. But for Aristotle, character is subservient to plot in a good play. cf. *Poetics* 1451a.

11. *Op. cit.* pp. 93ff.

Chapter 11

1. See: "Narratology and Deconstruction," forthcoming in *Proceedings of the First Annual Humanities Institute Meeting*, ed. Hayden White. Stanford: *Stanford Studies in Comparative Literature*.

2. Gerard Genette (1972) *Figures III*. Paris: Seuil. The book has appeared in English as *Narrative Discourse: An Essay in Method* (1980), tr. J. Lewin. Ithaca: Cornell University Press.

3. Wayne Booth (1961) *The Rhetoric of Fiction*. Chicago: University of Chicago Press. Roland Barthes (1975), An Introduction to the Structural Analysis of Narrative," in *New Literary History*, VI, 2 (Winter), pp. 237−272.

4. And today, not a few structuralists go even so far as to dismiss the idea of a "science of literature" (See Tzvetan Todorov (1980), *Introduction to Poetics*, tr. R. Howard, pp. XX−XXXII. Brighton (Sussex): The Harvester Press.).

5. Roman Jakobson (1960), "Closing Statement," in *Style in Language*, ed. Thomas Sebeok, pp. 350−377. Bloomington: Indiana University Press.

6. Genette, *Narrative Discourse*, p. 228.

7. What Genette calls: "this narrating instance that we have to look at, according to the traces it has left − the traces it is considered to have left − in the narrative discourse it is considered to have produced," p. 214.

8. Franz Kafka "Das Schweigen der Sirenen" (1935), *Parables*, pp. 74−79, (in German and English). New York: Schocken Books.

9. Homer (1957), *Odyssey*, ed. W.B. Stanford, XII, 194. London: MacMillan.

10. Homer (1967), *Odyssey*, tr. A. Cook., XII, 168 (p. 166). New York: Norton.

11. See: *Lexicon Homericum*, ed. H. Elding, I, p. 141 & II, p. 427. Hildesheim: Georg Olms Buchhandlung.

12. Cook translates "kallimon aoiden" by "lovely song" and E.V. Rieu (1960) (New York: Random) by "sweet song."

13. Homer, *Odyssey*, XII, 187, 183, 192.

14. *Odyssey*, VIII, 487–586.

15. Georg Lukacs (1971), *The Theory of the Novel*, tr. A. Bostock, II, 1, pp. 29–39. Cambridge, Mass.: MIT Press.

16. See: W.W. Horn and J. Wells (1928), *A Commentary on Herodotus*, p. 128. Oxford: Clarendon Press.

17. *Roman History*, V, 50, 5.

18. *Roman History*, V, 32, 6.

19. Howard R. Patch, "The Tradition of the Goddess Fortuna in Roman literature and in the Transitional Period," in *Smith College Studies in Modern Languages* (1922), III, 3 (April), pp. 130–177.

20. *The Republic*, X, 617.

21. *Iliad*, XXII, 209–10.

22. Georges Duby, *Le Dimanche de Bouvines*. Paris: Gallimard.

23. Jacques Derrida (1974), *Of Grammatology*, tr. G.C. Spivak, p. 36. Baltimore: The Johns Hopkins University Press.

24. Herodotus, *Histories*, VI, 112.

25. W.W. Horn & J. Wells, *A Commentary on Herodotus*, p. 108.

26. Elias Canetti (1978), *The Voices of Marrakesh: A record of a Visit*, pp. 22–26. New York: Continuum.

27. Saussure (1971), *Cours de Linguistique Générale*, ed. Ch. Bailly and A. Sechehaye, p. 98. Paris: Payot.

28. Roman Jakobson and Linda Waugh (1979), *the Sound Shape of Language*.

29. Hegel (1956), *The Philosophy of History*, tr. J. Sibree, I, 3, p. 199. (New York: Dover).

30. Canetti, pp. 23–24.

31. *Ibid.*, p. 25.

32. *Ibid.*, p. 100.

33. *Ibid.*, p. 102.

34. *Ibid.*, p. 103.

35. See, for instance, Mircea Eliade (1957), *Mythes, rêves et mysteres*, pp. 90–97. Paris: Gallimard.

36. Hans Georg Gadamer (1975), *Truth and Method*, pp. 190–191.

37. Hans Robert Jauss (1982), both *Aesthetic Experience and Literary Hermeneutics*, tr. Michael Shaw; and *Toward an Aesthetic of Reception*, tr. Thimoty Bathi. Minneapolis: University of Minnesota Press.

38. On narratives of experience, see: Michel de Certeau (1980), *L'invention du quotidien*, pp. 149–167. Paris: 10/18.

39. Homer, *Odyssey*, p. 3.

40. See: Alfred Schütz, *Structures of the Life-World*, tr. M. Zaner & T. Engelhardt, passim. Evanston: Northwestern University Press.

41. Charles Baudelaire (1927), "Au lecteur", *Fleurs du Mal*, in *Works*,

tr. A. Symons, New York: Albert Boni.
   42. *"La vie anterieure,"* p. 110.
   43. *"La Beauté,"* p. 92.

Chapter 12

1. See for instance Jacques Derrida, "Outwork, prefacing," in *Dissemination,* trans. Barbara Johnson (Chicago: University of Chicago Press, 1981).

2. Jacques Derrida, "Differance," in *Speech and Phenomena,* trans. David B. Allison (Evanston: Northwestern University Press, 1973), p. 130.

3. *Ibid.,* p. 141.

4. Martin Heidegger: "Our Western languages are languages of metaphysical thinking, each in its own way. It must remain an open question whether the nature of Western languages is itself marked with the exclusive brand of metaphysics, and thus marked permanently by onto-theo-logic, or whether these languages offer other possibilities of utterance — and that means at the same time of a telling silence," *Identity and Difference,* trans. Joan Stambaugh (New York: Harper and Row, 1969), p. 73. Cf. also, Martin Heidegger, *The End of Philosophy,* trans. Joan Stambaugh (New York: Harper and Row, 1973); and *Kant and the Problem of Metaphysics,* trans. James S. Churchill (Bloomington: Indiana University Press, 1962). Derrida picks up the theme, though he construes it in an entirely different way, as is suggested by the following cryptic catalogue of topics he means to investigate: "The *symtomatic* form of the return of the repressed: the metaphor of writing which haunts European discourse, and the systematic contradictions of the onto-theological exclusion of the trace. The repression of writing as the repression of that which threatens presence and the mastering of absence. The enigma of presence 'pure and simple': as duplication, original repetition, auto-affection, and *différance.* The distinction between the mastering of absence as speech and the mastering of absence as writing, "Freud and the Scene of Writing," in *Writing and Difference,* trans. Alan Bass (Chicago: University of Chicago Press, 1978), p. 197.

5. Jacques Derrida: "Despite appearances, the deconstruction of logocentrism is not a psychoanalysis of philosophy . . . . For example, logocentric repression is not comprehensible on the basis of the Freudian concept of repression; on the contrary, logocentric repression permits an understanding of how an original and individual repression

became possible within the horizon of a culture and a historical structure of belonging . . . . Logo-phonocentrism is not a philosophical or
historical error which the history of philosophy, of the West, that is,
of the world, would have rushed into pathologically, but is rather a
necessary, and necessarily finite, movement and structure: [it is] history
as *différance* which finds in philosophy as epistèmè, in the European
form of the metaphysical or onto-theological project, the privileged
manifestation, with worldwide dominance, of dissimulation, of general
censorship of the text in general," "Freud and the Scene of Writing," pp.
196, 197.

    6. Gayatri Chakravorty Spivak, "Translator's Preface," in Jacques
Derrida, *Of Grammatology*, trans. Gayatri Chakravorty Spivak (Baltimore: Johns Hopkins Press, 1975), p. liii.

    7. *Ibid.*, p. xliii.

    8. The thesis has much in common with Heidegger's existential-
ized theme of *Dasein*: "*More Originary [ursprünglich] than man is the
finitude of the Dasein in him*," *Kant and the Problem of Metaphysics*, p. 237;
cited by Spivak, *op. cit.*, p. 1.

    9. "Differance," pp. 140-141.

    10. Ferdinand de Saussure, *Course in General Linguistics*, ed. Charles
Bally *et al.*, trans. Wade Baskin (New York: McGraw-Hill, 1966), p. 67;
cited in *Of Grammatology*, p. 31. I am trying to keep to the passages Derrida himself selects.

    11. *Of Grammatology*, p. 30; *General Course*, p. 23.

    12. *Of Grammatology*, p. 31; *General Course*, pp. 23-24.

    13. *Of Grammatology*, p. 44.

    14. *Of Grammatology*, p. 33; *General Course*, p. 23.

    15. *Of Grammatology*, p. 40; *General Course*, pp. 33, 21.

    16. *Of Grammatology*, p. 40. Emile Benveniste confirms this inter-
pretation effectively, citing several occasional written remarks of
Saussure's that he takes to be central to his thinking: "Here is our pro-
fession of faith regarding linguistic matter: in other fields one can speak
of things *from such or such point of view*, certain that one will find oneself
again on firm ground in the object itself. In linguistics, we deny in principle that there are given objects, that there are things which continue
to exist when one passes from one order to ideas of another, and that
one can, as a result, allow oneself to consider 'things' in several orders,
as if they were given by themselves"; "The more one delves into the
material proposed for linguistic study, the more one becomes convinced
of this truth, which most particularly — it would be useless to conceal
it — makes one pause: that the bond established among things is preex-

istent, in this area, *to the things themselves*, and serves to determine them"; "The absolutely final law of language is, we dare say, that there is nothing which can ever reside in *one* term, as a direct consequence of the fact that linguistic symbols are unrelated to what they should designate, so that *a* is powerless to designate anything without the aid of *b*, and the same thing is true of *b* without the aid of *a*, or that both have no value except through their reciprocal difference . . .," *Problems in General Linguistics*, trans. Mary Elizabeth Meek (Coral Gables: University of Miami Press, 1971), pp. 35,36,37; cf. Ch. 8. Benveniste himself adopts Saussure's problem and concedes his (Benveniste's) not having solved it: "Language *re-produces* reality [he says]. This is to be understood in the most literal way: reality is produced anew by means of language . . . . At this point some serious problems immediately arise which we shall leave to the philosophers, notably that of the adequacy of the mind to express 'reality' . . . Language reproduces the world, but by submitting it to its own organization," p. 22.

17. The question is explored in a different idiom in Joseph Margolis, "Scientific Realism as a Transcendental Issue," unpublished.

18. This is why Derrida's notion of deconstruction must be carefully distinguished from Heidegger's notion of "de-struction" (not to be confused with "destruction"). Spivak remarks that Derrida did actually use Heidegger's term in the first version of *Grammatology, op. cit.*, p. xlix. Richard Palmer cites an instructive exchange between Heidegger and Eugen Fink regarding Heraclitus, in which Heidegger remarks: "We are both agreed that when we would speak with a thinker, we must pay attention to the unspoken in the spoken . . . the unthought in the thought." Palmer understands this deconstructively: "interpretation has to penetrate to what the earlier thinker himself was blind to, but which was the essential determination of his thinking. Interpretation is not destructive but deconstructive: it seeks for what is behind the manifest content of thought . . . this is a general characteristic of the hermeneutical − it discloses the hidden − which is the central trait of the Heideggerian path," "The Postmodernity of Heidegger," in William V. Spanos (ed.), *Martin Heidegger and the Question of Literature; Toward a Postmodern Literary Hermeneutics* (Bloomington: Indiana University Press, 1976), pp. 80, 81. If this is a fair reading (Derrida seems to incline toward it), then Heidegger attempts deconstruction only in a "shallow" sense − roughly, deciphering in the hermeneutic way (not unlike Freudian psychoanalysis: notice Palmer's use of the term "manifest") − whereas Derrida treats "alterity," "trace," *"différance"* as indicating that what he marks as absent *is not present-as-absent*. Heidegger's motivation, of course, is to overcome the metaphysical bent of Western thought; he links the entire effort to *aletheia*.

Derrida is quite explicit about all this: "On what conditions [he asks] is a grammatology [that is, the science of writing – in his sense of writing] possible? Its fundamental condition is certainly the undoing [*sollicitation*] of logocentrism. But this condition of possibility turns into a condition of impossibility," *Of Grammatology*, pp. 74, 4 (cf. footnote #4). This appears in the section titled "Of Grammatology as a Positive Science." The use of the term "positive" plays a double role (it seems): first, it is meant to undermine the pretension that grammatology is a science among other (positive) sciences (cf. p. 83ff), perhaps to undermine the views that grammatology conforms with positivistic views of science; and second, it may be meant to suggest an analogy with the theological technique of the *via negativa*; here, comparison with Heidegger appears instructive. For when Derrida speaks of "the *incompetence* of science which is also the incompetence of philosophy," he links the thesis to our need to acknowledge the "unnameable movement of *difference-itself*, that I have strategically nicknamed *trace, reserve,* or *differance* . . . " (p. 93). "The trace," he explicitly says, "*is nothing*, it is not an entity, it exceeds the question *What is?* and contingently makes it possible" (p. 75). And yet, the "science" of grammatology concerns *trace,* writing, *différrance*. A very striking clue to both the resemblance and difference between Derrida and Heidegger is given by the fact that "differance" appears only in the singular (and is unnameable and without structure) and "difference" appears only in the plural (and belongs within conceptual systems or networks); similarly, in Heidegger "Being" in its ontological sense appears only in the singular and "being" (or, better, "entities") in its ontic sense appears only in the plural. As Heidegger puts it: "The Being of entities 'is' not itself an entity"; "Ontological inquiry is indeed more primordial, as over against the ontical inquiry of the positive sciences," *Being and Time*, trans. John Macquarrie and Edward Robinson (New York: Harper and Row, 1962), pp. 26, 31. In part, then, Heidegger provides the positive way of approaching the *ontically* inaccessible reality of Being to Derrida's negative way of approaching "writing" or texts. But of course, Derrida also sees Heidegger, ultimately, as *ontologically* sanguine about his own project: "Our provisional aim is the Interpretation of *time* as the possible horizon for any understanding whatsoever of Being" (p. 1), that is, our understanding of "the meaning of Being" (p. 24).

19. *Of Grammatology*, p. 46.

20. *Of Grammatology*, p. 46.

21. For a discussion of the use of "foundational," see Joseph Margolis, "Skepticism, Foundationalism, and Pragmatism," *American Philosophical Quarterly*, XIV (1977) and "Pragmatism without Foundations," unpublished.

22. See, for example, the illuminating debate ("Truth") between John Austin and P.F. Strawson, *Proceedings of the Aristotelian Society*, Suppl. Vol. XXIV 1950).

23. Cf. Jacques Derrida, "The Supplement of Copula," trans. Josué V. Harari, in Josué V. Harari (ed.), *Textual Strategies* (Ithaca: Cornell University Press, 1979).

24. "Freud and the Scene of Writing," p. 196.

Chapter 14

1. The essay "White Mythology," has appeared in *Margins of Philosophy*, trans. A. Bass, Chicago: University of Chicago Press, 1982, pp. 207–271. It will be referred to under the following abbreviation: *M* in the text. For citation will be used also the following abbreviations of Derrida's works: *SP* for Speech and Phenomena, trans. D.B. Allison, Evanston: Northwestern 1973; *WD* for *Writing and Difference*, trans. A. Bass, Chicago: University of Chicago Press 1978; *OG* for *Of Grammatology*, trans. G.Ch.Spivak, Baltimore: The Johns Hopkins University Press 1976; *D* for *Dissemination*, trans. B. Johnson, Chicago: University of Chicago Press 1981; *VP* for *La Vérité en Peinture*, Paris: Flammarion 1978; *AF* for *L'Archéologie du Frivole*, Paris: Galilée 1973. – The present essay is part of a larger study entitled *The Tain of the Mirror: Deconstruction and Reflexivity*, to appear soon.

2. Jacques Derrida, "The *Retrait* of Metaphor," trans. Eds., *Enclitic*, Vol. 2, n. 2, 1978, p. 8.

3. Martin Heidegger, "My Way to Phenomenology," *On Time and Being*, New York: Harper 1972, trans. J. Stambaugh, p. 74.

4. See L. Bruno Puntel, *Analogie und Geschichtlichkeit. Philosophiegeschichtlich-kritischer Versuch über das Grundproblem der Metaphysik*, Freiburg: Herder, 1969.

5. As for the later Heidegger and the problem of analogy, we refer the reader to Puntel's study, pp. 455–531.

6. See Eberhard Jüngel, *Zum Ursprung der Analogie bei Parmenides und Heraklit*, Berlin: DeGruyter, 1964.

7. Puntel, p. 16.

8. Pierre Aubenque, *Le Problème de l'Etre chez Aristote*, 2nd edition, Paris: PUF 1966, pp. 199–205.

9. Paul Ricoeur, *The Rule of Metaphor*, trans. R. Czerny, Toronto: University of Toronto Press, 1977, pp. 259–280.

10. Aristotle, *Metaphysics*, trans. R. Hope, Ann Harbor: University of Michigan Press, 1975, 1003a 33–34.

11. Aristotle, 1016b 34.

12. Franz Brentano, *On the Several Senses of Being in Aristotle*, trans. R. George, Berkeley: University of California Press, 1975, pp. 58–66.

13. Puntel, p. 26.

14. Martin Heidegger, *Being and Time*, trans. J. Macquarrie and E. Robinson, London: SCM, 1962, p. 62.

15. p. 189.

16. pp. 104–105.

17. p. 201.

18. See pp. 196ff, but for more detail also see Martin Heidegger, *Logik. Die Frage nach der Wahrheit, Gesamtausgabe*, Vol. 21, Frankfurt: Klostermann 1976, pp. 153ff.

19. Jacques Derrida, "Economimesis," trans. R. Klein, *Diacritics*, Summer 1981, p. 13.

20. p. 19.

21. Derrida, "The *Retrait* of Metaphor," p. 28.

22. Henri Birault, "*Heidegger et la pensée de la finitude*," *Revue Internationale de Philosophie*, 1960, n. 52, pp. 135–162.

Chapter 15

1. G = Jacques Derrida, *De la Grammatologie* (Paris: Les Éditions de Minuits, 1967); the pages following the slash refer to the English translation: *Of Grammatology*, trans. G.C. Spivak (Baltimore: Johns Hopkins University Press, 1974).

2. "Translator's Introduction" in Jacques Derrida, *Dissemination* trans. Barbara Johnson (Chicago: University Press, 1981), p. vii.

3. Edmund Husserl, *Cartesian Meditations*, trans. Dorian Cairns (The Hague: Martinus Nijhoff, 1960), 20. p. 46.

4. This critique of Husserl is to be found throughout Derrida's early writings, but see in particular *Speech and Phenomena and Other Essays on Husserl's Theory of Signs*, trans. David Allison (Evanston: Northwestern University Press, 1973), chapters 3 and 5.

5. See Husserl's "Nachwort zu meiner Ideen" which appears as the "Author's Preface to English Edition" in *Ideas: General Introduction to Pure Phenomenology*, trans. W. Boyce Gibson, New York: Collier Paperbacks, 1962), p. 14; *Cartesian Meditations*, §62, p. 151.

6. This is the argument of *Ideas I*, §§44–6.

7. Martin Heidegger, *Zur Sache des Denkens* (Tübingen: Max Niemeyer, 1969), pp. 31–32; Eng. trans. *On Time and Being*, trans. Joan Stambaugh (New York: Harper and Row, 1972), pp. 29–30.

8. Martin Heidegger, *Gelassenheit* (Pfullingen: Neske, 1960), p. 26; Eng. trans. *Discourse on Thinking*, trans. E. Freund and J. Anderson (New York: Harper and Row, 1959), p. 55.

9. The most important texts on the transcendental signified upon which we base this claim are: G, 31−41/18−26; 70−73/48−50; 106−8/72−3; 214−5/149−50; 227−234/159−64.

10. Martin Heidegger, *The Essence of Reasons*, A bilingual Edition, trans. T. Malick (Evanston: Northwestern University Press, 1969), pp. 108−9.

11. Martin Heidegger, *Der Satz vom Grund* (Pfullingen: Neskle, 1957), p. 188.

12. . . . moving along lines that would be more Nietzschean than Heideggerean . . . " Jacques Derrida, *Positions*, trans. Alan Bass (Chicago: University Press, 1981), p. 10.

13. Martin Heidegger, *Gesamtausgabe*, B. 9, *Wegmarken* (Frankfurt: Klostermann, 1976), pp. 193−4.

Chapter 16

1. When citing Derrida's or Heidegger's works, I give the original French or German page (and occasionally the text) and then, in parentheses, the corresponding page in existing English translations, which can be found in the standard bibliographies. When several citations or references occur within the same paragraph, I frequently gather them in a single footnote at the end of the paragraph so as not to interrupt the reader.

I am grateful to Professors Thomas J. Harrison and Robert Pogue Harrison for their invaluable criticisms and suggestions in the revising of this paper.

2. The Cérisy lecture: in *Les fins de l'homme: A partir du travail de Jacques Derrida*, Paris: Galilée, 1981, pp. 445−479.

3. Anterior (plus "vieille" que): *Marges de la philosophie*, Paris: Minuit, 1972, p. 23 (22). Model oneself (*se modeler sur ce qu'on déconstruit*): *Positions*, Paris: Minuit, 1972, p. 70 (54).

4. Bruno Bauer, *Die Pausane des jüngsten Gerichts über Hegel den Atheisten und Antichristen: ein Ultimatum*, in *Die Hegelsche Linke*, ed. Karl Löwith, Stuttgart-Bad Cannstatt: Friedrich Frommann Verlag (Günther Holzboog), 1972, pp. 123−225. Selections in English translation are found in *The Young Hegelians: An Anthology*, ed. and trans. Lawrence S. Stepelevich, Cambridge: Cambridge U.P., 1983, pp. 177−186.

5. Jean-Paul Sartre, *Search for a Method*, trans. Hazel Barnes, New York: Knopf, 1963, p. 38.

6. Departure; extremely important, irreversible advance (écart; une avancée inédite, irréversible): *Positions*, 73 (54). Thought of presence (*la défence la plus "profonde" et la plus "puissante"* . . . pensée de la présence): *Positions*, 75 (55).

7. *Eigentlichkeit, das Eigene* as the continuous thread: *Positions*, 74 (54); *Eperons*, 116 (120); *Marges*, 74, n. 26 (omitted at 64 n. 39); *Marges* 152, n. 14 (omitted at 127, n. 21); 155 n. 16 (129, n. 25).

8. Proximity to, identical with, oneself (*cette proximité absolue de l'étant questionnant à lui-même*): *Marges*, 150 (125); (*l'identité avec soi du questionnant*): *ibid.*, 74 (64). Identical with being itself (*l'identité du questionnant et de l'interrogé*): *Marges*, 150 (126).

9. Phenomenology's principle of presence: *Marges*, 150 (126f.). *Au plus proche de soi* and temporality: *De la grammatologie*, Paris: Minuit, 1976, p. 33 (20). Man as the near of being: *Marges*, 160 (133). "Passes through the mouth": "Economimesis," Diacritics, June 1981, p. 14.

10. Living in thrownness (*die Übernahme der Geworfenheit*): *Sein und Zeit*, Tübingen: Neomarius, 1953 (7th ed.), p. 325 (373). Compare Michael E. Zimmerman, *Eclipse of the Self: The Development of Heidegger's Concept of Authenticity*, Athens, Ohio: Ohio U.P., 1981, pp. 102–118 and Gianni Vattimo, "Excerpts from 'On the Way to Silence,'" in *The Favorite Malice: Ontology and Reference in Contemporary Italian Poetry*, edited and translated by Thomas J. Harrison, New York: Out of London Press, 1983, pp. 329–335, esp. p. 330.

11. For example, *Grammatologie*, 64 (43).

12. Intellectual intuition of itself as intuition (*kai esti he noesis noeseos noesis*): *Metaphysics*, L, 9, 1074b 34f. Perfect interiority (*l'intimité de l'âme, la présence vivante de l'âme à soi*): *Grammatologie*, 46 (30).

13. Reads the imperfect from the perfect (*proteron de . . . to teleion men tou atelous*): *Physics*, TH, 9, 265 a 23, and (*proteron energeia dynameos*): *Metaphysics*, TH, 9, 1049 b 5. Reads movement from the standpoint of repose (*he gar genesis heneka tes ousias estin all' ouch he ousia heneka tes geneseos*): *De Partibus Animalium*, A, 640 a 18, and (*he genesis agoge eis ousian*): *Topics*, Z, 139 b 20. In God no obscurity (*me hylen echei*), nous and nooumenon are one (*to auto . . . kai . . . mia*): *Metaphysics*, L, 9, 1075 a 4 and 5.

14. Making all things intelligible (*ho de [nous] toi panta poiein*): *De Anima*, G, 5, 430 a, 16 f. Plato (*ek tou me ontos eis to on . . . poiesis*): *Symposium* 205 b. The most divine element in us (*en hemin to theiotaton*): *Nicomachean Ethics*, K, 7, 1177 a 16.

15. On Eckhart, see John D. Caputo, *The Mystical Element in Heidegger's Thought*, Athens, Ohio: Ohio U.P., 1978, esp. pp. 103–113. Re: human intellectualism vs. ontically-epistemically normative spirits, cf.: "*Rationale est differentia animalis, et Deo non convenit nec angelis*," Thomas

Aquinas, *I Sent.*, d. 24, q. 1, a. 1. (Following Boethius, Aquinas further compares *ratio* and *intellectus*: "*Unde dicit Boetius in IV* de Consol., [prosa 6], *quod similiter se habet ratio ad intellectum sicut tempus ad aeternitatem et circulus ad centrum*," In Librum Boetii De Trinitate Expositio, Lect. II, q. II, a. 1, ad tertium, in St. Thomas Aquinas, *Opuscula Theologica*, ed., M. Calcaterra, Rome: Marietti, 1954, II, 382.) *Non habet rationem termini*: Thomas Aquinas, *Summa Theol.*, II, q. 5, a. 7, ad 3.

16. Husserlian ideal of man and meaning (*l'être comme présence: proximité absolue de l'identité à soi*) (*la présence à soi de la vie transcendentale*): *La voix et le phénomène*, Paris: Presses Universitaires de France, 1967, p. 111 (99); (*cette proximité absolue du signifiant au signifié*): *ibid.*, 90 (80); (*la présence naturelle et prèmiere et immédiate du sens à l'âme dans le logos*): *Grammatologie*, 55 (37); (*sens, c'est-à-dire . . . la présence pleine du signifié dans sa vérité*): *ibid.*, 60 (40). Full language . . . its own father: *ibid.*, 45 (29); (30); 58 (39). Rousseau: *ibid.*, 354 (250). Archi-écriture as exteriority, etc.: *Grammatologie*, 39 (24); 41 (26); 55 (37); cf. "*ce qui ménace la présence*," *L'Ecriture et la différence*, Paris: Seuil, 1967, p. 293 (197).

17. These issues are presented in some detail in my "Heidegger's Philosophy of Mind" in *Contemporary Philosophy: A New Survey*, Vol. IV: *Philosophy of Mind*, ed., Guttorm Fløistad, The Hague: Nijhoff, 1983, pp. 287–318, esp. pp. 297–304.

18. Transcendental word (*le mot transcendental assurant la possibilité de l'être mot à tous les autres mots*): *Grammatologie*, 34 (20). Irreducible simplicity: *ibid.* 34 (21). *Unter-schied* etc.: *Identität und Differenz*, Pfullingen: Neske, 1957, 56f. (65); cf. *Zur Sache des Denkens*, Tübingen: Niemeyer, 1969, p. 16 (15): *auseinander . . . zueinander*. An excellent analysis of the text in *Identität und Differenz* is given by Prof. John D. Caputo in his *Heidegger and Aquinas: An Essay in Overcoming Metaphysics*, New York: Fordham U.P., 1982, pp. 147–154.

19. Teleologically promised ultimate signified: *Marges*, 152, n. 14 (127, n. 21). *Le désir*: *Marges*, 59 (52).

20. Ambiguous (*peut-être; ambiguité; non pas en deçà*): *Grammatologie*, 23f. (12), 36 (22), 38 (23); cf. last writing . . . first writing, *ibid.* 38 (23). "*Quelque platonisme*," *Marges*, 74 (89).

21. Blanchot, *L'Espace litteraire*, Paris, 1955, p. 202, cited in Paul de Man, *Blindness and Insight*, p. 63.

22. Italo Calvino, "The Written and the Unwritten Word," James Lecture (New York Institute for Humanities), March 30, 1983, printed in *The New York Review of Books*, May 12, 1983, p. 39; trans. William Weaver.

23. The living entities who have *logos* (*logon de monon anthropos echei ton zoion*): *Politics*, B, 1253 a 9f. Vanishes at daybreak: *Ecriture* 224 (151).

24. Primacy and relative priority: *protos* (Latin *primus*) and *proteros* (Latin *prior*), respectively superlative and relative or comparative degrees of *pro*. Anchibasie: Heraclitus, Frag. 122. Almosting it: J. Joyce, *Ulysses*, New York: Modern Library, 1961, p. 47.

25. Economy of the abyss (*faire l'économie de l'abîme*): "*Parergon, II*," in *La Vérité en peinture*, 45.

26. Criticism . . . krinein (*la critique en général, liée . . . à la possibilité du décidable, au* krinein): *La Dissémination*, Paris: Seuil, 1972, p. 267 (236f.). Critique of criticism (*une "critique" déconstructrice de la notion de "critique"*): *Positions*, 63 (46).

27. Heidegger on *krinein*: *Wegmarken*, Frankfurt: Klostermann, 1976, p. 264 (241).

28. In-duction: *Wegmarken*, 244 (225f), 264 (241). This topic is treated in my "Heidegger's Philosophy of Mind," pp. 296f.

29. Not assured exercise (*pas . . . un exercice de tout repos*): *Positions* 24 (14). "I am trying precisely": The Languages of Criticism and the Sciences of Man: The Structuralist Controversy, eds. Richard Macksey and Eugenio Donato (Baltimore: The Johns Hopkins Press, 1970), p. 267. Conversation on a Country Path: *Gelassenheit*, Pfullingen: Neske, 1960 (2nd. ed.), p. 35 (62).

30. Cf. "*Continuerons-nous ainsi dans la meilleure tradition apocalyptique à dénoncer les fausses apocalyptiques?*" *Les Fins de l'homme*, p. 472. For Heidegger's "apocalypse," see the texts cited in Reiner Schürmann, *Le principe d'anarchie: Heidegger et la question de l'agir*, Paris: Seuil, 1982, p. 158.

31. Silence about silence: *Unterwegs zur Sprache*, Pfullingen: Neske, 1971 (4th ed.), p. 152 (52).

32. Critique of religion: Karl Marx, *Contribution to the Critique of Hegel's Philosophy of Right: Introduction*, in *The Marx-Engels Reader*, ed., Robert C. Tucker, New York: Norton, 1978 (second edition) p. 53.

Chapter 17

1. Hugh Silverman, "Self-Decentering: Derrida Incorporated" in *Research in Phenomenology*, Volume VIII (Atlantic Highlands, NJ: Humanities Press, Inc., 1978), pp. 60-61.

2. Richard Rorty, "Derrida on Language, Being, & Abnormal Philosophy," in *The Journal of Philosophy*, Volume LXXIV, no. 11 (Lancaster, Pa.: Lancaster Press, Inc., 1977), pp. 676–77.

3. Jacques Derrida, "Restitutions of Truth to Size" in *Research in Phenomenology*, Volume VIII (Atlantic Highland, NJ: Humanities Press, Inc., 1978), p. 35.

4. Jacques Derrida, *La Verité en Peinture* (Paris: Flammarion, 1978), p. 363.

5. *Ibid.*, p. 371.

6. *Ibid.*, p. 381.

7. Derrida, "Restitutions of Truth to Size," p. 3.

8. *Ibid.*, p. 20.

9. Derrida, *La Verité en Peinture*, p. 407.

10. *Ibid.*, p. 403.

11. *Ibid.*, p. 292.

12. Derrida, "Restitutions of Truth to Size," p. 38.

13. *Ibid.*, p. 8.

14. *Ibid.*, p. 9.

15. *Ibid.*, p. 19.

16. *Ibid.*, p. 37.

17. Derrida, *La Verité en Peinture*, p. 383.

18. Derrida, "Restitutions of Truth to Size," p. 24.

19. *Ibid.*, p. 39.

20. Derrida, *La Verité en Peinture*, p. 399.

21. *Ibid.*, p. 404.

22. David Allison, "Destruktion/Deconstruction in the Text of Nietzsche" in *Boundary 2*, Volume VIII, no. 1 (Binghamton, NY: SUNY Binghamton, 1979), pp. 197–222.

23. Jacques Derrida, *Margins of Philosophy*, trans. Alan Bass (Chicago: University of Chicago Press, 1982), p. 124.

Chapter 18

1. Immanuel Kant, *Critique of Pure Reason*, trans. Norman Kemp Smith (New York: St. Martin's, 1965), p. 488 (A573/B601).

2. *Ibid.*, pp. 490–493 (A576–579/B604–607).

3. *Ibid.*, p. 56 (B22).

4. G.W.F. Hegel, *Faith and Knowledge*, trans. Walter Cerf (Albany: State University of New York Press, 1971), p. 81.

5. Kant, *op. cit.*, p. 163 (B149).

6. *Ibid.*, p. 513 (A613/B641).

7. G.W.F. Hegel, *Science of Logic*, trans. A.V. Miller (London: George Allen & Unwin, 1969), p. 107.

8. Martin Heidegger, *Being and Time*, trans. John Macquarie & Edward Robinson (New York: Harper & Row, 1962), p. 262 (H220).

9. Kant, *op. cit.*, p. 513 (A613/B541).

10. *Ibid.*, p. 514 (A614/B642).

11. *Ibid.*, p. 202 (A167/B209).

12. Immanuel Kant, *Anthropology from a Pragmatic Point of View*, trans. Mary J. Gregor (The Hague: Martinus Nijhoff, 1974), p. 55.

13. *Ibid.*, p. 84.

14. F.W.J. Schelling, *Of Human Freedom*, trans. James Gutmann (Chicago: Open Court Publishing Company, 1936), p. 21.

15. G.W.F. Hegel, *Science of Logic*, op. cit., p. 483.

16. G.W.F. Hegel, *Lectures on the Philosophy of Religion*, Vol. III, trans. Rev. E.B. Speirs (London: Kegan Paul, Trench, Trubner & Co., 1895), p. 353ff.

17. G.W.F. Hegel, *Science of Logic*, p. 50.

18. Friedrich Nietzsche, *The Will to Power*, trans. Walter Kaufmann and R.L. Hollingdale (New York: Random House, 1967), p. 64.

19. *Ibid.*, p. 300.

20. *Ibid.*, p. 301.

21. *Ibid.*, p. 278.

22. Immanuel Kant, *The Critique of Pure Reason*, op. cit., p. 451 (A511/B539).

23. Friedrich Nietzsche, *The Gay Science*, trans. Walter Kaufmann (New York: Random House, 1974), p. 336.

24. Friedrich Nietzsche, *Twilight of the Idols*, trans. R.J. Hollingdale (New York: Penguin Books, 1968), pp. 40–41.

25. G.W.F. Hegel, *Science of Logic*, op. cit., p. 461.

26. Friedrich Nietzsche, *The Will to Power*, op. cit., m p. 330.

27. Friedrich Nietzsche, *Thus Spoke Zarathustra*, trans. R.J. Hollingdale (New York: Penguin, 1961), p. 233. The German is taken from the *Kritische Gesamtausgabe* (ed.) Giorgio Colli, Mazzino Ontinari (Berlin: De Gruyter, 1968) Vol. VI, p. 267.

28. Friedrich Nietzsche, *On the Genealogy of Morals*, trans. Walter Kaufmann (New York: Random House, 1969), p. 45.

29. Nietzsche, *The Will to Power*, op. cit., pp. 332–333.

30. Freidrich Nietzsche, *Beyond Good and Evil* in *Basic Writings of Nietzsche*, trans. Walter Kaufmann (New York: Random House, 1968), p. 211.

31. Friedrich Nietzsche, *The Will to Power*, op. cit., p. 334.

32. Friedrich Nietzsche, "On Truth and Lie in an Extra Moral Sense" in *The Portable Nietzsche*, trans. Walter Kaufmann (New York: Viking Press, 1954), pp. 46–47.

33. Friedrich Nietzsche, *The Will to Power*, op. cit., p. 340.

34. Friedrich Nietzsche, *On the Genealogy of Morals*, op. cit., p. 79.

35. Friedrich Nietzsche, *The Will to Power*, op. cit., p. 290.

36. Martin Heidegger, *Nietzsche, Volume I: The Will to Power as Art*, trans. David Farrell Krell (New York: Harper & Row, 1979), p. 74.

37. William James, *Pragmatism and Other Essays* (New York: Washington Square Press, 1963), p. 98.

38. F.W.J. Schelling, *Of Human Freedom*, op. cit., p. 24.

39. See, for example, "The Elimination (*Ueberwindung*) of Metaphysics Through Logical Analysis of Language," trans. Arthur Pap in *Logical Positivism*, ed. A.J. Ayer (New York: The Free Press, 1959), p. 60ff.

40. Friedrich Nietzsche, *The Will to Power*, op. cit., p. 277.

41. Martin Heidegger, *Nietzsche, Vol. I, op. cit.*, p. 132.

42. Friedrich Nietzsche, *The Will to Power*, op. cit., p. 279.

43. *Ibid.*, p. 280.

44. Friedrich Nietzsche, *Ecco Homo*, trans. Walter Kaufmann (New York: Random House, 1969), p. 326.

45. Friedrich Nietzsche, *The Will to Power*, p. 291.

46. Cf. Martin Heidegger, *The Basic Problems of Phenomenology*, trans. Albert Hofstadter (Bloomington: Indiana University Press, 1982), pp. 39ff.

47. Martin Heidegger, *Nietzsche, Vol. IV: Nihilism*, trans. Frank A. Capuzzi (New York: Harper & Row, 1982), p. 191.

48. *Ibid.*, p. 192.

49. See Martin Heidegger, "On the Essence of Truth," trans. John Sallis in Martin Heidegger, *Basic Writings* (ed.) David Krell (New York: Harper & Row, 1977), p. 127.

50. Martin Heidegger, *The Essence of Reasons*, trans. Terrence Malick (Evanston: Northwestern University Press. 1969), pp. 127, 129.

51. Friedrich Nietzsche, *Thus Spoke Zarathustra*, op. cit., p. 191 (212).

52. Jacques Derrida, *Spurs: Nietzsche's Styles*, trans. Barbara Harlow (Chicago: The University of Chicago Press, 1979), p. 73.

53. Gilles Delueze, *Nietzsche and Philosophy*, op. cit., p. 220.

54. Jacques Derrida, *Spurs: Nietzsche's Styles*, op. cit., p. 103.

55. Martin Heidegger, "Recollection in Metaphysics" in *The End of Philosophy*, trans. Joan Stambaugh (New York: Harper & Row, 1973), p. 79.

56. Jacques Derrida, *Spurs: Nietzsche's Styles*, op. cit., p. 113.

57. Jacques Derrida, *Of Grammatology*, trans. Gayatri Chakravorty Spivak (Baltimore: The John Hopkins University Press, 1974), p. 61.

58. Jacques Derrida, *Spurs, Nietzsche's Styles*, op. cit., pp. 119, 121.

59. Martin Heidegger, "The End of Philosophy and the Task of Thinking" in *On Time and Being*, trans. Joan Stambaugh (New York: Harper & Row, 1972), p. 70.

60. *Ibid.*, p. 69.

61. Martin Heidegger, *Being and Time*, op. cit., p. 270 (H227−8).

62. See, for example, Friedrich Nietzsche, *The Will to Power, op. cit.*, pp. 278ff.

63. Martin Heidegger, *Being and Time*, op. cit., p. 268 (H226).

64. *Ibid.*, p. 271 (H229).

65. Martin Heidegger, "Recollection in Metaphysics," *op. cit.*, p. 78.

66. Martin Heidegger, "Overcoming Metaphysics" in *The End of Philosophy, op. cit.*, pp. 96–97.

67. Rudolf Carnap, "The Elimination of Metaphysics Through Logical Analysis of Language," *op. cit.*, p. 80.

68. Martin Heidegger, "The Question Concerning Technology" in *The Question Concerning Technology and Other Essays*, trans. William Lovitt (New York: Harper & Row, 1977), p. 24.

69. Kant, *op. cit.*, A472/B500.

70. Martin Heidegger, *Nietzsche IV, op. cit.*, p. 201.

71. Martin Heidegger, "The Word of Nietzsche: 'God is Dead'" in *The Question Concerning Technology and Other Essays*, op. cit., p. 111.

72. Phillipe Lacoue-Labarthe, *Le sujet de la philosophie* (Paris: Abbier-Flammarion, 1979), p. 127.

73. See Martin Heidegger, *What is Called Thinking?*, trans. J. Glenn Gray (New York: Harper & Row, 1968), Part II.

74. Martin Heidegger, "Summary of a Seminar on the Lecture 'Time and Being'" in *On Time and Being, op. cit.*, p. 45.

75. Martin Heidegger, *What is Called Thinking?, op. cit.*, p. 71.

76. G.W.F. Hegel, *Enzyklopadie der philosophischen Wissenschaft* I, (Frankfurt Am Main: Suhrkamp, 1970), p. 59.

77. Friedrich Nietzsche, *Thus Spoke Zarathustra, op. cit.*, p. 177 (195).

78. Martin Heidegger, "Letter on Humanism" in *Basic Writings, op. cit.*, p. 223.

Chapter 19

1. Jacques Derrida, *La Carte Postale: de Socrate à Freud et au-delà* (Paris: Aubier-Flammarion, 1980), p. 357. Henceforth the writings of Jacques Derrida will be bracketed within the text. All references will include essay title and text in which the essay is included, or the larger work, and page number. Translations for passages taken from *Glas*, *La Carte Postale*, and *La Verite en peinture* are mine. The following abbreviations will be observed:

(*AF*)   *The Archeology of the Frivolous: Reading Condillac*, trans., John P. Leavey, Jr. (Pittsburgh: Duquesne University Press, 1980).

(*CP*)   *La Carte Postale: de Socrate à Freud et au-delà*.

(Glas)	*Glas* (Paris: Éditions Galilee, 1974).
(OG)	*Of Grammatology*, trans., Gayatri Chakravorty Spivak (Baltimore: The Johns Hopkins University Press, 1974).
(POS)	*Positions*, trans. Alan Bass (Chicago: University of Chicago Press, 1981).
(SP)	*Speech and Penomenoa: and Other Essays on Husserl's Theory of Signs*, trans., David Allison (Evanston: Northwestern University Press, 1973).
(Spurs)	*Spurs: Nietzsche's Styles/Éperons: Les Styles de Nietzsche*, trans., Barbara Harlow (Chicago: University of Chicago Press, 1979).
(VP)	*La vérité en peinture* (Paris: Flammarion, 1978).
(WD)	*Writing and Difference*, trans., Alan Bass (Chicago: University of Chicago Press, 1978).
(YFS)	"Scribble (writing/power)," *Yale French Studies*, No. 58 (1979), pp. 116−147.
(OLR)	"Singsponge 1," *Oxford Literary Review*, Vol. 5, no 1/2 (1982), pp. 102−112.
(EN)	"The *Retrait* of Metaphor," *Enclitic*, Vol. II, No. 2 (1978).
(PFT)	"The time of a thesis: punctuations," *Philosophy in France Today*, edited by Alan Montefiore (Cambridge University Press, 1983), pp. 34−50.

2. G.W.F. Hegel, *The Phenomenology of Mind*, trans., J.B. Baillie (New York: Harper and Row, 1967), p. 251.

3. Rene Descartes, *Meditations on First Philosophy* in *The Philosophical Works of Descartes*, edited and trans., by E.S. Haldane and G.R.T. Ross (Cambridge: Cambridge University Press, 1981), p. 139 translation modified; cf., Rene Descartes, *Oeuvres Philosophiques*, Ferdinand Alquie (Paris: Classiques Garnier, 1963), Tome II, pp. 392−393.

4. Martin Heidegger, "The Turning," *The Question Concerning Technology and Other Essays*, trans., William Lovitt (New York: Harper and Row, 1977), p. 36.

5. Martin Heidegger, *Identity and Difference*, trans., Joan Stambaugh (New York: Harper and Row, 1969), p. 37/102.

6. Maurice Blanchot, *The Space of Literature*, trans. Ann Smock (Lincoln: University of Nebraska Press, 1982), p. 253.

7. Martin Heidegger, *The Basic Problems of Phenomenology*, trans., Albert Hofstader (Bloomington: Indiana University Press, 1982), p. 155.

8. Descartes, *Discourse on the Method for Rightly Conducting Reason and Seeking for Truth in the Sciences*, in Haldane and Ross, p. 83, volume I.

9. *Ibid.*, p. 124 translation modified; cf. *Oeuvres Philosophiques*, Tome I, p. 124.

Chapter 20

1. An exchange made public by Schapiro in an essay titled, "The Still Life as a Personal Object — A Note on Heidegger and Van Gogh". Meyer Schapiro, "The Still Life as a Personal Object — A Note on Heidegger and Van Gogh," *The Reach of Mind: Essays in Memory of Kurt Goldstein*, Ed. Marianne L. Simmel (New York: Springer Publishing Company, 1968) pp. 203–09.
2. Jacques Derrida, *"Restitutions/de la verité en Pointure,"* *La Verite en Peinture* (Paris: Flammarion, 1978) p. 312.
3. *Ibid*, p. 355.
4. *Ibid*, p. 302.
5. Martin Heidegger, "The Origin of the Work of Art," *Poetry, Language, Thought*, translated by Albert Hofstadter (New York: Harper and Row, 1971).
6. Derrida, *loc. cit.* p. 302.
7. *Ibid*, p. 323.
8. *Ibid*, p. 326.
9. *Ibid*, p. 323.
10. *Ibid*, p. 339.
11. Derrida, *loc. cit.* p. 342.
12. *Ibid*.
13. *Ibid*, p. 354.
14. Heidegger, *loc. cit.* p. 33.
15. *Ibid*.
16. Derrida, *loc. cit.* p. 341.
17. *Ibid*, p. 346.
18. *Ibid*.
19. *Ibid*, p. 347.
20. *Ibid*, p. 345.
21. *Ibid*, p. 343.
22. *Ibid*, p. 356.
23. *Ibid*, p. 331.
24. *Ibid*, p. 349.
25. *Ibid*, p. 347.
26. *Ibid*, p. 305.

Index

ABOUT THE EDITORS

Hugh J. Silverman is Professor of Philosophy and Comparative Literature at the State University of New York at Stony Brook. He is editor of *Piaget, Philosophy and the Human Sciences* (1980), co-editor of *Jean-Paul Sartre: Contemporary Approaches to his Philosophy* (1980) and *Continental Philosophy in America* (1983). He is translator of Merleau-Ponty's *Consciousness and the Acquisition of Language* and "Philosophy and Non-Philosophy since Hegel." He has published numerous articles in continental philosophy and literary theory. He is Executive Co-Director of the Society for Phenomenology and Existential Philosophy.

Don Ihde is Professor of Philosophy and past Chairman of the Department at the State University of New York at Stony Brook. He is author of *Hermeneutic Phenomenology* (1971), *Sense and Significance* (1973), *Listening and Voice* (1976), *Experimental Phenomenology* (1977), *Technics and Praxis* (1979), and *Existential Technics* (1983). He is co-editor (with R.M. Zaner) of previous volumes in this series, entitled *Dialogues in Phenomenology*, vol. 5 (1975) and *Interdisciplinary Phenomenology*, vol. 6 (1977). He is past Executive Co-Director of the Society for Phenomenology and Existential Philosophy.

DATE DUE